Robert Moscaliuc

9/11 Imaginaria
Writing Catastrophe, Memory, and the War on Terror

With a foreword by Giorgio Mariani

Robert Moscaliuc

9/11 IMAGINARIA
Writing Catastrophe, Memory, and the War on Terror

With a foreword by Giorgio Mariani

Bibliografische Information der Deutschen Nationalbibliothek
Die Deutsche Nationalbibliothek verzeichnet diese Publikation in der Deutschen Nationalbibliografie; detaillierte bibliografische Daten sind im Internet über http://dnb.d-nb.de abrufbar.

Bibliographic information published by the Deutsche Nationalbibliothek
The Deutsche Nationalbibliothek lists this publication in the Deutsche Nationalbibliografie; detailed bibliographic data are available on the Internet at http://dnb.d-nb.de.

ISBN (Print): 978-3-8382-1855-7
ISBN (E-Book [PDF]): 978-3-8382-7855-1
© *ibidem*-Verlag, Hannover • Stuttgart 2025

Leuschnerstraße 40
30457 Hannover
Germany / Deutschland
info@ibidem.eu

Alle Rechte vorbehalten

Das Werk einschließlich aller seiner Teile ist urheberrechtlich geschützt. Jede Verwertung außerhalb der engen Grenzen des Urheberrechtsgesetzes ist ohne Zustimmung des Verlages unzulässig und strafbar. Dies gilt insbesondere für Vervielfältigungen, Übersetzungen, Mikroverfilmungen und elektronische Speicherformen sowie die Einspeicherung und Verarbeitung in elektronischen Systemen.

All rights reserved. No part of this publication may be reproduced, stored in or introduced into a retrieval system, or transmitted, in any form, or by any means (electronic, mechanical, photocopying, recording or otherwise) without the prior written permission of the publisher. Any person who commits any unauthorized act in relation to this publication may be liable to criminal prosecution and civil claims for damages.

Printed in the EU

Table of Contents

Foreword III

Introduction 13

1. **Remapping Memory** 25

    1.1. From One Ground Zero to Another: The Discursive Weight of 9/11 25
    1.2 Theoretical Trajectories: Towards a Theory of *Selfish Events* 43
    1.3 Genes, Memes, and Relativity: An Event's Eye View of Culture 52

2. **A Cultural Symptomatology of *Selfish Events*** 61

    2.1 Plural Voices, Singular Views: Siri Hustvedt's *The Blazing World* and Other, *Stranger Things* 61
    2.2 Erasures of Locality, Impairment, and Diplopia: Don DeLillo's *Falling Man* 78
        2.2.1 *Against the Melancholic State and Other Misuses of Trauma* 84
    2.3 The Post-post-9/11 Novel: Cormac McCarthy's *The Road* 116
        2.3.1 *The Post-Nuclear Family* 126
    2.4 Apocalypse Then, Utopia Now: James Howard Kunstler's *World Made by Hand* 141

3. **Stabilising Disruptions** 151

    3.1 The Ghost-Writer Complex: Disintegrating Selves, Dis-integrating Narratives 151
        3.1.1 *Updike's Final Act of Ethnic Ventriloquism* 159
    3.2 Permutations of Everything: The Strange Case of Paul A. Toth's *Airplane Novel* 170
    3.3 The Americanising Gaze: Cultural Intrusions and the 'Third Space' in Ackerman's *Green on Blue* 176
    3.4 Reading Otherwise: Toward a *Reparative Reading* of Selfish Events 183

4. **Mapping a Way Out of the Selfish Event: Fiction, Journalism, and the Proximal-Ancillary Continuum 193**

    4.1 Theoretical Foundations: From Canons to Continuums 193
    4.2 Premises for a Proximal-Ancillary Coverage Continuum 195
    4.3 *Proximal Coverage*: From Functional Truth to Spheres of Consensus 200
    4.4 *Ancillary Coverage*: Personal Truth and the Demands of Narrative 204

5. **The Peacekeeping Novel Is a War Novel: Ancillary Coverage of the "War on Terror" as a Form of Cultural Selection 221**

    5.1 Men Against "Roaches" and Other Enemies 221
    5.2 The Peace Within War and the War Within Peace: A Literary Genealogy of the "War on Terror" 225
    5.3 The War Narrative Before the War: *The Things They Carried*, *Hystopia*, *The Sympathiser*, and *Anatomy of a Soldier* 232
    5.4 The War at Hand and the War Literature That Is Not .. 241

6. **Families and Their Soldiers, Soldiers and Their Families 255**

    6.1 Now Survive the Homecoming: Phil Klay's *Redeployment* 255
    6.2 The War Seen Through Somebody Else's Eyes: Elliot Ackerman's *Green on Blue* 264
    6.3 Parallel Views: Michael Pitre's *Fives and Twenty-Fives*, Matt Gallagher's *Youngblood*, and Roy Scranton's *War Porn* 273
    6.4 The Enemy at Home: Families at War 292

Conclusion 307

Bibliography 311

Acknowledgements 325

Foreword

In the first chapter of Herman Melville's *Moby-Dick*, as he tries to explain how he came to live the adventure narrated in the pages that follow, narrator Ishmael surmises that "doubtless, my going on this whaling voyage, formed part of the grand programme of Providence that was drawn up a long time ago. It came in as a sort of brief interlude and solo between more extensive performances. I take it that this part of the bill must have run something like this:

> 'Grand Contested Election for the Presidency of the United States.
> 'Whaling Voyage by one Ishmael.
> 'BLOODY BATTLE IN AFGHANISTAN'"

In the aftermath of the 9/11 attacks, several American literature scholars, as well as numerous common readers of Melville, were reminded of this passage, which appears, moreover, in a chapter titled "Loomings" and largely deals with Ishmael's reflections as he "circumambulate[s] ... your insular city of the Manhattoes." Of course, only a few readers were willing to endow Melville with prophetic powers. To many, it was only a startling coincidence that Ishmael would situate his apocalyptic voyage between the 1848 contested election of Zachary Taylor—who lost the popular vote but won the presidency in the Electoral College—and the 1841-42 revolt against British colonial rule in Kabul, which resulted in the annihilation of a retreating British battalion that only one man survived. And yet, *it was* a startling fact that what many consider the American epic par excellence would seem to carry anticipations of a national disaster sandwiched between the contested election of George W. Bush—who lost the popular vote to Al Gore but won the presidency in the Electoral College by one vote—and the many "bloody battles in Afghanistan" that would follow the Al Qaida attacks against the United States of America.

The most intelligent comments on these coincidences came from those who, like Alessandro Portelli in his short book *America, dopo* (*America, after*; Donzelli, 2002), refused to see Ishmael as a nineteenth-century Nostradamus and believed, instead, that it was more useful to ask why, in 1850-51, Melville write what he wrote. Thus, Portelli notes that at the time, the U.S. had just come out of a war of territorial expansion against the sovereign state of Mexico, and shortly, it would precipitate into a long and bloody Civil War. Abraham Lincoln would be assassinated, and his successor, Andrew Johnson, would be impeached and acquitted in the Senate by one vote. Later, in 1876, the most contested American presidential election ever was marked by electoral fraud and voter intimidation. Perhaps, Portelli surmises, the "hypo" Ishmael suffers from has something to do with a sickness corroding both the American world from within and affecting its relations with those far-away regions like Afghanistan. Melville could not read the future, but embracing a *longue durée* perspective, we might wish to situate the events of 9/11 and the "war on terror" that would follow, in the longer and wider historical frame of colonialism and imperialism — something that a scholar like Edward W. Said would in fact do, by arguing that rather than confront the U.S.'s condition as "an imperial power injured at home for the first time, pursuing its interests systematically in what has become a suddenly reconfigured geography of conflict, without clear borders, or visible actors," the Bush administration worked hard to funnel "collective passions ... into a drive for war that uncannily resembles Captain Ahab in pursuit of Moby Dick." ("'Islam' and 'the West' are Inadequate Banners," *The Observer*, 16 September 2001).

What is most striking about all this is not only how current events of a certain magnitude have the potential of redrawing the political and conceptual boundaries of the contemporary world, so that we have all by now become accustomed to thinking of 9/11 as a dividing line between a "before" and an "after." What is even more remarkable is that the social, political, and *cultural* weight of an event like 9/11 is such that we are prompted to re-read *even the past* with new eyes, thus calling into question traditional understandings of history as a chronologically linear affair. One of the greatest virtues of Robert Moscaliuc's *9/11 Imaginaria: Writing Catastrophe, Memory, and the War on Terror* is that it provides us with an original theoretical tool to think about a cultural constellation like the one I have been sketching in the preceding lines. By drawing on Richard Dawkins's concept of the "selfish gene," Moscaliuc asks us to read the event of 9/11 as a *selfish event*. Before looking at what Moscaliuc means by that and why I think his is an insight that breaks new ground in how we may conceptualise "9/11" — an umbrella term covering a potentially infinite range of political and cultural layers and ramifications — let me state at the outset that Moscaliuc is fully aware of both the advantages and the risks involved in the crossing of disciplinary boundaries. Interdisciplinarity is usually highly prized and recommended in academic circles, but it also often comes under critical scrutiny because there is nearly always someone who will be unhappy with the way a concept taken from one discipline is "reworked" to fit the demands of a different area of study. This is most often the case when the fields of science and literary studies are brought together. In some extreme cases, attempts at cross-pollination have been accused of being not only the work of dilettantes but outright fraudulent. In other cases, however, while remaining controversial, the use of ideas taken from the field of science to study literary phenomena has yielded quite interesting results. One may think, for example, of Franco Moretti's efforts to see literary forms as involved in a sort of "evolutionary" struggle to establish their supremacy over other forms less equipped to survive on the literary market. Even the most elaborate, guarded, and intelligent of these interdisciplinary conversations, however, must, in the end, acknowledge that the social and cultural world, on the one hand, and the world of nature and biology, on the other, are two different entities. And yet, we live in both worlds, and one may wish to observe that even a biological notion like that of the "selfish gene" is in itself cross-cultural. Genes do not have anything resembling human consciousness. Their "selfishness" is the invention of Dawkins' metaphorising imagination. To advance his thesis and take a bold new look at the world of biology, Dawkins must resort to employing an eminently moral/ethical (and therefore cultural) concept like "selfishness."

Moscaliuc never tries to hide the metaphoric quality of his insight. He is not suggesting that the "body" of a nation like the U.S. may be comparable to a natural organism. What he *is* proposing, instead, is that — in his own words — the concept of the *selfish event* is useful to make sense of a historical event "of such overpowering cultural, symbolic, and psychological significance that it dominates and reconfigures surrounding narratives, discourses, and cultural artefacts to ensure its perpetuation within collective memory." While Moscaliuc, given the nature of his inquiry, is interested in how a selfish event like 9/11 "absorbs and repurposes" contemporaneous and subsequent "cultural outputs," he does not rule out the possibility that selfish events may reorient also the way we look at the past, and the flood of articles, comments, cartoons, etc. on *Moby-Dick* and 9/11, and *Moby-Dick* and the "War on Terror," are a clear exemplification of what Moscaliuc identifies as the "gravitational pull" of the selfish event. Moreover, rewritings and appropriations of the past like that of Melville's masterwork, are perfectly consistent with another important point that Moscaliuc makes when he observes that one of the main reasons why 9/11 can be read as a selfish event is that "due the severe effects of its occurrence, [it] does not have the time and the cultural resources and content to generate a discourse of its own that could reflect upon and explain its complexity, and as such it resorts to cultural artefacts that happen to be in its proximity." If we think of "proximity" not only as a spatial and temporal concept but also in cultural and metaphorical terms, then even a text written a century and a half before the selfish event took place may provide both a prop to reinforce its centrality and an interpretive lens for making sense of it.

Selfish events are indeed to be understood as motors of "cultural hegemony," and the purpose of Moscaliuc's work is, among other things, to explore how this process unfolds by examining a wide range of novels and stories belonging to what, for better or for worse, has come to be identified as "post-9/11 literature." The reader will no doubt appreciate the way in which Moscaliuc manages to discuss primary texts side by side with a remarkable, indeed nearly gargantuan, number of critical interventions. In navigating these spacious, deep, and troubled waters, the notion of the selfish event provides him with a compass rather than a set of inflexible principles. As he writes, "*selfish events* do not dictate strict rules of production and procedure," and the same may be said of his own readings of "post 9/11 literature" in light of the selfish event. The interpretations offered in the book do not wish to suggest that all novels and stories that may be considered "about" 9/11 are mechanical reproductions of a dominant matrix. On the contrary, the author shows that literature has tried to come to terms with the selfish event in a variety of different ways by adopting styles and narrative strategies often at odds with one another. This is the reason why, early in his book, Moscaliuc writes that his notion of the selfish event may be likened to Norman Fairclough's definition of "interdiscursivity" as a "structural entity which underlies discursive events, rather than the individual formation or code." Perhaps Moscaliuc could have thrown in this theoretical mix one more illustrious figure, as I wonder whether the "discursive event" of 9/11 may not be also investigated on the basis of Michel Foucault's concept of "discursive formation," especially if one thinks of how the emergence of this selfish event is in several ways inseparable from the "war on terror" and the subsequent invasions of both Afghanistan and Iraq. In other words—at least in my view—what Moscaliuc identifies as the "enduring imprint" of the selfish event could also be decoded as a reconfiguration of power-knowledge whose political and historical consequences we are still trying to make sense of.

The discussion of what is commonly identified as "post-9/11 literature" accounts for only the first half of Moscaliuc's impressive book. The second half deals with what is usually referred to as the "war on terror" literature—a literature that covers the wars triggered by the selfish event covered in the first half of the book. I think this is a perfectly understandable and logical choice, as seeing both the Al Qaeda attacks on America and the wars that followed "on a *continuum* rather than as *isolated incidents* might shed light on how the discourse surrounding them informs and is informed by those events." But Moscaliuc is not after historical continuity *per se*. He suggests, instead, that we pay attention to the continuity in how these separate though related events are "depicted in literature." To see this may require a certain effort on the reader's part, as in switching to the second half of his inquiry, the author's theoretical pole star is not so much the selfish event as the cognate, though different, notion of the *proximal-ancillary coverage continuum*. This is not to say that the concept of the selfish event bears only a loose connection to the critical tool employed in the second half of his study. Indeed, Moscaliuc argues that selfish events "in a typical fashion, *prescribe* their representation in the media," which means that what he calls *proximal coverage* – the "direct, immediate, and often journalistic representations that focus on the events as they unfold" – is bound to speak the language of the selfish event, while the *ancillary coverage* is in a position to translate that language into a different idiom, even though Moscaliuc adds that the "frame-modifying capacities" of the ancillary coverage is intrinsically limited.

After the lessons of the New Journalism and, more recently, the insights informing Hayden White's work as well as the work of the New Historicists, there are probably very few people who would be willing to disagree with Moscaliuc on the theoretical soundness of the *proximal-ancillary coverage continuum*. Though, personally, I wish he had spent a few pages to clarify how his own understanding of the factual-fictional continuum diverges from previous theorisations, my impression is that Moscaliuc's main point is not so much to emphasise that proximal (i.e. journalistic) coverage is at the end of the day not easily distinguishable from outright ancillary (i.e. fictional) coverage, as to insist that the notion of a continuum between these two representative strategies should not rule out the fact that they "are inherently distinct" in terms of both style and function. In particular, they are distinct in the way they conceive of both "truth" and "narrative necessity," as while journalism is bound by rule to give us an accurate depiction of objective facts – or at least it must try its best to do so – fiction accords the writer a different latitude, "offering a narrative freedom that can defy established truths or even subvert them. *Ancillary coverage* can express a conflict's emotional and psychological scope, providing insights that *proximal coverage* may not capture."

This may sound like a somewhat traditional defence of literature as an uncontaminated space of freedom, but in fact Moscaliuc's effort to "emancipate discourse from the grip of the cultural egotism of the *selfish event*" draws on Eve K. Sedgwick's influential distinction between *paranoid* and *reparative* reading and is by no means a naïve attempt at resurrecting some blind faith in the aesthetic. By opposing such paranoid notions like that of *inevitability*, reparative readings resurrect "the pleasure of discovery" and—most importantly perhaps—"the hope for things turning out differently from the way they did." This is a praiseworthy reading strategy, especially when one aims to read texts that are about war with the hope that they may provide us with the intellectual and emotional means to see, beyond the horrors and devastation of war, a horizon of peace. Concerning this last point, however, I must admit that while I sympathise with the objectives of a reparative reading strategy, I would also insist that this is indeed a *reading* strategy, and it depends to a significant extent on the position that the *reader* assumes vis-à-vis the text. In his polite disagreement with one of the arguments I have tried to develop in my book *Waging War on War* (University of Illinois Press, 2015), Moscaliuc laments that "whenever the burden of proof shifts onto the reader, the interpretive outcomes invariably oscillate, depending on the sociocultural and historical context in which the narrative is consumed," and he hopes to find a solution to this problem by exploring "how these narratives explore the 'physical' knowledge produced through war, particularly in their representation of human bodies." Again, while I sincerely sympathise with his desire to anchor reparative readings to the objective configuration of the texts, I remain sceptical concerning the viability of this project. In particular, Moscaliuc's idea that the "peacefighting" aspect of these narratives "does not come down to convincing people that war is wrong but instead creates a sense of fear, a heightened sense of anxiety in those who have not experienced war directly," leaves me wondering how "fear" and "anxiety"—the same feelings exploited by warmongers to drag the U.S. into military adventures that have cost the lives of hundreds of thousands of people—may provide an emotional (and therefore pre-political) basis on which a more peaceful world could be edified.

Be that as it may, I strongly believe that regarding these matters, disagreements may be productive and stimulate further research and discussion. Here, however, I would like to conclude by calling attention to one of the most original points to be found in Moscaliuc's reading of the war-on-terror literature (but let me also add parenthetically that his book is, among other things, a veritable treasure chest of brilliant "local" insights). The narratives he discusses, Moscaliuc concludes, "seem to show that the most crippling affliction [the] soldiers suffer from does not stem from their exposure to battle and bloodshed but from having to return to a system of values that is incapable of re-integrating them within itself.... These soldiers' return home ... is akin to a 'redeployment' to a different kind of battlefield." By reversing the readers' expectations, offering them a home that is not peaceful and a battlefield that is not belligerent—or not as belligerent as one would at first think— these narratives can indeed be seen, as Moscaliuc suggests, "as a set of simultaneous discursive practices meant to *reform* the very way we gaze at war." Most significantly, perhaps, by collapsing the distinction between the "front" and the "home front," these stories also call into question comfortable and all-too-easy distinctions between the soldiers sent to the war and the civilian population embroiled in the politico-cultural context that is responsible for sending the soldiers to war in the first place. Novels like Ben Fountain's *Billy Lynn's Long Halftime Walk*, Michael Pitre's *Fives and Twenty-Fives*, and Roy Scranton's *War Porn*, as well as the stories collected in Phil Klay's *Redeployment*, are all efforts in Moscaliuc's view, to create "a point of no return into the consciousness of the readers," by opening "a space from which the reader can return home with the same sense of unfamiliarity that returning soldiers experience." This line of interpretation, I believe, may be especially fruitful in reading the wars of the new millennium, given that thanks to advances in communicative technology, the line separating civilian from military life has indeed become rather thin. But I also wonder whether it may not be applied to previous war literature, from such texts as Hemingway's "Soldier's Home" and Faulkner's *Soldier's Pay* to Tim O'Brien's *The Things They Carried* and many, many other fictional and autobiographical accounts of war devoting considerable space to how war is usually far from over once the soldier comes back home.

In proposing that Moscaliuc's interpretive insight be also applied retroactively, I would not want to suggest that we may discover that a set of identical features marks the "redeployment" of war veterans across different ages. In fact, my suspicion is that while we may well identify a number of recurring structural and emotional situations running from stories of World War I veterans to the narratives of veterans of the "War on Terror," we may also uncover numerous differences in the way American society has tried, failed, or in some cases succeeded in reintegrating returning soldiers within itself. As we embark on this kind of research, we may wish to supplement Moscaliuc's insight with the notion of a "post-bellum complex": a term employed by Jennifer L. Baldwin to describe the set of medical, cultural, and social practices that over the last few decades VA hospitals have created to enable the veterans' transition from the battlefield to civil society (cfr. *Ácoma* 11, 2016). Considerable attention has been paid to the "military-industrial complex," but the existence of a "post-bellum complex" has been too often ignored, and the concept of "redeployment" as understood by Moscaliuc may provide a useful mediating term to develop a dialectical understanding of these two distinct but related "complexes." His work is, therefore, not only of considerable significance for what it accomplishes but also—like all important books—for opening up new paths for future research.

Giorgio Mariani
Rome, January 15, 2025

Introduction

Much like history books, works of fiction often include maps, typically positioned at the beginning to depict real or imaginary locations. Whether genuine or fictional, these maps feature intricate lines and boundaries that delineate spaces adorned with the names of cities, landmarks, rivers, lakes, seas, and oceans. However, readers frequently view these maps from a different perspective, as if the context in which they are placed *diminishes* their realism, particularly when they illustrate supposedly *real* places. Readers often disregard these maps, feeling they offer little assistance in navigating the fictional world they are about to enter, as the reality they portray seems suspended, suggesting a parallel universe. The north, as indicated by the small compass at the bottom of the map, ceases to be our own; instead, it represents a fictional north existing alongside the real one. The map, and by extension, the world it depicts, becomes a "metaverse" — a space that is both *recognisable* and *alien*, existing alongside our reality but governed by different rules.

However, the ability to suspend disbelief and distinguish fiction from fact is crucial for the functioning of literature and intellectual discourse. Without this ability, writers could face arrest and imprisonment, and we would struggle to converse politely. History books would lose their value, as we would not know whom to trust. We must separate these aspects to appreciate *fictional* literature, as this differentiation enables us to recognise the distinct roles that fiction and non-fiction play in helping us understand the world. "The historian," Jane Smiley argues in *Thirteen Ways of Looking at the Novel* (2005), "is required to give up dramatic interest in the pursuit of accuracy, but a novelist must give up accuracy in the pursuit of narrative drive and emotional impact" (Smiley 2006, 21). Nevertheless, sacrificing accuracy does not necessarily mean sacrificing *significance*; it can lead to gains in other areas.

The knowledge gained from fictional accounts *is* accurate and valuable. They are *precise* in showing what happens when accuracy is no longer paramount. "The personal isn't by definition false," Charles D'Ambrosio told Leslie Jamison in an interview for *The New*

Yorker, "nor is confession, but in writing, both have to meet [...] the demands of language" (Jamison 2014). Nor is this knowledge simply emotional or subjective. The writer's dual allegiance, D'Ambrosio concludes, "to the truth of the thing and [...] the truth of writing, inevitably takes you away from the merely heartfelt" and "maps a path out of the self" (Jamison 2014). Fiction also charts a course beyond the limitations and rigidity of facts.

In this study, I aim to demonstrate that, under certain circumstances, the fictional and the non-fictional can be viewed as part of a *continuum*. To achieve this, I have divided my book into two parts. The first discusses the circumstances that necessitate a reconsideration of the truth-fiction dichotomy. The second investigates how interpreting these concepts as a *continuum* can be more productive under these conditions. With this in mind, I base my arguments on two theoretical constructs, which will be explained in the initial pages of each part and below. The first part of my book presents the notion of *selfish events* and will primarily focus on the literature related to and arising from the terrorist attacks of September 11, 2001. The second part puts forward the idea of a *proximal-ancillary continuum* and will concentrate mainly on the literature regarding the American "war on terror" in Iraq and Afghanistan.

The first part of my book is divided into three chapters, each addressing a theoretical element alongside a specific selection of texts. While the first chapter outlines the theoretical trajectories upon which my argument is based, the second and third chapters will integrate theory and practice through in-depth text analysis. In this first part, I contend that the terrorist attacks of September 11, 2001, created an *ethos of perception and cultural production* that can be traced in the texts discussing the events either directly or indirectly. Consequently, 9/11 can be defined as a *selfish event*—one that, due to the *severe* effects of its occurrence, lacks the time, cultural resources, and content to generate a discourse of its own that could reflect upon and explain its complexity. As such, it resorts to cultural artefacts that happen to be in its proximity.

A *selfish event* thus refers to an occurrence of such *overpowering* cultural, symbolic, and psychological significance that it *dominates* and *reconfigures* surrounding narratives, discourses, and cultural artefacts to ensure its perpetuation within collective memory. Much like Richard Dawkins's "selfish gene," which prioritises the survival of its genetic material through any means necessary, *selfish events* exert a gravitational pull on proximate cultural outputs, *absorbing* and *repurposing* them to reinforce their centrality. This process leads to a form of *cultural hegemony*, where the event reshapes both contemporaneous and subsequent interpretations of related and even unrelated phenomena, thereby embedding itself within the cultural consciousness. This *appropriative* move translates into a *cultural practice* and is reflected in narratives that employ similar appropriative strategies but address different topics.

This first part also traces the *cultural symptomatology* of *selfish events* by discussing notions such as the *erasure of locality, impairment*, and *diplopia*. It will examine how these concepts, viewed as signature elements of the *selfish event*, operate within narratives like Don DeLillo's novel *Falling Man* (2007) and Cormac McCarthy's *The Road* (2006). Furthermore, I shall address the issue of which texts have *not* been absorbed or tainted by the *selfish event* and discuss why a text like James Howard Kunstler's novel *World Made by Hand* (2008) escapes the cultural egotism associated with the event.

The third chapter will focus on the event's *signature element*, namely the disintegration of the *narrating self* and the *coerced integration of otherness*. This chapter will explore narratives such as Paul A. Toth's *Airplane Novel* (2011) and Elliot Ackerman's novel *Green on Blue* (2015). Finally, the last section of the third chapter presents a "reparative reading" of post-9/11 fiction that seeks to liberate discourse from the grip of the cultural egotism of the *selfish event*. Following Eve K. Sedgwick's distinction between *paranoid* and *reparative reading*, the chapter will conclude that engaging in a reparative reading practice would also mitigate the culturally expansive tendencies of a *selfish event* and potentially free reality from the fear of the inevitability of another attack.

The second part of my book is also divided into three chapters. It focuses primarily on the *proximal-ancillary coverage continuum* and its application to interpreting literature concerning the wars in Iraq and Afghanistan. The *proximal-ancillary coverage continuum* is a conceptual framework that distinguishes between two types of cultural this idea when he states that semantics "is about the relation of words to reality — the way that speakers commit themselves to a shared understanding of the truth and the way their thoughts are anchored to things and situations in the world" (Pinker 2008, 3). The words and terms we select are not merely abstract concepts but mechanisms that dictate how events are perceived and remembered.

This narrative continuity extends beyond historical analysis into the realm of literature. As I will argue in the following pages, specific literary techniques forged in the fictional representations of 9/11 have been carried into the fiction surrounding the "war on terror" in Iraq and Afghanistan. This suggests not only a continuity in historical events but also in how we frame and process those events through storytelling.

The type of analysis undertaken in this book is not without precedent. Given the richness of this emerging field, several scholars have discussed aspects that I consider and challenge further. In particular, the study that has most influenced my research is Adam Hodges' *The 'War on Terror' Narrative: Discourse and Intertextuality in the Construction and Contestation of Sociopolitical Reality* (2011). Hodges' analysis aims to illustrate how language *shapes* sociopolitical reality. By analysing George W. Bush's speeches given in the immediate aftermath of 9/11, Hodges sets out to demonstrate "how political rhetoric can pave the way for justifying war in the hope that such an understanding might raise awareness and develop the critical ethos needed to avoid future wars" (Hodges 2011, x). Sandra Silberstein performs a similar analysis in *War of Words: Language, Politics and 9/11* (2002), where she "explores the use of language in developing the public understanding of, and response to, the events that surrounded 9/11" and concludes that public language (re)created national identity in the aftermath of these events (2004, xvii). Much like Hodges and Sandra Silberstein, I cultivate a similar critical awareness regarding post-9/11 literature and discourse, viewing language as instrumental in shaping or dismantling reality and its perception.

There are numerous studies analysing post-9/11 literature. Among these, I consider Kristiaan Versluys's *Out of the Blue:*

September 11 and the Novel (2009) and Richard Gray's *After the Fall: American Literature Since 9/11* (2011), both of which play a significant role in establishing a 9/11 canon. While Versluys examines the challenges writers face in representing 9/11 and is particularly intent on demonstrating that it is a traumatic event, Gray seeks to differentiate himself from Versluys by expanding the 9/11 canon. Thus, Gray includes not only those texts that focus explicitly on 9/11 but also works that depict what it is like to live in a post-9/11 world. Moreover, Gray is among the first to incorporate Cormac McCarthy's *The Road* (2006) into the canon, arguing that post-9/11 fiction should also encompass narratives that do not directly reference the events.

Georgiana Banita's *Plotting Justice: Narrative Ethics and Literary Culture After 9/11* (2012) takes a step further, arguing that the terrorist attacks of September 11 triggered profound changes on cultural and moral levels. In this regard, Banita contends that "the aim of the post-9/11 novel is not to cease judging the Other, but to show we are judging even when we think we are not, how we have judged wrongly, and how to make amends for it" (Banita 2012, 26). In other words, these novels challenge readers to recognise their biases and prejudices, highlighting how reparations might be made. Tim Gauthier's *9/11 Fiction, Empathy, and Otherness* (2015) and Daniel O'Gorman's *Fictions of the War on Terror: Difference and the Transnational 9/11 Novel* (2015) both follow in Banita's footsteps, asserting that "the impact of 9/11 on literary fiction has reached far beyond the limits of the 9/11 genre: it has given rise to a cultural condition that permeates contemporary literature more broadly" (O'Gorman 2015, 13). Both analyse how *difference* is framed, focusing on the role of literature in shaping and critiquing issues of difference.

Undoubtedly, Birgit Däwes's *Ground Zero Fiction: History, Memory, and Representation in the American 9/11 Novel* (2011) is the most comprehensive study of post-9/11 literature and discourse. Däwes's approach is systematic and provides a taxonomy of post-9/11 fiction that helps to structure what might otherwise appear as an amorphous and elusive literary field. Rather than treating post-9/11 literature as a monolithic genre, Däwes distinguishes between its subcategories and seeks to correct earlier critical tendencies that either overemphasised the singularity of 9/11 fiction or subsumed it entirely within existing genres, such as the trauma novel or postmodern-historiographic-metafiction.

Däwes proposes six subcategories of post-9/11 fiction: "metonymic approaches" (including novels such as Paul Auster's *Brooklyn Follies* and Bret Easton Ellis's *Lunar Park*, which replace the subject with its characteristics or something related and leave the burden of meaning-making to the reader), "salvational approaches" (which focus on preservation or salvation from destruction using various narrative techniques and rely heavily on religion, politics, and American mythology), "diagnostic approaches" (which situate 9/11 within broader historical and geographical contexts and reassess the status of American identity, as Susan Sontag did when she used her reaction to 9/11 to question and critique American cultural and political assumptions), "appropriative approaches" (including novels such as John Updike's *Terrorist* and Don DeLillo's *Falling Man*, which transcend the limits of otherness and (re)construct the voice of the perpetrator, thus balancing the dominant discourse of 9/11 against diverse ethical and political responsibilities), "symbolic approaches" (including works such as Richard Quan's *Siren's Silence* and Jonathan Franzen's *Freedom*, which use 9/11 as a symbolic backdrop and provide a parallel and contrasting context for stories of personal hardship, grief, or decline), and "writerly approaches" (including novels such as Richard Powers' *The Echo Maker* and Siri Hustvedt's *The Sorrows of an American*, which overcome the representational challenges of the event by rearranging them into semantic, structural, or formal innovations, including multiple perspectives, non-linear narration, and various other such experiments).

Adhering to specific principles of New Historicism, particularly the idea that fictional texts and historical contexts are mutually constitutive rather than discrete entities, Däwes's study aims to illustrate how fictional texts have contributed to shaping and establishing the cultural memory of 9/11. Most importantly, rather than treating literature as a reflection of historical events, she demonstrates how narrative choices, ideological framings, and aesthetic strategies have influenced how 9/11 is remembered, mythologised, and integrated into national discourse.

Stuart Croft follows a similar path in his work, *Culture, Crisis, and America's War on Terror* (2006), where he argues that "a focus on the cultural can enlighten international relations and security studies" (2006, 34). His central claim is that culture does not merely *reproduce* discourse in the aftermath of 9/11 but actively *co-produces* it. This implies that cultural outputs such as films, books, news media, and public rhetoric are not simply passive reflections of events or the dominant narratives shaped by political leaders and institutions. Instead, Croft posits that these cultural forms dynamically create, shape, and transform the discourse surrounding terrorism, security, and national identity. Unlike Däwes and other scholars who focus primarily on textual artefacts, Croft adopts a more expansive understanding of culture and extends his analysis to a broader range of media and public discourses.

Academic work focused exclusively on the literature of the wars in Iraq and Afghanistan remains inchoate as of this writing, yet the canon continues to grow each year. Noteworthy in this regard is Catherine Mary Mcloughlin's *Authoring War: The Literary Representation of War from the Iliad to Iraq* (2011), which aims to identify, similar to Versluys' *Out of the Blue*, "what makes war impossible or very difficult to write about" and "to explore the means by which it has, nevertheless, been written about with some success" (2011, 8). David A. Buchanan's *Going Scapegoat: Post-9/11 War Literature, Language, and Culture* (2016) may not match Mcloughlin's ambition, but it presents a compelling argument regarding how language *shapes* reality and *prescribes* certain behaviours. Buchanan adapts Kenneth Burke's *scapegoat mechanism* for the critique of literature and applies it to three novels addressing the wars in Iraq and Afghanistan: Ben Fountain's *Billy Lynn's Long Halftime Walk* (2012), David Abrams' *FOBBIT* (2012), and Kevin Powers' *The Yellow Birds* (2012). Additionally, Buchanan dedicates a significant portion of his book to genre discussions and the concept of "combat gnosticism," which has long influenced the production and consumption of war literature.

Another authoritative source on the literature regarding the wars in Iraq and Afghanistan is Peter Molin's blog, *Time Now: The Iraq and Afghanistan Wars in Art, Film, and Literature*. This blog not only offers constant updates about new releases but also provides readers with reviews of nearly everything available in terms of text *and* images related to these conflicts. At the end of each year, Molin publishes a comprehensive list of all books, films, and documentaries released up to that point. Michiko Kakutani's articles for *The New York Times*, "Human Costs of the Forever Wars, Enough to Fill a Bookshelf" and "A Reading List of Modern War Stories," both published in 2015, aim to furnish readers and scholars with a list of books on the topic, charting a territory that remains largely uncharted and will continue to be so for years to come.

The numerous articles published in newspapers and magazines are also noteworthy. One notable piece is George Packer's "Home Fires: How Soldiers Write Their Wars" (Packer 2014), published in *The New Yorker* (April 7, 2014), in which he discusses Paul Fussell's notion of irony and analyses texts such as Kevin Powers' *The Yellow Birds* (2012), Brian Turner's collections of poems *Here, Bullet* (2005) and *Phantom Noise* (2010), and Phil Klay's collection of short stories *Redeployment* (2014).

Brian Castner's extensive article "Afghanistan: A Stage Without a Play," published in the *Los Angeles Review of Books* (October 2, 2014), maps this uncharted territory and contends that, unlike the war in Iraq, the war in Afghanistan has produced far fewer literary works. From Castner's perspective, the literature surrounding the Afghanistan war has deviated from the expected conventions of modern war writing—the tropes of combat narratives, homecoming sagas, and moral reckoning—due to the nature of the conflict. Because of this, its literature remains formally and thematically unsettled, struggling to establish a coherent discourse around a war that lacked clear objectives or resolution.

Roy Scranton's "The Trauma Hero: From Wilfred Owen to 'Redeployment' and 'American Sniper,'" published in the *Los Angeles Review of Books* (January 25, 2015), is another extensive article that examines a trend and seeks to make both readers and writers of war narratives aware of its harmful tendencies. In it, Scranton posits that the prevailing "myth of the trauma hero" has led to an increased reliance on *combat gnosticism* — the notion that only those who have experienced war firsthand can truly understand it — and reinforced an insular, soldier-centred perspective that marginalises broader political and ethical considerations. The myth has also acted as a "scapegoat function" by discharging "national bloodguilt" and "substituting the victim of trauma, the soldier, for the victim of violence, the enemy" (Scranton 2015). In other words, war narratives often shift collective guilt away from national responsibility by recasting soldiers as the primary victims of trauma rather than acknowledging the suffering of those affected by American military violence. As I will argue in the concluding sections of the second part, Scranton attempts to disrupt this pattern in his novel *War Porn* (2016), which challenges the sentimentalisation of the American soldier and exposes the moral ambiguities of war.

Ácoma, the international journal of North American studies, has devoted one of its issues to the theme of war. Published in 2016 and edited by Giorgio Mariani, whose work on the concept of war I shall discuss in the second part of my book, this issue features a diverse range of articles that address aspects of war's representation in cinema, literature, and art. Additionally, it includes an article on how the United States Veterans Affairs (VA) provides care to returning veterans, as well as one discussing the *military-literary complex* — a term describing the relationship between the military establishment, cultural production, and the publishing industry — which has shaped how writers approach the representation of war in fiction and beyond. Unlike other scholarly studies that focus on American-authored war narratives, this issue offers a more transnational approach to war literature by including Iraqi perspectives. Furthermore, it contains an article that later served as the foundation for a chapter in the second part of this book.

While my study adopts a slightly different approach — one that examines a diverse range of seemingly unrelated texts — it does so to establish a theoretical framework that can serve as a foundation for future research. Although its breadth may seem ambitious, the concepts of *selfish events* and the *proximal-ancillary coverage continuum* could evolve into umbrella concepts to address the vast amount of material generated daily within this field. They may also be applied to other discourses and events. While other scholarly works endeavour to map this uncharted and ever-changing terrain, my book can be likened to the compass at the bottom of the map that guides exploration, refines direction, and provides a means to orient oneself within this composite landscape.

1. Remapping Memory

> Memory is life, borne by living societies founded in its name. It remains in permanent evolution, open to the dialectic of remembering and forgetting, unconscious of its successive deformations, vulnerable to manipulation and appropriation, susceptible to being long dormant and periodically revived. History, on the other hand, is the reconstruction, always problematic and incomplete, of what is no longer. Memory is a perpetually active phenomenon, a bond tying us to the eternal present; history is a representation of the past.
> (Pierre Nora, *Between Memory and History: Les Lieux de Mémoire*, 1989)

1.1. From One Ground Zero to Another: The Discursive Weight of 9/11

Three months after the 9/11 attacks, Liberty Island reopened to the public, but the tourist information plaques had yet to be updated to reflect the *altered* Manhattan skyline. A noticeable *absence* marked the location where the Twin Towers of the World Trade Centre once stood—a void that felt, in Don DeLillo's words, "critically missing" (*Falling Man*, 2007). Writing in *The New Yorker*, John Updike described this *absence* as existing "amid the glittering impassivity of the many buildings across the East River" under a sky that was "pure blue, [...] uncannily pristine by the absence of jet trails." (*The New Yorker* 2001). Three months after the events, one of those tourist plaques, situated at the edge of Liberty Island from which visitors could view the tip of Manhattan, still featured the *old* Manhattan skyline, in which the two towers stood intact—an image that no longer corresponded to the physical reality visitors now saw before them.

The contrast between *reality* and its *representation* was profoundly unsettling. The engraving on the tourist plaque, juxtaposed with the view, created a moment of visual dissonance between the old skyline and the new. This interplay between *reality* and *representation* cast a foreboding shadow over the day now known as 9/11, reflecting a mindset that somewhat *compulsively* revisited the traumatic spectacle of the falling towers to comprehend the profound *absence* in the once-familiar skyline. It was a portrayal of *before* and *after*, resembling the structured contrasts of television commercials for anti-ageing creams or shampoos that promise transformation. Like a brainteaser puzzle that challenges players to spot minute differences between two nearly identical images, the discrepancy between the plaque's engraving and the real skyline invited a macabre game of recognition, forcing viewers to confront what was missing rather than what remained. Besides being a documentation of change, this disjunction also signalled a *transfer* or *shift in cultural weight* beyond the physical landscape, where the towers became a site of mythmaking.

Jean Baudrillard provocatively and ironically explains that the disintegration of the towers transported them into a "definitive imaginary space" where they became nothing less than "the world's most beautiful building — the eighth wonder of the world!" (Baudrillard 2012, 36–37). In his view, their physical destruction paradoxically elevated them to an almost mythical status, a monumental cultural icon within the collective imagination. Given the magnitude of the event, filling the gap in the majestic stillness of Manhattan's skyline demanded something far greater than mere concrete and physical labour.

The plaque on Liberty Island was not the only one to offer such uncanny commentary on a shifting landscape. More than a decade after 9/11, in November 2015, while staying in New York City, I stumbled upon a similarly ominous plaque during one of my morning runs in Astoria Park. The green plaque, which is located halfway between the Robert F. Kennedy Bridge and the Hell Gate Bridge, faces the East River and overlooks Manhattan's skyline. Despite lacking images, the plaque recounts the tragic 1904 *General Slocum Disaster*, when a steamboat carrying 1,300 people caught fire and sank in the East River, leaving only about 280 survivors.

What caught my attention, however, was the last sentence of the first paragraph, which notes that *before* September 11, 2001, "the burning of General Slocum had the highest death toll of any disaster in New York City history" ("Astoria Park Highlights — General Slocum Disaster: NYC Parks," n.d.). Besides the seemingly innocuous comparison this piece of information presents — most likely intended to help New Yorkers and tourists gain a sense of perspective regarding the scale of the tragedy and the importance of such an event—I could not help but think about how a plaque dedicated to something that occurred nearly a century earlier is *incidentally* much more about what transpired in the aftermath of 9/11 than about the General Slocum Disaster. Although distant and somewhat disconnected from Ground Zero—the two towers would not even have been visible from there—the spot on the East River appeared to carry a significance beyond its intended historical scope.

The commemorative text *juxtaposes* the two events, much like the two versions of Manhattan's skyline, creating a dialogue between them. However, in this instance, the comparison shifts from the dynamic changes in a familiar landscape to how culturally resonant events *overshadow* specific occurrences in a city's collective memory. This *simultaneity* acts as a testament to the extent to which 9/11 has become a defining moment in the city's collective identity, so much so that most visitors are unlikely to recall a century-old steamboat disaster attributed to "organisational and leadership failings" ("Astoria Park Highlights—General Slocum Disaster: NYC Parks," n.d.). More than just a historical footnote, this comparison also positions 9/11 as a *yardstick* or *conceptual benchmark*— a disaster against which others are measured, suggesting that the General Slocum Disaster cannot be comprehended in isolation.

Moreover, comparing the two events conveys a sense of historical *competitiveness*, akin to that of world records. The wording of the tourist plaque suggests that as time progresses, higher death tolls could be anticipated, potentially surpassing the current record. In the future, another disaster of 9/11's magnitude could become the defining tragedy in the city's history. Smaller events will also continue to reference it and borrow from its symbolic weight to establish historical authority. This logic implies that disasters are not only remembered but also positioned in a hierarchy, where new tragedies reshape the collective understanding of past ones.

This competitive framing is evident even in media discourse. For instance, when reporting on the 2017 truck attack in lower Manhattan, *The Guardian* noted that the suspect "appears to have been inspired by ISIS in the deadliest terror attack on New York City since 9/11" (Staff 2017), reinforcing 9/11 as the benchmark against which all subsequent acts of massive violence in the city are measured.

In addition, the spatial proximity of the two tragedies suggests a form of *semantic transfer* or *conceptual blurring*, in which the categorisation of one event influences the perception of the other. Since the General Slocum Disaster is explicitly labelled a *disaster*, 9/11 could also be perceived as a disaster, thereby triggering the emotional responses associated with large-scale civilian tragedies.

The events of September 11 and the General Slocum Disaster are interconnected in a manner that each serves as a commentary on the other. Following the thorough investigation led by President Theodore Roosevelt's commission, those responsible for the General Slocum tragedy were identified, and accountability was established. In response, stringent safety measures were implemented to prevent such a disaster from occurring again, and the U.S. Coast Guard now enforces strict adherence to maritime safety regulations. A fountain in Tompkins Square Park serves as a dedicated memorial to the victims, featuring an annual ceremony to honour their memory. This process — investigation, accountability, reform, and commemoration — creates a sense of *closure*, as the victims are memorialised within a framework of justice and institutional change.

In contrast, 9/11 does not provide the same sense of *closure*, both in terms of historical narrative and emotional resolution. The threat continues to loom in new and evolving forms, even though the alleged perpetrators — key figures in terrorist organisations — have been identified and removed. While commemorative ceremonies are held each year at the 9/11 Memorial, they do not function as markers of closure in the way that the Tompkins Square Park memorial does for the General Slocum victims. Instead, the ceremonies highlight the threat's enduring nature and the need for continued vigilance, reminding people that the danger has not been entirely eradicated.

There is also a sense that no security measures or other efforts could ever eliminate or even lessen the threat posed by terrorism and the cunning of malevolent terrorists. Unlike a singular, localised disaster, where the damage can be assessed, repaired, and ultimately historicised, terrorism is an ongoing, amorphous threat with no clear endpoint or resolution. Ultimately, the feeling of terror and the emotions associated with it function specifically through the notion that since the object of terror is somewhat obscured—as it is linked to an ongoing and uncertain threat—it can never be entirely removed, and therefore, closure, whether emotional or psychological, can never be achieved.

The inclusion of 9/11 on the commemorative plaque for the General Slocum Disaster establishes a historical connection or hierarchy between the two events, thereby diminishing the significance of the latter. This kind of downplaying or *narrative displacement* is emblematic of post-9/11 memory culture, in which past tragedies are often rewritten—or even subsumed—by the dominant discourse of 9/11. One striking example of this phenomenon is the transformation of the term "Ground Zero"—originally a military term referring to a site of nuclear detonation—now used to designate the location where the towers once stood:

> The term not only captures [...] the tension between the attacks' initial indescribability, on the one hand, and the need to discursively place them within a historical order and thus within the knowable, on the other; but it also overwrites another event, in which the United States was responsible for the deaths of some one hundred thousand civilians. By appropriating the original meaning, "Ground Zero" erases its historical pretexts—from the nuclear bombing of Japan in World War II to the fears and threats emanating from the Cold War. (Däwes 2011, 15)

This shift not only recontextualises 9/11 within the semantics of total devastation but also illustrates how the event has assimilated pre-existing historical and linguistic markers, effectively overriding their previous connotations.

The proximity of 9/11 to the General Slocum Disaster grants it an authoritative force—a type of cultural gravity that overshadows the latter. The event's numerical shorthand, 9/11 or September 11, functions much like an emergency telephone number—deeply ingrained in the global cultural imagination and evoking an immediate, visceral reaction due to its association with crisis and catastrophe. This abbreviation, as argued by Marc Redfield in "Virtual Trauma: The Idiom of 9/11" (2007), is not merely descriptive. It "presents itself as a constative, if deictic, description [...] that simultaneously unfolds as a performative and imperial command (you shall have no other September 11ths; should you mention others, they will be secondary to this absolute, toxic punctum: if you wish, say, to refer to Chile, you will have to speak of 'the other September 11'" (Redfield 2007, 59). In other words, 9/11 does not simply mark a date—it asserts its primacy as an uncontested focal point, erasing or subordinating historical events that share the same temporal designation. It functions as both designation and decree.

Noam Chomsky, in his discussion of Chile, adheres to Redfield's prescription by describing it as "the first 9/11: September 11, 1973, when the US succeeded in its intensive efforts to overthrow the democratic government of Salvador Allende in Chile with a military coup that placed General Pinochet's brutal regime in office" (Chomsky 2011, 23). However, paradoxically, even in his attempt to challenge the dominant cultural and historical primacy of the 2001 attacks, Chomsky inadvertently reinforces their linguistic authority. By labelling Chile's coup as *the first 9/11*, he concedes that the term 9/11 now primarily pertains to the attacks on the Twin Towers, demoting all other September 11ths to a status that necessitates qualification. Redfield thus posits that employing the term transforms it into a *principality*, an absolute referent—a structuring mechanism in cultural discourse that exerts power over how historical events are categorised, remembered, and discussed.

This incidental "overwriting," as Brigit Däwes describes it in *Ground Zero Fiction: History, Memory, and Representation in the American 9/11 Novel* (2011), occurs frequently enough to be regarded as a *recurring pattern* or *defining feature* of the *selfish event*. A similar, albeit unconscious, instance of overwriting can be observed in Joan Didion's *The Year of Magical Thinking* (2007), when she juxtaposes the "ordinary Sunday morning" of Pearl Harbor with the "ordinary beautiful September day" that preceded 9/11, emphasising how moments of violent rupture and change often emerge from seemingly normal, unremarkable circumstances (Didion 2007, 4).

However, the comparison Didion makes is not entirely a stretch or merely rhetorical. Much like Pearl Harbor, 9/11 was an act of aggression carried out on American soil that prompted widespread shock and significant military and political responses. Nevertheless, the comparison also reveals an essential difference in terms of historical memory: while Pearl Harbor is framed within a narrative of retribution and eventual victory, 9/11 remains an unresolved, continually invoked event that still shapes political discourse, security policies, and cultural anxieties. In this sense, Didion's parallel does more than link two moments of American vulnerability—it reveals how 9/11, as a *selfish event*, reconfigures past trauma in its image, to the extent that even earlier national crises are remembered through its framework.

Didion was far from alone in drawing this parallel. American professor and political writer David Ray Griffin boldly named his book on the Bush Administration post-9/11 *The New Pearl Harbor* (2004), a title that directly equates the administration's post-9/11 policies with the U.S. response to the 1941 attack. Much like Pearl Harbor, 9/11 represented a defining rupture in American history that warranted a forceful and immediate military response. In the wake of the attacks, politicians from across the political spectrum further solidified this connection in their speeches and public discourse, thus framing military intervention as not just a choice but a historical imperative.

Thus, there is an observable *transfer* of cultural significance between these interconnected events: 9/11 features a high death toll and global impact, surpassing that of the *General Slocum* disaster, while carrying a gravity and solemnity that the latter, now largely forgotten, fails to evoke. At the same time, Pearl Harbor provides a nation-unifying narrative template and a historical precedent for military action. Moreover, although far less significant in cultural memory, the *General Slocum* disaster contributes to the historical context of tragic events in New York City, further highlighting the uniqueness of 9/11 by contrast. All three events complement one another and function as points of reference within a hierarchy of national memory. However, in this constellation of historical trauma, 9/11 stands out as a culmination of past traumas.

The media's efforts to equate the attacks on the World Trade Centre and the Pentagon to the Japanese attack on Pearl Harbor did not resonate sufficiently, according to Susan Faludi's *The Terror*

Dream: Fear and Fantasy in Post-9/11 America (2007). This failure was primarily due to the fundamental differences in the nature of the enemy and the structure of the threat. Pearl Harbor represented a clearly defined military assault by a nation-state (Japan), which resulted in a direct and conventional military conflict (World War II). In contrast, 9/11 was an attack by a non-state terrorist organisation (Al-Qaeda), leading to a more ambiguous and protracted "war on terror" without clear battle lines or an endpoint, fought against an indistinct enemy.

When these comparisons failed to capture the public imagination, the media shifted its focus to a more psychologically resonant historical framework: "the 1950s Cold War," which seemed a more fitting reference point (Faludi 2007, 3). Hidden deep in the mobilising of forces against an enemy that remained as undefined and contextual as the plural personal pronoun "they," there were renewed discussions about the "enemy among us" and the unity of the American nuclear family, symbolised by the pronoun "us" and the need for solidarity in confronting this elusive adversary. Thus, the "war on terror" was framed not only as a military conflict abroad but as a cultural and ideological battle at home, which required resilience, morality, and collective vigilance.

Like the "Reds" of the Cold War, the perceived 9/11 adversary was framed as uncompromising, ideologically rigid, and intent on exporting a value system fundamentally incompatible with American principles. In his State of the Union address following the attacks, former President Bush reinforced this binary by declaring that Al-Qaeda's goal "is not making money; its goal is remaking the world—and imposing its radical beliefs on people everywhere" (*The Guardian* 2001). His rhetoric mimicked Cold War-era narratives, where the struggle was framed as an existential battle between incompatible worldviews—one in which the enemy was defined not only by their actions but by their ideology.

Farish A. Noor extends this comparison, arguing that after 9/11, the world was suddenly split "along the faultlines of religion, culture and civilisation, and as the discourse of terror was invented and articulated by the proponents of American hegemony it should come as no surprise if America and the West are configured in terms almost entirely positive" (Noor 2010). The discourse of the "war on terror," Noor suggests, strongly resonated with that of the "war on Communism" of the McCarthy era. Just as the Cold War generated fears of communist infiltration within American society and fuelled purges and loyalty oaths, the post-9/11 era ignited fears of terrorist cells or sympathisers hidden within the country and summoned Americans to band together in the face of adversities. In this way, the "war on terror" was not merely a geopolitical strategy but a domestic ideological campaign.

In his book *The Muslims Are Coming: Islamophobia, Extremism, and the Domestic War on Terror* (2014), Arun Kundnani extends the Cold War analogy and asserts that the "war on terror" operates as a Cold War against Islamism, shaped by long-standing anti-Islam and anti-Muslim prejudices in the West. Kundnani notes that "war on terror liberals reproduced the weaknesses of the conceptual scaffolding they inherited from the Cold War" by locating "the problem of radical political challenges [...] in alien ideologies that [...] were bound to produce violence" (Kundnani 2014, 114). This parallels Cold War logic, which cast communism as an ideological contagion that required containment, and which obscures the historical and geopolitical roots of political violence by reducing sociopolitical struggles to a 'clash of civilisations' narrative. However, by framing Islamism as the new communism, post-9/11 discourse legitimised racialised forms of surveillance, policing, and counterterrorism that disproportionately targeted Muslim communities in the U.S. and Europe.

Other scholars also emphasise this parallel between the Cold War and the post-9/11 era. Giovanna Borradori, in her introduction to *Philosophy in a Time of Terror* (2003), argues that "the spectre of global terrorism haunts our sense of the future because it kills the promise upon which a positive relation with our present depends. In all its horror, 9/11 has left us waiting for the worst" (2003, 21). In other words, she suggests that global terrorism, by its very nature, undermines any sense of security or optimism about the future as it introduces a constant, lingering threat, disrupting our ability to maintain a positive relationship with the present, which thus becomes fraught with feelings of terror. In this way, 9/11 does not simply represent a single traumatic rupture but rather a restructuring of temporal experience itself, one reinforcing a perpetual 'state of waiting' that mirrors Cold War-era fears of an unpredictable future.

Given the pervasive sense of fear and insecurity following 9/11, the subsequent narratives extensively employed the family trope, reflecting a collective yearning for security, emotional support, and national unity in the face of trauma. Alongside the estimated $55 billion in physical damage inflicted on New York City (Carter, AM, and Cox, 2011), media and cultural narratives increasingly shifted their focus to the emotional toll on families, framing the attacks as a domestic tragedy that affected American households. Furthermore, stories highlighting the impact on families somewhat humanised the event, bringing the abstract concept of terrorism down to a personal level that readers could empathise with and develop coping mechanisms for.

However, the issue with these parallelisms was that they all pointed to an inherently flawed reaction—a retreat into myth rather than an engagement with reality. "We reacted to our trauma," Susan Faludi rightly remarks, "not by interrogating it but by cocooning ourselves in the celluloid chrysalis of the baby boom's childhood" (2007, 4), staging reenactments of the fifties Western and other comforting narratives from the past. Rooted in nostalgic visions of moral clarity, national unity, and heroic masculinity, these narratives *reframed* the response to 9/11 as a simplistic good-versus-evil battle rather than a nuanced confrontation with a transformed global landscape.

This reliance on retrograde narratives meant that the discourse surrounding September 11 was less about the event itself and more about the reactivation of pre-existing ideological frameworks that took on new significance in these unprecedented circumstances. Following the event, specific items—such as terrorism, national security, and even freedom—underwent a *semantic shift* and acquired unfamiliar connotations as they were scrutinised, contested, and redefined. Their implications were thus *repositioned*. The event's compelling symbolic power, immediacy, and ability to permeate global media channels created a *symbolic emergency*, prompting a re-evaluation of *naming* and *procedural* practices.

This *relocation of cultural weight*—the shifting of semantic meaning and emphasis in the wake of 9/11—can be understood through psychological mechanisms such as the "availability heuristic" (Kelman, 2011) or "illusory correlation" (Chapman & Chapman, 1969). First identified by Israeli psychologists Amos Tversky and Daniel Kahneman in 1973, the "availability heuristic" is a *cognitive shortcut* used to assess the likelihood or frequency of events based on how easily examples of those events come to mind. This heuristic can "generate biased or incorrect judgments, as when people are asked whether the English language contains more words beginning with the letter *k* or more words with *k* as the third letter, most people find it easier to think of instances of words beginning with *k* and therefore concluding that there are more words beginning with *k*, whereas a typical long text contains twice as many words with *k* as the third letter" (Colman 2009). Essentially, if something is more readily remembered or vivid in a person's mind, it is likely to be perceived as more common or significant than it truly is.

Closely related to the "availability heuristic," the phenomenon of "illusory correlation" further explains how perceived but inaccurate associations between events, ideas, or groups can shape cultural memory. First introduced by American psychologists Loren J. Chapman and Jean Chapman in 1967, "illusory correlation" refers to the tendency to perceive a relationship between variables when no such relationship exists (Chapman and Chapman, 1969). This phenomenon can occur when specific pairings are more memorable or vivid, leading individuals to believe they are correlated even in the absence of empirical evidence. In the context of cultural memory, this may imply that certain events or ideas are interconnected in the public consciousness, not because they are *objectively* related, but instead because they are frequently mentioned together or because one is so prominent that it overshadows others.

In the context of post-9/11 discourse, the term "illusory correlation" contributed to a widespread yet often unfounded association between Islam and terrorism. The relentless juxtaposition of

Muslim identity with terrorist imagery in media coverage, political speeches, and security discourse established a cognitive link in the public consciousness, despite statistical evidence indicating that most Muslims worldwide had no connection to violent extremism. A report by the Centre for Strategic & International Studies (CSIS) debunks the "clash of civilisations" thesis, providing empirical evidence that most Muslims overwhelmingly reject extremism and terrorism. The report emphasises that the primary concerns of Muslims across diverse regions are not ideological conflicts but instead economic stability, governance, and security, concerns that mirror those of non-Muslim populations. Particularly revealing is the report's finding that Arab youth, often misrepresented as radicalised or susceptible to extremism, do not support violence. Even the highest estimates of so-called "foreign fighters" cited in media discourse represent "a negligible portion of the total number of young men who might join in such movements" (Cordesman 2017).

The consequences of this *manufactured* correlation were profound, becoming the driving force behind Islamophobic narratives, increased surveillance of Muslim communities, racial and religious profiling, and restrictive immigration policies. In his book *How Does It Feel to Be a Problem? Being Young and Arab in America* (2008), Moustafa Bayoumi argues that following 9/11, "Arabs and Muslims are the new 'problem' of American society," subjected to systemic suspicion and scrutiny because they "now hold the dubious distinction of being the first new communities of suspicion after the hard-won victories of the civil rights era" (Bayoumi 2008, 2-3). This shift mirrored historical patterns in which marginalised groups have been framed as existential threats during moments of national crisis. Just as Japanese Americans were interned after Pearl Harbor (Daniels 2002), and African Americans were criminalised through the War on Drugs (Nunn 2002), the "war on terror" justified and normalised practices such as airport profiling, mosque surveillance, and indefinite detention under the Patriot Act (Cole 2004; McKelvey 2013).

A self-reinforcing cycle, as Daniel Kahneman argues in *Thinking, Fast and Slow* (2011), emerges within the availability heuristic, shaping how information flows between media outlets and consumers. "People tend to assess the relative importance of issues," Kahneman writes, "by the ease with which they are retrieved from memory—and this is largely determined by the extent of coverage in the media. [...] In turn, what the media choose to report corresponds to their view of what is currently on the public's mind" (Kahneman 2011, 11). The implications of the "availability heuristic" and those of the "illusory correlation" thus extend beyond mere psychology and influence how the entire apparatus of perception operates, determining whose fears are validated, whose rights are curtailed, and whose lives are subject to state scrutiny. These phenomena not only distorted perceptions of risk but also reshaped legal frameworks, public discourse, and the lived experiences of specific communities.

When applied in the context of the commemorative plaque, the "availability heuristic" reveals that whoever conceived the text provided readers with a mental shortcut or an easily recalled narrative by relying on immediate examples that come to mind when evaluating, for instance, the death toll of the General Slocum disaster. However, it also illustrates how historical framing is deliberately shaped through cognitive shortcuts that offer readers an immediate, easily recollected narrative rather than encouraging deeper engagement with the event. Furthermore, by concentrating on a precise, striking number, such as the number of deaths, the text ensures that the death toll becomes a defining aspect of how the event is understood, making it easily retrievable from memory whenever the disaster is mentioned.

Furthermore, akin to how the media and the public's mindset create a continuous feedback loop, the juxtaposition of the two historical events on the commemorative plaque encourages a similar process of mutual influence and reinterpretation. The significance, emotional impact, and how each event is memorialised may shift due to their proximity. The reader's understanding of the General Slocum disaster might be shaped through the lens of 9/11, prompting a cultural reframing where the earlier disaster is recontextualised as part of a broader narrative of New York City's tragic history. Thus, the commemorative plaque does not serve as a neutral record of history but as a site where historical memory is actively constructed and negotiated. It becomes, in Pierre Nora's words, a "lieux de mémoire" or a site of memory as opposed to a "milieux de mémoire" or real environments of memory (Nora 1989, 7). To put it differently, historical memory is no longer preserved through organic, lived traditions; instead, it relies on designated sites — such as plaques, memorials, and museums — to artificially anchor the past in the present.

Nevertheless, using the availability heuristic as an interpretive tool remains inherently restrictive. Rather than offering insight into the intrinsic nature of the events themselves, it primarily reveals the mental framework of the plaque's authors and readers, as well as the broader post-9/11 cultural atmosphere in which this memorialisation occurred. In this sense, the heuristic serves as a lens through which the act of commemoration — rather than the historical events themselves — becomes illuminated. The presence of 9/11 within the plaque's text creates a shared cognitive space, one that is immediately recognisable not only to its authors but also to its readers. Within this space, historical meaning is not static but instead negotiated, as both groups understand which mental images, emotions, and associations to evoke in order to make sense of the General Slocum disaster — and vice versa. This process reflects what Maurice Halbwachs describes as "collective memory," the notion that historical understanding is shaped not just by facts but by the social frameworks through which those facts are recalled and interpreted. "Our memories remain collective," Halbwachs explains, "and are recalled to us through others even though only we were participants in the events or saw the things concerned" (Halbwachs and Douglas 1980, 23). In this way, the plaque functions as a site of historical convergence, where two temporarily distinct events are brought into dialogue through shared mnemonic structures.

Considering this perspective, I assert that this *dialogic simultaneity* — the ongoing interplay between past and present events — marks a fundamental shift in the world's "primal scenes." These deep-seated mental shortcuts or frames of reference act as interpretive lenses through which historical meaning is constructed and perceived. The prominence of 9/11 in contemporary cultural memory has not only reoriented our frames of reference but also reshaped the way new events are understood, processed, and narrated. "Many people," George Packer argues in *The Assassins' Gate: America in Iraq*, "allowed historical analogies to do their thinking for them" (Packer 2007, 86). Rather than perceiving events in isolation, individuals interpreted them in conjunction with past occurrences, employing these comparisons as cognitive tools that shaped their understanding of new situations.

In the case of the "war on terror," launched in response to the events of September 11, two dominant "primal scenes," or historical reference points, shaped public understanding: World War II and the Vietnam War. These analogies provided familiar narrative templates, allowing individuals and policymakers to view the new conflicts through the lens of past wars. However, drawing parallels between the "war on terror" and WWII or Vietnam posed its own set of challenges. While such comparisons offered a sense of reassurance, they also restricted individuals' ability to comprehend the *exceptional* aspects of these new challenges. WWII, often mythologised as a morally unambiguous war, and Vietnam, remembered as a protracted conflict without a definitive victory, offered contrasting perspectives that shaped how individuals and governments approached the unprecedented issues arising from the events of 9/11. They also oversimplified the nature of post-9/11 conflicts, ignoring the asymmetrical, decentralised structure of terrorism, the lack of a conventional battlefield, and the absence of clear victory conditions (Stepanova 2008, 3).

The commemorative plaque for the General Slocum disaster introduces an added layer of complexity to this argument. The plaque suggests that the remembrance of the General Slocum disaster has been *influenced* by the cultural prominence of 9/11. Although the disaster occurred nearly a century before the September 11 attacks, the scale and impact of 9/11 have reshaped the hierarchy of tragedies in New York's—and the nation's—public consciousness. While ostensibly commemorating a significant and distinct historical tragedy, the plaque *implicitly* acknowledges this shift: 9/11 has overshadowed earlier tragedies, becoming the dominant mnemonic anchor for how the city and its inhabitants comprehend and contextualise disaster and massive loss.

The broader implication of this shift is that 9/11 has rewritten the script for public tragedy, revealing that collective memory is not fixed but continually reconfigured as new events enter the public consciousness. Whereas before 9/11 public tragedies were typically localised in scope, the terrorist attacks introduced a new paradigm of mourning and memorialisation, characterised by large-scale memorials, media saturation, and rituals of remembrance.

This transformation is evident in annual commemoration rituals, where "family members of the victims read aloud the names of those killed in the 9/11 attacks" ("Commemoration | National September 11 Memorial & Museum," n.d.). The phrase "never forget" is widely used by politicians across the political spectrum and in news broadcasts, as if to ensure that the loss is not diminished by the passage of time. With its emphasis on personal stories, heroism, and resilience, 9/11 transformed a public tragedy into a national experience rather than a local one. This shift aligns with what Marita Sturken describes in *Tourists of History: Memory, Kitsch and Consumerism from Oklahoma City to Ground Zero* (2007) as the transformation of grief and mourning into a spectacle. "In the years since September 2001," Sturken explains, "Ground Zero has become [...] a place inscribed by local, national, and global meanings, a neighbourhood, a commercial district, a tourist destination, a place of protest, and a site of memory and mourning" (Sturken 2007, 168). It has evolved into a contested space where memory, mourning, politics, and commercial interests intersect.

Given these premises and by analysing both fictional and non-fictional texts as well as other cultural artefacts from various fields, this study examines how culturally resonant events, such as the September 11 terrorist attacks and the ensuing "war on terror," function as *selfish events* — phenomena that dominate, reshape, and subsume surrounding narratives, discourses, and cultural expressions. Due to their overwhelming cultural and symbolic significance, such events do not simply exist within collective memory; they actively generate an *ethos* of *production* and *perception* designed to sustain their primacy within historical consciousness. I aim to illustrate that this *reconfiguration* or *reinterpretation* is particularly impactful when artefacts engage in simultaneous dialogues with those carrying what Susan Willis refers to in *Portents of the Real: A Primer for Post9/11 America* (2005) as "sliding signifiers" — concepts whose meanings are unstable and contingent, shifting in response to evolving cultural narratives (Willis 2005, 15). The interpretive flexibility of these signifiers allows artefacts to negotiate their place within the mnemonic landscape, either by reinforcing the culturally hegemonic narrative of the *selfish event* or resisting its totalising influence.

In Susan Willis's framework, a "sliding signifier" refers to symbols or concepts that move fluidly through different cultural contexts, shifting in meaning as they adapt to new circumstances. Among the examples of such signifiers Willis provides are the American flag, which was ubiquitous and thus paradoxically trivialised by the media and government authorities, and the Anthrax scare, which came to represent the pervasive state of fear that characterised the post-9/11 atmosphere. Willis also includes images from the Abu Ghraib prison scandal as "sliding signifiers," stating that these images took on different connotations — symbols of military misconduct or necessary evils in the fight against terrorism — depending on the viewer's perspective (Willis 2005, 116). She argues that the release of these images on CBS's *60 Minutes* shattered the myth of American moral superiority "in a way that news reports of the war's carnage have failed to achieve" (Willis 2005, 116). Unlike statistics or abstract policy debates, these graphic representations of torture brought the violence and ethical failings of the war directly into the living rooms of ordinary Americans, thus challenging their complacency and ignorance about the consequences of U.S. actions abroad.

Through an examination of works such as Don DeLillo's *Falling Man* (2007), Siri Hustvedt's *The Blazing World* (2014), Cormac McCarthy's *The Road* (2006), and Elliot Ackerman's *Green on Blue* (2015), along with other texts that engage with the discourses surrounding 9/11 and the "war on terror," I argue that these dialogues between artefacts and concepts lead to *forceful interpretive interventions* or *intrusions* in both subsequent and preceding cultural discourses. These texts do not simply reflect the events and ideologies linked to 9/11; instead, they *actively* reinterpret and, in some cases, *disrupt* dominant cultural narratives.

Like the commemorative plaques on Liberty Island and Astoria Park, these artefacts serve as representations of what Andreas Huyssen might describe in *Present Pasts: Urban Palimpsests and the Politics of Memory* (2003) as mnemonic palimpsests, where layers of historical consciousness overlap. Within them, "the strong marks of present space merge in the imaginary with traces of the past, erasures, losses, and heterotopias" (Huyssen 2009, 7). Just as urban spaces transform through successive layers of historical inscription, these literary works embed themselves within the evolving cultural memory of the events, becoming ongoing sites of symbolic production.

However, the concept of dialogue used in my argument does not inherently imply *intertextuality* in the traditional sense, nor does it align with what Norman Fairclough refers to in *Discourse and Social Change* (1992) as "manifest intertextuality" — a process in which "specific other texts are overtly drawn upon within a text" (Fairclough 2009, 117). Instead, my argument is more closely aligned with Fairclough's concept of "interdiscursivity" (or "constitutive intertextuality"), which describes how a discourse type is constituted through an interplay of multiple discursive formations rather than direct textual borrowing (2009, 118). While specific texts may appear to communicate directly, the connections between them are often implicit and emerge only when they are juxtaposed within the analytical framework of an external observer. Fairclough's notion of "interdiscursivity" is instrumental here because it suggests that "the complex interdependent configuration of discursive formations [...] has primacy over its parts and has properties which are not predictable from its parts" (2009, 68) and because it makes a clear distinction between wholes and parts. In other words, the totality of these discursive shifts creates a new interpretive framework that extends beyond the sum of its textual components. This distinction shall be helpful in my theoretical discussion of *selfish events*.

Fairclough's definition of "interdiscursivity" as a "structural entity which underlies discursive events, rather than the individual formation or code" (2009, 68) is relevant to my analysis of selfish events. Unlike conventional historical narratives, which often impose fixed interpretive frameworks, *selfish events* do not create rigid textual dependencies or prescriptive rules of representation. Instead, the cultural artefacts associated with these events arise within a shared symbolic framework and develop a range of *acceptable* interpretative strategies. These cultural artefacts, while interrelated, do not always exhibit intertextuality; however, they maintain discursive coherence through their relationship to the event's symbolic structure. In other words, the common foundation of these artefacts lies not in their textual links to one another, but in their shared function as vehicles for negotiating the memory, trauma, and ideological weight of the *selfish event*.

These artefacts can be compared to planets orbiting selfish events, and in most cases, their characteristics do not explain why they are attracted to these events. Although the authors of these artefacts may acknowledge influences from other cultural works and authors, suggesting a certain degree of interconnectedness, the extent of this influence is not explicitly stated within the texts themselves. Consequently, the notion of dialogue here suggests *simultaneity*. This is most apparent when these texts and cultural artefacts are combined in interpretative processes, where their intersections are identified and discussed.

1.2 Theoretical Trajectories: Towards a Theory of *Selfish Events*

The concept of *selfish events* arises from the extensive cultural, political, and intellectual engagement with the terrorist attacks of 11 September 2001. The events offered a platform for writers and artists to share their perspectives alongside philosophers, intellectuals, and policymakers from diverse backgrounds. There was a collective desire to soften the events' intensity and immediacy, providing, if not a *stabilising* narrative, at least a means to come to terms with them. These responses were not merely efforts to narrate or document the attacks; instead, they contributed to the construction of 9/11 as a culturally dominant event, one that absorbed, redefined, and overshadowed competing histories.

Although none of the streams of thought I refer to and discuss in the following pages employ the same terminology, each contains hints of the unifying metaphor that the concept of *selfish events* seeks to map, as well as insights into how it might function within cultural memory, historical discourse, and political frameworks. By examining each of them and outlining their main ideas, this chapter endeavours to reverse-engineer the concept of *selfish events* by identifying key theoretical precedents and tracing its intellectual lineage. While this discussion does not claim to be exhaustive, it positions selfish events within a broader system of thought.

One area that garnered significant discussion in this context was philosophy. Since philosophy concerns itself with fundamental concepts related to existence, knowledge, and language, philosophers were among the first to engage with the singularity of this event. It was not merely the novelty and scale of the event that perplexed observers; it was also its ability to evade established frameworks of interpretation, exposing gaps in political, legal, and ethical thought.

The concept of 'terrorism,' which gained widespread usage in the aftermath of 9/11, came under intense scrutiny. "Despite the marked differences in their approaches," Giovanna Borradori writes in her preface to *Philosophy in a Time of Terror* (2003), both Habermas and Derrida "hold that terrorism is an elusive concept that exposes the global political arena to imminent dangers as well as future challenges" (Habermas and Derrida 2003, xii). For Derrida, in particular, terrorism is "the symptom of an autoimmune disorder," a self-destructive mechanism that threatens the very structures it purports to protect—democracy, legal institutions, and the separation of religion and politics (2003, 20). Given its threatening nature, in Derrida's view, the focus of terrorism is "always on the future, somewhat pathologically understood as promise, hope, and self-affirmation" (2003, 22). From this perspective, Derrida posits that terrorism is not an aberration but an inevitable symptom of more profound systemic contradictions—contradictions that 9/11 merely rendered visible.

While Jacques Derrida framed terrorism as an autoimmune disorder—a crisis that compels democratic states to undermine their principles—Alain Badiou focuses on the linguistic weaponisation of the term itself. In *Polemics* (2011), Badiou challenges the way 'terrorism' has been redefined in contemporary discourse. While historically the term referred to "a particular figure of the exercise of state power," in the post-9/11 context, it has been co-opted as a tool of political delegitimisation. "The word has finally come," Badiou argues, "to designate, from the viewpoint of the dominant, anyone who, using whatever means available, commits to a combat against the prevailing order that the latter judges […] unacceptable" (Badiou and Winter 2011, 18). As a result, the notion acquired propagandistic implications and "had become an essentially formal term," stripped of any "neutral currency," thus it "no longer designates either a political orientation or the possibilities inherent to such and such a situation; instead, it exclusively designates the form of action" (2011, 19). With its semantic weight, the *selfish event* necessitated a re-evaluation of the lexicon through which history is interpreted and framed.

When asked about whether 9/11 should be considered an unprecedented event, Jürgen Habermas stressed the novelty of the event by arguing that not only was the "monstrous act" behind it new, but also its "symbolic force." "Perhaps," Habermas suggests, "September 11 could be called the first historic world event in the strictest sense: the impact, the explosion, the slow collapse—everything that was not Hollywood anymore but, rather, a gruesome reality, literally took place in front of the 'universal eyewitness' of a global public" (Habermas and Derrida 2003, 28). In the symbolic milieu created by the force of the events, the protagonists themselves, figures such as Osama bin Laden and his acolytes, almost serve "the function of a stand-in" or symbolic placeholders for an elusive opponent. This is, Habermas explains, what lends terrorism a "new quality," namely the impossibility of identifying the opponent and making any realistic assessment of the danger (2003, 29).

According to Habermas' reasoning, September 11 was a fortuitous alignment of various elements that amplified the force of the event strictly because of their differences. This concept is crucial to understanding *selfish events*. Like a gravitational centre around which discourse perpetually revolves, they exert dominance by ensuring that they remain conceptually unresolved. Their protagonists and antagonists are adaptable, their meanings continuously altered, and their significance consistently reaffirmed. Without the "universal eyewitness," perhaps referring to television, news, and the Internet—mediums capable of storing and replicating data endlessly—the event would not have had the same magnitude.

"With the attacks on the World Trade Center in New York City," Jean Baudrillard writes in *The Spirit of Terrorism* (2003), "we might even be said to have before us the absolute event, the 'mother' of all events, the pure event uniting within itself all the events that have never taken place" (Baudrillard 2012, 3). It is an event that both exceeds representation and becomes indistinguishable from its representation. In Baudrillard's view, this event possesses a somewhat unusual status because, at its core, 9/11 embodies a guilty desire or the fulfilment of an unconscious cultural script—not simply the desire for destruction, but the latent fantasy of witnessing the downfall of hegemonic power. It represents the coronation of something we have all dreamt of and seen rehearsed in film, political discourse, and the Western imaginary.

This thought is "unacceptable to the Western moral conscience" because it implies an unspoken cultural investment in disaster, a fascination with catastrophe that threatens both material assets and human lives. Although this complicity is denied, Baudrillard rightly points out, "[without] this deep-seated complicity, the event would not have had the resonance it has, and in their symbolic strategy the terrorists doubtless know that they can count on this unavowable complicity" (Baudrillard 2012, 5). Thus, there was no "purely destructive logic" (2012, 20) behind the terrorist acts of 9/11; instead, it was a tactic that resulted in "an excess of reality." This excess not only exposed vulnerability within the system but also fulfilled the system's logic to an extreme degree, making its collapse appear both spectacular and inevitable. Baudrillard thus suggests a dual agency at work in 9/11: on the one hand, the alleged perpetrators, the orchestrators of the attack, who executed the event; on the other hand, the event itself, which operated like an autonomous force, accelerating the contradictions of global capitalism to their breaking point. The towers did not simply collapse; in Baudrillard's reading, they had to collapse—an outcome already embedded in the symbolic fabric of the West's hyperreal condition.

The event was also a form of *radicalisation* that did not pit two civilisations against one another, as argued in its immediate aftermath[1], but image against reality. As Baudrillard claims, it was the *symbolic* collapse of the towers that preceded and even necessitated their physical destruction. Much like Andy Warhol's *Death and Disaster* series (1963), where the repetition of violent imagery transforms the subject into both spectacle and abstraction, the image of the two burning towers became serially replicated *ad infinitum* in global media, growing more intense yet increasingly detached from the event with every replay. This is why, Baudrillard argues,

> the terrorists exploited the 'real-time' of images, their instantaneous worldwide transmission, just as they exploited stock-market speculation, electronic information and air traffic. The role of images is highly ambiguous. For, at the same time as they exalt the event, they also take it hostage. They serve to multiply it to infinity, and, at the same time, they are a diversion and a neutralization (this was already the case with the events of 1968). The image consumes the event in the sense that it absorbs it and offers it for consumption. Admittedly, it gives it unprecedented impact, but impact as image event. (Baudrillard 2012, 21)

In this collision between image and reality, as Baudrillard puts it, the image becomes hegemonic—not because it represents the real, but because it *engulfs* it. The event itself is less tangible than the "real-time of images" that broadcasts and reproduces it. However,

---

[1] The notion of the "clash of civilisations" was coined by Samuel P. Huntington and first appeared in an essay published in the Summer 1993 issue of *Foreign Affairs*. Entitled "The Clash of Civilisations?," Huntington's essay posits that after the Cold War, the "fundamental source of conflict" will be a "conflict between civilisations" rather than "among princes-emperors, absolute monarchs and constitutional monarchs attempting to expand their bureaucracies, their armies, their mercantilist economic strength and, most important, the territory they ruled" (Huntington 1993). Huntington's idea resurfaced in the aftermath of 9/11, classifying the event as a symptom of that "clash of civilisations." Following this resurgence, the notion faced heavy criticism and was repeatedly dismissed by prominent figures such as Noam Chomsky, Slavoj Žižek (2012, 51), and Jürgen Habermas (2003, 36).

this *absorption* is directly connected to the *replicability* of the image. The image becomes hegemonic because it is *numerically* superior to the event itself, thus *overwhelming* the event and separating from it at the same time:

> In this case, then, the real is superadded to the image like a bonus of terror, like an additional *frisson*: not only it is terrifying, but what is more, it is real. Rather than the violence of the real being there first and the *frisson* of the image being added to it, the image is there first, and the *frisson* of the real is added. Something like an additional fiction, a fiction surpassing fiction. (2012, 22)

Baudrillard's argument thus reverses conventional thinking: rather than the image being a product and an aftershock of the real, the real attaches itself to the image, as if seeking legitimacy through its spectacle. This excess of imagery does not just mediate reality—it produces a hyperreal event, an aestheticised catastrophe that consumes itself in its endless replication.

Slavoj Žižek makes a similar point in *Welcome to the Desert of the Real* (2002). Following Karl Heinz Stockhausen's assertion that 9/11 was essentially the ultimate work of art, Žižek argues that the collapse of the towers can be seen as the "climactic conclusion of twentieth-century art's 'passion for the Real'" (Žižek 2012, 13). The event punctured the postmodern condition, which had long been defined by a "passion for the semblance" — an obsession with simulacra, virtuality, and surface. Žižek sees this departure from the postmodern virtualisation of reality as both traumatic and perversely satisfying, noting that:

> [The] 'terrorists' themselves did not do it primarily to provoke real material damage but *for the spectacular effect of it*. When, days after September 11, 2001, our gaze was transfixed by the images of the plane hitting one of the WTC towers, we were all forced to experience what the 'compulsion to repeat' and *jouissance* beyond the pleasure principle is: we wanted to see it again and again; the same shots were repeated *ad nauseam*, and the uncanny satisfaction we got from it was *jouissance* at its purest. (Žižek 2012, 13)

Akin to Baudrillard, Žižek observes that the spectacle of 9/11 ultimately overshadowed the event itself, culminating in what he describes as its "apparent opposite" — a "theatrical spectacle" (2012, 10). The event is not only an image but also a reality. It thwarted the postmodern virtualisation of the real that deprives products "of their malignant properties: coffee without caffeine, cream without fat, beer without alcohol," and just as these products come to be experienced like "the real thing," so "virtual reality is experienced as reality without being so" (2012, 12). The event is simultaneously a "virtualised" version and a real one.

The precedents for this kind of setting had been prepared by the Hollywood motion picture industry, whose productions had corrupted the perception of the real thing, so much so that for us, "the landscape and the shots of the collapsing towers could not but be reminiscent of the most breathtaking scenes in a big catastrophe production" (2012, 17–18). This effect was not accidental. Žižek notes that "a group of Hollywood scenarists and directors, specialists in catastrophe movies, had been established at the instigation of the Pentagon, [to imagine] possible scenarios for terrorist attacks and how to fight them" (2012, 18). The boundaries between simulation and reality, fiction and catastrophe, had already been blurred long before the towers fell. Without this pre-existing "phantasmatic background" created by the Hollywood motion picture industry, 9/11 would not have had the same spectacular effects (2012, 19).

Thus, where Baudrillard sees the image consuming the real, Žižek suggests something even more unsettling: the real arrived because we had already imagined it. The event was not simply "hijacked" by media spectacle; it was pre-scripted within the logic of disaster cinema, national security simulations, and a culture primed to consume catastrophe as entertainment. In this sense, 9/11 was not just a terrorist attack—it was a "virtualised" event that collapsed into its hyperreal premonition.

Unlike Baudrillard, Žižek does not attribute agency to the image itself; instead, he explains its *replicability* as stemming from the viewers' pathological compulsion, in Freudian terms, to repeatedly look at the pictures of the planes hitting the two towers. The rewatching of 9/11 footage, Žižek argues, is less about witnessing reality and more about an unconscious attempt to process an event that cannot be fully integrated into experience:

> The Real which returns has the status of a(nother) semblance: precisely because it is real, that is, on account of its traumatic/excessive character, we are unable to integrate it into (what we experience as) our reality and are therefore compelled to experience it as a nightmarish apparition. This is what the compelling image of the collapse of the WTC was: an image, a semblance, an 'effect', which, at the same time, delivered the 'thing itself'. (Žižek 2012, 22)

In this sense, Žižek elucidates the process by extending the argument beyond Baudrillard's fatalistic media determinism. He not only separates the images/effects from the event but also places them under the viewer's tutelage. There, they are objectified and thus replicated to such an extent that they overwhelm the event. It is not the image that has power over us, but our compulsive desire to return to it.

However, these images/effects illuminate not the event itself but another semblance, namely, another image/effect. In the clash between image and reality, as Baudrillard posits, reality is always at a disadvantage, for every time the images/effects emerge, they do not draw the viewer closer to the "reality" of the event but rather increase the distance between the two. In this endless cycle of image producing another image, we consume not the event itself but an excess of its mediation. The more we watch, the further we are from the real.

The virtualisation of the Real, as Žižek puts it, is also the primary focus of Paul Virilio's *Ground Zero* (2002), where he frames 9/11 within a more significant trajectory of artistic and technological decline. Within this trajectory, which inevitably leads to decadence, the anarchist, the terrorist, and the avant-garde artist are increasingly indistinguishable. However, Virilio does not directly address this in his book; instead, he attempts to demonstrate that things have deteriorated since the Renaissance. Within this dialectic of decadence, September 11, as a thwarted form of art, occupies a relatively small space:

> The artists of the twentieth century, like the anarchist with his home-made bombs, the revolutionary suicide bomber or the mass killers celebrated by the mass-circulation press, would themselves become wielders of plastic explosives, visual mischief-makers, anarchists of colour, form and sound before coming to occupy the gutter press's gallery of horrors. (Virilio 2002, 48)

Here, Virilio inverts the causal order: rather than terrorism becoming art, it is art that has long been preparing the conditions for terrorism as spectacle. Through an increasingly technologised imagination, artistic production in the twentieth century evolved towards explosions of meaning, aestheticised destruction, and the spectacularisation of violence. In this context, the September 11 attacks do not introduce anything new; they merely realise the latent potential of an aesthetic logic already established. For Virilio, Ground Zero is not just the physical site of the Twin Towers' collapse but a metaphorical threshold where reality and its representation collapse into one another.

At this point, the event's dual nature becomes unmistakable in the works of Baudrillard, Žižek, and Virilio. The material rupture of 9/11, embodied in the vacancy left in the Manhattan skyline, coexists with its symbolic rupture, which reshapes cultural, political, and linguistic frameworks. On the one hand, the attack produced changes in what we perceive as "real"—security policies, urban landscapes, and global geopolitics. On the other hand, it created a semantic void that necessitated a re-evaluation of older notions or the creation of new ones. There is also a sense that once this dual nature is established, the symbolic, which is generally prone to alterations through frequent use, tends to diverge from the physical and develop its autonomy. In this sense, reality becomes superfluous as the symbolic circulates and gains momentum.

The compulsion to replay the events, as posited by Žižek, can be viewed as a symptom of the malleability of the event's symbolic nature. With each replay, the event accrues new meanings and perspectives until the necessity for further replay dissipates, as the event is already present and only a minimal stimulus is required to evoke it again. This phenomenon of *recollection*, akin to Proust's *involuntary memory* that "comes unsolicited, often with explosive force, to unsettle the individual in the present" (Gross 2000, 47), is simultaneously grounded in the event's permanence in visual terms. Although the "real" becomes unnecessary in terms of tangible participation in the unfolding of the event, it is the "real" and the underlying tragedy that renders the symbolism so pervasive and compelling since the denial of the image would ultimately lead to a denial of the "real' — a movement that is first and foremost countered by the sheer volume of both amateurish and professional material that could serve as proof of its existence.

However, in the case of Proust's involuntary memory, while the uniqueness of the triggering stimulus (i.e. the Madeleine) may evoke different experiences for different users, in the case of *selfish events*, this order is reversed: diverse triggering stimuli point to a singular experience — not of having been present when it occurred, but of witnessing the event through other means. One of the most recurring tropes in discussions about 9/11 was *recalling* where one was when it happened, a phenomenon that reaffirms the event's structuring role in both personal memory and historical consciousness. The event, therefore, exerts a centripetal force, drawing disparate situations towards itself. These varied situations offer insight into the event within this gravitational vacuum.

Ultimately, *selfish events* are not just remembered; they actively shape the *conditions* of memory itself. They impose a structure in which all paths return to the event, reinforcing its status as an undeniably real and endlessly reproducible point of reference in cultural discourse and individual recollection.

1.3 Genes, Memes, and Relativity: An Event's Eye View of Culture

The concept of the *selfish event* I advocate is rooted in two primary ideas from distinct research fields. The first is derived from evolutionary theory and addresses how individual organisms compete for survival in challenging and changing external environments. This notion is based on Richard Dawkins' idea of "selfish genes," extensively discussed in his 1976 book, *The Selfish Gene*, where he suggests that genes behave as self-replicating entities, competing for survival by ensuring their transmission across generations. Similarly, *selfish events* do not passively exist in historical memory but actively work to sustain and propagate themselves, shaping the narratives, ideologies, and discourses that surround them.

The second foundational idea, used in conjunction with the concept of the "selfish gene," derives from physics and pertains to the relationship between spacetime and matter, as well as how these two elements interact and influence each other. Albert Einstein proposed and developed this concept in his renowned work, *Relativity: The Special and General Theory* (1916). Just as massive objects distort spacetime by creating gravitational wells that pull other bodies into their orbit, *selfish events* bend cultural and historical discourse around themselves, ensuring their continued relevance and primacy. They become gravitational centres of meaning, drawing disparate discussions, memories, and narratives toward them while simultaneously reshaping the landscape of collective consciousness.

Richard Dawkins' *The Selfish Gene* (1976) presented a provocative shift in evolutionary thought, arguing that genes, and not organisms, are the actual units of selection. His analysis *anthropomorphised* genes by allotting them decision-making powers that animated their struggle for survival, thereby explaining evolution better. In his preface to the second edition, Dawkins explains that rather than focusing on individual organisms, the book "takes a gene's-eye view of nature" (2006, xv). This perspective profoundly affects how we see organisms, which, in Dawkins's almost fictional rendition, become secondary to genes. In this equation, higher-order organisms, such as humans and animals, become mere "machines created by our genes" to ensure *their* survival over the ages (2006, 2). The genes, also known as *replicators*, of which modern humans and animals are carriers, "indirectly control the manufacture of bodies" by overseeing, for example, the production of proteins, which "not only make up much of the physical fabric of the body" but also "exert sensitive control over all the chemical processes inside the cell, selectively turning them on and off at precise times and in precise places" (2006, 23). From this perspective, bodies are not replicators because they do not reproduce themselves. The sole aim of bodies is to "propagate their replicators" by functioning in such a way as to preserve those replicators (2006, 254).

In this sense, the genes are like computer programmers because all they can do is "set up" one of their survival machines to work independently from the beginning (2006, 52), much like policymakers who instruct their machines to do what they believe is best to ensure their survival (2006, 60). Thus, considering the indirect influence that genes exert on these processes — an impact that extends well beyond protein production — a body comes to be perceived as "the gene's way of preserving the genes unaltered" (2006, 23). The stronger the body, the greater a gene's chances of long-term survival.

Much like genes programme bodies to ensure the survival of their genetic material, *selfish events* programme language, literature, media, and political rhetoric to reinforce their dominance. The stronger the narrative structures surrounding the event, the greater its longevity within historical consciousness. In this sense, historical events do not merely occur and fade away; instead, they strive for mnemonic survival, competing with other events for a place in the collective memory. The more robust the ideological, symbolic, and institutional framework surrounding an event, the greater its ability to overcome and outlast competing narratives, making it, in a very real sense, *selfish*.

Dawkins' notion of selfish genes was met with intense criticism, and it is not difficult to understand why. The shift to genes as the true agents of survival also implies a shift away from the individual as the centre of evolutionary importance. In Dawkins' framework, individuals are ephemeral, transient carriers, while genes are the true immortals, leaping from one generation to the next, outlasting the organism they inhabit:

> Another aspect of the particulateness of the gene is that it does not grow senile; it is no more likely to die when it is a million years old than when it is only a hundred. It leaps from body to body down the generations, manipulating body after body in its own way and for its own ends, abandoning a succession of mortal bodies before they sink into senility and death.
> The genes are the immortals, or rather, they are defined as genetic entities that come close to deserving the title. We, the individual survival machines in the world, can expect to live a few more decades. But the genes in the world have an expectation of life that must be measured not in decades but in thousands and millions of years. (Dawkins 2006, 34)

Thus, every action the individual performs must be seen as an action a gene undertakes to ensure its survival, meaning that "any individual body is just a temporary vehicle for a short-lived combination of genes" (2006, 25). At the time, Dawkins' theory was akin to that of Copernicus, robbing us of the belief that we were at the centre of the universe.

Just as genes 'leap' across generations by embedding themselves within organisms, *selfish events* leap across time by embedding themselves within narratives, institutions, rituals, and cultural memory. Similar to genes, which do not exist in isolation but must be replicated within biological carriers, *selfish events* cannot survive independently — they require continual reenactment, commemoration, and discursive reinforcement.

Another compelling aspect of Dawkins' theory of selfish genes, which will be helpful when discussing how *selfish events* operate, is his idea of cooperation as a form of *affinity* between genes. Collaboration among genes in the early stages of development and between members of a species or across species is based on similarities between genes. Good genes, Dawkins asserts, "must be compatible with, and complementary to, the other genes with whom it has to share a long succession of bodies," just as a gene for "plant-grinding teeth is a good gene in the gene pool of a herbivorous species, but a bad gene in the gene pool of a carnivorous species" (2006, 84). In other words, a gene's success depends on its compatibility with other genes within a given biological system.

When discussing *selfish events*, as the following chapters will argue, the concepts of *cooperation* and *affinity* chiefly pertain to how these occurrences attract and utilise only those cultural artefacts with which they share a specific affinity or those that possess *gliding signifiers*. Much like a *replicator*, a *selfish event* replicates itself solely within the optimal cultural environments for its growth. It aligns with those that enhance and perpetuate its symbolic and political significance.

Like Dawkins' concept of "selfish genes," my notion of *selfish events* adopts an event-centric perspective on cultural phenomena, viewing cultural transmission as comparable to genetic transmission. This may seem like a leap of faith, but I believe that a reversal of roles might shed light on how events like 9/11 create a ripple effect in a cultural context. Dawkins alludes to this type of transmission when he addresses memes, defining them as "the new replicators" (2006, p. 189). Memes, or units of *imitation*, can encompass a range of elements from "tunes, ideas, catch-phrases" to "clothes fashions, ways of making pots or of building arches" (2006, 192) and can propagate from one mind to another:

> Just as genes propagate themselves in the gene pool by leaping from body to body via sperm or eggs, so memes propagate themselves in the meme pool by leaping from brain to brain via a process which, in the broad sense, can be called imitation. [...] When you plant a fertile meme in my mind you literally parasitise my brain, turning it into a vehicle for the meme's propagation in just the way that a virus may parasitize the genetic mechanism of a host cell. (Dawkins 2006, 192)

While genes are deemed successful when they create gene machines that survive the longest, a meme's success rate originates from its "great psychological appeal" (2006, 193). Dawkins argues that its appeal stems from the fact that a meme "provides a superficially plausible answer to deep and troubling questions about existence" (2006, 193). However specious that answer may be, it must also be concise and convey the essence of a complex situation, or at least provide some alleviation, a means to mitigate harmful situations beyond our control, such as the destructive forces of nature.

According to Dawkins, the concept of God exemplifies a successful meme because it has survived for so long. Although we do not know how it originated in the meme pool, we do know that part of its success lies in its suggestion that "injustices in this world may be rectified in the next" (2006, 193) and that those who are good will receive their due reward. "Memes for blind faith," Dawkins suggests, "have their own ruthless ways of propagating themselves," which is also true of "patriotic and political as well as religious blind faith" (2006, 198). In other words, memes serve as a shorthand for culturally complex situations or matters that are too difficult to express otherwise. A significant part of their success depends on their ability to be concise, easily understood, and remembered.

Both 9/11 and the ensuing "war on terror" serve as shorthand for culturally and politically complex situations. The "war on terror," in particular, became shorthand for a variety of actions on both domestic and international levels, to the extent that it "emerged as a powerful ideological frame," one that provided not only "linguistic cover for widespread political change in the name of national security," but also "an institutionalised way of seeing the world" (Reese and Lewis 2009). Additionally, as the following chapters will suggest, the "war on terror" can be viewed as a *sub-meme*, or a subordinate *frame*[2], of 9/11, meaning that, at least from a structural perspective, the discourses surrounding the wars in Iraq and Afghanistan partly follow trends established in the immediate aftermath of the events of September 11, 2001.

This discursive continuity is particularly evident in literary responses to 9/11 and the "war on terror." Early post-9/11 fiction often employed fragmented narratives told by various narrators to cope with the semantic void created by the events, as well as cultural appropriation to bridge the gap between the alleged perpetrators and the victims. The literature on the "war on terror" similarly utilised these mechanisms. Most narratives analysed in the second part of this book exhibit a similar reliance on fragmentation, polyvocality, and acts of cultural appropriation, suggesting that the storytelling strategies formulated in response to 9/11 were later reiterated and adapted in the context of the wars in Iraq and Afghanistan.

Like Dawkins' intuitive study of genes and memes, Albert Einstein's exploration of relativity marked a departure from traditional scientific paradigms. Upon its publication, *Relativity: The Special and General Theory* (1916) offered readers a brand-new theory of gravity in elegant and straightforward language, rendering Sir Isaac Newton's theory nearly obsolete. Furthermore, while Newton's theory described apples being pulled down by the Earth's

---

[2] Stephen D. Reese's definition of *frames* closely aligns with Dawkins' definition of memes. In "Finding Frames in a Web of Culture: The Case of the War on Terror," included in *Doing News Framing Analysis: Empirical, Theoretical, and Normative Perspectives* (2009), Reese defines frames as "organising principles that are socially shared and persistent over time, that work symbolically to meaningfully structure the social world" (D'Angelo and Kuypers 2010, 17). Although the concepts of both authors are quite similar in this respect, their definitions emphasise different aspects. While Dawkins' definition of a meme focuses on its viral component, specifically its ability to travel rapidly and efficiently from mind to mind, Reese's definition of a frame highlights its power to organise the surrounding social and political reality.

gravity, Einstein's theory introduced a new perspective on the universe.

In Einstein's view, the gravitational pull of a massive object, such as the Sun or the Earth, affects not only physical objects, like Newton's apple, but also light, radio waves, and space-time. "An atom," Einstein argues in Appendix 3c, "absorbs or emits light of a frequency which is dependent on the potential of the gravitational field in which it is situated" (Einstein, Lawson, and Calder 2006, 119). For this reason, stars near a massive body like the sun may appear displaced when observed from the Earth because "rays of light are propagated curvilinearly in gravitational fields" (2006, 70). Conversely, light rays propagate linearly in the absence of gravitational fields and on a smaller scale. Within this framework, Einstein concludes, "the general principle of relativity permits us to determine the influence of the gravitational field on the course of all those processes which take place according to known laws when a gravitational field is absent, i.e. which have already been fitted into the frame of the special theory of relativity" (2006, 92). Einstein suggests that massive bodies distort space and time in their immediate vicinity. This distortion wanes as we move away from these massive bodies, and their gravitational pull diminishes.

Selfish events, like massive celestial bodies, prompt similar cultural distortions — distortions that are particularly visible and measurable when examining cultural artefacts produced before the event. These artefacts, which may have initially held independent meanings, undergo a phenomenon I will call *interpretive intrusion*: a forced reconfiguration of their meaning under the gravitational influence of the selfish event.

One striking example of such an *interpretive intrusion* is George Segal's sculpture *Woman on Park Bench*, which will be examined in depth in the following section. In the wake of 9/11, the whiteness of Segal's sculpture, once an aesthetic and conceptual choice detached from any catastrophe, became involuntarily recontextualised. When situated within the "gravitational field" of *selfish events*, cultural artefacts that bear some *affinity* with the nature of the selfish event appear displaced as their interpretations mutate to acknowledge the presence of the *selfish event*. In conjunction with images of men and women covered in ash running away from the falling towers, the whiteness of Segal's sculpture no longer conveys its initially intended meaning. Instead, it becomes an echo of those men and women, and only a *reparative reading* that deliberately abstracts from the presence of the selfish event can recover the artwork's original semiotic space.

Considering these varied perspectives, I propose the concept of "selfish events" to capture the dualistic nature of significant occurrences that shape and reshape cultural and symbolic landscapes. A "selfish event" has such a profound impact that it exerts a gravitational pull on surrounding cultural artefacts, media, and societal narratives, *reorienting* them toward its core. Like Dawkins' "selfish genes," which prioritise their replication through the survival of their host organisms, selfish events *dominate* and *appropriate* adjacent discourses to ensure their *perpetuation* and *prominence* in collective memory.

These events, through their overwhelming symbolic and real-time immediacy, distort the cultural and interpretive frameworks in which they are situated. They achieve this by *absorbing* existing narratives, symbols, and media, recontextualising them to reinforce the events' authority and significance. This phenomenon results in a unique form of *cultural* and *interpretive hegemony* in which the selfish event, much like a massive celestial body in Einstein's theory of relativity, bends the spacetime of cultural narratives, creating an enduring imprint that influences both contemporary and subsequent interpretations of related and unrelated phenomena.

Understanding selfish events in this way allows us to see how singular occurrences like 9/11 do not simply leave an impact — they embed themselves deeply within the fabric of cultural and historical discourse, continuously reshaping the collective psyche and dictating the horizon of interpretation for years to come.

2. A Cultural Symptomatology of *Selfish Events*

2.1 Plural Voices, Singular Views: Siri Hustvedt's *The Blazing World* and Other, *Stranger Things*

To fully understand the influence of selfish events on cultural narratives and how they shift cultural weight, we must explore how dialogic simultaneity and cultural transfer function in literature. In this context, cultural weight refers to the significance and interpretive influence that a cultural artefact or event holds over a society's collective consciousness and interpretive frameworks. This concept includes both the immediate effect and the lasting impact of the artefact or event within cultural discourse. Post-9/11 literature offers many illustrative examples in this regard. One significant instance of cultural transfer is well documented in Siri Hustvedt's *The Blazing World* (2014), a novel that constructs the identity of Harriet Burden, a fictional artist, through a collection of fragmented voices.

The novel serves as a *mise-en-abyme* of the post-9/11 cultural landscape, illustrating how external factors can significantly influence the interpretation of an event or a work of art. Hustvedt's polyphonic narrative forces readers to confront the issue from different angles and see how shifting perspectives influence meaning. The novel uses distinct narrators for each chapter, inviting readers to inhabit different frames of reference throughout their reading experience.

The chapters themselves do not crystallise into a unified narrative. They are, in fact, clippings from various sources gathered by an enigmatic editor whose introduction, placed at the very beginning of the novel, bestows an investigative aura upon the work if not one of journalistic integrity. The unity implied by the so-called "editor" emerges from these different perspectives. "The best policy," the editor explains towards the end of the introduction, "may be to let the reader of what follows judge for him- or herself exactly what Harriet Burden meant or didn't mean and whether her account of herself can be trusted" (Hustvedt 2014, 6). However, the final judgment the reader can render is always limited by these diverse yet restricted points of view.

At times, the editor's introduction sounds more like a warning, particularly when the editor, who is not the novel's author and whose gender and identity remain unclear except for some vague allusions, declares that Burden's writings often descend into sheer psychosis. There is even talk of mental breakdowns, mental illness, and the artist's self-diagnosed "intellectual loneliness" (Hustvedt 2014, 6). Some of the notebook entries were dated, while others were not. Additionally, Burden "had a system of cross-referencing the notebooks that was sometimes straightforward but at other times appeared byzantine in its complexity or nonsensical," and her handwriting often oscillated between vanishing into illegibility and disappearing behind "drawings that intrude into the written passages" (2014, 4). Despite the documentary value of the notebooks, at times, the editor seems to throw up their hands in near despair. "I sometimes had the uncomfortable feeling," the editor confesses, "that the ghost of Harriet Burden was laughing over my shoulder. She referred to herself several times in her journals as a 'trickster,' and she seems to have delighted in all kinds of ruses and games" (Hustvedt 2014, 10).

The editor's unclear identity raises doubts about the reliability of the entire narrative despite the reputable academic credentials presented to the reader. At one point, the editor's introduction mentions a heavy teaching schedule that interfered with the investigation into Harriet Burden's works, the public scandals she caused, and a subsequent sabbatical the editor took to "work on my book *Plural Voices and Multiple Visions*" (2014, 2). This writing project somewhat mirrors the one found within the pages of *The Blazing World*. The novel serves as a form of adjacent research that resonates with the editor's intellectual interests. *The Blazing World* is an intellectual exercise exploring "plural voices and multiple visions." The editor's identity playfully overlaps with that of Harriet Burden, the "trickster" (2014, 10), the focal point around which the narrative revolves, leading one to wonder whether the editor and the protagonist are, in fact, the same person.

Burden's burden (pun intended) is also multi-layered. She is a female artist, and after having lived in the shadow of her art-connoisseur-dealer husband for so long, she devises an experiment by concealing her female identity behind three male artists who agree to present her work as if it were their own. The purpose of the experiment, as Burden explains in her numerous journal entries, was to expose the art world's biases against female artists, who were often portrayed as victims of a phallocentric perception of art. "All intellectual and artistic endeavours," goes the opening quote attributed to Burden, "fare better in the mind of the crowd when the crowd knows that somewhere behind the great work [...] it can locate a cock and a pair of balls" (Hustvedt 2014, 1). Burden is thus simultaneously setting a trap that, in a self-fulfilling manner, reveals what she, and allegedly others, have long suspected but failed to articulate fully.

The experiment succeeds — at least to a certain extent. Critics dismiss works signed under Burden's name as "high-flown, sentimental, and embarrassing," redolent of a "half-baked Existentialism" (2014, 170). Yet, when exhibited under the names of male artists, the same works suddenly gain critical legitimacy. The experiment's outcome, Fernanda Eberstadt claims in her review of Hustvedt's novel for *The New York Times*, seems "to vindicate [Burden's] thesis about the art world's biases" (Eberstadt 2014). Anton Tisch, the first of the three male fronts, becomes an overnight sensation, only to morph into a "monster" of Burden's own making. His success proves the accuracy of her critique and the limits of her control over the system she seeks to expose. The second male mask, Phineas Q. Eldridge, does not capture Tisch's attention and is not featured in Gap-style ads for sneakers the way Tisch was, but secures a gallery show — a privilege that Burden herself, despite her talent, had struggled to obtain.

However, the experiment unravels when the third and final male front, an artist known as Rune, plays a double game, secretly making claims against Burden while publicly benefiting from the exposure. The true betrayal, however, does not lie in Rune's duplicity alone but in the art critics' refusal to acknowledge Burden's authorship. As the novel makes clear, the real antagonist is the male-oriented inertia of the art world, which actively resists rewriting its established narratives. Oswald Case, a prominent art critic whose written statement appears in the novel, suggests that Rune may have used Burden as a muse because the show mounted under the male artist's name "looks nothing like those squishy Burden works [...] being shown" (Hustvedt 2014, 168). The problem, it seems, lies with the "indefatigability of denial," as Rachel Cusk puts it in her *Guardian* review of the novel (Cusk 2014). The fault in choosing Rune, the story suggests, is that, unlike the other two male artists, who were relatively obscure, Rune's artistic persona overshadowed that of Burden. His existing critical acclaim gave him an interpretive advantage, one that art critics like Oswald Case used to reinforce the art world's prevailing structural biases.

Burden's art experiment is a fitting metaphor for the post-9/11 cultural atmosphere, where perception, context, and naming power shape an artefact's meaning and reception. *The Blazing World* examines the susceptibility of "the mind of the crowd" (2014, 1) to external influences and demonstrates how a slight shift in attribution can dramatically alter interpretation. Burden's works take on new meanings under different names. Once her work is separated from her persona and associated with another name, it transforms into something entirely different.

This process mirrors Mary Douglas's observations in *Purity and Danger* (1966), wherein discarded food and wrappings shift from being "unwanted bits of whatever it was they came from" and thus dangerous to acquiring a new and more stable identity within the structured category of a rubbish heap (Douglas 2002, 197–98). In both instances, meaning is not inherent but contingent upon classification. Likewise, Burden's works, when viewed in isolation, lack significance; however, once they are categorised as authored by a male artist, they gain recognition and critical legitimacy.

This transformation in perception, where neutral or unrelated attributes become symbolically charged due to historical or cultural shifts, is a defining feature of the post-9/11 landscape. In *Ethics, Evil, and Fiction* (1999), Colin McGinn provides a striking example of this process through Adolf Hitler's moustache. Although inherently free of moral or ethical attributes, the toothbrush moustache "comes to seem the very mark of organised viciousness, a sort of death signature." The moustache carries no intrinsic moral weight, yet it becomes "fearful and repellent" (McGinn 1999, 145) through association.

A similar semiotic transformation occurred in the wake of 9/11, particularly regarding facial hair. Beards, a common feature of Islamic tradition, became a cultural shorthand for radicalism, extremism, and, in many cases, terrorism in the Western imagination. This shift in perception is central to Mohsin Hamid's novel *The Reluctant Fundamentalist* (2007), where the first-person narrator, Changez, urges his unnamed American interlocutor to disregard his beard because he is, in fact, "a lover of America" (Hamid 2008, 1). Despite this plea, Changez later acknowledges that his decision to grow a beard might have been a "form of protest" on his part amid the tensions stemming from the American response to 9/11 (2008, 130). Like Hitler's moustache in McGinn's example, his facial hair ceases to be a neutral aesthetic choice and becomes a loaded political and cultural signifier. Following the *selfish event*, even a seemingly insignificant detail, such as a man's beard, assumes new meanings that ultimately trace back to the event itself.

This semiotic transformation highlights the selfish event's ability to influence cultural artefacts retrospectively. Hustvedt's novel presents one of Burden's art installations, suggestively titled "The Suffocation Rooms," as a prime example of this effect. Although the installation had been completed before the September 11 attacks, the public's perception of it was inevitably shaped by the event's aftermath:

> The show was mounted the spring after New York was attacked, and the little mutant that crawled out of the box had the haunting look of a damaged survivor or a new being born in the wreckage. It didn't matter that the work had been finished well before 9/11. The increasing heat in the rooms contributed to the interpretation; the last, hot room felt ominous. At the same time, my debut was an insignificant casualty of the falling towers. (Hustvedt 2014, 129)

In Hustvedt's fragmented narrative, Burden's art installations are not the only ones that succumb to this retrospective reinterpretation occasioned by the violence of the "falling towers" (Hustvedt 2014,

129). The earlier works of one of her male counterparts, Rune, face the same interpretation, with the notable exception that his works were exhibited well before September 11. The narrative thus chronicles how, after 9/11, Rune's "coloured crosses" exhibition (2014, 169) took on an entirely different meaning. "Modelled on the Red Cross symbol in different colours," Oswald Case explains in his written statement included in the novel, "they could have been an ironic reference to the whole history of Christianity or [...] the Crusades. After 9/11, they looked prescient: East-and-West conflict, civilisations at war" (Hustvedt 2014, 170). Akin to a deflector in space, the *selfish event* acts as a gravitational force, pulling unrelated artefacts into its interpretive field and distorting their meanings in ways their creators could not have anticipated.

The novel also explores how, in the wake of 9/11, artists felt compelled to alter their aesthetics in response to the event's overwhelming cultural gravity. In an interview with the same Oswald Case, Rune allegedly admitted that he had never experienced awe before 9/11. "He called it 'emotional superconductivity,'" Case recounts, "he wanted it in the work" (Hustvedt 2014, 168). Profound cultural events like September 11 do not merely alter understanding; they impose an *imperative* for artistic evolution, compelling artists to push beyond the limitations of representation. In its aftermath, every artist grappled with whether it was possible to depict a tragedy already saturated with images and narratives in a meaningful way. One could argue that such events establish an ethos of artistic creation and perception that must acknowledge the presence of these events as a regulatory "primal scene," a foundational moment that regulates creative expression and determines the boundaries of acceptable interpretation.

Roland Bleiker argues in "Art after 9/11" that the September 11 attacks "engendered a more fundamental breach in human understanding," a rupture that security experts struggle to grasp but that aesthetic insights can illuminate (Bleiker 2006). A testament to this rupture, Bleiker suggests, is the surge of creative expression that followed the attacks. However, Bleiker somewhat fails to acknowledge in his survey of artistic representations of these events that, in addition to the pressing cultural need to represent the *unrepresentable*, of which that outpouring of creativity was a symptom, there is also a more pragmatic dimension: the element of opportunism that inevitably accompanied this surge. Artists created because they felt compelled to contribute their understanding of the events *and* because the attacks provided a platform from which to project their work. As with any seismic historical moment, the gravity of 9/11 both demanded artistic engagement and facilitated new creative trajectories, positioning the attacks as both an object and a springboard for visibility.

This dual process of aesthetic transformation and symbolic contamination became the focal point of a 2012 exhibition at the Museum of Modern Art. Titled *"September 11,"* the exhibition marked the tenth anniversary of the attacks and ran from September 11, 2011, to January 9, 2012. For the exhibition, MoMA PS1 curator Peter Eleey assembled a collection of artworks, most of which were not directly related to 9/11 but were close enough to compel the audience to confront the notion that, while the works themselves had not changed in that time, their perception had transformed in the wake of the events. "The exhibition," as Michael H. Miller notes in the *Observer*, "is more about how September 11, 2001, changed the experience of viewing art after the fact and less about the day itself. This new context gave certain works a more menacing appearance" (Miller 2011). In his catalogue essay, Eleey articulated a similar perspective, stating that the exhibition aimed to create "a setting that directly challenges visitors to read 9/11 into the art (or to reject such a context)," ultimately interrogating "the persistence of [9/11] in the mind" (Eleey 2011). The exhibition thus served as an experiment in interpretive inevitability.

An instance of this persistence of interpretive contamination can be found in Don DeLillo's novel *Falling Man* (2007), where a still-life painting by Giorgio Morandi—originally depicting an arrangement of mundane household objects (boxes, biscuit tins, and bottles)—becomes imbued with an uncanny prescience concerning 9/11. As in Rune's "coloured crosses" from Hustvedt's *The Blazing World*, Morandi's painting was conceived and exhibited decades before the attacks, yet its visual composition allows for an eerie reinterpretation in their aftermath:

> Two of the taller items were dark and sombre, with smoky marks and smudges, and one of them was partly concealed by a long-necked bottle. The bottle was a bottle, white. The two dark objects, too obscure to name, were the things that Martin was referring to. 'What do you see?' he said. She saw what he saw. She saw the towers. (DeLillo 2011, 49)

The two dark shapes in Morandi's painting could represent any ordinary objects, but in the post-9/11 interpretive field, their ambiguity transforms into specificity. The resemblance to the Twin Towers becomes not incidental but inescapable, as if the image has been lying in wait to be retroactively activated by the event. DeLillo's novel suggests that in the cultural atmosphere surrounding 9/11, even abstraction cannot shield artworks from being repurposed by the event's overwhelming symbolic gravity.

A similar interpretive shift occurs in the case of George Segal's sculpture, *Woman on a Park Bench*, included *in MoMA PS1's September 11 exhibition*. When the show was displayed at MoMA in 2012, the artist had been deceased for over ten years, and his work first emerged well before 9/11. However, the ghostly whiteness of the woman in the sculpture could easily be interpreted, like the 'little mutant' in Burden's art installation, as one of the survivors fleeing the clouds of dust from the collapsing towers (LUAG, n.d.). The sculpture's lack of distinctive features, rather than shielding it from reinterpretation, renders it an ideal vessel for cultural projection, demonstrating the extent to which *selfish events* retroactively claim artefacts, repurposing them within their gravitational field.

In some cases, the intrusion of the *selfish event* into interpretative processes that are otherwise disconnected from it is even more forceful, violently restructuring meaning in ways that seem irreversible. Peter, one of the narrators of David Levithan's *Love is the Higher Law* (2009), illustrates this phenomenon when he witnesses the smoke rising from the Twin Towers while standing in Washington Square. At that moment, the reality embedded in the music he loves suddenly fractures:

> I know if I press play, the song will never be able to work for me again because instead of the song playing under the moment, the moment will weigh on top of the song, and I am never going to want to remember this, I am never going to want to remember this, I am never going to want to be here

again, so I walk without anyone else's words in my ears, and all the music falls away from the world, because how can you have music on a day like today? (Levithan 2010, 39)

Here, the music remains unchanged, but the event prescribes how it is heard and experienced. Peter resists pressing play because he understands that the event will become embedded in the song, irrevocably altering its meaning. The "moment," as Peter describes it, asserts itself as a *hegemonic* discourse, eclipsing all other narratives and rendering them subservient.

The acknowledgement of this interpretive intrusion recurs almost obsessively in Peter's narrative, partly due to his passion for music, an art form especially vulnerable to external contamination. Music, with its *gliding signifiers* and context-dependent meanings, becomes a prime example of how selfish events distort perception. "We all understand that this is just music," Peter notes during a Travis concert he attends in New York City, "[we] all understand that these songs were written Before—there is no way the band could have known how we would hear them After" (2010, 87). Yet, despite this awareness, both Peter and the audience inevitably surrender to the event's shifting signifiers. Their collective experience is reshaped by the very forces they recognise but cannot resist.

September 11 also changed Peter's relationship with a U2 album released nearly a year before the attacks. Before that day, Peter appreciated the album "but didn't need it," but afterwards, his perception underwent a profound shift. "The song I latched onto most," Peter explains, "the song that I would play ten times in a row because I needed to hear it all ten times, was 'Walk On.' It was that unexpected, almost religious thing: the right song at the right time" (2010, 119). The reasons for this alignment between reality and representation also highlight the *selfish* nature of the event, as another historical trauma of a similar nature and scope is considered. "I think one of the reasons [U2 spoke] to so many Americans right after 9/11 is because they know what we're going through. They lived through Ireland in the '70s and the '80s. They know what it's like to be bombed and threatened and afraid. They know what it's like to walk on. They're not just singing it" (Levithan 2010, 119–

20). Much like the commemorative plaque in Astoria, which places the General Slocum disaster in dialogue with 9/11, these songs connect two initially unlinked events, providing new meanings to the recent event, which acts as a *primal scene*, a dominant interpretive framework through which other tragedies are understood.

The phenomenon of *intrusive* and *dialogic simultaneity* is equally evident in the discourses surrounding the American "war on terror," particularly in the cultural artefacts that, while not explicitly addressing post-9/11 realities, are nonetheless filtered through its interpretive frameworks. A striking example emerges in *Stranger Things*, Netflix's original series released in July 2016. Although set in 1983, the show's depiction of government surveillance inevitably resonates with contemporary anxieties stemming from the Edward Snowden leaks and the subsequent mass surveillance scandals.

This interpretive slippage is especially apparent in the seventh episode of the first season. When Mr Wheeler—the archetypal oblivious father—assures his wife that they should trust the government agents who have infiltrated their home, insisting that the government is always on their side, the line carries unintended irony. Following revelations about extensive state surveillance post-9/11, the audience is primed to view his naïve faith in authority as profoundly misguided. The show's Cold War setting and narrative align it with 1980s paranoia about covert government operations, but in a post-Snowden, post-Patriot Act era, its themes acquire a secondary meaning. The series, like other cultural artefacts of its kind, thus becomes a site of *mnemonic convergence*, where past and present fears about state overreach collapse into one another.

The series subtly implies that the government was on no one's side, except, perhaps, for Jim Hopper (played by David Harbour), the lone policeman whose involvement in the events is driven more by personal than professional duty. This narrative of governmental indifference and secrecy is not purely fictional; it is rooted in historical precedents. As *Rolling Stone* journalist Cady Drell observes, while *Stranger Things* is heavily influenced by cinematic giants like Steven Spielberg and literary icons like Stephen King, "some of its creepiest source material comes from the real world" (Drell, n.d.).

A CULTURAL SYMPTOMATOLOGY OF *SELFISH EVENTS* 71

"Past the plot points about the Upside-Down and the slime monsters," Drell writes, "there are references to government mind-control programs and covert experiments in telepathy that actually took place in the U.S. throughout the 20th century—like MKUltra and the Stargate Project" (Drell, n.d.). Throughout the series, Eleven (Millie Bobby Brown), the girl with the bizarre ability to move objects, including cars, with her mind, frequently experiences flashbacks of mind-control experiments conducted by Dr. Martin Brenner (Matthew Modine). After the experiments, the girl remains emotionally crippled, mirroring the experience of those involved in the MKUltra experiments. In this context, Eleven functions as a fictional cypher for the very real victims of state-sponsored psychological experimentation.

On August 28, 1982, journalist Jack Anderson reported in the *Washington Post* that, following revelations about the horrors of the MKUltra program and the wave of lawsuits that followed, the CIA was forced to admit that it had conducted experiments on individuals without their informed consent. The agency was unable to produce written consent forms upon request, and, in many cases, no medical personnel were present when subjects were drugged. "One of the plaintiffs," Anderson reported, "Farrell V. Kirk, was used as a chemical mixing bowl" despite the agency's awareness of his fragile mental and emotional state. The experiments had devastating consequences—Kirk attempted suicide multiple times, at one point trying to burn himself, hang himself, and even gnaw off his own arm (Anderson 1982, 17). *Stranger Things* subtly nods to these historical atrocities and embeds their echoes within its fictionalised portrayal of government-sanctioned mind control.

Stranger Things also makes extensive references to sensory deprivation techniques, which, as Drell notes, were used "to coerce testimony out of suspected terrorists at government black sites." Drell's reference to CIA torture methods is particularly revealing. Released in 2016, the series was probing the still-open wounds left by the *Senate Intelligence Committee Report on CIA Torture*, which had been declassified in late 2014. Drell points out that in the series, "sensory deprivation tanks are used to trigger [one character's] powers to help her listen in on far-away conversations and sneak up on the monster from the Upside Down. In real life, they mostly trigger hallucinations" (Drell, n.d.). This echoes real-life accounts from the report, which describes sensory deprivation as one of many "advanced interrogation techniques" deployed by the CIA to extract intelligence from detainees.

One footnote in the declassified document details how prisoners at a CIA black site were subjected to "techniques that were not recorded in cable traffic, including multiple periods of sleep deprivation, required standing, loud music, sensory deprivation, extended isolation, reduced quantity and quality of food, nudity, and 'rough treatment'" (n.d., 107). Following a *selfish event*, namely one that, due to its resonance, relocates and reshapes meaning, cultural artefacts acquire new meanings, and they narrativise not only their initial signifier, in this case, the MK-Ultra experiments and the atmosphere of state surveillance of the 1980s but also their acquired signifier, state surveillance and torture in the post-9/11 world. In this way, the *selfish event* layers historical precedents onto more contemporary fears.

With its stark division between a familiar "real" world and an ominous "Upside Down" that mirrors it while harbouring malevolent, *Stranger Things* — much like Peter's songs in Levithan's novel — resonates with both contemporary anxieties *and* the political atmosphere of the 1980s. Just as the terrorists turned passenger planes into weapons of destruction, the creatures from the "Upside Down" infiltrate and destabilise the known world, spreading fear and disorder. Moreover, much like the artworks in Hustvedt's and DeLillo's novels, these images become prescient, as if they were warnings ignored by those who, in their complacency, had not seen *it* coming even in the 1980s. For viewers, state surveillance in the 1980s seems distorted and is informed by recent events, creating a layered, dialogic relationship between past and present.

Upon examining these instances, a common thread emerges. While these depictions do not explicitly reference the events of September 11 or the ensuing "war on terror," they exhibit what Susan Willis calls "circulating signifiers" (Willis 2005, 15) — symbols that can be readily co-opted by a culturally dominant or *selfish* event, following Richard Dawkins' notion of the "selfish gene" (Dawkins

2006). However, Willis' concept suggests more than just circulation; it implies that the signifier becomes *objectified* and *reified* in different contexts, its meaning evolving to reflect shifting policies. This process also presupposes an underlying affinity between the signifier and the situation in which it is repurposed. A case in point is the national flag, which Willis identifies as a prime example of this transformation:

> Not only is the flag displayed at fixed positions, on homes, freeway overpasses, and storefronts, [but] it has also become a *circulating signifier*. The flag raised Iwo Jima style over New York's Ground Zero was subsequently shipped to Afghanistan, where it was raised over the Kandahar airport. Passed from the hands of firefighters to those of the Marines, the flag designates a shift in America's interest away from a host of domestic needs left pending after 9/11 and towards a politic aimed at military operations overseas, whose repercussions on the domestic is, then, the militarization of the homefront under the guise of Homeland Security. (Willis 2005, 15)

Through this process of reification, the flag evolves into what Willis calls a "supersymbol," an empty signifier capable of embodying multiple, sometimes contradictory, referents without losing its perceived coherence (2005, 16). "Like the shroud of Turin," Willis adds, "this flag speaks for a form of patriotism raised to the level of religion" (2005, 16).

However, Willis largely overlooks the fact that national flags have always served as abstract representations of a broad spectrum of meanings, even in a pre-9/11 world. By their very nature, flags are "supersymbols," standing for concepts such as nation, empire, and collective identity. Their capacity to accommodate disparate referents is not a new phenomenon but rather an inherent feature, especially in a multicultural society like the United States. Therefore, the abundance of flags Willis refers to does not necessarily indicate a mutation of meaning. Instead, it pertains to an oversaturation of reality with the abstract notions that flags have *always* symbolised. In the wake of 9/11, the flag did not necessarily transform into an "empty signifier" but instead became hyper-visible, reaffirming national unity at a moment of heightened existential urgency.

Given the limitations of Willis' concepts of "circulating signifiers" and "supersymbols," I argue that a more suitable concept to explain this process—namely, the cultural relocation between two signifiers that do not necessarily share an affinity—is that of the *gliding signifier*. This notion is borrowed from phonology, where *gliding sounds*—such as /w/ and /y/—adapt to their phonetic environment, absorbing traits from adjacent sounds and, in turn, altering both themselves and their surroundings (McMahon 2010, 42). To put it more directly, *gliding sounds* 'intrude' upon their neighbouring sounds to achieve phonological stability. Similarly, selfish events 'intrude' upon artefacts to attain interpretative stability, reshaping them in the process. This interpretative *intrusion* occurs not only at the level of subsequent cultural discourses—such as the shifting interpretations of Burden's artworks in Hustvedt's novel—but also at the level of preceding ones, as exemplified by the Morandi painting in DeLillo's *Falling Man*, which retroactively acquires new significance in light of 9/11. Over time, even artefacts that originally bore no inherent connection to the events begin to appear prescient, as though anticipating a catastrophe that would later define their meaning.

A striking example of this retrospective re-signification can be found in an episode of *Johnny Bravo*, an American animated television series created by Van Partible, which aired on *Cartoon Network* on April 27, 2001. Titled "Chain Gang Johnny," the episode features a seemingly innocuous movie poster in the background of one scene, depicting a burning skyscraper with the ominous tagline "Coming Soon." The absence of a title on the poster further fuelled speculation among conspiracy theorists, who later interpreted it as an eerie premonition of the September 11 attacks. Similarly, an episode of *The Simpsons* that aired on May 2, 1997, also fell into the same 9/11 conspiracy narrative. Titled "To Surveil with Love," this episode shows a magazine cover where the dark silhouettes of the Twin Towers appear alongside the magazine's price ($9), unintentionally forming a visual representation of 9/11. The conspiracy theory gained renewed traction with Trump's rise to power, another event that *The Simpsons* had famously "predicted."

Even more ominously, and perhaps with an unsettling irony, on the night of September 10, 2001, comedian George Carlin took the stage in Las Vegas to perform what he called a "red-hot closing bit" for his upcoming HBO special. In it, he told the audience that he enjoyed "fatal disasters with a lotta [sic] dead people" (Edgers, n.d.). Adding to the eerie timing of his routine, Carlin had also joked earlier in the show about Osama bin Laden and aeroplane explosions resulting from the accumulation of flammable flatulence at the back of the plane:

> These planes get flying so fast that all the most vicious, lethal, volatile, flammable, unstable farts get pushed toward the back of the airplane, where they begin to build up pressure [...] and they build, and they build, and they build until they reach critical fart density—C.F.D.—and they continue to build throughout the flight, until finally, some kid turns on a Game Boy and *boom!* The whole back end of the plane blows off. And you know who gets blamed? Osama bin Laden. Terrorists get blamed for these explosions that are nothing more than cabbage-fart detonations. (Crouch 2016)

Following the events of the next day, the HBO special was considered too controversial for release and remained shelved for fifteen years, eventually published posthumously by Carlin's daughter and collaborators. In a "Culture Desk" feature, Ian Crouch, writing for *The New Yorker*, described Carlin's work as showcasing "shocking prescience on the night before 9/11" and noted how, at a time when comedians struggled with the solemnity required by the situation, "there were some things [...] that even the combative Carlin considered off-limits" (Crouch 2016). Carlin purportedly withheld the release out of concern for taste, although he did not shy away from the topic in later performances, including a show in New York City.

Nevertheless, Crouch—along with others who remarked on Carlin's so-called "prescience" —was careful to ground his observations in rationality. Toward the end of his article, he reflects on how releasing a lost performance to the public always creates an uncanny effect because the piece "is both old, a capsule of the moment when it was recorded, and new, and thus heard in the context of the present" (Crouch 2016). This uncanny duality, a product of temporal dissonance, mirrors the interpretive shifts that occur in cultural artefacts following a *selfish event*. However, unlike Carlin's recording, which was deliberately withheld and later reintroduced into public discourse, most of the cultural artefacts discussed thus far had been available well before the event. In this sense, *selfish events* also serve as a cultural reset, altering the trajectory of all future interpretations.

Philip Noyce's *The Quiet American* (2002), an adaptation of Graham Greene's novel of the same name, was initially scheduled for release shortly after September 11. However, Miramax's fears that the film might be perceived as unpatriotic delayed its distribution for over a year. Set in early 1950s Saigon, the film explores the early stages of U.S. involvement in Vietnam, foreshadowing the war that would follow. Its postponement reflects the heightened sensitivity surrounding narratives that challenged American foreign policy during a time of national crisis.

Although *The Quiet American* was initially withheld from release due to concerns over "matters of taste" and its misalignment with the mournful atmosphere of post-9/11 America, its eventual release in 2002 proved unintentionally timely. The film's depiction of U.S. intervention in Vietnam eerily paralleled the political climate of 2003 as the United States prepared to invade Iraq. In the film, Alden Pyle (Brendan Fraser), an American idealist and CIA operative, is dispatched to Vietnam to manipulate the conflict in favour of the United States. His actions are guided by the theories of York Harding, an American foreign policy strategist who advocates for a "third force" to oust the French colonialists and placate the Vietnamese rebel forces. In pursuit of this vision, Pyle covertly arms a Vietnamese splinter group led by a corrupt militia, resulting in terrorist bombings in Saigon that claim innocent lives. The blame is then strategically placed on the communists, who become convenient scapegoats for escalating American involvement in Vietnam.

The situation depicted in *The Quiet American* is not inherently unpatriotic. Stanley Kubrick's *Full Metal Jacket* (1987) and Francis Ford Coppola's *Apocalypse Now* (1979) also critique the chaos and recklessness of American involvement in the Vietnam War. However, the issue that Miramax had with *The Quiet American* arose from its concerns that, in the post-9/11 context, the film might be perceived — much like Susan Sontag's short piece in *The New Yorker* — as a critique of U.S. foreign policy at a time when such re-evaluations were unwelcome. Unlike the solemn and reverent tone expected in the aftermath of a national tragedy, the film presented an unsettling reflection on American interventionism, one that risked conflicting with the prevailing patriotic sentiment.

By 2003, when *The Quiet American* was finally released, the situation in Afghanistan, one of the central battlegrounds in the United States' global "war on terror," bore striking similarities to the events depicted in the film. The Taliban's resurgence was gaining momentum, and American forces, allied with Afghan troops, launched "Operation Mongoose" against militant fighters. However, the roots of the Afghan conflict stretched back to 1979, when the CIA's active encouragement, along with support from Pakistan's ISI (Inter-Services Intelligence), led to "35,000 Muslim radicals from 40 Islamic countries [joining] Afghanistan's fight between 1982 and 1992" against the Soviet Union (Rashid 1999, 31). The full extent of this support eventually led to "more than 100,000 foreign Muslim radicals [who] were directly influenced by the Afghan jihad" (Rashid 1999, 31). "U.S. government support of the Mujahideen," Michel Chossudovsky argues in "Al-Qaeda and the 'War on Terrorism,'" was depicted as "a 'necessary response' to the 1979 Soviet invasion of Afghanistan in support of the pro-communist government of Babrak Kamal" (Chossudovsky 2008). At the time, this intervention was framed as imperative, leaving little room for dissent or debate.

In the long run, the covert support provided by the United States government and authorised by President Carter laid the groundwork for al-Qaeda. A similar trajectory unfolded during the 2003 Iraq invasion, which ultimately led to the emergence of ISIS. As Robert Wright notes in *The New Yorker*, after the invasion, "Abu Musab al-Zarqawi, a Jordanian who led an obscure group of radical Islamists, rebranded it as an Al Qaeda affiliate and used the wartime chaos of Iraq to expand it" (Wright 2015). That once-obscure affiliate eventually evolved into the ISIS we recognise today.

As *The Quiet American* illustrates, in both Afghanistan and Iraq, the U.S. sought to create a "third force" to combat terrorism.

However, within the broader context of the "war on terror," this force repeatedly turned against its original backers. Although the film was released after these developments, it effectively highlighted U.S. foreign policies even in 2003. The only way to identify the parallels between the two conflicts was to disregard *the locality* or the historical setting portrayed in the film and superimpose the new geopolitical landscape onto it. Had *The Quiet American* been released immediately after 9/11, when patriotism surged, and critical reflection was unwelcome, it might have been yet another "victim" of the falling towers.

Put differently, culturally resonant events have the power to *contaminate* cultural artefacts that happen to be in their proximity, reshaping how an interpretative community interprets them. This contamination is not unidirectional in a chronological sense; rather, it operates fluidly across time. When cultural artefacts containing *gliding signifiers* are placed in dialogic simultaneity — whether temporally or spatially — with *selfish events*, they are often *absorbed* into the discourse of those events. This is particularly true when the events themselves are still in the process of constructing a stable narrative, existing as what might be called 'cultural stumps.' Much like Dawkins' "selfish machines," these events prioritise their own cultural survival at all costs (Dawkins 2006, 66). The more artefacts they subsume, the greater their chances of securing a lasting presence within the cultural landscape.

2.2 Erasures of Locality, Impairment, and Diplopia: Don DeLillo's *Falling Man*

The cultural *contamination* discussed in the previous section reflects, to some extent, the disruptive impact of the terrorist attacks themselves. As Birgit Däwes observes, these attacks "deeply unsettled the relationship between image and reality" (Däwes 2011, 26). One striking manifestation of this rupture in representation and perception is how any two aeroplanes flying near tall buildings now instinctively evoke images of the World Trade Centre's destruction. The enduring cultural influence of 9/11 lies in its ability to imprint itself onto other cultural artefacts, either through direct evocation or structural replication. Once an event of this magnitude becomes embedded in a group's cultural lexicon—a shared system of symbols, narratives, and interpretative frameworks—through media coverage or other means of transmission, it exerts a gravitational pull over meaning-making processes. Even when discussing entirely unrelated events, this newly dominant cultural vocabulary persists, reshaping discourse in ways that foreground the memory and resonance of 9/11.

The interpretative reframing applied to Segal's sculpture and Morandi's paintings can be directly linked to the visual representations that emerged in the immediate aftermath of the attacks. In the days and months that followed, images of devastation became embedded in the collective consciousness, shaping perceptions of subsequent artworks. For instance, *New York Magazine*'s *Encyclopaedia of 9/11* includes a photograph depicting men and women fleeing from the dense cloud of debris that engulfed Lower Manhattan as the towers collapsed (*New York Magazine*, n.d.). The ash and dust are so thick that the individuals' faces are barely discernible as they shield their mouths and faces. The surrounding environment is rendered almost unrecognisable, its defining features erased, making it appear as if it could be anywhere—a void stripped of specificity. This loss of locality, both literal and symbolic, speaks to how the attacks disrupted spatial and visual markers.

Hauntingly titled "Gray Escape," the photo effectively *dissolves* New York City's identity, transforming it into an anonymous space consumed by dust and debris. In the foreground, a man with a loosened yellow tie pulls his shirt collar up over his nose; his entire body is coated in a layer of grey ash. His facial expression is nearly indistinguishable. The watch on his wrist appears eerily luminous, as if the shock of the situation has affected its ability to tell time.

In the background, a man clasps a woman's hand tightly, their shoulders nearly touching. Although the woman's gesture resembles those of others, it seems more like a reaction of shock than a protective gesture; her raised hand appears more like a fist. The man beside her, acting as an almost instinctive barrier between her and the chaos, does not cover his mouth; instead, he gazes outward at the devastation unfolding around him. Their lack of distinct features, with their bodies coated in the same suffocating dust, renders them spectral figures, reminiscent of Segal's *Woman on a Park Bench* (LUAG, n.d.).

This *erasure of locality* is evident in several works featured in MoMA PS1's *September 11* exhibition. One such piece is William Eggleston's dye-transfer print, "Untitled (Glass on Plane) (1965-74)," which shows a hand inserting a straw into a glass filled with a brown-red liquid and ice cubes. Sunlight streaming through the aeroplane window illuminates both the glass and the tray table that supports it. A magazine is visible in the back pocket of the seat in front, just behind the tray table, a familiar detail that anchors the scene in the realm of commercial air travel. The hand in the image wears a ring on the middle finger, while the rest of the surroundings remain out of view, leaving the viewer with a composition that feels both intimate and eerily anonymous.

Like the "Grey Escape" in *New York Magazine*, Eggleston's photograph occupies an ambiguous space, taken in a setting that is both familiar and yet stripped of specificity. This lack of clear context creates a semantic void — what Eleey describes as the mental persistence of 9/11 — allowing the event to imprint itself onto otherwise unrelated images. This persistence of 9/11 in the collective consciousness transforms the photograph into a kind of pre-existing template, a mental shortcut that invites interpretation through the lens of the tragedy.

The image, though taken decades earlier, could easily be mistaken for a moment aboard one of the hijacked planes on that fateful morning. Once this realisation takes hold, the photograph gains emotional and transformative weight. Despite the dates in the caption, the interpretation almost feels *predetermined* by the gravity of historical hindsight. The drink in the image evokes an unsettling parallel, resembling a final indulgence akin to an inmate's last meal before execution. Was the traveller about to enjoy the drink, unaware of what was unfolding or where the plane was headed? Is the moment immortalised in the frame an instance of calm before the storm? The image, though static, now carries the ghostly presence of an event that, although temporarily distant, remains culturally omnipresent.

However, Eggleston's "Untitled (Glass on Plane) (1965-74)" relies on the viewer's prior knowledge of 9/11 to enact this *erasure of locality*. It requires an additional layer of understanding—one that extends beyond the frame and into collective memory. If the significance of 9/11 were to diminish over time, the image would inevitably shed its current connotations, reverting to a more neutral interpretation. Viewers might simply recall their personal experiences aboard an aeroplane, enjoying a drink, rather than associating the image with impending catastrophe.

However, the ideological and institutional contexts in which the photograph is now presented—such as MoMA's September 11 exhibition and the broader post-9/11 atmosphere in New York City—preclude such a benign reading. Essentially, the photograph has been *recontextualised* due to its interpretative flexibility, allowing for multiple interpretations. A similar reframing occurs with Alex Katz's 1994 painting "10:00 AM," another piece featured in the exhibition. The painting's grey and white lines, suggestive of ripples on water against a muted greenish-grey backdrop, contain two indistinct, smoky forms that appear as reflections on the water's surface. The painting's title, uncannily echoing the timeframe of the attacks, along with its erasure of locality, enhances its openness to recontextualization, enabling it to absorb the weight of the event and transform under its gravitational pull.

To a certain degree, DeLillo's *Falling Man* builds upon the same interpretive fluidity and *erasure of locality*. Additionally, the novel embeds the transition from a pre-9/11 to a post-9/11 world through temporal markers. A similar transformation is articulated in the opening of H. M. Naqvi's *Home Boy* (2009), where the narrator recalls how, after 9/11, he and his friends became "Japs, Jews, Niggers," even though they "weren't before" (Naqvi 2011, 3). DeLillo's novel opens with a similarly abrupt recognition of change: "It was not a street anymore," the narrative begins, "but a world, a time and space of falling ash and near night. [...] This was the world now" (2011, 3).

Here, the street has ceased to be merely a street; its original function and meaning have been irrevocably altered. Using Mary Douglas' theoretical framework, in the world of "falling ash and near night" (DeLillo 2011, 3), the street exists in a state of liminality — it is "recognisably out of place," its "half-identity" as a street still clinging to it, yet its presence distorts the clarity of the scene it inhabits (Douglas 2002, 197). Because it no longer fits within its former conceptual framework, its continued presence in the narrator's memory becomes almost absurd. How could it have ever been just a street, given its current condition, submerged in "falling ash and near night"? How does it integrate into this new, disorienting reality? The question itself highlights the story's exploration of a milieu where familiar landmarks have become shifting signifiers, forever altered by the gravity of the event.

The *impairment* Douglas describes amplifies the violence of the following sentence in *Falling Man*, where "anymore" gives way to "now," and "the roar" of the collapsing towers lingers in the air. The world may have been different before, but this — this altered reality — is how it exists *now*. At this moment, the "street" sheds its "half-identity" and is fully subsumed into a newly defined place, a world dictated by the event's aftermath. In this world, even fundamental structures like streets, which impose order through traffic regulations and spatial continuity, have become obsolete. "The world was this as well," the narration continues, as if to underline this *suspension* of prior rules and categories: "figures in windows a thousand feet up, dropping into free space, and the stink of fuel fire, and the steady rip of sirens in the air" (DeLillo 2011, 4). The vortex created by the falling towers does not merely distort perception — it entirely *restructures* it, overriding the street's prior identity and replacing it with a world governed by spectacle, destruction, and disorientation.

Nevertheless, in *Falling Man*, as in "Grey Escape," the *erasure of locality* extends beyond the external world, consuming even the internal coherence of the protagonists. The event, as James Berger suggests, "had taken over reality entirely" (Berger 2003, 54). As DeLillo's protagonist, Keith Neudecker — a 39-year-old lawyer working in the World Trade Center — joins the stream of survivors fleeing the wreckage, he maintains an eerie sense of detachment as if insulated from the immediate chaos. "Things inside were distant and still," the narrator observes as if pointing to an inner core untouched by the rumble of the collapsing towers: "[it] happened everywhere around him, a car half buried in debris, windows smashed and noises coming out, radio voices scratching at the wreckage" (DeLillo 2011, 3–4). Unlike those around him, Neudecker does not run; he walks, his movements deliberate, almost mechanical. When a woman offers him a bottle of water, he does not snatch it in desperation but carefully sets down the suitcase he has been carrying before accepting it. Each of his gestures is described with meticulous precision. Even as he drinks, he is acutely conscious of the water moving down his throat.

However, as Neudecker moves away from the smoke and dust, and as the world comes into focus again—he crosses Canal Street, emerging from the cloud of smoke that engulfed him—he is violently pulled back into the vortex by the sound of the north tower collapsing. In that instant, the boundary between self and catastrophe dissolves entirely. "That was him coming down," the third-person narrator states, "the north tower" (DeLillo 2011, 5). The striking use of the personal pronoun *him* to refer to the tower has been interpreted by Kristiaan Versluys as a symptom of the stream-of-consciousness technique that the novel extensively employs. "External observation," Versluys argues, "seamlessly flows into internal impressions" until the passage signals "a reordering of reality, a shift in reference" (Versluys 2009, 41). The collapse of the tower is not just an external event but an existential one that reflects the dissolution of the self in the face of the overwhelming nature of the event.

This interpretation aligns seamlessly with Versluys' psychoanalytic reading of the novel. He regards this seemingly minor slip as almost Freudian, suggesting that it reflects "compulsion, an obsessive fixation, and, since the referent of the personal pronoun remains cryptic, it also indicates the repression of the traumatic memory, the refusal to remember" (2009, 42). However, rather than framing the novel's protagonists or even the narrator as psychiatric patients, I propose an alternative reading. The shift in the use of the personal pronoun at the very beginning of the novel signals the presence of a *selfish event*. In that moment, Neudecker's individuality is subsumed by the overwhelming gravitational pull of the event itself. The "soft awe of voices" that accompanies the tower's collapse is not merely an external observation; it marks a profound *erasure* of selfhood, an *appropriation* of voice, wherein the event momentarily speaks through him.

The initial sense of composure and clarity that Neudecker maintained within the cloud of dust abruptly dissipates the moment he steps beyond it, as if that clarity had been essential only while he remained inside — or as if the event itself had consumed it. Once outside, he struggles to affirm his own existence: "[he] tried to tell himself he was alive, but the idea was too obscure to take hold" (DeLillo 2011, 6). Beyond the cloud of dust, the characters seem stripped of a part of their individuality, as if the event had drained them of something vital. It is only when "an old panel truck" pulls up and offers him a ride that Neudecker realises where "he'd been going all along" (2011, 6). Within the dust cloud, individual time is suspended, creating a *hiatus* in the protagonist's personal narrative, severing him from the world he inhabited before the event. In this temporal void, even his name ceases to be relevant. It is within this rupture that the event itself begins to assert its agency.

2.2.1 Against the Melancholic State and Other Misuses of Trauma

DeLillo is among many who have observed the stark contrast between the experience inside and outside selfish events. In the wake of the September 11 attacks, there was a noticeable *shift* in perception as one moved farther away from New York City and Ground Zero. Joan Didion captures this phenomenon in *Fixed Ideas: America Since 9.11* (2003), recounting a book promotion trip she took just seven days after the attacks. "[Like] most of us who were in New York that week," she reflects, "I was in a kind of protective coma," merely following a schedule that had been arranged before the gravity of the situation had fully registered (2003, 3-4). The dissonance between those immersed in the immediate aftermath and those further removed from the epicentre highlights how selfish events distort perception and create an internal reality that feels sealed off from the outside world.

Much like Keith Neudecker, who is suddenly confronted with the raw truth of his existence, Joan Didion undergoes a moment of *emergence* from the "protective coma" that had enveloped her during her time in New York City. While in San Francisco, standing on stage during a promotional event, she is handed a book and asked to read a few lines from an essay she had written in 1967 about New York. Believing herself safe from the emotional and ideological entanglements of the present, given the essay's distance in time, Didion begins to read with a degree of confidence. The passage opens with the words, "New York was no mere city," a line that once evoked a romanticised, mythical urban dream. It continues, describing the city as an "infinitely romantic notion, the mysterious nexus of all love and money and power, the shining and *perishable* dream itself" (2003, 4, emphasis added). The word that resonates with unexpected force with her and the audience is "perishable." For a fleeting moment, it seemed as though an essay written in 1967 had foreseen the tragic event. The past and present collapse into one another and the essay is transformed into a premonition.

Yet this realisation is not the only insight Didion gathers during her book promotion tour. The geographical distance separating New York City from the cities she visits — San Francisco, Los Angeles, Portland, and Seattle — also manifests as a *cognitive* and emotional divide. Removed from the immediate spatial violence of the attacks, the people she encounters perceive the unfolding situation through a markedly different lens. "These people to whom I was listening," she observes, "were making connections I had not yet thought to make in my numbed condition: connections between that political process and what had happened on September 11, connections between our political life and the shape our reaction would take and was [...] already taking" (Didion 2003, 5). This moment of epiphany, one in which Didion realises that others have begun parsing the events within a broader ideological and political framework, shocks her, and the reverberations of that shock do not subside. Didion elaborates in this sense:

> These people understood that when Judy Woodruff, on the evening the President first addressed the nation, started talking on CNN about what "a couple of Democratic consultants" had told her about how the President would be needing to position himself, Washington was still doing business as usual. They understood that when the political analyst William Schneider spoke the same night about how the President had "found his vision thing," about how "this won't be the Bush economy anymore, it'll be the Osama bin Laden economy," Washington was still talking about the protection and perpetuation of its own interests.
> These people got it.
> They didn't like it. (2003, 6–7)

Didion witnesses not only the onset of a new political consciousness among those geographically distanced from the attack site but also the first signs of disillusionment—the awareness that even in the face of national trauma, political opportunism thrived. The people she meets grasp something that she, still enveloped in the psychic fog of Ground Zero, has not yet been able to name.

Didion eventually recognises this perceptual dissonance most acutely upon her return to New York City. Unlike in San Francisco or Los Angeles, where critical reflection and political interpretation shaped public discourse, in New York, she encounters a markedly different atmosphere—one in which the event has slipped out of conversation and instead been supplanted by the visual grammar of nationalism. "I came in from Kennedy," she writes, "to find American flags flying all over the Upper East Side, at least as far north as 96th Street, flags that had not been there in the first week after the fact" (2003, 7). In New York, the attacks were no longer being spoken about; they were being *ritualised*. They were becoming "systematically leached of history and so of meaning, finally rendered less readable than it had seemed on the morning it happened" (2003, 8–9). The rawness of the original experience—its immediate clarity, its emotional urgency—was already giving way to a *curated* narrative. Didion felt that the event had imposed a new reality, one in which every location in New York City, every street corner, every skyline silhouette, and every mundane route through the city carried the imprint of the attacks, transforming the urban landscape into a permanent site of mnemonic entrapment.

Given this initial appropriation of individuality by the event, *Falling Man* cannot, as Richard Gray proposes in *After the Fall: American Literature Since 9/11* (2011), be dismissed as "immured in the melancholic state, offering a verbal equivalent of immobility" (Gray 2011, 28). The characters' apparent inertia is not the result of resignation or emotional paralysis, nor is it a simple descent into melancholy. Rather, it is the product of a psychic depletion—of having been drained by the gravitational pull of the selfish event, which imposes a cognitive loop that precludes any forward movement or narrative closure. Keith Neudecker's physical routines, whether compulsively going to the gym or succumbing to the fugue state of gambling, are *not* escapist attempts at emotional numbness. They are instead gestures of coping with the loss of narrative agency, efforts to fill the void left by a mind entrapped within the event's interpretive vortex.

This looping logic becomes apparent when Martin and Lianne observe the Morandi still life. What they see is not a painting, per se, but a *projection* shaped by the event. DeLillo renders the moment in two short sentences that mimic the rhythm and existential symmetry of Hamlet's "to be or not to be": "She saw what he saw. She saw the towers" (DeLillo 2011, 49). This mental loop does not imply immobility but rather a compulsive oscillation between two poles: a passive mental state in which the paintings exist innocuously in the background and an overactive interpretive state in which those same objects are re-inscribed with catastrophic significance. What Gray interprets as paralysis is, more accurately, a symptom of interpretive excess—a hyper-mobility of meaning in which the symbolic weight of the towers colonises perception itself.

Gray is not the only critic to fall into this interpretive trap—namely, the temptation to read *Falling Man* through the lens of what a "9/11 novel" is expected to perform rather than what it articulates. In *Out of the Blue: September 11 and the Novel* (2009), Kristiaan Versluys similarly characterises DeLillo's work as "the darkest and the starkest" of its kind and argues that "[to] an unusual extent, the novel is death-driven" (Versluys 2009, 20-21). What is particularly telling, however, is how subtly but markedly Versluys' reading is shaped by DeLillo's essay "In the Ruins of the Future" (2001), published in *The Guardian* shortly after the attacks. That initial, contemplative response becomes, for Versluys, a blueprint for interpreting *Falling Man*, so much so that he reads the novel almost as an extended prose elaboration of the essay's premises.

It is, then, no coincidence that Versluys frames the novel predominantly in psychoanalytical terms. He describes it as "pure melancholia without the possibility of mourning," a narrative in which trauma is endlessly re-enacted and never resolved (2009, 20). The result, he claims, is a cast of characters who are "minimally alive," numbed and weighed down by "an overwhelming sadness that they cannot shake off" (2009, 23). But like Gray's reading, Versluys's interpretation reflects less a response to the novel's internal rhythms, and more an adherence to the expectations of what a 9/11 novel should be. Because *Falling Man* addresses 9/11, the logic goes, it must therefore be elegiac, trauma-inflected, and melancholically subdued. The tone *must* align with a broader cultural demand for solemnity — a demand rooted not in the text but in the symbolic weight of the event it confronts. What such readings overlook, however, is how the novel interrogates and resists *precisely* these prescribed responses, refusing to present a narrative of easy mourning or cathartic resolution.

This tendency, as Georgiana Banita notes in *Plotting Justice: Narrative Ethics and Literary Culture after 9/11* (2012), resulted in a critical valorisation of Jonathan Safran Foer's *Extremely Loud & Incredibly Close* (2005), which was lauded as "the only compassionate vision" of 9/11, while Don DeLillo's *Falling Man* was castigated as a "heartless and alienating rendering of horror corresponding to 'nothing in this life'" (Banita 2012, 63). Such a reception is not only disconcerting but also revealing, for it sheds light on the ideological expectations imposed by the post-9/11 publishing industry. In the aftermath of the attacks, the implicit message was unequivocal: literary works that offered consolatory narratives, undergirded by emotional accessibility and empathy, were to be celebrated; those that confronted the trauma obliquely or that withheld emotional transparency risked being branded as unpatriotic or morally deficient. In this climate, *tone* became as decisive as content—if not more so. The demand was not simply for literature *about* 9/11 but for literature that *performed* a particular effective stance, privileging emotional catharsis over aesthetic ambiguity or ethical provocation.

These market-driven expectations only intensified as a wave of affect-driven novels began to dominate the literary landscape. Among them, David Levithan's young adult novel *Love Is the Higher Law* (2009) stands out for its explicit focus on the emotional reverberations of the September 11, 2001, attacks. Structured through a fragmented narrative that alternates between multiple perspectives, the novel offers what might be termed a 'compassionate vision' of the event, foregrounding the interior lives of those either directly or tangentially affected. It suggests that forming an emotional community is the most effective way to combat or mitigate the hatred underpinning terrorist violence.

The novel thus prescribes a form of emotional pedagogy, suggesting that community *can* and *should* emerge from collective suffering. "And suddenly I'm feeling this," one of the narrators confesses, "I guess you could call it tenderness—for people I never even liked before" (Levithan 2010, 82). The novel thus taps into the clichéd notion that profound adversity fosters human connection and presents it as the most viable option under the circumstances. A few pages later, Claire tells Jasper, another narrative voice, that the event functions as a kind of moral instruction. "I think we were walking around like we were invincible," Claire tells Jasper after assuring him that she harbours no hidden intentions behind her judgment, "[and] maybe that's a bad way to live your life. Because you're not invincible. Nobody is. And maybe now that we've learned that, we'll be better" (2010, 105). Implicit here is a framework in which catastrophe becomes the crucible for ethical refinement. Yet, as the narrative unfolds, it becomes clear that these sentimental conclusions—though comforting—are not the only ideological prescriptions the novel advances.

Levithan demonstrates a keen understanding of his young adult readership and writes with that in mind. The three protagonists in *Love Is the Higher Law* are convincingly drawn teenagers who express concerns that resonate with both younger and older readers. Claire's observation about America's sense of invulnerability—"we were walking around like we were invincible"—gestures towards a broader critique of American exceptionalism and echoes the intellectual admonitions of figures such as Susan Sontag and Noam Chomsky. Most explicitly, it recalls Slavoj Žižek's analysis: "On September 11, the USA was given the opportunity to realise what kind of world it was part of. It might have taken this opportunity—but it did not, instead opting to reassert its traditional ideological commitments: out with feelings of responsibility and guilt towards the impoverished Third World, *we* are the victims now" (Žižek 2012, 58). Like Žižek, Claire implies that the tragedy of 9/11 did not exist in an ideological vacuum—that it was, at least in part, shaped by America's historical postures and foreign entanglements.

Yet, Levithan's narrative is careful not to allow this view to dominate. Almost immediately, Claire's moment of critical lucidity is undercut by Jasper's sardonic retort: "Or we'll bomb the shit out of Afghanistan" (Levithan 2010, 105). Jasper cannot help but say this, for not saying it would be tantamount to succumbing to a *soft view* of the event. His comment serves as a rejoinder to sentimentality, highlighting the tension between reflection and reaction that characterises much of the post-9/11 discourse.

The two characters, Claire and Jasper, are also strategically positioned in this context. Claire, a girl, expresses a more compassionate and considerate approach, while Jasper, a boy, advocates a more aggressive and confrontational stance. Claire's perspective fosters thoughtful discussion and reflection. In contrast, Jasper's viewpoint presents violence as the primary solution, using language that echoes George W. Bush's demands on the Taliban in his State of the Union address following the attacks. "These demands," the then U.S. President said, "are not open to negotiation or discussion" (*The Guardian* 2001). The injunctions were thus issued. There was no time for self-reflection and no room for contemplation.

In contrast to Levithan's novel and other affect-driven narratives that foreground emotional response as a vehicle for meaning, Don DeLillo's *Falling Man*, as Georgiana Banita contends, deliberately resists the imperative to "[advance] affective responses to the

9/11 events" (Banita 2012, 64). While the novel gestures towards "media narratives of trauma and survival," it simultaneously interrogates and subverts their emotional saturation by enacting what Banita terms an "anesthetisation of emotion in everyday life" (2012, 64). According to Banita, this aesthetic restraint, far from being an evasion or an absence, is a critical strategy: it enables the novel to chart the deeper and more insidious repercussions of the events without becoming ensnared in the emotionally charged nationalism that proliferated in their aftermath. Banita's observation is crucial because it helps us understand that DeLillo's muted emotional register is not a matter of stylistic aloofness or authorial whim (though he is no stranger to those) but a deliberate tactic. By damping down affect, *Falling Man* forgoes the cathartic consolations readers may expect and instead invites a meditation on how trauma disrupts not only the lives of individuals but also the very structures through which we seek to comprehend and narrate catastrophe.

The turn towards affect-driven responses to 9/11 had already taken root well before the publication of *Falling Man*, permeating virtually every stratum of public discourse. Journalists were among the first to adopt this emotionally resonant tone, a shift driven in part by the institutional constraints that shape the field of journalism. The affective register employed by political leaders in the immediate aftermath of the attacks set the rhetorical standard, and the press, under intense pressure to reflect national sentiment, largely complied. As Michael Schudson observes in "What's Unusual About Covering Politics as Usual," included in the second edition of *Journalism After September 11* (2011), reporters "felt thrust into the sphere of consensus" (2011, 48), where deviating from the dominant narrative risked being perceived as unpatriotic or insensitive. In this context, journalistic neutrality gave way to what Schudson describes as a "priestly or pastoral mode," a tone marked by quiet solemnity, akin to "speaking at a funeral" (2011, 48). The range of acceptable responses thus narrowed considerably, and any expression of ambivalence, critique, or political complexity was either marginalised or avoided altogether.

Thus, journalism in the wake of 9/11 was no longer about finding scapegoats — a point Susan Sontag tentatively raised in her brief yet incendiary response in *The New Yorker* (September 24, 2001). There, she criticised "the voices licensed to follow the events," claiming they appeared "to have joined together in a campaign to infantilise the public" (*The New Yorker* 2001). At a time of national mourning, she argued, searching for scapegoats was deemed not only inappropriate but morally untenable.

As Michael Schudson later observed, "post-September 11 journalism sought to provide comfort or reassurance, not just information or analysis" (2011, 48). In this sense, the events of 9/11 inaugurated a new journalistic *ethos* — one defined less by objectivity and critical distance than by emotional resonance and ritualistic solemnity. This shift made dissent perilous, as those who voiced alternative interpretations were swiftly condemned. In *The Weekly Standard* (October 2001), Sontag was accused of "unusual stupidity," "moral vacuity," and "sheer tastelessness" and was lumped together with a host of other "chattering asses" (Bottum 23:01) for her refusal to adopt the sanctioned tone of grief and patriotism. In this light, the outburst Jasper delivers in David Levithan's *Love Is the Higher Law* — "bomb the shit out of Afghanistan" — belongs to the same rhetorical field as Bottum's insult. Both express, in different registers, a refusal to entertain deviation from the affective script.

Literary criticism, by extension, also succumbed to the emotional inflexion that permeated much of the post-9/11 cultural discourse. In the immediate aftermath of the attacks, many literary critics reflexively turned to trauma studies as the most fitting interpretive framework, assuming that the shocking spectacle and scale of devastation necessarily placed literary responses within the domain of collective trauma. Birgit Däwes critiques this assumption, noting that it stems from the mistaken belief that events such as 9/11 are intrinsically traumatic — that their destructive impact on urban space and human life automatically confers traumatic status. Yet, as Jeffrey Alexander et al. contend in *Cultural Trauma and Collective Identity* (2004), trauma is not simply the result of empirical harm or sudden catastrophe; rather, it is a cultural attribution. "Trauma," he writes, "is attributed to real or imagined phenomena, not because of their actual harmfulness or their objective

A CULTURAL SYMPTOMATOLOGY OF *SELFISH EVENTS* 93

abruptness, but because these phenomena are believed to have abruptly and harmfully affected collective identity" (2004, 10). What defines a cultural trauma, therefore, is not pain alone but the successful embedding of that pain into the symbolic core of a group's self-understanding (2004, 10). To put it differently, the violence of one event, regardless of how sudden or prolonged it is, does not guarantee that event's traumatic status.

This distinction proves crucial. As Däwes observes, the attacks on the World Trade Center, while horrifying and deeply unsettling, did not obliterate New York City as a functioning community, nor did they dismantle the broader infrastructure of American society or Western civilisation at large (Däwes 2011, 64). In contrast, historically traumatic events such as the Buffalo Creek flood or the genocidal forced relocation of Native American populations during the Trail of Tears left enduring scars on the social and political fabric of entire communities. By comparison, the status of 9/11 as a trauma was not an inevitability – it had to be narrativised, interpreted, and reinforced as such. That narrative construction served ideological ends, enabling and justifying a series of political and military actions whose legitimacy was grounded in the premise of a wounded national identity in need of restoration or retribution.

The persistent misapplication of trauma theory to literary texts in the wake of 9/11 also arises from the intrinsic vagueness of the term "trauma" itself. Originally a clinical concept, trauma referred to physical injury or psychological harm experienced by individuals. However, with the advent of Holocaust Studies and the increasing focus on collective suffering, the term was gradually expanded to include the experiences of communities, nations, and even entire cultures. This expansion, while fruitful in many contexts, has also led to theoretical imprecision. As Birgit Däwes rightly notes, one common error among those who hastily apply trauma studies to literary texts is the failure to recognise that "fictional characters are not subject to natural or medical laws" (2011, 67). Characters in fiction function not as patients or victims in a clinical sense but as symbolic vehicles through which societies articulate and encode meaning. They do not *experience* trauma in any empirical sense; rather, they *represent* or *assign* traumatic significance to events within a broader cultural narrative.

In this symbolic framework, literature acts as a repository of collective memory and meaning-making, shaping how events are remembered and understood. It is only when a violent occurrence has been narrativised—when its cultural repercussions have been acknowledged and institutionalised—that trauma studies can offer valuable insights. Even when trauma claims are grounded in real suffering, they must still pass through an "imaginative process of representation" to become legible as trauma. Alexander explains this process by disentangling the material violence of an event from the social claims of victimhood that follow. He underscores that it is not the event itself that defines trauma but how it is framed, narrated, and politically mobilised:

> It is not that traumas are never constructed from nonexistent events. Certainly, they are. But it is too easy to accept the imagined dimension of trauma when the reference is primarily to claims like these, which point to events that either never did occur or to events whose representation involves exaggerations that serve obviously aggressive and harmful political forces. [...] Imagination informs trauma construction, just as much when the reference is to something that has [...] occurred as to something that has not. It is only through the imaginative process of representation that actors have the sense of experience. Even when claims of victimhood are morally justifiable, politically democratic, and socially progressive, these claims still cannot be seen as automatic or natural responses to the actual nature of an event itself. (Alexander 2004, 9)

Within this framework, the discursive aftermath of the September 11 attacks—particularly the reactions of the media, publishing industry, and political elite—can be read not merely as the documentation of a traumatic event but as the *construction* of one. The cultural production that followed often relied on narrative exaggeration and emotive framing that, to borrow Alexander's phrasing, served "aggressive and harmful political forces." In this way, 9/11 was not only remembered as trauma; it was *manufactured* as such, rendered traumatic through symbolic repetition, institutional reinforcement, and the emotional tone imposed upon its interpretation.

Ulrike Tancke identifies a similar trajectory in her essay "Uses and Abuses of Trauma in Post-9/11 Fiction and Contemporary

Culture," included in *From Solidarity to Schisms: 9/11 and After in Fiction and Film from Outside the US* (2009). She argues that the concept of trauma has been widely adopted as a heuristic for navigating the complex entanglement of individual and collective responses to 9/11 and that it has been credited with engendering a "new subjectivity based on a collapse of history and memory, time and space" (Cilano 2009, 78)." According to Tancke, this cultural construction of trauma was not spontaneous but rather anticipated by Hollywood cinema, which had already furnished the visual and narrative grammar through which the attacks would be understood. In this sense, the events of September 11 were not received as unprecedented ruptures but were rapidly enfolded into existing semiotic and affective frameworks—into what Tancke refers to as "prefigured processes of signification" (2009, 78).

Crucially, Tancke asserts that the trauma framework, rather than providing a neutral or solely psychological perspective, can be utilised for ideological purposes. Her argument coincides with Jeffrey Alexander's assertion that trauma is not an inherent or automatic reaction to violence, but a constructed and mediated discourse influenced by social and political forces. Tancke suggests that trauma is not simply a raw emotional state; instead, it is a cultural and political artefact—one that can be selectively employed to validate certain narratives while obscuring others.

The process of instrumentalisation becomes starkly apparent in the widespread suppression of dissenting voices, both in the media and the broader cultural sphere. Individuals who expressed even mild reservations about the Bush administration's decisions—whether concerning the wars in Iraq and Afghanistan, the expansion of domestic surveillance, the use of military tribunals, or the indefinite detention of suspects—were swiftly branded as unpatriotic or un-American and subsequently marginalised. This climate of conformity was reinforced by a pervasive wave of sentimentality that swept through New York City and beyond in the aftermath of the attacks. As Joan Didion observes in *Fixed Ideas: America Since 9.11* (2003), the event was rapidly distilled into a set of emotionally charged but intellectually vacant symbols—"the loved ones," "the families," and "the heroes" (2003, 9)—that, while ostensibly honouring the victims, served to foreclose critical inquiry and dissent, and thus precluded a more nuanced understanding of the event and its consequences.

The victims of the attacks were to be commemorated as if their deaths were the result of a noble sacrifice on a battlefield—martyrs of a defining national conflict rather than casualties of a singular and complex catastrophe. In his address to the nation on the evening of September 11, George W. Bush framed the tragedy in overtly symbolic and quasi-mythological terms, declaring, "America was targeted for attack because we're the brightest beacon for freedom and opportunity in the world. And no one will keep that light from shining" (*The Guardian* 2001). The rhetoric was carefully calibrated: the invocation of light as a metaphor for national virtue cast the United States not merely as a victim but as a redemptive force in a struggle between good and evil. The violence, in this framing, was not only real but also symbolic, and it necessitated a retaliatory spectacle that would affirm national identity and resilience in the face of an existential threat.

Given the critical reception of both Jonathan Safran Foer's *Extremely Loud & Incredibly Close* and Don DeLillo's *Falling Man*, it becomes clear that post-9/11 literary production was not only expected to reckon with trauma but to do so in a tone that reaffirmed national ideals. It had to ensure that, despite the challenges posed by a group of people allegedly inherently hateful and envious of America's freedom, that freedom was more alive than ever and would ultimately triumph. Literature, like journalism, was tacitly encouraged to adopt what Michael Schudson calls the "priestly or pastoral mode," a move designed to comfort rather than challenge, to soothe rather than scrutinise. It had to participate in the "campaign to infantilise the public," as described by Sontag, and reduce narratives to moral simplicity and emotional immediacy.

Foer's novel, intentionally or not, yielded to precisely this cultural demand. By filtering the events through the consciousness of nine-year-old Oskar Schell—whose father perishes in the attacks—the novel adopts a register that borders on the childlike, if not the outright sentimental. It is difficult to conceive of a more literal embodiment of the "infantile" perspective Sontag decried. Oskar's grief is transformed into a metaphysical quest, a kind of emotional scavenger hunt propelled by his vivid imagination, which deflects rather than confronts the political dimensions of the tragedy. The novel's affective mode tends to sublimate national trauma into domestic sorrow, thus aligning with the broader cultural imperative to preserve the sanctity of American innocence.

One episode in *Extremely Loud & Incredibly Close* that most strikingly exemplifies the novel's tendency toward infantilisation is Oskar's school presentation on the bombing of Hiroshima. As part of a class project, he plays a recording of an interview with Kinue Tomoyasu, a survivor of the atomic blast. The classmates' reaction is telling, given the solemnity that such a topic requires: "The girls were crying," Oskar observes when he presses stop on the boom box, "and the boys were making funny barfing noises" (Foer 2006, 189). Only the teacher, Mr Keegan, offers a vaguely appropriate reaction, nervously dabbing his forehead with a handkerchief. The juxtaposition of emotional immaturity and tragic subject matter produces an uneasy dissonance that feels more evasive than illuminating. In his review for *The Guardian*, Michel Faber reads this moment as emblematic of Foer's overall strategy: "A painfully serious topic is given a whimsical spin to make a painfully serious point" (Faber 2005). The subject that Oskar addresses in his class presentation and the type of language that Foer attributes to the nine-year-old seem out of place within the novel's context. The historical weight of the topic is subordinated to the novel's sentimental arc, which mirrors the broader post-9/11 cultural tendency to render traumatic history digestible, even palatable, through a lens of innocence and emotional accessibility.

Although Oskar Schell can be situated within a literary tradition of hyper-intelligent and precocious youths—ranging from Holden Caulfield in *The Catcher in the Rye*, Christopher John Francis Boone in Mark Haddon's *The Curious Incident of the Dog in the Night-Time* (2003), and even his namesake Oskar Matzerath from Günter Grass' *The Tin Drum* (1959)—he remains, ultimately, a composite figure lacking organic vitality. As Michael Faber notes in his *Guardian* review, Foer's Oskar is "constructed not from freshly materials but from embroidered scraps of language, poetic notions, allegorical conceits" (Faber 2005). Michiko Kakutani, writing for *The New York Times*, similarly characterises the novel as bearing a dual nature, "contrived and improvisatory, schematic and haphazard," and suggests that its protagonist feels more like a "synthetic creation" cobbled together from fragments of literary precursors than a fully realised fictional consciousness (Kakutani 2005).

The character's self-conscious eccentricities, while perhaps intended to endear, have instead alienated many readers and critics. In his review for *The New York Review*, Keith Gessen labels him "a genuinely annoying nine-year-old" (Gessen 2005), and John Updike admits to being "boggled" by the sheer implausibility of a child navigating the five boroughs of New York alone, methodically visiting "two hundred and sixteen different addresses listed in the phone book under the name 'Black'" (Updike 2005). This suspension of disbelief is further strained by Oskar's unrestricted access to the internet, which leads him to Portuguese-language websites featuring videos of people falling to their deaths. "Whenever I want to try to learn about how Dad died," he confides to the enigmatic tenant in his grandmother's apartment, "I have to go to a translator program and find out how to say things in different languages, like September…" (Foer 2006, 256). His frustration crystallises in the bitter realisation that "people all over the world can know things that I can't," a thought that fills him with impotent rage (2006, 256). While these details may underline Oskar's psychological and emotional precocity, they also stretch the limits of plausibility and contribute to the sense that he is less a grieving child than a literary device.

Nevertheless, Foer's *Extremely Loud & Incredibly Close* succeeded in eliciting the emotional response required for lasting cultural resonance and wide replicability. Its affect-driven narrative struck a chord with audiences in ways that aligned with the post-9/11 ethos of vulnerability, resilience, and sentimental healing. As a result, the novel became emblematic of a certain literary response to the attacks, to the point that when post-9/11 fiction is discussed, it is often the first title that comes to mind, even if the words in the title are frequently misremembered or jumbled. Its cultural currency was further cemented with the 2011 film adaptation, directed by Stephen Daldry, which featured high-profile actors such as Tom Hanks and Sandra Bullock.

All this notwithstanding—and despite the novel's calculatedly poignant, occasionally saccharine moments, such as Oskar's imagined invention of "a special drain that would be underneath every pillow in New York" to collect the tears of those who cry themselves to sleep (Foer 2006, 38)—the trauma of 9/11, within the economy of the novel, appears somewhat hollow, a formal shell infused with meaning primarily through association with other, historically prior traumas. Thus, the novel's emotional design relies less on the intrinsic weight of the September 11 attacks and more on the transference of affect from events such as the firebombing of Dresden. Oskar's grandfather, the elder Thomas Schell, loses his beloved fiancée, Anna, in the Dresden inferno of February 1945—a loss so profound that it renders him mute. From that moment onward, he relinquishes speech in favour of written communication, a gesture emblematic of trauma so totalising that it exceeds language.

Mirroring this inherited grief are the haunting dreams of Oskar's grandmother, in which "people apologised for things that were about to happen, and lit candles by inhaling" (Foer 2006, 311), visions that express a longing to forestall catastrophe, to perform retroactive absolution. This temporal reversal finds a visual analogue in one of the novel's narrative conceits: a sequence of photographs placed at the end of the book depicting a man falling from the World Trade Center. When flipped in reverse order, the images animate the man's ascent back into the building—a childlike fantasy of undoing, of denying the irreversibility of loss. In this way, 9/11 becomes the gravitational centre around which other, older traumas orbit, lending it emotional substance through analogy rather than immediacy.

Within the broader constellation of historical traumas, such as the Dresden bombing, the emotional gravity of 9/11 in *Extremely Loud & Incredibly Close* appears somewhat displaced. Foer's decision to juxtapose these events, effectively creating a chronology or genealogy of trauma, suggests that 9/11, as a cultural and emotional wound, remains in a formative stage. It has yet to acquire the historical texture and moral legibility that older traumas have accrued over time. In this light, 9/11 requires the emotional scaffolding of previous catastrophes to gain narrative depth and resonance. By layering these traumas, Foer enables readers to position the events of September 11 within a broader framework of collective suffering. The novel's emotional economy thus depends less on the singularity of 9/11 than on its alignment with a lineage of loss that lends it both context and symbolic density.

However, this narrative placement also functions on a deeper, more critical level. In her analysis of *Extremely Loud & Incredibly Close*, Birgit Däwes argues that by aligning the trauma of 9/11 with other historical atrocities—such as the atomic bombing of Hiroshima—Foer actively undermines the myth of an innocent America unjustly victimised (Däwes 2011, 380). This juxtaposition sheds light on the broader context of violence and serves as a reminder of the political implications of representing 9/11 as a traumatic event. By employing these dialectics of violence, Foer also establishes a framework that seeks to temper sensationalised portrayals of the event and permits readings that may differ from acceptable ones.

This need for *cultural scaffolding* becomes particularly evident in the character of the grandmother, who remains unable to relinquish her memories of Dresden. "In her mind," Kristiaan Versluys observes, "Dresden has become an absolute event, so totalising in its impact that it no longer has a definable place in space or time" (Versluys 2009, 96). Even as she watches the events of September 11 unfold on television, her attention remains absorbed by the past: "she is occupied with memories of Dresden" (2009, 97). In this juxtaposition, 9/11 emerges as the 'weaker' of the two events, not in terms of spectacle or geopolitical consequence, but in its inability to eclipse or displace a trauma that has, for her, ossified into something absolute.

The novel counterposes the enduring trauma of Dresden with a tentative sense of hope following 9/11, offering a form of emotional closure that borders on redemptive. The tensions that animate the narrative are, to some extent, resolved by the mother's sudden declaration of love for her son—a moment that seems to magically dissipate Oskar's grief, particularly his "frustration over his father's unceremonious farewell and lack of affectionate parting words" (Versluys 2009, 118). It is as if, by narrative sleight of hand, the emotional core of the novel is reduced to a miscommunication within the nuclear family, and once addressed, the larger trauma can be safely neutralised. Versluys, in his concluding remarks, suggests that love has the power to mend what violence has shattered, to restore a semblance of lost security, and to make speech possible once more (2009, 118). In other words, Foer's novel guides the reader toward an emotionally 'appropriate' reaction — one that reaffirms human connection and domestic intimacy as the ultimate salve for historical rupture.

Interrogating the limitations of this interpretation, which assumes that certain feelings are more appropriate to events like 9/11, can drastically reshape how readers and critics perceive key moments in DeLillo's *Falling Man*. A particularly revealing episode occurs when Keith and Lianne, the estranged couple at the centre of the novel, find themselves momentarily reconciled while watching television footage of the attacks. As they re-experience the unfolding horror on-screen, a fragile intimacy is re-established — not through dialogue or shared understanding, but through a kind of synchronised *surrender* to the images. It is as if immersing themselves in that recursive loop, where the event is played and replayed, serves to align their interior landscapes.

Yet this alignment is not restorative in the sentimental sense; rather, it is the event itself — relentless in its symbolic and psychic imposition — that orchestrates the moment. In this context, the protagonists' apparent selflessness in their surrender to the images does not imply heroic solidarity or noble sacrifice but rather a profound *evacuation* of subjectivity. They are not *choosing* to be selfless; they have been hollowed out by the gravitational force of the event's narcissistic repetition. The selfish event leaves no room for individual agency. It occupies the psychological terrain so completely that the characters are rendered mute, passive, and interchangeable.

In stark contrast to Foer, who portrays 9/11 as a catalytic rupture that ultimately leads to familial reconnection around a distilled, almost childlike conception of love, DeLillo resists such narrative closure. *Falling Man* presents a family that was already fractured prior to the event. The novel does not suggest that trauma heals, redeems, or reconstitutes the domestic sphere. While some may interpret the moment of shared viewing between Keith and Lianne as indicative of renewed intimacy or emotional solidarity, such a reading overlooks the notion that their apparent togetherness merely stems from the *unique* (i.e., inimitable, one-of-a-kind) nature of the *selfish event* itself. Their apparent togetherness is less a consequence of personal reconciliation than a byproduct of synchronised exposure to the same overwhelming spectacle. This simulated unity mirrors the collective experience of 9/11 as it unfolded in real-time: millions across the globe became, for a moment, a singular interpretive community — not through shared values or emotional alignment, but through simultaneous spectatorship.

The novel's second chapter reveals the underlying dysfunctions in Keith and Lianne's relationship, particularly through a conversation between Lianne and her mother, Nina Bartos. When Keith arrives at Lianne's apartment, "grey soot head to toe" (DeLillo 2011, 8), Nina, a retired university professor who left academia after a knee replacement surgery, offers a pointed yet understated critique of the couple's dynamic. "Why didn't he go straight to a hospital?" she observes, "[Why] didn't he go to a friend's place?" The word "friend" does not pass unnoticed; for Lianne, it carries an implicit meaning —*friend* translates as *girlfriend* (2011, p. 9). Nina's tone, marked by restrained scepticism, subtly discourages an emotional reading of Keith's return. "He was in grave danger, I know," she concedes, but cautions her daughter, "[but] if you let your sympathy and goodwill affect your judgment" (DeLillo 2011, 10). Nina's remark leaves the consequence unstated, but the implication is clear. With the context we are given, it becomes evident that Nina sees the rekindling of their relationship not as a healing gesture but as a misstep.

To some extent, Nina's remarks function not only as a cautionary note to her daughter but also as a subtle admonition to the reader, hinting at the emotional restraint that characterises *Falling Man* as a whole. Her words carry a distinct weight as DeLillo frames Nina within a carefully composed minimalist ambience, reflective of her intellectual reserve. The north wall of her New York City apartment is adorned with two still-life paintings by Giorgio Morandi—compositions that, much like Vermeer's interiors, offer a contemplative window into Nina's inner life. Later in the novel, when Lianne visits her mother and her partner, Martin, Nina seems to emerge from the subdued tonalities of these paintings. Dressed "in a dark skirt and a white blouse," she moves with deliberate, "segmental" precision, leaning on her cane (DeLillo 2011, 44). The interplay of dark and light in her clothing, combined with her slow, restrained movements, renders her almost a still life in motion—a living embodiment of Morandi's colour palette and meditative form.

However, there is no indication that this embodiment or personification is a result of the September 11 attacks, further challenging the view that *Falling Man* is a symptomatic portrayal of post-traumatic melancholy. Nina's stillness and introspective gravity predate the event, resisting the interpretive gravitational pull that the selfish event seeks to exert. When Martin confides in Lianne that ever since his arrival from Europe, Nina has offered him nothing but grief, Lianne quietly affirms that grief is Nina's job (2011, 45). The line is both dry and revealing: Nina's grief is *not* new. It is a mode of being, an existential temperament, not a direct response to 9/11. Yet, as with the two darkened, ambiguous forms in the Morandi paintings that hang on her apartment wall, the event recontextualises her disposition. Her grief, like the paintings, is drawn into the symbolic orbit of the event. In this way, the selfish event appropriates her general melancholy, misreading it as post-9/11 grief, thus flattening the depth and complexity of her character into yet another echo of catastrophe.

The notion that the characters have been supplanted, replaced like changelings or hollowed out by the *selfish event*, reverberates throughout *Falling Man*. When Lianne first sees Keith after the towers collapse, she is momentarily uncertain of his identity. "When he appeared at the door," the narrator observes, "it was not possible; a man comes out of an ash storm, all blood and slag, reeking of burnt matter, with pinpoint glints of slivered glass in his face" (DeLillo 2011, 87). The image is almost mythic in its intensity: Keith does not return so much as he emerges, transformed, less a survivor than a spectral envoy of the event. Lianne, instinctively protective, turns off the television to protect him "from the news he'd just walked out of" (2011, 87), as though the broadcast might reabsorb him into its loop. Her actions convey not merely care but a recognition that Keith's identity has become porous, shaped by something larger and more invasive than trauma alone. When she brushes dust from his clothes, she discovers the blood on them is not his, an unsettling detail that suggests a kind of symbolic substitution (2011, 88).

The blood, like the ash, carries the weight of another's death — it marks him as a bearer of loss, not simply a victim. The moment resembles a ritual cleansing or a rite of passage, a rebirth into a new self, shaped within the ordeal of the selfish event. Later, when Keith returns a suitcase he found amid the wreckage to its owner, Florence, the encounter intensifies this transformation. He finds in her a strange kinship, not rooted in romance but in a shared sense of *contamination*.

The shared experience of the event cultivates a sense of belonging and camaraderie between Keith and Florence, yet simultaneously diminishes their individuality. When they interact, Keith struggles to shake the impression that Florence sees him as someone else entirely — as if he is expected to say and do what anyone in such a situation would naturally say and do (DeLillo 2011, 138). In their conversations, Versluys notes, "[neither] of the interlocutors is fully present to him- or herself. Lacking a [...] sense of identity, they cannot express themselves fully or authentically" (Versluys 2009, 26). Although the protagonists' lives visibly begin to unravel after the event, it soon becomes clear that their disintegration had already commenced, with the event merely exposing pre-existing fault lines. These characters have not awakened from a dream and been transported to a reality fundamentally different from the one they experienced before the event, as they have not emerged from the American Dream. The issues existed all along; they were simply unaware of them.

To some extent, the intensely visual nature of the event has appropriated the characters' sense of sight, fundamentally altering their perception of the world. "The fire and ash," Banita argues regarding Keith's sight following the event, "instead of impairing [it], only [lowered] the threshold of his perception. In contrast, life before 9/11 suddenly strikes him as a form of blindness, where not noticing used to be both a quality and a condition of living" (Banita 2012, 65). Returning to his apartment, Keith experiences not a surge of loneliness or melancholy, but instead comes face-to-face with "the overwhelming emptiness of his life" (2012, 65). This acute awareness of emptiness underscores the shift from the world of "then" to the changed world of "now" introduced at the novel's outset:

> When he entered his apartment, he stood for a while, just looking around. The windows were scabbed in sand and ash, and there were fragments of paper and one whole sheet trapped in the grime. Everything else was the same as it had been when he walked out the door for work that Tuesday morning. *Not that he'd noticed*. He'd lived here for a year and a half since the separation, finding a place close to the office, centering his life, content with the narrowest of purviews, that of not noticing.
> *But now he looked*. Some light entered between splashes of window grit. He saw the place differently now. Here he was, seen clear, with nothing that mattered to him in these two and a half rooms, dim and still, in a faint odour of nonoccupancy. (DeLillo 2011, 26)

DeLillo's portrayal of Keith's apartment is somewhat paradoxical, employing a deliberate juxtaposition of conflicting metaphors. I contend that this dual narrative movement—simultaneously directed *inward* and *outward*—constitutes another hallmark of the selfish event. The windows, typically symbols of *observation* and outward *perception*, are obscured by debris from the towers, suggesting an impaired field of vision. This visual impairment redirects Keith's focus *inward* toward the interior of his apartment, prompting him to notice details he previously overlooked. Thus, the sharp clarity of his inward gaze contrasts with the hazy view outward. Such nuances underscore that the characters do not descend into mental apathy following the event, as Gray suggested in his interpretation. Rather, *selfish events* compel them toward a heightened mental alertness reminiscent of detectives.

DeLillo's Keith Neudecker is not alone in experiencing an abrupt awakening to a new inward reality. In "Living Up to It," the opening essay of *Interesting Times: Writings from a Turbulent Decade* (2009), George Packer recounts the story of an investment banker who "[in] the minutes after the South Tower fell on September 11, [...] had an epiphany" (Packer 2009, 24). Stumbling through the debris and confusion in Lower Manhattan, the banker eventually finds himself inside a church in Greenwich Village. Yet, despite the surroundings and expectations, his epiphany does not involve religious insight. When a policeman tries to reassure him by suggesting he is probably in shock, the banker insists that, quite to the contrary, he is exceptionally clear-headed, asserting he has never before felt so "cognizant" of his own life. According to Packer, this heightened awareness transcended the category of investment bankers. Matthew Timms, an unemployed video producer, attempted to film the attacks but realised his camera had died. Packer describes how Timms became so disturbed by his own sense of detachment that he wanted "his blood drawn [...] to overcome it" (Packer 2009, 24). It is almost as if the event briefly made him self-aware.

Many New Yorkers shared a similar sentiment in the aftermath of the attacks, feeling acutely aware that "[they] had not been living as they would have liked; the horrors of the day before had woken them up; they wanted to change" (2009, 26). DeLillo, too, captures this widespread impulse to act, irrespective of whether such action was truly necessary or even helpful. As Neudecker moves away from the collapsing towers, a woman offers him a bottle of water. Later, upon arriving at Lianne's apartment, she, too, hands him water. "Everybody's giving me water," Keith exclaims, almost in desperation (DeLillo 2011, 87), as though water distribution had become the universally sanctioned response to the event. Similarly, hundreds of New Yorkers rushed to donate blood, only to be turned away due to an oversupply. Regardless of the actual need, the compulsion to act, to participate in some way, became one of the most common reactions to the crisis.

The *diplopia*, or double vision, engendered by the selfish event creates a sense of *duplicitousness* and internal *separation*, resembling the experience of distancing oneself from a former identity. It establishes a fundamental *rift*. This duality often emerges due to the unsettling nature of the event, which *disrupts* conventional interpretive frameworks and gives rise to a fractured, layered perception. Within cultural narratives, *diplopia* signifies the simultaneous coexistence of two conflicting interpretations or perceptions in a single cultural artefact. This phenomenon highlights how profoundly influential events, such as 9/11, can impose a new, dominant narrative that overshadows and competes with previous interpretations, resulting in a split vision. Cultural artefacts thus become sites of interpretive contestation, spaces where pre-existing narratives and new, intrusive meanings uneasily coexist, giving rise to interpretive dissonance.

When Keith peers into his refrigerator, he observes the bottles and cartons as though they belong to someone else, even though he himself is "the man who used to live here" (DeLillo 2011, 27). Standing in the hallway, he addresses no one in particular, acknowledging his own presence, yet receives no response. The narrative continues ironically, remarking that "in the movie version, someone would be in the building, an emotionally damaged woman or a homeless old man, and there would be dialogue and close-ups" (DeLillo 2011, 27). Here, DeLillo underscores the sense of detachment and isolation, juxtaposing Keith's fragmented reality with the familiar tropes of cinematic representation, thus highlighting the artificiality of conventional narrative expectations in the aftermath of the event.

Nevertheless, there is no "emotionally damaged woman," as that would mean succumbing to the sentimental cliché exemplified by Foer's novel. *Extremely Loud & Incredibly Close* functions as the cinematic embodiment of such tropes, both figuratively and literally. Abby Black, whom Oskar encounters during his quest and who resides in "the narrowest house in New York" (Foer 2006, 90), inexplicably bursts into tears during their interaction. Another character, Ada Black, inhabits a beautiful apartment, possesses two Picasso paintings, and employs an African American woman as her maid. When Oskar praises the maid's uniform, Ada chastises him for embarrassing her, quickly asserting that "[she] does a serious job, and I pay her well" (Foer 2006, 150). Georgia Black, a Staten Island resident, "had turned her living room into a museum of her husband's life. She had pictures of him from when he was a kid, and his first pair of shoes, and his old report cards" (Foer 2006, 239). Each of these characters is emotionally scarred in distinct ways, and Oskar's presence—analogous to the intrusion of the event in De-Lillo's novel—acts as a catalyst that brings their hidden traumas vividly to the surface.

The individuals Oskar encounters, David Holloway argues in *9/11 and the War on Terror* (2008), are "invariably as damaged, scarred, unstable or fixated as he, and their experience seemed to be offered as the personification of the narrative interiorisations practised by the novel—each of them gripped, like Oskar, by private tragedy so all-consuming that they became private universes in which their victims endured blighted and asocial lives" (Holloway 2008, 116). When Oskar cries out into the void, much like Keith standing silently in the hallway declaring that he is "standing here" (DeLillo 2011, 27), he symbolically receives responses from the various characters he encounters throughout his quest to uncover the mystery behind the key discovered in his father's study. In contrast, DeLillo deliberately withholds such reassuring interactions from his characters. Instead, they are met only with silence— an echo produced solely by the selfish event itself.

As Versluys suggests in relation to DeLillo's novel, the collapse of the towers creates an environment where the very concept of genuineness "has become a staged condition," leaving the characters feeling as though they are merely "playing their own lives, [...] actors on a movie set" (Versluys 2009, 26). When these characters attempt to express their authentic selves, they encounter only distorted representations. Both Florence and Keith, Versluys further explains, "have the sense that they have been expropriated, that their own lives have their centres somewhere outside themselves, somewhere distant and out of control," resulting in a profound "feeling of self-othering" (Versluys 2009, 27). Within the repetitive mental loop established by this *selfish event*, individuals experience a loss of autonomy, as if their identities have become diluted, elusive, or even consumed entirely.

Versluys highlights this *slipperiness* of identity by examining the titles of the novel's three parts, each reflecting a fluidity of self that others can easily alter or reshape. "Bill Lawton," the title of the novel's first part, is a playful, innocent modification of Bin Laden's name coined by Justin, Keith and Lianne's son. By renaming Bin Laden, Justin neutralises the name's sinister associations, allowing it to function as a clandestine term among teenagers, reminiscent of euphemisms like "You-Know-Who" or "He-Who-Must-Not-Be-Named" from the Harry Potter series. This act of renaming exemplifies the appropriation and malleability of identity in the aftermath of a selfish event.

The second title, "Ernst Hechinger," further emphasises the mutability of identity. Hechinger, an art dealer and the partner of Lianne's mother, Nina, adopts the alias "Martin Ridnour" to escape his association with a militant left-wing organisation in Germany. The third title, "David Janiak," also reflects identity fluidity, with the crucial distinction that it denotes the real identity of a person publicly recognised by a different, symbolic name: the Falling Man. Janiak, a performance artist, recreates Richard Drew's iconic photograph, "The Falling Man," published in *The New York Times*, by repeatedly leaping from tall buildings around New York City while secured by a safety harness. Janik's performances thus embody the internal conflict or repetitive mental loop generated by the selfish event, repeatedly re-enacting a highly mediatised and emotionally charged moment from the original tragedy.

This same mental loop recurs when Lianne, sorting through her mail, discovers a postcard sent by a friend visiting Rome. Her attention is immediately captured by the image on the front of the card, "a reproduction of the cover of Shelley's poem in twelve cantos, first edition, called *Revolt of Islam*" (DeLillo 2011, 8). Although she recognises that the postcard was sent a week or two earlier — well before 9/11 — Lianne cannot dismiss the uncanny sense of prescience surrounding its arrival. "It was a matter of simple coincidence," she rationalises, "that a card might arrive at this particular time bearing the title of that specific book" (DeLillo 2011, 8). DeLillo's *Falling Man* thus does not represent, as Gray suggests, a "verbal equivalent of immobility" (Gray 2011, 28). Instead, it conveys the verbal equivalent of a mental gravitational pull and illustrates how every cultural artefact, object, or detail, no matter how seemingly insignificant, becomes imbued with the significance of the selfish event.

In DeLillo's novel, identity and memory are intricately intertwined, with memory frequently threatening to overwhelm and subsume identity. This tension becomes particularly apparent in the narrative's persistent engagement with Alzheimer's disease, a topic that borders on obsession. Keith, the protagonist, mentions in the fourth chapter that he attends "his poker game, six players, downtown, one night a week" (DeLillo 2011, 29) as a means of maintaining mental focus. His affiliation with this group symbolically marks his separation from Lianne, who aligns herself with another community. Lianne participates in "her storyline sessions, in East Harlem, also weekly, in the afternoon, a gathering of five or six or seven men and women in the early stages of Alzheimer's disease" (2011, 29). During these meetings, patients spend roughly twenty minutes writing about their lives and subsequently share their writings aloud. The narratives they produce revolve around deeply personal experiences—ranging from family moments to "hard times, happy memories, daughters becoming mothers" and "the revelation of writing itself" (2011, 31)—experiences that will inevitably fade as their illness advances. After 9/11, however, the narrative observes that "[there] was one subject the members wanted to write about, insistently, all [...] but Omar H. It made Omar nervous, but he agreed in the end. They wanted to write about the planes" (2011, 31). It is as though the event itself has co-opted their impulse to document and preserve their individual lives and experiences.

The novel's commentary on the nature of the selfish event in this episode may initially puzzle or, at the very least, intrigue readers. Alzheimer's disease is a progressive condition that leads inevitably to profound memory loss, dementia, and significant cognitive impairment. Although no cure exists, treatments can help delay the disease's progression. When Lianne proposes to increase the frequency of the storyline sessions, Dr Apter cautions her against it, suggesting that such a move could be counterproductive. "Their situation will become increasingly delicate," he advises, "[these] encounters need space around them. You don't want them to feel an urgency to write everything down or say everything before it's too late" (DeLillo 2011, 60).

Yet, this is precisely the heart of the issue. The writing sessions moderated by Lianne aim to *preserve* the patients' memories, safeguarding them from being irretrievably lost. They offer a structured approach to documenting and interpreting the patients' mental experiences, which serves both the authors and their readers and listeners. Given the critical urgency of this recording and re-coding process, especially as the disease advances and threatens their cognitive abilities, the intrusion of the event—depriving them of the mental space necessary to recall a reality beyond the event itself— amounts to a form of *suppression*. Consequently, the selfish event imposes a form of self-censorship and self-denial, establishing a regime that ensures its continual self-replication, even within vulnerable minds whose memories teeter on the brink of dissolution.

Like Keith, who finds solace in the repetitive ritual and reliable structure of his poker games, Lianne discovers a comparable comfort in her writing session with the Alzheimer's patients. She engages the patients with a curiosity that extends beyond mere professional duty. When the patients write about "where they were when it happened" or about "the people they knew who were in the towers, or nearby" (2011, 60), she detects in their narratives an almost experimental form of hedonism, recognising that even these individuals, whose circumstances differ profoundly from her own, are wrestling with similar emotional and cognitive struggles related to the event. "She wanted to hear everything," the narration elaborates, "the things everybody said, ordinary things, and the naked statements of belief, and the depth of feeling, the passion that saturated the room. She needed these men and women. [...] It was possible that the group meant more to her than it did to the members" (DeLillo 2011, 61). As Lianne desperately attempts to escape the mental loop imposed by the event, she realises that she cannot find true refuge in the experiences shared by her patients. The relentless mental loop endures, and the only consolation she obtains from the sessions lies in the reassuring yet modest recognition that she is not alone in her predicament.

In this context, I argue that the comfort Lianne derives from these group meetings transcends mere sympathy or professional obligation. Beyond embodying "the living breath of the thing that killed her father" (DeLillo 2011, 62) — Jack Glenn, who chose suicide to avoid enduring the progressive deterioration of senile dementia (2011, 40) — these patients and their writing sessions offer Lianne a reassuring exit from the mental loop imposed by the event in at least two significant ways. On one level, the routine nature of these scheduled meetings simultaneously mirrors and disrupts the repetitive, obsessive cycle triggered by the event. On another level, as Alzheimer's advances among the participants, the sharpness and intensity of their memories, including their recollections of the traumatic event itself, gradually diminish. This diminishing intensity provides a subtle reassurance to Lianne and to readers alike: even the most vivid and painful memories, comparable in significance to those cherished moments and family histories that shape one's identity, eventually succumb to the degenerative entropy of memory. Thus, despite its initial overwhelming clarity, the obsessive recurrence of the event's memory will ultimately soften with the passage of time.

The patients are not merely peripheral characters in *Falling Man*; rather, they are central in shaping the novel's narrative and symbolic architecture. Their presence operates as a synecdoche for the broader post-9/11 condition, embodying the (de)individualisation that emerges in proximity to a selfish event. These individuals, on the brink of cognitive dissolution due to Alzheimer's, mirror the cultural and psychological fragmentation triggered by the attacks. As Versluys notes, their progressive erasure "is anticipated in the way they are written about. Lightly sketched, known only by their first name and initial, they remain shadowy presences, partly rubbed out already, getting more and more vague as time goes by" (Versluys 2009, 35). However, this reading overlooks the narrative subtlety DeLillo employs. The anonymity of the patients, while possibly attributable to Lianne's professional obligation to uphold confidentiality, is also deliberately stylised. As the narration reveals, it was Lianne's "affected" decision to treat them "as if they were characters in European novels" (DeLillo 2011, 30), lending their presence a literary rather than medical opacity. They are not inherently shadowy; they are made so through Lianne's lens—her stylised, perhaps distancing, way of coping with their stories and her own.

The reference to "European novels" may appear incidental to a casual reader, yet it reveals significant implications about Lianne's psychological orientation and the broader affective landscape of the post-9/11 world. Embedded in this remark is an almost pathological gesture of distancing. That the patients are imagined as characters not merely from literature, but specifically from *European* novels, suggests that, in Lianne's internal geography, they are situated within a cultural and emotional *elsewhere*, removed from the American immediacy of trauma. Europe, in this instance, becomes a metaphorical space of detachment, a locus of melancholic narrative and aesthetic restraint, seemingly untouched by the towers' collapse. This invocation constructs a form of psychological insulation for Lianne: by casting the patients as foreign, stylised figures from an old-world literary tradition, she can mediate their suffering through an aestheticised lens. In doing so, she displaces their proximity to the event and thereby maintains a manageable distance from their dissolution—a coping mechanism that also mirrors the broader post-9/11 impulse to narrativise, aestheticise, and contain trauma.

On the other hand, this aesthetic and emotional distancing results in a subtle form of *objectification*, as the patients become vehicles for Lianne's own narrative desires. This dynamic is especially evident when she deliberately *steers* the group toward a conversation about the terrorists despite their hesitations. "She prompted them," the narrator observes, "[there] has to be something you want to say, some feeling to express, nineteen men come here to kill us" (DeLillo 2011, 64). The urgency in her request reveals more than a therapeutic prompt; it is a search for validation, a desire to elicit a certain emotional or ideological response. This pressure is particularly fraught in the case of Omar H., whose Arabic-sounding name makes him a likely target of suspicion or discomfort in such a context. And yet, Lianne persists.

Like many prompts, hers is not entirely neutral; it subtly embeds the contours of the answer she hopes to receive. Although the narrator tells us she is unsure "what it was she wanted to hear" (2011, 64), the text contradicts this uncertainty. When Anna, another patient, claims that the terrorists cannot be named because "they're a million miles outside your life" (2011, 64), Lianne silently translates this into a desire for retribution: "the small intimate wish, however useless in a hellstorm," and internally "welcomes" the sentiment (DeLillo 2011, 64). In this moment, the patients, like many figures in *Falling Man*, are reframed not as autonomous individuals but as participants in a carefully constructed moral tableau — a set of literary case studies through which Lianne *rehearses* the permissible range of post-9/11 emotions.

Don DeLillo's *Falling Man* and H.M. Naqvi's *Home Boy* embed the loss into their very syntax, announcing from their opening lines a rupture between the pre- and post-9/11 worlds. Other novelists, such as Mohsin Hamid, encode the same loss more obliquely, allowing it to emerge through subtle narrative gestures. In *The Reluctant Fundamentalist*, the protagonist and narrator, Changez, declares himself a "lover of America," but it soon becomes clear that the America he loves is a fading illusion — a country surrendering to "a dangerous nostalgia" (Hamid 2008, 113). That nostalgia finds symbolic embodiment in Erica, whose name unmistakably echoes "Am*erica*," carrying within it the phonetic trace of a lost ideal. Like Keith Neudecker's dissociation in the dust cloud of DeLillo's novel or the splintered identities of the three narrators in *Home Boy*, Changez finds himself drawn into a void — an emotional and symbolic hiatus — contained within the Erica/(Am)Erica analogy.

This fracture comes into focus during an intimate encounter with Erica. As Changez becomes aware of her withdrawal and emotional absence, he realises she remains haunted by the memory of her deceased lover, Chris. The name "Chris," as Richard Gray has observed, may itself be a subtle invocation of Christopher Columbus, gesturing toward a mythic origin of America that carries colonial weight (Gray 2011, 62). In an act of desperate empathy — or perhaps *erasure* — Changez tells her, "Then pretend, pretend I am him" (Hamid 2008, 105). In this moment, he becomes a stand-in, a cypher absorbed into another person's narrative. Like a cultural artefact subjected to the gravitational pull of a selfish event, Changez is subsumed into a story, not of his own making. His individuality, like that of DeLillo's characters, is appropriated by a dominant discourse—a mythos of grief, nationhood, and idealisation from which he remains alienated.

Changez's willingness to inhabit the role of Erica's deceased lover, as Martin Randall argues in *9/11 and the Literature of Terror* (2011), signifies a profound erosion of his "real self" (2011, 141). Yet, this is not the first indication of his identity's malleability. Randall notes that Changez "mimics the financial high-flyers he works with at Underwood and Sampson," performing the polished confidence of American corporate success, only to later adopt a contrasting persona—growing a thick beard and assuming what many Americans read as the visual shorthand for "terrorist" (2011, 141). This series of transformations points to a deeper existential instability. In attempting to fill the psychic and cultural void left by the loss of home, belonging, and authenticity, Changez becomes a vessel for borrowed identities, each of which intensifies his alienation. The roles he adopts are not additive but *subtractive*; each one pulls him further from an originary sense of self until even his claim to that self becomes uncertain.

Much like DeLillo's Keith Neudecker, who eventually realises where "he'd been going all along" (DeLillo 2011, 4), Changez's post-9/11 awakening is marked by disillusionment. As Randall observes, the shock of 9/11 "wakes Changez from his dream of America" (Randall 2011, 143). But this awakening is not liberating—it is traumatic. What Hamid's novel ultimately reveals is that the American dream, as experienced by the outsider, may require the forfeiture of authenticity. The promise of assimilation is predicated on a subtle and continuous erosion of the self in favour of an external repertoire of gestures, values, and appearances—each of which draws the dreamer further from home, both geographically and psychologically.

The proliferation of fictional characters across the texts discussed above foregrounds a recurrent thematic concern in post-9/11 literature: the decentering of identity. This decentering—an acute and destabilising displacement of self — is one of the defining characteristics of selfish events. Such events assert their dominance not only by directing cultural attention but also by reshaping the interpretive frameworks through which individuals and artefacts are understood. While cultural artefacts, such as the Morandi paintings in DeLillo's *Falling Man*, undergo symbolic recontextualisation — absorbing the aura of the event and becoming unwilling receptacles of its echoes — the human characters in these narratives experience a more precarious fate. Their identities are not merely overshadowed but are constantly at risk of being supplanted.

This threat is not merely metaphorical. For characters like Mohsin Hamid's Changez or H.M. Naqvi's three narrators in *Home Boy*, the post-9/11 atmosphere renders their identity as American citizens or legal immigrants tenuous and provisional. Their ethnic and religious backgrounds become the primary lens through which others interpret them. In this reconfiguration of meaning, the "self" becomes a contested site, always vulnerable to appropriation or misreading. What emerges is not the replacement of identity with another but the persistent possibility of that replacement — the looming presence of a prescribed identity, that of the Islamic fundamentalist, which becomes culturally legible irrespective of the characters' allegiances, values, or histories. The selfish event does not simply reframe the world; it rewrites its subjects.

2.3 The Post-post-9/11 Novel: Cormac McCarthy's *The Road*

The three novels discussed thus far each centre their narrative weight on the moment of transition between a pre-9/11 and post-9/11 atmosphere. Whether overtly or obliquely, they engage with the dialectic of before and after, wrestling with the immediacy, singularity, and cultural aftermath of the event. Cormac McCarthy's *The Road* (2006), though not explicitly a "9/11 novel" — except, perhaps, for the *accident* of having been published in the wake of the attacks — assumes a markedly different position within the post-9/11 literary assemblage. Rather than recounting the moment of rupture, McCarthy's narrative unfolds in the long shadow of disaster. It offers a meditation not on the event itself but on its lingering afterlife—a devastated world wherein the rupture has become the norm.

In *The Road*, the world in which the father and his young son travel is not the site of cataclysmic *becoming* but rather of *ongoing* ruin. The cataclysm, whose origin is never named, never fully described, has already occurred. The characters inhabit a scorched and ash-covered landscape, where loss is no longer traumatic but has become quotidian. The past—the "before"—survives only in the fragile recollections of the father, while the present is defined by stark survival and silence. The novel transforms the "valley of ashes" from Fitzgerald's *The Great Gatsby* and echoes of T. S. Eliot's *The Waste Land* into a universal condition, one that mirrors the psychological and cultural desolation wrought by the events of 9/11. However, McCarthy's terrain is more than metaphorical; it stages the world as permanently altered, its destruction not the work of enemies or ideology but of an unnameable erasure.

It is in this sense that we should read *The Road* as a *post*-post-9/11 novel. Unlike those narratives that grapple directly with the singularity of the event or attempt to reconstruct its immediacy, McCarthy's novel imagines a temporal horizon *beyond* the event—a post-apocalyptic future in which the trauma has become an elemental part of the landscape. The novel gestures, faintly, toward the possibility of redemption or return, yet it does so without ever abandoning the burden of loss. The past may shimmer in memory, but the conditions of its return are foreclosed. What remains is not hope in the conventional sense but a quiet reckoning with *irreversibility*—a world where the fire may still be carried, but the world that once contained it is gone.

The *indeterminacy* surrounding the disaster that ravages the world in *The Road*, leaving behind a scorched and featureless wasteland, is one of the key reasons the novel lends itself so readily to post-9/11 interpretation. This ambiguity is not incidental but structurally embedded in the narrative, allowing for resonances with 9/11 to emerge naturally. As David Holloway notes, the novel's grounding in apocalyptic trauma inevitably brings to the fore "poetic resonances with 9/11 and the war on terror," making such associations, in his words, "explicit and unavoidable" (Holloway 2008, 110). McCarthy thus constructs a narrative that deliberately oscillates between revelation and concealment. As Richard Gray observes, the novel simultaneously speaks and withholds, enacting a form of narrative silence that gestures toward the unspeakable nature of the catastrophe without ever fully articulating it (Gray 2011, 39).

Yet, Gray's reading ultimately hinges on a problematic reduction. He attributes McCarthy's narrative restraint to the ineffability of trauma itself, insisting that trauma must be approached "by circuitous means, by indirection," and that *The Road* thus operates "a symbolic narrative, a powerful but also slippery tale of something, some trauma that seems to resist telling" (Gray 2011, 40). In doing so, Gray reinscribes the novel within a now-familiar interpretive framework that seeks to stabilise ambiguity by assigning it a culturally legible signifier—in this case, 9/11. His reading positions McCarthy's silence not as a rhetorical or philosophical gesture but as a *symptom* of trauma, thereby aligning the novel with a broader compulsion in post-9/11 criticism to read indeterminacy as indexical.

This interpretive move echoes the behaviour of the art critics in Hustvedt's *The Blazing World,* who project their anxieties onto Harriet Burden's "Little Mutant," seeing in it the figure of a 9/11 survivor. Similarly, viewers of George Segal's *Woman on a Park Bench* may discern in the sculpture a dust-covered refugee of the Twin Towers, despite its pre-9/11 provenance. In each case, an absence or ambiguity is filled by the gravitational pull of 9/11 as a cultural "primal scene." Gray's reading follows the same logic, whereby McCarthy's refusal to name the cataclysm becomes yet another surface onto which the event's symbolic weight is projected. This interpretive reflex suggests less about McCarthy's narrative strategies than it does about the lingering need to inscribe 9/11 into every silence, every void, every textual aporia that remains unnamed.

The novel quietly *resists* the kind of oblique interpretation that seeks to subsume every narrative ambiguity under the shadow of 9/11, and this resistance may, in fact, constitute McCarthy's tacit admonition *against* interpreting the text solely through the lens of familiar cultural referents. *The Road* is, at its core, a meditation on radical indeterminacy. It is a novel that *dwells* in ambiguity—not incidentally, but *insistently*. The persistence and recurrence of its indeterminacies—regarding the nature of the catastrophe, the specifics of temporal and geographic setting, and even the names of its central characters—form an assemblage of narrative absences that may, at first glance, appear to critique the novel's own refusal to anchor itself in a singular, definitive signifier.

Yet this very refusal is what gives the novel its interpretive openness. The absence of a fixed point of reference does not signal narrative deficiency but rather constitutes the novel's philosophical stance. It resists being enclosed by reductive allegories, especially those that would tie it too neatly to the cultural trauma of 9/11. In doing so, *The Road* not only complicates attempts to read it as a post-9/11 allegory but also challenges readers to engage with a broader existential landscape marked less by historical specificity than by metaphysical and ethical inquiry.

Building on this line of reasoning, the expansive *aperture* that *The Road* constructs and preserves throughout its narrative serves as a subtle injunction *against* interpretive overreach. The novel's refusal to identify the precise nature of the cataclysm is not merely a stylistic choice but a thematic gesture that invites readers to meditate on how the reverberations of distant, often invisible catastrophes are absorbed into the fabric of daily life. The fact that the disaster lies well beyond the father and son's grasp, never named, never explained, mirrors the lived reality of global conflict: the ways in which wars and crises, especially those unfolding overseas, insinuate themselves into the lives that remain formally untouched by their immediate violence. We experience their consequences, economic instability, refugee flows, cultural paranoia, and ecological degradation, without ever confronting the conflict itself. In this sense, McCarthy's rendering of the catastrophe as a ghostly, unnamed absence becomes a commentary on the spectral influence of distant suffering: how the world can burn, quite literally, and leave behind survivors who know only the ash, not the fire.

The earliest indicators of catastrophe in *The Road* are understated yet ominous: the clocks halt at 1:17, and what follows is described as a "long shear of light and then a series of low concussions" (McCarthy 2010, 54). There is no gradual escalation of tension, no foreboding signs of geopolitical unrest — only an eerie tranquillity preceding the rupture. Even before the event, the world is rendered as peculiarly subdued and inert. The only visible trace of the calamity is the "dull rose glow in the window glass" that succeeds the mysterious flash (2010, 54). Though visually distant and deceptively gentle, the event irreversibly fractures reality. The man, registering the shift, instinctively turns on the light, only to find the power already gone. He then rushes to fill the bathtub with water — an act of preparation prompted not by direct knowledge of the threat but by the intuition of impending collapse.

Marc Redfield's concept of "spectrality," developed in *The Rhetoric of Terror: Reflections on 9/11 and the War on Terror*, is particularly instructive in this context. McCarthy's disaster is not witnessed in the hyper-mediated, televisual fashion of 9/11. It is, instead, refracted — projected not onto a television screen but onto the more primal surface of a window glass. This shift displaces the spectacle into something more liminal. Redfield speaks of trauma's "virtual" nature, noting how "virtual intends to suggest the trembling of an event on the edge of becoming present: one that is not fully or not properly 'actual'" (2009, 2). This precisely characterises the event in *The Road* — not yet fully manifest, not yet concretely nameable, but already exerting pressure on the characters' reality. The trauma lingers in latency: its signs have appeared, but its full implications remain suspended. In this interstitial space between *recognition* and *devastation*, McCarthy captures an existential poise — the moment before descent, where human intuition confronts an inexplicable world.

The "virtual nature" of the catastrophe in *The Road* is further underscored by the fact that the novel is, ultimately, a work of fiction. Like war literature, the literature of disaster — what one might term the narrative aftermath — carries with it the inherent risk of misinterpretation. As Lynne Hanley observes in *Writing War: Fiction, Gender, and Memory* (1991), fiction does not merely distort reality through factual manipulation; more insidiously, it can promote "a false sense of security" (Hanley 1991, 5). No matter how "vivid and gripping the account," Hanley warns, the reader will never experience one of disaster's most defining characteristics: "the immediate and entirely legitimate fear of losing one's life, limbs, or senses, or of seeing the person next to one lose his" (1991, 5). A catastrophic event is, above all, not something one experiences while "settling down in an easy chair with a good book" (1991, 5).

McCarthy's novel seems to radicalise this insight by withholding not only the emotional immediacy of disaster but also the narrative scaffolding that might typically render such an event comprehensible. If the protagonists are severed from the origin of the catastrophe, the reader is even more distanced — twice removed, one might say — by the layers of narrative indirection and ontological ambiguity that shape the novel's form. The disaster becomes not merely unspeakable but unreachable, suspended in a state of narrative deferral. It resists even metaphor, functioning like a failed objective correlative — a signifier whose referent remains elusive. This is fiction, not as a witness but as estrangement. McCarthy's most unsettling provocation lies in this: the disaster, already virtual for its characters, becomes even more so for us.

To a significant extent, despite the many indeterminacies that surround it, the cataclysm in *The Road* resists contextualisation. Though the past occasionally returns in the form of fleeting recollections — glimpses conjured by the father, who alone possesses the cognitive resources to remember — it is a past without anchorage. These memories drift through the narrative, unmoored from any discernible spatial or temporal framework, blending seamlessly with the grey, ash-laden present. They are not situated but suspended, mere impressions without coordinates. The fire that transforms the world arrives without origin or warning, acquiring the scale and symbolism of a biblical conflagration.

This deliberate *evacuation of context* and the parallel *erasure of locality* converge with the logic of the selfish event: an event so singular and voracious that it devours preceding and surrounding narratives, becoming the gravitational centre around which all other meanings orbit. In this sense, McCarthy's fire becomes a ready vessel for cultural relocation, a cypher that can be filled with the traumatic weight of other catastrophes, 9/11 chief among them. Like the fire invoked in the title of James Baldwin's *The Fire Next Time* — the fire promised after the flood — it embodies judgment, erasure, and apocalyptic reckoning.

And yet, as Richard J. Gray observes, McCarthy's novel simultaneously reconfigures one of American literature's most enduring tropes: the journey. "The journey here," Gray writes, "is not a linear progress, from the East to the West, a liberatory flight from the old to the new as in the classic American Western. It is a turning back, from the North to the South, across an unobstructed space that triggers not a sense of freedom but a feeling of empty immensity" (Gray 2011, 36). This reimagined topography, vacant, unyielding, and stripped of symbolic promise, undermines the very narrative structure upon which American exceptionalism is often built. It is a journey not toward destiny but through entropy. Not a frontier to be claimed but a void to be endured.

The pervasive greyness of the landscape makes it difficult to pinpoint specific locations, and despite carrying a map, the two protagonists travel through unnamed places. The narrative deliberately refrains from revealing the names of these locations. Though the characters spend extended periods on the road, they either overlook road signs or encounter signs that have been altered to reflect the contemporary geography: billboards painted over to discourage visitors, now serving as "a pale palimpsest of advertisements for goods which no longer existed" (McCarthy 2010, 135). During the nights, the boy meticulously studies the maps by the fire, memorising the names of towns and rivers and tracking their progress (2010, 229). Nevertheless, the novel deliberately withholds the names of these towns and rivers, as if McCarthy intentionally sought to keep the journey obscure. Unlike fans of Jack Kerouac's *On the Road*, who can retrace the famous journey from East to West, readers cannot undertake a similar pilgrimage in this case.

Aside from the sea at the novel's end, the narrative offers few, if any, identifiable landmarks. The buildings the protagonists encounter are as featureless as the ash that blankets them — houses, like the one where the father once lived (2010, 24), or looted supermarkets, indistinguishable in their desolation. The cities they traverse are smothered by the greyness, bearing no signs of life. "Cars in the street caked with ash," the narrator observes, "everything covered with ash and dust" (McCarthy 2010, 11). Ground Zero, where DeLillo's Neudecker found himself on the day of the event, is extended here into a global condition, brought to its logical and apocalyptic conclusion: the entire world has become Ground Zero. The only proper names to punctuate this semantic void are Tenerife—home of the Pájaro de Esperanza, the ship the father ransacks for food—and London, etched onto the Hezzaninth marine sextant he finds onboard. A third name appears as a ghost of an advertisement on the side of a log barn glimpsed on their journey south. "See Rock City," the slogan silently commands in "faded ten-foot letters" (2010, 20). Like the billboard bearing the eyes of Doctor T. J. Eckleburg in F. Scott Fitzgerald's *The Great Gatsby* (1925), such signs function less as bearings and more as spectral commentary on a landscape that no longer speaks.

The novel's understated commentary on these three quasi-accidental references leans towards a quietly anti-capitalist stance. Tenerife, once capable of conjuring idyllic images of sun-drenched beaches and carefree tourism, now exists only as a ghostly echo of vanished leisure. Likewise, the antique brass Hezzaninth sextant evokes a world once governed by exploration, precision, and empirical certainties, a world that could be measured, navigated, and mapped. Both mental images stand in stark contrast to the landscape McCarthy conjures. The beach to which the father and son eventually arrive is not white and inviting but grey and lifeless, "with the slow combers rolling dull and leaden and the distant sound of it. Like the desolation of some alien sea breaking on the shores of a world unheard of" (McCarthy 2010, 230). There is no trace of the oceanic blue promised by the maps the boy pores over at night beside the fire. The sextant, emblem of orientation and mastery, lies useless, a relic of a world no longer worth charting. When the boy asks his father whether anything lies beyond the sea, the father replies that there is *nothing*—or perhaps, he concedes, "there's a father and his little boy, and they're sitting on the beach" (2010, 231). In McCarthy's stark, biblical imaginary, the world beyond is simply a mirror image of the world at hand: equally stripped, equally barren, and locked in the same relentless quest for survival.

The colour of the ash itself evokes a place stripped of identity, neither white nor black, but caught in a liminal grey that suggests not only the erasure of distinguishing features but also a state of *purgatory*. Much like DeLillo's "bubble of dust," McCarthy's ashen landscape becomes the apotheosis of erased locality. Yet *The Road* takes this one step further, layering an erasure of temporality upon spatial dissolution. On waking one indistinct morning, the father surveys the land stretching southward, "[barren], silent, godless," and with it, the collapse of chronological certainty. "He thought the month was October," the narrator notes, "but he wasn't sure. He hadnt [sic] kept a calendar for years" (McCarthy 2010, 2). Even the volumes they find in an abandoned house remain unnamed, their most salient features being the rot and dampness that mark their slow disintegration (2010, 138). Whatever words or titles they may still bear are, at best, *vestigial*. Though these fragments of a prior culture may register with the father and son, they no longer hold interpretive or explanatory power. What seizes the father's attention instead is something as banal and historically weighted as a can of Coca-Cola dislodged from a vending machine (McCarthy 2010, 22), a symbol less of consumer culture than of vestigial comfort and fleeting familiarity. In this world, explanation has lost its currency; thought has been dethroned. What remains is bare instinct, sheer necessity, the skeletal scaffolding of survival.

The narrative structure of *The Road* mirrors the desolate indeterminacy of the landscape the protagonists cross. McCarthy eschews chapter divisions entirely, offering readers no clear markers of progression, no milestones, no turning points. The only semblance of pause from the relentless, toothless terror of the world's ashen expanse comes in the form of occasional paragraph breaks, themselves spare and withholding. The novel unfolds as an unbroken stream of indistinct days, marked only by haunting dreams, gnawing hunger, and fleeting, often heartrending encounters with other survivors. The dialogue, rendered with McCarthy's characteristic parsimony and frequently left unattributed, feels directionless, its threads of communication fraying in the bleak silence of the post-apocalyptic void. The world has long ceased to participate in any meaningful semiotic exchange; language, like the landscape, is stripped to its barest elements.

Even the father's efforts to preserve a semblance of meaning through bedtime stories — tales of courage and justice, told as he remembers them (McCarthy 2010, 42) — are exposed as hollow gestures. "Those stories are not true," the boy asserts after witnessing a moment of brutal necessity in which his father kills another man, "in the stories we're always helping people and we dont [sic] help people" (2010, 287). In that moment, the child repudiates inherited fictions, and the moral scaffolding they once provided collapses under the weight of lived experience. The symbolic order these stories once upheld no longer applies. They are not merely inadequate; they are *dishonest*. The world that once required narrative as a stabilising force has withered into one in which narrative is a vestige of *denial* — a comfort for a reality that is no longer possible.

The father's stories of "courage and justice" (2010, 42), like the vivid dreams "so rich in colour" of a world that has vanished, serve less as reflections of reality than as *temptations* — artefacts of a moral order that no longer applies (2010, 20). Both are rendered inadequate, not only because they fail to align with the lived experience of the post-apocalyptic world but because they attempt to impose narrative simplicity on a reality that no longer permits it. When the father invites his son to reverse roles and tell a story himself, the boy refuses, implicitly admonishing him: the boy's stories are "more like real life" (2010, 287), while the father's stories are idealised fiction. The child's rejection marks a profound shift — not merely a stylistic diversion but a deeper epistemological break. His imagination, shaped by a world stripped of colour, light, and moral clarity, can no longer accommodate heroic paradigms.

While the father's dreams grow increasingly lush and luminous, an ominous sign he earlier associated with the nearness of death, the boy's interior landscape is defined by absence. When questioned about his dreams, his reply is stark and devastating in its brevity: "Nothing" (2010, 194). It is not just that he has no dreams worth recounting; it is that the very faculty for dreaming, for picturing a world different from the one he inhabits, has been eroded. The greyness of the external world has seeped into his inner life as well. Thus, McCarthy presents not only a ruined world but also a generation whose very capacity to imagine restoration has been extinguished. In this bleak exchange between father and son, the novel articulates its most heartrending revelation: that the catastrophe has not only destroyed the past but foreclosed the future.

2.3.1 The Post-Nuclear Family

The generational gap between the father and the child in McCarthy's *The Road* carries profound implications, becoming increasingly pronounced as the narrative progresses. David Holloway observes that the novel is deliberately structured to highlight both "the young child's awful vulnerability to the predations of the post-apocalypse (extreme cold, starvation, illness, rape, slavery, cannibalism) and the likely death of the father who protects him" (Holloway 2008, 110). In Holloway's view, the novel thus dramatises the genre's recurring preoccupation with figures — particularly children and civilians — left exposed in a world where neither parental nor state protection remains (2008, 110–11). In this context, the state has entirely abdicated its foundational role; it no longer functions as a guarantor of safety and stability. In its absence, the father steps in as a surrogate authority, a human embodiment of the lost institutional scaffolding, though he, too, is doomed, increasingly ravaged by illness and fatigue.

Yet the father's substitution is not merely practical — it is also spiritual and symbolic. In his eyes, the child assumes a messianic significance: "If he is not the word of God, God never spoke" (McCarthy 2010, 3). This declaration reveals the father's investment in transcendence, in the belief that meaning may yet be salvaged from desolation. However, the child does not share his father's theological orientation. More than the father, the child internalises the new order of things. While the father attempts to shield him with inherited moral categories, the boy quietly resists such impositions, bearing witness to a future that can no longer be built on the assumptions of the past.

Towards the novel's end, while the man prepares a meagre dinner, the boy constructs a miniature village in the sand, complete with a rational "grid of streets" (McCarthy 2010, 261). Yet even before the father speaks, the child already knows that the sea will soon wash the village away. This scene underscores the boy's growing awareness—not simply of impermanence but of the natural order of devastation in the world they inhabit. He no longer requires an adult to explain how things work. This erosion of innocence is both subtle and total. A particularly resonant moment comes when the man dreams of strange, otherworldly creatures after discovering an underground shelter stocked with food and basic comforts. The passage showcases the irreversible generational rupture the novel explores:

> Maybe he understood for the first time that to the boy, he was himself an alien. A being from a planet that no longer existed. The tales of which were suspect. He could not construct for the child's pleasure the world he'd lost without constructing the loss as well, and he thought perhaps the child had known this better than he. He tried to remember the dream, but he could not. All that was left was the feeling of it. He thought perhaps they'd come to warn him. Of what? That he could not enkindle in the heart of the child what was ashes in his own. (McCarthy 2010, 163)

The boy, born into devastation, belongs to a new ontological category. He is not just a bearer of innocence, but a herald of a generation incapable of imagining the world otherwise—a generation that, as Don DeLillo famously put it, must learn to live "in the ruins of the future" (DeLillo 2001). This unbridgeable gap is particularly evident in the scene where the father carves a flute and gives it to the boy. The music that emerges is described as "formless music for the age to come. Or perhaps the last music on earth called up from out of the ashes of its ruin" (McCarthy 2010, 81). In its very formlessness, the music reflects the aesthetic of the world around them—bereft of structure, meaning, or tonal resolution. The boy, momentarily possessed by the spirit of the sound, "seemed some sad and solitary changeling child announcing the arrival of a travelling spectacle in shire and village who does not know that behind him the players have all been carried off by wolves" (2010, 81). The flute becomes an object of eerie prophecy, its sound a lamentation — an elegy for a lost world.

Family matters constitute a persistent preoccupation in the post-9/11 novel. Foer, DeLillo, and McCarthy each weave familial relationships into the fabric of their narratives as if such a thematic engagement were an unspoken criterion for membership in what might cynically be called the 9/11 fiction canon. When Pankaj Mishra, writing for *The Guardian*, includes Ken Kalfus' *A Disorder Peculiar to the Country* (2006) among the key works in this genre, the rhetorical question he poses almost in passing feels entirely expected: "Are we meant to think of domestic discord," Mishra muses, "as a metaphor for post-9/11 America?" (Mishra 2007). That the breakdown of the family unit might mirror national disarray is a metaphor too apt to resist.

Yet the fixation on familial turmoil is not merely symbolic. As Arin Keeble observes in his overview of post-9/11 fiction for *The Independent*, these narratives frequently explore how "privileged Americans absorb and respond to trauma" (Keeble, n.d.). What often goes unacknowledged, however, is that they are equally saturated with the latent guilt of an older generation — an inherited human burden rooted in the belief that something precious, perhaps irretrievably so, has been destroyed under its stewardship. Nowhere is this generational guilt more deeply embedded than in McCarthy's *The Road*. Here, fatherhood is a sheltering role and a reminder of complicity. The father bears within him the knowledge that the world he passes on is no longer viable, and a quiet self-indictment shadows his every act of protection.

"What emerges most powerfully as one reads *The Road*," Michael Chabon contends in his review for *The New York Review of Books*, "is not a prognosticatory or satirical warning about the future or a timeless parable of a father's devotion to his son," but rather an overpowering "testament to the abyss of a parent's greatest fears" (Chabon 2007). These fears are not abstract anxieties about distant dangers; they are visceral and immediate: the terror of leaving one's child alone, of dying before the child has learned to navigate the mechanisms and risks of a hostile world, or before the child has found someone else to face those dangers with. Most hauntingly, Chabon argues, what the father in McCarthy's novel struggles with throughout is the unbearable fear that he might, one day, be compelled—out of mercy and necessity—to commit violence against his son, to end his life for his "peace and comfort" (Chabon 2007).

This ever-present fear, Chabon notes, transcends the specific circumstances of McCarthy's imagined apocalypse and touches upon a more profound, almost primal generational anxiety. It is the fear, "as every parent fears—that you have left your children a world more damaged, more poisoned, more base and violent and cheerless and toxic, more doomed, than the one you inherited" (Chabon 2007). This underlying unease, I would argue, is precisely what secured *The Road*'s immediate inclusion among the canon of post-9/11 novels, despite the absence of direct allusions to the attacks. The novel captures, with a devastating economy, the unspoken dread of an older generation: the fear of bequeathing to their children a world irrevocably scarred, where the memory and legacy of 9/11—whether in its literal forms or the atmosphere of perpetual aftermath it fostered—linger as the new normal. Though rarely articulated openly, this fear permeates McCarthy's bleak landscape, heavy and inescapable.

However, this is only one instance where McCarthy comments on the generational gap that structures *The Road*. Deep into the novel, the boy and the father watch from a distance as a group of people—whom the man later designates simply as "the bad guys" (2010, 97)—advance along the same road:

> An army in tennis shoes, tramping. Carrying three-foot lengths of pipe with leather wrappings. [...] The phalanx following carried spears or lances tasselled with ribbons, the long blades hammered out of trucksprings in some crude forge upcountry. [...] Behind them came wagons drawn by slaves in harness and piled with goods of war and after that the women, perhaps a dozen in number, some of them pregnant, and lastly a supplementary consort of catamites illclothed against the cold and fitted in dogcollars and yoked each to each. (McCarthy 2010, 96)

The brutal social hierarchy of this procession is immediately apparent, and its violent nature is inscribed both in the weapons it bears and in the exploitation of the weak. While such a structure would be vehemently rejected in the framework of modern Western society, McCarthy's depiction suggests that this is the inevitable configuration of humanity stripped of its civilizational features. This is the sort of world the father seeks desperately to shield his son from, aware that exposure to such cruelty might forever shape the boy's perception of existence.

Yet McCarthy's vision goes further. Echoing Shreve's grim musing in Faulkner's *Absalom, Absalom!*—a future in which every man would have "sprung from the loins of African kings" (Faulkner 1995, 378)—McCarthy presents an equally sobering glimpse of an inescapable legacy: the children borne by the enslaved, pregnant women of the phalanx, like the father's boy, will inherit this blasted, hierarchical world and will themselves be either victims or enforcers within it. Perhaps that is why the father commands the boy to avert his eyes—to protect him not merely from the sight of the passing horde but from an unbearable foreknowledge of the future. The description of the "phalanx," with its crude regalia and tribalistic overtones, strikingly recalls the depiction of the "legion of horribles…clad in costumes attic or biblical or wardrobed out of a fevered dream" (2015, 48) in *Blood Meridian* (1985). In both cases, McCarthy envisions societies devolved into primal displays of violence, where the future is no longer a dream but a repetition.

At the opposite side of the spectrum—where "the good guys" would nominally belong—is another type of itinerant family, described in more modest, almost pitiful terms, and this time ob served from a distance without any explicit request for viewer discretion:

> They came down the road and crossed the bridge. Three men and a woman. The woman walked with a waddling gait, and as she approached, he could see that she was pregnant. The men carried packs on their backs, and the woman carried a small cloth suitcase. All of them wretchedlooking beyond description. Their breath steaming softly. They crossed the bridge and continued on down the road, but they vanished one by one into the waiting darkness. (McCarthy 2010, 208)

In stark contrast to the earlier phalanx, this one has no discernible social hierarchy or evident signs of aggression. They seem, if anything, closer to the ill-clothed catamites than to the armed men: ill-equipped for the hostile environment, fragile, spectral. Yet this group's way of life resonates with the father, even if he remains cautious, unwilling to expose himself and the boy to the risks of contact. Like the father and son, these wanderers have chosen — or been forced — to remain outside the orbit of larger, more organised groups, rejecting the false security such communities offer when they devalue and dehumanise life to its most brutal essence.

By contrast, the "bad guys," as the father calls them, have created a social order where survival is predicated on domination and atrocity, culminating in acts of cannibalism as a grotesque means of survival. The father and son are soon exposed to the full horror of this reality when they discover one of the marauders' hideouts: a basement where human beings are kept like livestock, awaiting slaughter. Even before that, an earlier encounter with another roving band of "bad guys" nearly cost them their lives. In McCarthy's universe, the dignity of wandering alone, bereft of even the minimal protection of numbers, becomes one of the last affirmations of humanity.

The father openly expresses his disdain for the bad guys' way of life, even as his and the boy's own situation becomes increasingly desperate. With food and water scarce and few viable options left, their bodies begin to fail them, worn down by persistent hunger and mounting exhaustion. The toll is most starkly evident in the boy's physical deterioration. The father observes with anguish the child's "taut face and hollow eyes," a visage marked by "[a] strange beauty" (2010, 108), "like something out of a deathcamp. Starved, exhausted, sick with fear" (2010, 123). Later, the boy appears almost otherworldly: "The boy's candlecoloured skin was all but translucent," and "[with] his great staring eyes he'd the look of an alien" (2010, 137). In this context of extreme deprivation — where all human comforts are reduced to shadows, and survival becomes the only compass — *The Road* acquires unmistakable moral undertones. The world is shrunk to what McCarthy calls "a raw core of parsible entities" (2010, 93), and the novel's structure begins to reflect an us-versus-them dichotomy resonant with the atmosphere that emerged in the immediate aftermath of 9/11.

The narration sometimes adopts a biblical tone, particularly in its depictions of the "bad guys," whose moral depravity is reflected in their grotesque appearance. One such figure is described with a stark, almost apocalyptic precision:

> Eyes collared in cups of grime and deeply sunk. Like an animal inside a skull looking out the eyeholes. He wore a beard that had been cut square across the bottom with shears, and he had a tattoo of a bird on his neck done by someone with an illformed notion of their appearance. He was lean, wiry, rachitic. Dressed in a pair of filthy blue coveralls and a black billcap with the logo of some vanished enterprise embroidered across the front of it. (2010, 65)

This is not simply a portrait of a man but of a fallen state where the body carries outward signs of inner corruption. The grotesque is not symbolic—it is *anatomical*. When the father later revisits the episode and contemplates the corpse of the man he was forced to shoot—now devoured by his companions—the figure assumes the shape of something nearly mythic, even satanic: "My brother at last," the father muses, "[the] reptilian calculations in those cold and shifting eyes. The grey and rotting teeth. Claggy with human flesh" (2010, 79). In this hellish vision, the boundary between man and beast collapses entirely, and the novel's moral compass becomes intimate and absolute.

To put it differently, and to draw on Colin McGinn's "aesthetic theory of virtue," the "bad guys" in McCarthy's narrative serve as "visible embodiments of evil," operating on the premise that evil is inherently a form of ugliness. "If the evil spirit were to become visible," McGinn writes, "*this* is how it would look—as 'ugly as sin'" (McGinn 1999, 144). Their arrival is foreshadowed not only by the rattle of their crude truck but also by the sound of coughing—bodily decay made audible. Following McGinn's line of reasoning, the evil otherness the "bad guys" represent becomes a "reification of the soul made ugly through vice and innate depravity" (McGinn 1999, 145). Their external disfigurement is not a mask but a manifestation of their moral and spiritual disfigurement. In them, the outer life is not merely indicative of the inner life—it is the same.

Matters differ somewhat from the other group of wanderers the two protagonists meet. The essential distinction between the two groups lies in their choices, or more precisely, in the way they persist in those choices. There is a shared stubbornness—a refusal to yield to circumstance—on both sides, but it takes radically different forms. Whereas the "bad guys" exhibit a grotesque alignment between their physical degradation and their moral depravity, the supposed "good guys" offer a quiet refusal of that alignment. Their destitution does not mirror any spiritual failure. They remain human despite their wretched appearance, and this is reflected in the hushed dignity of their passage. Unlike the cacophonous arrival of the bad guys, theirs is marked by stillness. "Their breath steaming softly" (2010, 208) is the only sign of their presence. Their goodness is inscribed not in declarations or deeds but in an absence—in their refusal to disturb, to dominate, to devour.

Moreover, while the wretchedness of appearance functions as a fitting punishment for the "bad guys," it carries no such moral resonance in the case of the "good guys." For the latter, their destitution feels not like the result of transgression but rather like an unjust burden imposed upon them by a world gone awry. Their threadbare clothing and hollow faces seem less like the visible imprint of sin than the undeserved fallout of a catastrophe they neither chose nor caused. As the father bleakly observes, "in the history of the world, it might even be that there was more punishment than crime" (2010, 33). This quiet recognition highlights the moral dissonance at the novel's core. The "good guys," including the father and his son, are acutely aware of their degradation and go to subtle lengths to shield it from view, as though to preserve some residual dignity in a world that no longer makes room for such distinctions.

The father feels a certain kinship with this second group of wanderers, not only because of their silent dignity but also because, in their quiet perseverance, he sees an echo of the family he has lost. Among them is a pregnant woman—a sight that pierces him with memories of a life that might have continued but did not. Unlike the unnamed woman who carried life forward, his wife chose instead to walk into nothingness. Her presence in the novel is spectral, surfacing only in fragmentary recollections. In one especially charged flashback, she pleads with the father to end all their lives.

"We're the walking dead in a horror film," she tells him bitterly, "sooner or later, they will catch us, and they will kill us. They will rape me. They'll rape him. They are going to rape us and kill us and eat us, and you wont [sic] face it. You'd rather wait for it to happen" (2010, 57–58). Her argument is devastating in its finality — there is no refutation because the world outside offers no redemption, no moral reckoning, only annihilation. "And she was right," the man concedes later, recalling the countless nights spent "arguing the pros and cons of self-destruction with the earnestness of philosophers chained to a madhouse wall" (2010, 60). And yet, the mere sight of this other family trudging onward, however battered, suggests a faint glimmer of hope — an alternative in the face of despair.

Seen through the lens of this Manichean division between "us" and "them," *The Road* can almost be read as one of those stories of courage and justice that the boy, with instinctive scepticism, finds unconvincing. This becomes particularly evident in the father's repeated assurances that they could not possibly die — because they were "the good guys" and because they were "carrying the fire" (2010, 87, 136). Like the arc of a traditional moral narrative, the implication is that virtue will be rewarded, and some form of redemption or "happily ever after" will follow. Yet, as so often in McCarthy's work, this clarity is undermined by a persistent ambiguity.

The novel's ambivalence and its silence on crucial matters obscure any definitive interpretation of the "fire" the protagonists are said to carry. If we were to rely solely on the us-versus-them binary, the "fire" might stand for a moral code — an ethical inheritance stubbornly preserved in the ruins of civilisation. Despite unrelenting hardship, the man and the boy uphold this code. They refuse to resort to cannibalism, and they offer help, however limited, when they can: sharing a can of food and a few words with Ely, the elderly drifter they meet after emerging from the subterranean shelter. They use violence only in self-defence, never out of malice or opportunism. In a world where the remnants of morality are threadbare and belief in human goodness scarce, the father's hope that the boy might someday contribute to a better world imbues the narrative with its faint but persistent transcendence.

Nonetheless, the fire they carry may reflect the other fire that once ravaged the world, leaving it in its current state. Amidst the love and protection that the father promises his child, a suggestion lingers that their unwavering faith in the inherent goodness of humanity may have contributed to their predicament. Adding to this interpretation is the ambiguity surrounding both fires mentioned in the novel. The physical fire that ravaged the world lacks context, scale, causes, and a foreseeable outcome. Likewise, the metaphorical fire that the boy and his father carry resists fixed interpretation. Is it the moral stance that the characters adopt during their journey? Is it the preservation of a supposedly moral species that the father so obstinately seeks to safeguard? Is the novel presenting a story in which physical adversity leads to a spiritual revelation? If so, what is this spiritual revelation? Is it that one must persist in their beliefs regardless of the circumstances?

The idea of "carrying the fire" lies at the heart of the grand narrative the father constructs for his son—a sustaining myth that suspends the ever-present shadow of death, embodied in the single bullet that remains in the father's gun. Though the man never articulates precisely what the fire represents, it functions as a talisman and mantra. As Michael Chabon notes, "from this hopeful fiction or hopeless truth the boy seems to intuit a promise: that life will not always be thus; that it will improve, that beauty and purpose, sunlight and green plenty will return; in short that everything is going to be 'okay,' a word which both characters endlessly repeat to each other, touching it compulsively like a sore place or a missing tooth" (Chabon 2007). The father's insistence on this word, this fragile affirmation, functions like a ritualistic incantation—akin to a form of cognitive behavioural therapy—arming the boy with the psychological scaffolding necessary to resist despair and endure the greyness of the world surrounding them.

Considering the novel's persistent refusal to offer definitive moral or symbolic clarity, "carrying the fire" emerges less as a statement of ethical position and more as a performative gesture—a ritual of *persistence*. Rather than presenting moral purity or human goodness, as some interpretations suggest, the fire in *The Road* can be seen as a placeholder for meaning in a world where meaning has become untenable. It functions much like a *selfish event*: a centripetal force that draws everything into its orbit, not through its intrinsic clarity, but through its repetitive invocation. The father and son repeat the phrase obsessively, touching it "like a sore place or a missing tooth," as Michael Chabon observes, precisely because it suspends the total collapse of the narrative. The fire is not a symbol of salvation nor a moral imperative—it is the act of saying *something* in a world without the conditions for saying anything. In this sense, McCarthy's novel resists the interpretive closure so often demanded of trauma fiction. It refuses to offer redemption and instead provides the barest scaffolding upon which a future might be imagined, however bleak. The fire burns only insofar as it is carried—its value lies not in what it illuminates but in the fact that it persists.

To a certain extent, McCarthy withholds from his readers any definitive resolution to the questions raised throughout the novel. When, after his father's death, the boy is approached by a stranger and asks whether he too is "carrying the fire," the man's response—tempered with gentle amusement—is that the boy might be "kind of weirded out" (2010, 303). Still, the narrative suggests that the boy's story is not over. He accepts the man's invitation to join his group, and, in this gesture, the boy's narrative realigns with that of another community. The circle is closed with the reappearance of maternal care, as a woman—presumably the man's wife—embraces him and speaks to him about God. Yet the spiritual axis of the boy's life remains his father. In the final lines, he attempts to talk to God but ultimately finds greater solace in addressing the memory of his father: "He tried to talk to God, but the best thing was to talk to his father, and he did talk to him and he didnt [sic] forget" (2010, 306). The ambiguity of the fire's meaning persists, but what remains clear is that memory, not divinity, becomes the boy's source of moral and emotional continuity.

In these final pages, the image of the father begins to merge with that of God, and the novel closes on an unmistakably religious note. Throughout the narrative, the father increasingly resembles a Christ-like figure, particularly in moments of doubt and despair, such as when he nearly curses God's name (2010, 120). After their first encounter with the bad guys, he assures the boy that he has been "appointed by God" to protect him (2010, 80), which casts his paternal devotion in a sacred light. Particularly arresting in this regard is a brief fragment in the novel's second half, in which a voice—ambiguous in origin, perhaps divine, perhaps internal, or even diabolical—challenges the purpose of the father's moral commitment. "Do you think your fathers are watching," it asks, "[that] they weigh you in their ledgerbook?" (2010, 209). The immediate rebuttal—"There is no book, and your fathers are dead in the ground" (2010, 209)—unsettles the moral axis of the novel. If all systems of judgement and divine accounting have collapsed, what remains to justify goodness in a godless world?

Yet even as the father succumbs to death, the narrative quietly restores a sense of sacred continuity. The woman who receives the boy at the novel's end offers a counterbalance to the nihilistic voice. "The breath of God was his breath yet though it pass from man to man through all of time," she tells the boy (2010, 306). Her words suggest that moral inheritance persists through human connection and memory, not divine judgment. Strikingly, her statement might even extend to the "bad guys," who, despite their depravity, also carry "the breath of God." In this light, the breath is not a moral seal of approval but a shared human condition that does not discriminate between good and evil but testifies to the fragility and persistence of life itself.

In contrast to the religious sensibility of the "older generation," embodied in the father, the boy represents a quiet secularism—an ethics unmoored from theology but nonetheless deeply felt. His most persistent concern is not divine judgment or salvation but the fear of failing to "do the right thing." In this sense, the novel enacts what David Roman, writing for the *Los Angeles Review of Books*, describes as an "ethical game," with the boy—not the father—as its master tactician. For most survivors in the novel, particularly the "bad guys," life and death constitute the stark binary upon which this new world is built. The boy, by contrast, "wants to keep some semblance of humanity" (Roman, n.d.). He clings to the ethical norms of a world where theft, cannibalism, rape, and murder are more than mere risks of survival—they are moral aberrations.

Yet this ethical drive does not arise from faith in God or obedience to religious doctrine. Those frameworks, like the prelapsarian world of the father's memory, are alien to the boy. "By not clinging to his religion," Roman argues, "and abstaining from using God's law as a cover for the ethical impulse, the son cuts a more appealing figure for the average modern reader" (Roman, n.d.). The boy becomes, in effect, the ethical seed of a new world, carrying not divine fire but the embers of decency. For Roman, the novel's ethical game is precisely this: "to ensure that the next civilisation to emerge from the ruins of the blight is not built by those who have survived by savagery" (Roman, n.d.). From this vantage point, *The Road* does not merely depict the aftermath of disaster but anticipates future conflict—a moral reckoning between those who, like the boy, navigate ruin with conscience intact and those who have survived by reducing morality to obsolescence.

The novel's final paragraph reads as a reverse genesis, a quiet undoing of creation. This antithetical genesis is foreshadowed repeatedly throughout *The Road*. "[Beyond] the numbness and the dull despair," the father occasionally senses that the world is "shrinking down" to a raw core, "[the] names of things slowly following those things into oblivion. Colours. The names of birds. Things to eat. Finally, the names of things one believed to be true" (McCarthy 2010, 93). In contrast to Adam and Eve in *Genesis* 1:28, who are granted dominion over creation through naming, McCarthy's characters inhabit a world where the act of un-naming marks the loss of dominion, a slow erasure of human centrality and meaning. In this reversal, language itself unravels alongside the natural order.

Yet the novel closes not in nihilism but with a haunting vision of the vanished world: the image of "trout in the streams of the mountains," whose "vermiculate patterns" resemble "maps of the world in its becoming. Maps and mazes. Of a thing which could not be put back. Not be made right again. In the deep glens where they lived, all things were older than man, and they hummed of mystery" (2010, 307). In this way, McCarthy does not end with apocalypse but with awe—a posthuman reverence that gestures beyond survival toward the sublime.

The reversed genesis at the novel's conclusion constitutes yet another symptom of the *diplopia* engendered by the selfish event—a cognitive double vision in which the outward gaze is redirected inward. The indeterminacy of the world outside, with its features blurred by the ever-present ash covering everything, contrasts with the father's internal life, perhaps the only moral or cognitive consciousness to which the reader is granted access. As the external world is reduced to essentials, demanding only survival without deliberation, ornament, or ethical nuance, its inner mechanics are revealed. As in *Blood Meridian*, where nature is portrayed as indifferent and lethal, here, too, an absent or hostile nature turns its indifference into a pressure that drives the individual inward, forcing a confrontation with a psychological terrain as bleak and arid as the physical one.

McCarthy also enhances this doubling of the gaze by performing a narrative feat that makes the novel gaze inwardly. Holloway argues that, in this sense, the novel, albeit replete with literary clichés such as "the wasteland, civilisations in ashes, the endless road, the child as a repository of goodness, hope, innocence," uses those very clichés to make a point against the proliferation of apocalyptic imagery in Western culture. "McCarthy's real achievement," Holloway adds, "was to evoke prevailing sensibilities with such poetic poignancy by infusing hackneyed tropes with resonant meaning and fresh emotional depth" (Holloway 2008, 111). Thus, the novel's diplopic vision not only disorients the reader's relationship to narrative and setting but also critiques the cultural mechanisms through which apocalypse is imagined.

The Road is, in this sense, a meditation on the genre itself, which simultaneously highlights the kind of trap that writers of post-apocalyptic fiction might fall into as they address the topic. Like the father, who disregards the mother's choice, which seems most appropriate given the current conditions, McCarthy repeatedly contemplates how to conclude things. Chabon claims in his review that the author himself is ensnared and his hell undone by the paradox that lies at the heart of every story of apocalypse. The only true account of the world after a disaster as nearly complete and as searing as the one McCarthy proposes, drawing heavily on the 'nuclear winter' scenario first proposed by Carl Sagan and others, would be a book of blank pages, white as ash. But to annihilate the world in prose, one must simultaneously write it into being. (Chabon 2007)

To say that the trees were dead and the leaves had turned to ashes as he crushed them between his fingers is to build this new world on the foundations of the previous one, where trees and magnolias were still possible. One must first possess that world to render it dead.

The voice in the novel's final paragraph echoes the divine voice that nearly persuades the father to yield to the flawed moral code of the new world. This is the voice of the narrative itself. The mysteries it hints at, which have been violently exposed during the cataclysm, suggest that any effort, whether gentle or aggressive, to disclose the workings of the world carries severe repercussions for the mysteries involved. Moreover, a quest, like the one pursued by the son and father, is necessary to restore the balance between good and evil. On the other hand, these elements also indicate that, regardless of the nature of the revealing cataclysm, a point of no return has been crossed. The mysteries that sustain the world cannot be recreated, as any attempt to do so would necessitate confronting the loss inherent in any social, political, or cultural structure that may emerge in its aftermath.

Nevertheless, this notion has been previously discussed. Throughout the novel, the father alludes to images that cannot be erased once they are placed there. "What you put in your head," the father warns the child, "is there forever" (2010, 203). In McCarthy's novel, the "persistence in the mind" that Peter Eleey refers to in his catalogue essay for MoMA's *September 11* exhibition is rendered tangible, yet not in the sense of creating an image that relates to the events themselves, but rather in the sense of imagining a world in which reality itself bears within it the signs *and* the symptoms of the event.

In this sense, *The Road* offers a more radical articulation of the selfish event than the other texts examined in this chapter. Whereas the 9/11-centered narratives explored earlier demonstrate how a singular event draws all meaning, memory, and discourse into its gravitational field, McCarthy's novel stages a scenario in which the event has already obliterated those structures. The catastrophe in *The Road* is not framed as an event to be remembered or interpreted but rather as one that restructures the conditions of experience. It permits no external reference point and displaces all frameworks for understanding—temporal, moral, geographic, and linguistic. In this respect, *The Road* exemplifies a fully internalised selfish event in which the event no longer demands narrative attention because it has already subsumed the world it left behind.

2.4 Apocalypse Then, Utopia Now: James Howard Kunstler's *World Made by Hand*

One of the few novels that has yet to be incorporated into the post-9/11 imaginarium, and thus largely overlooked by literary critics, is James Howard Kunstler's *World Made by Hand* (2008). The reasons for this exclusion remain uncertain, particularly given that Kunstler's novel addresses themes comparable to many of the most acclaimed post-9/11 works. As this chapter will demonstrate, however, Kunstler's treatment of the post-apocalyptic scenario shows minimal affinity with the prevailing concerns of other post-9/11 novels. Like McCarthy's *The Road*, *The World Made by Hand* portrays a post-disaster American society, though in a manner arguably more grounded in realism than McCarthy's allegorical landscape.

Part of the reason why Kunstler's novel has been excluded from the post-9/11 canon may lie in its tonal divergence. While most post-9/11 novels are steeped in a melancholic post-traumatic sensibility, *World Made by Hand* offers a vision of a society suspended in a nostalgic yearning for the lost comforts of a capitalist system unable to imagine its own collapse. Kunstler's narrative is also a tale of resignation and quiet surrender—an emotional register less appealing to a readership still unsettled by the shadow of low-flying aeroplanes. The characters are not searching for those responsible for the cataclysm that fractured their world; instead, they have resigned themselves to a numbing continuity that echoes the rhythm of their former lives.

Moreover, the novel's "eco-millenarian" perspective—a term coined by Paul Greenberg in his review for *The New York Times Sunday Book Review*—highlights the narrative's emphasis on post-apocalyptic regeneration rather than retrospective trauma. This orientation, which privileges ecological renewal and the possibility of a fresh start, runs counter to the darker, trauma-inflected visions that critics typically associate with post-9/11 fiction (Greenberg 2008). In this sense, *World Made by Hand* resists interpretation through the lens of trauma theory, situating itself instead within a more redemptive, albeit ambivalent, utopian framework.

Trauma is undoubtedly present in the characters' recollections; however, it never gains momentum or manifests in self-destructive behaviours. On the contrary, the novel's protagonists consistently reject any form of return, traumatic or nostalgic, to the pre-cataclysmic era. The world has not been reduced to ash, as in *The Road*, but rather to a pastoral society where everyone has become a labourer. This refusal to look back arises not from dissatisfaction with their new status as "noble savages" but from accepting the impossibility of reclaiming what was lost, except through renewed effort and innovation. "It's not healthy to obsess about the past," Robert Earle, the novel's protagonist, tells Loren, the Reverend of their community (Kunstler 2009, 2). Simply reflecting on "how well the world used to work and how much we'd lost" (2009, 4) is perceived as chilling and counterproductive. A fragile balance has been restored in the community where Robert Earle and Loren reside, and human interactions are mediated by mutual exchange. The past is no longer a source of hope or nostalgia; it has become something to avoid, a repository of loss and regret.

Yet the past is not entirely erased in Kunstler's novel. It re-emerges periodically, but always for contrast. "In the early twenty-first century," the narrator observes, "[we] got our food from the supermarket, and not everybody cared where the supermarket got it as long as it was there on the shelves" (2009, 5). In this former world, agriculture had nearly vanished, eclipsed by capitalist enterprise. "Now, in the new times," the narrator continues, "[farming] was back. That was the only way we got food" (2009, 5). The sharp distinction between these two modes of living, one ruthless in sustaining an ever-expanding population, the other modest, impoverished, and rooted in subsistence, is further underscored when Robert and Loren, returning from a fishing trip, encounter a man named Brother Jobe. He offers to pay a thousand dollars for Loren's meagre catch. The gesture is almost absurd: the "old persuader," as Jobe calls money, has lost its power to persuade in the new world, though many still pretend otherwise. "A dollar isn't what it used to be," Robert tells him (2009, 10). Though currency has become functionally meaningless, people continue to use and hoard it, clinging to the illusion that it might one day recover its former value.

Another possible reason for the novel's exclusion from the post-9/11 literary canon may lie in what Paul Greenberg identifies as the cyclical nature of literary utopias, which tend to reemerge "when an appropriate niche opens up" (Greenberg 2008). The cultural atmosphere following 9/11 arguably created such a niche. In this sense, *World Made by Hand* can be understood as a product of broader socio-political and economic dynamics, extending well beyond the events of the terrorist attacks themselves. In the world of the novel, the bombings that decimate Washington and Los Angeles coincide with the depletion of global oil reserves and escalating political instability in the Middle East. These attacks function as a tipping point that precipitates the collapse of the American state and the erosion of its technological supremacy, both domestically and abroad. In many ways, Kunstler's narrative reads as a fictional counterpart to his nonfiction work, *The Long Emergency: Surviving the Converging Catastrophes of the Twenty-First Century* (2005), in which he theorises the devastating consequences of a global decline in oil production.

Notably, the novel does not portray the terrorist attacks as a singular cause, but rather as part of a broader chain of systemic failures. This framing aligns with the controversial views of public intellectuals such as Susan Sontag, who, in the wake of 9/11, suggested that the attacks should be interpreted within a broader historical and political context, a view ostracised by the mainstream public discourse at the time. As I previously argued, selfish events shape their representations by silencing or sidelining interpretations that diverge from dominant narratives and explore discursively inaccessible paths.

In Kunstler's universe, the American state persists, but only as a symbolic vestige—an idea rather than an active force—while citizens have assumed responsibility for fostering community at the local level. State symbols, as one might expect, have been overtaken by vegetation, and a quiet sense of resignation saturates the landscape:

> The once meticulously groomed grounds of the state capitol building, an impressive limestone heap in the Second Empire style, were now choked with box elders, sumacs, and other woody shrubs. Knapweed, vetch, and blue chicory sprouted from the cracks between the broad front steps where a few ill-nourished layabouts sat listlessly surveying the scene. Inside the grand old building, every surface had been stripped down to the bare masonry. Carpets, draperies, chestnut wainscoting, metal fixtures, all gone, probably long gone. The stink of urine and excrement told the rest of the story. (Kunstler 2009, 166)

Kunstler's storytelling unfolds on a grand scale, which comes with its own narrative challenges. The setting has already been reclaimed by nature, requiring readers to accept the premise of societal collapse without extensive exposition. The characters, notably, have already made peace with their circumstances before the narrative even begins, and this adjustment occurs within a strikingly short temporal window. The novel takes place at a point when little can still be done in response to the terrorist attacks—when the urgency of survival has eclipsed the pursuit of culprits. In this way, *World Made by Hand* diverges sharply from the thematic concerns of most post-9/11 fiction, which tends to dwell on trauma and re-interpretation. Instead, Kunstler's novel propels the reader into a future that must be reckoned with on its terms. Its subdued yet persistent optimism seems almost discordant with the broader cultural mood at the time of its publication.

The novel also depicts a kind of comfortable inertia that runs counter to the emotional climate of the post-9/11 era. Overrun with weeds, the Capitol building becomes a metaphor not only for the erosion of political faith but also for the passivity of the survivors. Rather than attempting to rebuild the structures of the past, these individuals establish small communities governed by the dominant religious beliefs of their members. "The lack of county code enforcement," the narration observes, "had a positive effect on the creative side of things there. Many of the trailers and cottages had totem poles in front, too. Totem pole carving was something that seemed to have taken the place of TV and motor sports for them" (Kunstler 2009, 268). Such details suggest a retreat into a new form of localised culture that replaces mass entertainment and bureaucratic oversight with artisan expression and community rituals.

While this lifestyle might appear appealing, especially in its slower pace and rejection of modern excess, it did not find resonance within the broader post-9/11 literary atmosphere. Kunstler's novel proposes that the violence which shattered the old world did not provoke a turn toward introspection or catharsis, as in many post-9/11 narratives, but instead initiated a wholesale societal shift away from capitalist imperatives. In Kunstler's *World Made by Hand*, the pursuit of wealth and progress is no longer valid. What remains is not a hunger for growth but a more subdued yearning to endure, persist, and continue existing without an articulated telos. In this vision, the author offers neither lamentation nor outrage but a quiet, almost fatalistic acceptance of a new world order.

Kunstler's new world, however, evolves on a different plane, one that is primarily religious. While the physical world has been downgraded and reduced to a more rudimentary and labour-intensive mode of life, it becomes fertile ground for tightly knit groups such as the New Faith Brotherhood. In this sense, the novel functions as a cautionary tale. The liberal community of Union Grove, where Robert and Reverend Loren reside, is operational but held together by little more than a shared civic sense of duty. While Robert and his fellow townspeople have turned the refusal to mentally return to a pre-catastrophe past into a credo, they also lack a compelling vision of the future. Their principal aim is to maintain the basic functionality of the community, providing what the state once offered, rudimentary services such as running water and primary healthcare. Clinical concepts like depression, Robert explains, have fallen out of use "because despair was a spiritual condition that was as real to us as the practical difficulties we struggled with in everyday life" (2009, 17). The imagination of Union Grove's inhabitants does not extend beyond the immediate present and relies on nothing more than "the goodwill of the neighbours" (2009, 70).

In demographic terms, Robert's community appears to be at a disadvantage. This becomes particularly evident in the novel's portrayal of the women in the New Faith Brotherhood:

> The New Faith women dressed differently than our people. They wore a kind of uniform: a long, herb-dyed linen shirt and a sun-bleached white muslin blouse buttoned primly at the throat. The only real difference between them was in the sleeves. Some long, some short, and some no sleeves. But their figures were on display despite the superficial modesty. They apparently did not wear anything in the way of underwear. Perhaps they dressed for the summer heat, but their muslin blouses were surprisingly sheer, and here and there, if one of them was standing in the light a certain way, you could see her figure outlined through the fabric. Our women were generally older, and despite the décolletage on display, and the variety of fabrics and styles they wore, they came off more modestly than the New Faithers. (2009, 211–12)

Despite the uniformity and solemnity of their attire, these women appear more attractive than the varied and ageing female population of Union Grove, where Robert has been elected mayor. Robert is uniquely situated to observe and assess these differences. A former software executive, he has lost his wife to encephalitis—an illness untreatable in the post-collapse world—his daughter to influenza, and his son to the general upheaval. He is also engaged in an affair with Jane Ann, the wife of his best friend, Reverend Loren. Much like Rayford Steele, the airline pilot from Tim LaHaye and Jerry B. Jenkins's *Left Behind* novel series, Robert is a man unmoored: stripped of family, faith, and material stability. His religious beliefs are only disclosed late in the novel, and when they surface, he quickly dismisses them. From this perspective—both in terms of genetic viability and moral compass—Robert Earle hardly emerges as the ideal candidate to ensure the continuation of the human species in a post-apocalyptic world.

In a manner that is both dystopian and utopian, Robert Earle functions as a kind of visitor guide, designed to help the reader navigate this reconfigured society. He clearly resembles Samuel Butler's *Erewhon* narrator, Higgs, whose observations and judgements shape the reader's understanding of a radically altered world. This narrative function may be yet another reason why *World Made by Hand* failed to gain traction in the post-9/11 literary canon. Unlike novels such as DeLillo's *Falling Man* or even McCarthy's *The Road*, Kunstler's book offers a distinctive and, at times, didactic perspective, articulated through a robustly masculine voice that does not sit easily alongside the fragmented, grief-stricken narratives typically associated with post-9/11 fiction.

For instance, when Shawn Watling, a farmworker, is shot by Bunny—one of Wayne Karp's men—the villagers respond not with outrage but with resignation. Shawn's wife displays anger but not sorrow. Robert, ever observant, weaves the episode into a broader critique of the justice system:

> Surprisingly little curiosity was expressed about the incident that had left Shawn dead, once I had related what I knew two or three times, and it got around to all present. It was eerie, a portentous signifier of our true social condition beyond the conventions of a funeral. Nobody wanted to disturb Wayne Karp and his bunch anymore than they would poke a nest of rattlesnakes with a stick. We all knew the apparatus of justice had dissolved. (2009, 57)

Another particularly telling episode that highlights Robert's sense of authority—and perhaps superiority—over this new world is his encounter with Mrs Raynor, a solitary woman who offers shelter and the promise of a feast to Robert and his companions. What they receive, however, is grotesquely farcical:

> 'Potatoes and peas coming right up,' Mrs Raynor said, and she came back in with two serving bowls. I took the one full of potatoes. It was not the least bit warm. I took one and put it on my plate. It was a rock. I passed the bowl left to Seth, and he took his and so on. When the peas came around, I took a helping. It was grass. The lamb stew on our plates was watered up dirt: mud. Mrs. Raynor told us to dig in. I pantomimed eating, and the rest did as I did, except Brother Minor, who could barely conceal his mirth. Of course, I did not regard this as a mirthful situation, and I doubt the others did either. (Kunstler 2009, 130)

This distorted reenactment of a family meal positions Robert as the master of ceremonies, orchestrating the group's behaviour and emotional response. More broadly, he assumes the role of a moral instructor, frequently casting judgment on the pre-apocalyptic world. At the novel's outset, he remarks that "not everybody cared where the supermarket got [the food] as long as it was there on the shelves" (2009, 5), in a tone that borders on condescension. The blame for the catastrophe, in Kunstler's vision, lies not exclusively with the terrorist attacks but with the conditions that enabled them — namely, a culture of unchecked consumption and capitalist complacency. It is almost as if Robert believes this world deserved to be undone, given the heedless and dehumanising way people lived before the collapse.

This tentative shift of blame is another reason *World Made by Hand* feels estranged from the dominant contours of post-9/11 fiction. In terms of the reaction it advocates, Kunstler's novel, true to the implications of its title, resonates more closely with Susan Sontag's controversial response to the 9/11 attacks than with the rhetoric that permeated much of the cultural and literary output in the immediate aftermath. Like Sontag, Kunstler's protagonist adopts a non-belligerent stance toward the perpetrators and instead turns inward, focusing on the systemic issues at the heart of American society. "Where is the acknowledgement," Sontag asked in her brief, but incisive response published in *The New Yorker*, "that this was not a 'cowardly' attack on 'civilisation' or 'liberty' or 'humanity' or 'the free world' but an attack on the world's self-proclaimed superpower, undertaken as a consequence of specific American alliances and actions?" (*The New Yorker* 2001).

Similarly, Kunstler imagines a world where the attacks inadvertently produce unforeseen and arguably redemptive consequences. Although the characters occasionally lament the loss of modern conveniences such as electricity, motor vehicles, and the ease of communication, there is a prevailing sense that this return to a pre-modern mode of existence has allowed for a renewed attentiveness to aspects of life once obscured by technological noise. This return reconfigures human relationships with the natural world and one another. "Back in the machine times," Brother Jobe tells Robert after his visit to Mary Beth Ivanhoe, the charismatic leader of the New Faith Brotherhood, "there was so much noise front and back, so to speak, it kept us from knowing what lies behind the surface of things. Now it stands out more." (2009, 263). In the symbolic economy of Kunstler's narrative, the bombs that fell on Los Angeles and Washington D.C. act less as instruments of destruction than as revelatory catalysts—events that stripped away illusion and exposed the enduring truths beneath.

The novel abounds with quiet revelations that strike at multiple cultural and political nerves. Notably, the "act of jihad" that precipitates the collapse is not portrayed as an incomprehensible horror but rather as a calculated and "extraordinarily successful" operation (2009, 23). The atomic bombs that devastated Los Angeles and Washington, D.C., effectively "tanked the whole U.S. economy." In the wake of the attacks, international trade faltered, not because of a lack of demand or goods but due to escalating security measures and paralysing border controls. Fear of further attacks seized American authorities, leading to delays so extensive that cargo ships were often forced to return to port with their holds still full. Gradually, the global economic network that had sustained the United States began to disintegrate. What remained was a world governed not by market flows or digital systems but by local strongmen, barter economies, and the hard labour of subsistence. The novel thus charts a regression—not to chaos, but to primitive order where one must once again earn sustenance by the sweat of one's brow.

However, if 9/11 created fertile ground for the resurgence of dystopian and utopian narratives, it also paradoxically marked the demise of certain expressions within that genre. Because of its specificity and prescriptive tone, Kunstler's speculative fiction failed to resonate with the post-9/11 apocalyptic atmosphere. Unlike McCarthy's *The Road*, whose depiction of catastrophe leaves open interpretive space regarding the origins and nature of the disaster, *World Made by Hand* is anchored in concrete events: two atomic bombs and their far-reaching consequences on the U.S. economy. By defining the catastrophe in such explicit terms, Kunstler distances his fictional disaster from the symbolic and psychological terrain of 9/11. While *The Road* allows for a reading that overlays the novel's unnamed calamity with the trauma of 9/11, Kunstler's narrative constructs a parallel event—adjacent but never fully convergent. The atomic bombings in *World Made by Hand* resemble the rhetorical analogies employed by politicians in the immediate aftermath of 9/11: metaphors that expand the event's meaning while simultaneously displacing it.

When two disasters converge, the most immediate and culturally resonant one often supplants the other, particularly if the latter's long-term consequences are too far-reaching or its interpretive frameworks risk displacing culturally sanctioned forms of blame. Moreover, the timing of *World Made by Hand's* publication in the wake of 9/11 inevitably shaped how it was received. The responses it appeared to advocate—self-sufficiency, community-based governance, and a radical re-evaluation of modernity—seemed too demanding and prematurely offered. Its perspective on the past lacked the emotional affinity or rhetorical urgency typically required for a cultural artefact to be absorbed into the affective atmosphere of national trauma. While thematically aligned with many of the tropes that came to define the post-9/11 novel, Kunstler's work fails to resonate with the mood of that moment.

The novel also seems to issue a warning—one that, though legitimised by the pervasive "Muslim scare" infiltrating every level of American society in the immediate aftermath of 9/11, was seldom voiced openly by the American public. The New Faith Brotherhood emerges as a group that, while not overtly extremist or fundamentalist, is marked by a scepticism toward reason and a pronounced reverence for charismatic figures such as its "queen bee." In contrast, the "old faith," represented by Earle and the people of his community, ossifies and stagnates, clinging to a civic ethos that fails to inspire. The novel thus intimates that, in a post-apocalyptic environment, reconstituting communal bonds through shared belief systems, whether religious or spiritual, proves more adaptive and generative than the sterile secularism Robert embodies. In this sense, *World Made by Hand* gestures toward a counterintuitive conclusion: resilience in the wake of catastrophe may depend less on rational governance than collective mythmaking and the spiritual nourishment it affords.

3. Stabilising Disruptions

3.1 The Ghost-Writer Complex: Disintegrating Selves, Dis-integrating Narratives

In the introduction to *Culture, Crisis, and America's War on Terror* (2006), Stuart Croft argues that "behaviour patterns can be reproduced through cultural power" (2006, 4). While it is tempting to see popular culture merely as a vessel that reproduces or amplifies dominant discourse, Croft insists it must also be understood as a *co-producer* of discourse (2006, 9). "Those responsible for the production of a decisive intervention," Croft argues, "one capable of shaping a policy programme following the creation of a shared understanding of a particular crisis, *have to include the creators of popular culture* in a society such as that of contemporary America" (2006, 8–9). For Croft, politics and culture are inextricably linked; neither can be adequately articulated without the other.

Croft's argument, however, is neither novel nor exceptionally provocative. Marxist and sociological literary critics have long maintained similar positions and would likely view his claims as reaffirmations rather than revelations. In the introduction to *Ground Zero Fiction: History, Memory, and Representation in the American 9/11 Novel* (2011), Birgit Däwes explicitly situates her approach within the framework of New Historicism, concluding that "fictional texts and historical contexts are not independent entities" (Däwes 2011, 10). She argues that fiction reflects the "various manifestations of the 9/11 imaginary" and actively reshapes it, reopening dominant narratives to new interpretations (2011, 16). From this perspective, popular culture, and literature in particular, is not defined by "timeless artistic criteria," but instead emerges as a product of the "economic and ideological determinants specific to that era" (Abrams 1999, 149). Each era, in turn, reconfigures how such narratives are received and understood, underscoring the malleability and contextual dependence of cultural meaning.

Croft's argument is, in essence, a tailored iteration of Althusserian thought. Louis Althusser conceptualised society as a heterogeneous structure composed of various "ideological state apparatuses" — the Church, political parties, trade unions, and others — that function "both by repression and by ideology" while maintaining a "relative autonomy" (Althusser 1984, 23). Croft extends this framework by suggesting that, in the post-9/11 context, the political and the cultural have relinquished even that relative autonomy. Instead, they operate synchronously, shaping one another in unexpected and reciprocal ways. In Croft's view, the artistic no longer reflects the ideology of elite political structures; it co-produces it:

> This is to say, in effect, that the political elite and some producers of popular culture are mutually constructed in the contemporary United States. One cannot articulate a political project without impact upon popular culture; popular culture is not comprehensible without considering the political. [...] [The] articulation of a particular understanding of crisis, the formation of discourse, occurs both at the level of the political elite and that of popular culture. (Croft 2006, 9)

This convergence, Croft argues, was pivotal in shaping the American response to the 9/11 attacks. It underpins his broader contention — one that will be central to my argument later in this chapter — that post-9/11 cultural discourse cannot be disentangled from the narrative of the "war on terror." According to Croft, this war was not merely a political reaction, but a discursive construct forged through shared cultural and political storytelling in the wake of the attacks.

In this sense, Croft identifies four key narrative elements that structured the crisis and enabled the "war on terror" to take shape:

> The first was an articulation of self and other: the heroic, resilient American self and the absolute evil of the enemy. The second concerned inclusivity, an attempt to create a sense of identity with all Americans at home, and with all non-terrorist Muslims abroad. The third focused on American claims to exceptionalism that the United States embodied the best values and was a beacon for the world. The fourth was a claim to global leadership in pursuit of those values and interests. (Croft 2006, 149)

This narrative framework dictated which actions were permissible, which attitudes were sanctioned, and which visions of the future were to be pursued. In doing so, it legitimised some discourses while foreclosing others. Thus, storytelling does not merely reflect reality but participates in constructing it, shaping public consciousness, guiding political behaviour, and defining the ethical contours of collective memory.

The notion of *crisis* is central to this dynamic, as it fosters the conditions for an intensified synchronisation between the cultural and political spheres and stimulates public consumption of their textual and material productions. "In all crisis situations," Croft argues, "a meta-narrative of crisis is constructed, which then frames each individual narrative" (Croft 2006, 73). This meta-narrative operates as a scaffolding upon which various cultural and political discourses are built, providing cohesion and direction to otherwise disparate responses. In their influential article "A Dependency Model of Mass-Media Effects" (1976), S.J. Ball-Rokeach and M.L. DeFleur similarly contend that public reliance on media narratives peaks "when a relatively high degree of change *and* conflict is present in society" (1976, 7).

Such moments of upheaval, those that demand a fundamental reassessment of a society's core values, create fertile ground for the fusion of political messaging and cultural expression. In these instances, the interplay between politics and culture exerts its most potent and lasting influence. Yet, the consequences of these events are not always confined to official narratives or grand policy shifts. They often manifest in more mundane, seemingly apolitical actions — habits, behaviours, and beliefs that persist long after the crisis has faded from public consciousness. These residual effects may be the aftershocks of an earlier moment of synchronisation, or early signs of more profound structural changes still underway.

In times of national crisis, Americans often turn to running, quite literally. Historical data reveal a notable rise in long-distance running during periods of social and political upheaval. As Christopher McDougall recounts in *Born to Run* (2009), one of the earliest surges occurred during the Great Depression, when over two hundred runners traversed the country in the "Great American Footrace," covering distances of up to forty miles a day (McDougall 2010, 11). Another spike emerged in the early 1970s, coinciding with the collective disillusionment brought about by the Vietnam War, the energy crisis, and a prolonged economic downturn. Following the September 11 attacks, trail running again surged in popularity, becoming "the fastest-growing outdoor sport in the country" (McDougall 2010, 12). These patterns suggest that in moments of cultural rupture, running becomes a symbolic and physical form of recalibration, a solitary yet communal effort to restore personal agency amid uncertainty.

These recurring surges in physical activity, particularly running, during times of national crisis, suggest a deeper societal response to collective trauma. The tendency to choose "flight" over "fight" resonates with evolutionary survival strategies, especially in moments when real or imagined threats dominate the cultural psyche (McDougall 2010, 12). Whether these runners were seeking escape from a tangible adversary or the ambient anxiety permeating the national mood remains uncertain. Nonetheless, the widespread adoption of specific physical routines in the wake of traumatic events underscores how even seemingly mundane behaviours can become symbolic enactments of more profound societal shifts.

The nature of perceived threats has evolved over time. Whereas our Pleistocene ancestors ran from sabre-toothed cats in a literal struggle for survival, today's humans contend with more abstract but equally destabilising dangers: terrorist attacks, economic collapse, and the slow erosion of cultural resilience. Unlike our ancestors, however, we are increasingly preoccupied with evading these threats *and* understanding their agents. While there is little evidence to suggest that early humans speculated about the inner lives of their predators, contemporary societies have become deeply invested in probing the psychology of modern adversaries. This tendency is particularly evident in the literature that emerges in the wake of national crises, such as the aftermath of the 9/11 attacks. Literature, as one of the most vital and enduring repositories of cultural consciousness, provides extensive insight into this phenomenon and offers an archive of the collective effort to comprehend, narrate, and cope with the forces that threaten societal stability.

This cultural and literary preoccupation with the enemy has evolved over time, shifting gradually from the act of observing and describing the enemy to an empathetic effort to imagine the world from the enemy's point of view. A formative example of this transformation is John Gardner's novel *Grendel* (1971), which retells the Old English epic *Beowulf* through the eyes of the antagonist. Gardner reconfigures Grendel not as a senseless beast driven solely by violence but as a sentient, introspective creature grappling with existential questions. This inversion of perspective may seem to defy instinct. Where fear typically urges us to flee from our adversaries, such a narrative choice compels us to confront and understand them. In doing so, it raises significant questions about the ethical and political implications of representing the so-called "hostile other," particularly in times of crisis when cultural narratives often gravitate toward binary oppositions of good and evil.

Yet, as in Gardner's *Grendel*, the literary fascination with the inner life of the "enemy" also reflects a more profound yearning to reframe the very category of enmity. This imaginative gesture — and attempt to humanise, even rehabilitate, the antagonist — has its own complications. What happens when the language of otherness is not ours, when its cultural codes remain opaque or untranslatable? More pressingly, how should we respond when that otherness does not arrive peacefully, but violently, when it takes the form of four hijacked commercial airliners crashing into American soil? These questions expose the questions of cross-cultural empathy and highlight the dissonance between liberal humanist ideals and the realities of geopolitical conflict.

Grendel is a product of literary imagination; the 9/11 terrorists were real actors driven by the collision of two ideologies. One ideology, embodied in the Twin Towers, championed endless growth, with skyscrapers resembling vertical bar graphs in a capitalist progress report. The other upheld a vision of finite resources and improvised weapons, the four commercial airliners transformed into crude instruments of destruction — almost, one might say, physical manifestations of Caliban's curses. In this ideological confrontation, the planes, like the thousands of flags that proliferated across New York in the aftermath, had their original meanings — what Martin Amis calls their symbolism of "indigenous mobility and zest" — violently stripped away and re-inscribed with death. As Susan Willis argues in *Portents of the Real* (2005), such elements become "circulating signifiers" (Willis 2005, 15), mutable tokens in a volatile semiotic economy. Their meaning, in crisis, is not fixed but constantly rewritten.

Nonetheless, these were not the only elements stripped of their original significance and reinscribed with new meaning. In the days following the attacks, the only way to interpret the event was through the lens of disrupted routines and everyday spaces. Suddenly, everyone became hyper-aware of what they had been doing at the moment of impact. John Updike was visiting relatives in Brooklyn Heights. Denis Johnson was in New York City. Everyone, it seemed, was *doing* something when it happened. On a broader level, this shared compulsion to locate oneself at the moment of the attacks sparked a cultural phenomenon: a desperate need to fill a semantic void with significance.

In this vacuum of understanding and conversational gravity, "circulating signifiers" absorbed meanings suited to the emotional and political urgency of the moment. The term "*terrorist*," for example, as Alan Badiou observes in *Polemics* (2011), was transformed into "an intrinsically propagandistic term," no longer pointing to a specific political position or context, but rather referring solely to a type of action (Badiou and Winter 2011, 19). The image of the terrorist likewise became overdetermined. "Osama bin Laden's name and face," Edward Said wrote in *The Guardian*, "have become so numbingly familiar to Americans as in effect to obliterate any history he and his shadowy followers might have had before they became stock symbols of everything loathsome and hateful to the collective imagination" (Said 2001). This semiotic collapse also applied to "terrorism" itself, and to the indefinite wars waged against it. As Badiou further argues, "We have war as an abstract form of the *theatrical capture of an adversary* ('terrorism'), which is in its essence vague and elusive. The war against nothing: itself subtracted from the very idea of war" (2011, 28–29). If the enemy was vague and elusive, the actions taken against it could mirror that ambiguity —

symbolic, theatrical, and unmoored from a clear geopolitical purpose.

However, Badiou hesitates to acknowledge an equally crucial dimension. "Theatrical capture" need not involve boots on the ground or conventional combat. If "flight" — manifest in the post-9/11 running boom — became an instinctual response to an invisible threat, then the need to "capture" the enemy gave rise to its own cultural expression. In the absence of a tangible enemy, substitutes emerged — constructed, as surrogates often are, to meet predetermined expectations. Within the Hollywood-like cultural apparatus of post-9/11 America, these substitutes closely resembled the fictional Vietnamese of Viet Thanh Nguyen's *The Sympathizer* (2015): people "herded into the roles of the poor, the innocent, the evil, or the corrupt." If, as Nguyen's narrator wryly puts it, the French were naive enough to believe they needed to visit a country to exploit it, "Hollywood was much more efficient, imagining the countries it wanted to exploit" (Nguyen 2016b).

"Hollywood's high priests," and, by extension, those who possessed considerable cultural capital in the United States (writers such as John Updike, Martin Amis, and others), "understood innately the observation of Milton's Satan, that it was better to rule in Hell than serve in Heaven, better to be a villain, loser, or antihero than virtuous extra, so long as one commanded the bright lights of centre stage" (Nguyen 2016b). These American culture capitalists occupied the centre stage in this "theatrical capture" of the enemy not only because they controlled the mass-cultural means to do so, but also because of the symbolic nature of 9/11 itself and the act of appropriation embedded in its "enactment." They were cast as victims, and this victimhood catalysed a form of narrative entitlement: a *ghostwriter complex*.

If, for a brief historical moment, the terrorists commandeered the narrative by steering four airliners into the towers of the World Trade Centre, the American continuation of that same narrative proved far more invasive. While the perpetrators *appropriated* four American commercial planes, the American cultural apparatus appropriated their language, images, identities, and cultural histories. Comprised of politicians, oligarchs, and corporate and intellectual elites, this apparatus divided "the world into us versus them and good versus bad, the more easily to build alliances and target enemies" (Nguyen 2016a, 11). From the very instant George W. Bush wondered aloud why "they" hated "us," appropriation became a governing cultural logic.

The motif of the ghostwriter resurfaces in Nguyen's later work, particularly in his short story collection *The Refugees* (2017). The opening story, "Black Eyed Women," features a Vietnamese American woman who ghostwrites memoirs for individuals with powerful stories but lacking the skill, or perhaps the authority, to tell them. To one prospective client, the sole survivor of a plane crash, she sends a sample book she had previously ghostwritten: a memoir allegedly authored by the father of a school shooter (Nguyen 2017, 11). Much like Nguyen's narrator, writers in the aftermath of 9/11 often found themselves involuntarily positioned as ghostwriters of other people's trauma. Semantic voids, while seemingly offering a clean slate, become battlegrounds of interpretation. Unlike Nguyen's narrator, who willingly receives and retells others' stories with care and consent, post-9/11 literature frequently enacts a more coercive integration, where the "other's" story is not merely told, but subsumed, rewritten, and domesticated to serve the ghostwriter's narrative frame.

Martin Amis, too, adopts the role of cultural ghostwriter in *The Second Plane* (2008), where he defines terrorism as a form of "political communication." This definition affords him the rhetorical leverage to assert that the message broadcast on 9/11 was unequivocal: "America, it is time you learned how implacably you are hated" (Amis 2009, 3). Yet, Amis's claim to cultural clairvoyance is not borne out by the facts. The hijackers did not, like Major Kong in Stanley Kubrick's *Dr. Strangelove* (1964), ride the four commercial airliners while shouting their hatred for America. That version of events lives almost exclusively in Amis's imagination, where the spectacle of 9/11 is inflated to mythic dimensions: the four aeroplanes, the Pentagon, and the World Trade Centre are recast as quintessential "American artefacts," now defiled by what he describes as "morally barbaric" terrorists (Amis 2009, 3).

In the hands of such ghostwriters, every gesture attributed to the perpetrators is transformed into a performance of barbarity, not necessarily because of the violence itself, but because that violence is seen as a transgression against the cultural superiority implicitly claimed by the West. This is the ghostwriter complex at its most insidious: the re-inscription of moral hierarchies through the act of narrating the other's crime.

3.1.1 Updike's Final Act of Ethnic Ventriloquism

The impulse to narrate otherness at a time of fervent nationalistic display may seem counterintuitive. Yet, as David Holloway observes in *9/11 and the War on Terror* (2008), the early 9/11 novel often relied on "heightened subjectivities and interiorised or 'narcissistic' narrative voices" (Holloway 2008, 107). In his view, the most "exaggeratedly narcissistic" example is Jonathan Safran Foer's *Extremely Loud & Incredibly Close* (2005), a novel that foregrounds deeply interiorized characters who, through Oskar's narrative, are thrust out of their personal withdrawal and reinserted into a shared public narrative. According to Holloway, "almost everything" about Foer's novel pulls "the attention of the reader inward, into the private agonies of the traumatised self and away from any meaningful contextualising of 9/11 in public or historical space" (Holloway 2008, 114).

Holloway's caution in using the qualifier "almost" is warranted, for moments of contextualisation do punctuate Foer's narrative. For instance, on the observation deck of the Empire State Building, Oskar imagines another plane hurtling toward him. In the seconds before the imagined impact, he sees the terrorist's eyes conveying hatred (Foer 2006, 244). Yet the word "hate," and the violent intent it implies, never fully materialise. In this case, Oskar becomes not so much a victim of trauma as of *over-contextualisation*, burdened by meaning that is felt but never fully articulated. What Martin Amis fails to concede, and what Foer's underage narrator begins to intuit, is that terrorism, if it is a form of communication, necessitates a *coercive integration* of the perpetrator into the victim's discourse when the original message is either unintelligible or untranslatable.

Birgit Däwes identifies a similar phenomenon in her taxonomy of "ground zero fiction." Among the six narrative categories she outlines, classified according to their respective strategies in unearthing the cultural imaginary of 9/11, she includes those that adopt an "appropriative approach" (2011, 19). These works, which narrate events from the perspective of the allegedly inimical Other, often disclose less about the Other's psyche than they do about their creators' cultural and political anxieties. While they may claim to explore the complexities of the antagonist, their deeper function, Däwes argues, is revelatory: "As acts of 'ethnic ventriloquism,'" a term she borrows from Mita Banerjee, "they tell us more about the location of their origins (i.e., non-Muslim, Western writers)" and "expose a remarkably profound unease at the heart of Western identity" (Däwes 2011, 249–50). Such texts, in essence, reflect the invisible forces shaping a crisis, and while those forces may remain opaque, their imprint on cultural production is tangible.

John Updike performs a similar, albeit cautious, act of "ethnic ventriloquism" in his novel *Terrorist* (2006). Although the novel's third-person narrator maintains a degree of distance from Ahmad Ashmawy Mulloy, the titular "terrorist," this narrative positioning does not preclude a form of imaginative appropriation. Like Martin Amis, Updike's narrator tends to inflate individuals into archetypes, what Anna Hartnell calls "hollow stereotypes" (Hartnell 2011, 450). Through this inflation, Ahmad acquires an almost mythic stature. His worldview, saturated with political, social, and metaphysical abstractions, far exceeds the cognitive frame of a high school student. "Ahmad feels his pride of isolation and willed identity," the narrator explains, "to be threatened by the masses of ordinary, hard-pressed men and plain, practical women who are enrolled in Islam as a lazy matter of ethnic identity" (Updike 2007, 177). Though native-born, Ahmad views American reality as "a sprawling ferment for which he feels the mild pity owed a failed experiment" (2007, 177). His mental cadence is obsessive, reminiscent of the conspiratorial fervour of Lee Harvey Oswald in Don DeLillo's *Libra* (1988). In this light, Ahmad appears not as a psychologically coherent adolescent but as a vessel for broader historical anxieties, carried along by the undertow of civilizational conflict. He is, decidedly, not your average high school senior.

Despite these disconcerting permutations in the portrayal of its protagonist, *Terrorist* has been praised for its audacious engagement with post-9/11 taboos, especially its refusal to deny readers the possibility of empathising, however fleetingly, with the putative enemy other. At a moment when the dominant fictional mode in post-9/11 America foregrounded the interiority of traumatised, and therefore innocent, Western victims, Updike's novel sought to disrupt that moral architecture. In "Violence and the Faithful in Post-9/11 America," Anna Hartnell argues that the novel represents "an attempt on the part of one of America's most well-known and prolific writers to confront the complexities of the relations between Islam and the United States in the wake of 9/11," resisting "the temptation to consolidate the presumption of American unity and innocence that has formed the popular horizon for understanding the 2001 attacks" (Hartnell 2011, 478). Notably, the novel distances itself from the frequent stereotype of the sexually repressed Muslim male, a trope that saturates post-9/11 discourse. In contrast to authors such as Foer and DeLillo, who explore the internal reverberations of national trauma, Updike turns inward, grappling instead with what Hartnell calls "the unnamed source of America's post-9/11 fear: the Islamist enemy within" (Hartnell 2011, 480). That he does so through a literary strategy that grants a degree of complexity to Ahmad, while simultaneously insulating both the novel and its author through narrative distance, positions *Terrorist* as both a cultural provocation and a subtle exercise in self-protection.

The impulse behind this apparent sympathy is, at least ostensibly, noble. Appropriating the culture of the enemy other, as Updike does in *Terrorist*, seemingly gestures towards reconciliation. In moments of national crisis, rendering the adversary's worldview intelligible, both linguistically (through English) and culturally (through familiar narrative frames), is a frequent and strategic practice. Such appropriation aims to temper collective resentment, humanise the enemy, and build symbolic bridges between warring cultures. For a readership inundated in the post-9/11 years by persistent speculation about the roots of anti-American sentiment and the many reductive answers circulated within U.S. political discourse, *Terrorist* may well appear as the most elaborately constructed attempt to grapple with that sentiment.

Anna Hartnell suggests that "Updike does not ask this question from the standpoint of American innocence, since his work long ago began to grapple with American exceptionalism *as* a problem. What emerges in *Terrorist* as the Islamist critique of American society is in many ways Updike's own" (Hartnell 2011, 484). The suggestion is disarming in its symmetry: they hate us, *because* of who we are—and *this* is who we are. Ahmad's indictment of American cultural emptiness, consumerism, and moral decay acquires legitimacy because it is, in fact, Updike's indictment, albeit refracted through a fictional, culturally dissonant voice. The critique may be foreign in its idiom, but it is unmistakably domestic in origin.

Updike's safety net is thus firmly in place. As Hartnell notes early in her article, *Terrorist* is "the daring product of a writer who, amid a literary landscape often overdetermined by caution, has never shied away from the risks of representation" (Hartnell 2011, 480). Yet this claim risks obscuring an essential fact: Updike could afford to take those risks precisely because, by 2006, he occupied a position of untouchable eminence within the American literary establishment. Unlike less institutionally ensconced figures, he was permitted to transgress the taboos of post-9/11 representation. For instance, Martin Amis, who ventured into controversial territory with a short story centred on Mohamed Atta, was met with scathing criticism. Reviewers dismissed his efforts as clumsy, laboured, and even morally questionable, accusing him of providing "flat-footed" explanations for an event that defied simplification (Kumar 2006). Updike, by contrast, was not in a phase of his career when such missteps would cost him; he was, as Jem Poster puts it with gentle irony in *The Guardian*, "at a stage at which he might be forgiven for resting on his well-earned laurels" (Poster 2006). That he chose instead to tackle such a volatile subject was framed not as a risk but as a literary triumph. In this context, Ahmad's critique of America reads less like the unsettling view of a cultural outsider than the mediated lament of America's most prolific insider. His disillusionment is Updike's, and by extension, a national one. Hartnell's praise, then, verges on suggesting that *Terrorist* merits a kind of critical exceptionalism, a suspension of the standards ordinarily applied to post-9/11 fiction—precisely because its author is, to borrow a phrase from financial parlance, "too big to fail."

From this perspective, Hartnell's analysis becomes paradoxical, or at the very least, it gestures toward a paradox embedded within *Terrorist* itself. She contends that the novel "enacts a fascinating reversal whereby the interiority of the potential perpetrator of trauma is penetrated and exposed" (Hartnell 2011, 483). Yet the very interiority that Updike claims to access, or that Hartnell attributes to him, turns out to be largely external in its construction. "John Updike is wary of the internet," but for *Terrorist*, "he ventured onto the Web to research bomb detonators" (McGrath 2006). He also observed airport security checkpoints to correct his assumptions about X-ray scanners and consulted graduate student Shady Nasser for Arabic transliterations of Quranic verses. Even more revealingly, Updike admits that his "conscience was pricked by the notion that I was putting into the book something that I can't pronounce" (McGrath 2006). What is revealed, then, is not the inner world of a would-be terrorist, but Updike's own vision, shaped by the limits of linguistic competence, cultural distance, and the mediated knowledge afforded by Western institutions. When Hartnell concedes that Updike's depiction is couched in "strikingly religious terms, terms that threaten to reinstate, rather than transcend, the myth of hermetically sealed and timelessly opposed cultures" (2011, 484), she seems to hold fast to the belief that some transcendence nonetheless occurs. One is left to wonder: if this kind of mythmaking can be transcended with the aid of Wikipedia and secondhand Arabic, perhaps we are not making full use of the internet.

The apparent superficiality with which Updike approaches the theme of cultural difference may reflect a broader cultural fatigue with the promises of cross-cultural empathy through appropriation. However, it may also stem from his reliance on physicality, particularly bodily sensation, as a primary means of representing otherness. As Birgit Däwes observes, Updike tends to foreground metaphors of "food and digestion" (2011, 250) to articulate cultural dissonance. His characters' somatic reactions to American life—especially their inability to process certain foods—become markers of their alterity. "Pitting the imageries of purity and contamination against each other on Atta's plate," Däwes notes, "the story draws a clear semantic demarcation line between vitality and strength on the one hand (the insurgent Arab), and weakness, degeneration, and toxicity (the American hegemon) on the other" (2011, 251). This symbolic boundary not only unsettles the literal Middle Eastern stomach but also challenges the hegemonic self-image of the United States as robust and invincible.

Mr Levy's overweight wife becomes an emblem of this cultural gluttony. Her shift to subsisting on baby carrots functions as a parodic gesture toward self-correction. She wants to lose weight fast, or die trying, it seems. Her dietary transformation offers no real redemption, only another caricature of imbalance, precisely the moral and existential void Ahmad seeks to annihilate by blowing up a tunnel during rush hour. The novel's conclusion somewhat awkwardly aims to reconcile these oppositions through a clichéd invocation of American inclusiveness. "Hey, come on," Mr Levy tells Ahmad, "we're all Americans here. That's the idea, didn't they tell you that at Central High? Irish-Americans, African-Americans, Jewish-Americans; there are even Arab-Americans" (Updike 2007, 301). His appeal to multiculturalism comes on the heels of a monologue that acknowledges the conditional and selective nature of such inclusivity, albeit obliquely. Delivered with the cadence of a motivational speech—one part idealism, one part desperation—Mr Levy's words attempt to paper over structural divisions with the language of unity, echoing the performative optimism of a coach rallying a fractured team in the final quarter of a losing game.

Yet the paradox at the heart of *Terrorist* extends beyond its gesture of cultural appropriation. While Jonathan Safran Foer's novel critiques its own narcissism by dispersing narrative authority across multiple, stylistically distinct narrators, Updike opts for the seeming objectivity and safety of a singular, omniscient narrator. Unlike Faulkner's *Absalom, Absalom!*, where narrative fragmentation complicates and defers interpretive responsibility, *Terrorist* centralises authority in a voice that navigates, and to some extent contains, its characters' conflicting ideologies. This strategy allows Updike to present a spectrum of controversial viewpoints under the guise of narrative neutrality. The result is not a dispersal of responsibility, but rather a controlled orchestration of voices, where even the most provocative perspectives are filtered through a voice that remains unmistakably authorial.

The voice of Updike's narrator moves, undisturbed, through multiple minds and situations. This narrative omniscience is more than a stylistic choice; it enacts what I refer to as *coercive integration*, a process by which diverse, often conflicting perspectives are absorbed into a single discursive authority that retains control over how those perspectives are framed and interpreted. The very subject matter of *Terrorist* seems to demand such control. "Updike's narrative voice," Hartnell further adds, "is lent not only to Ahmad but also to a range of characters espousing contradictory and conflicting views. In so doing, the novel foregrounds a symbolic play on realist conventions; though the complexity of characterisation is to an extent sacrificed in order for individual characters to act as mouthpieces for specific viewpoints, taken together, they nonetheless present an America purged of moral authority" (Hartnell 2011, 496). But Hartnell ultimately stops short of acknowledging the deeper mechanism at work: the narrator's choices of what to include, whom to ventriloquise, and how to structure the polyphony are themselves expressions of narrative power. The so-called loss of moral authority is illusory; it is, in fact, carefully curated by a voice that orchestrates multiplicity while eliding accountability.

Nguyen's *sympathiser* would likely have scoffed at this narrative manoeuvre, detecting the latent contempt behind a narrator like the one in Updike's *Terrorist*. Yet Updike, like a skilled attorney adept at exploiting the loopholes of his legal system, has carefully shielded himself from direct accountability. The narrator inhabits characters with such divergent and contradictory worldviews that it becomes nearly impossible to determine which, if any, reflects Updike's own position. Is the author's voice aligned with Ahmad's righteous rage? With Jack Levy's disillusioned secularism? Or does it reside in a more aloof, omniscient plane, immune to ideological entanglement?

This ambiguity, however, produces at least one notable, and perhaps unintended, result: it opens the novel to a meditation on the corruption of ideas, on how ostensibly pure or innocent ideals are susceptible to manipulation and appropriation by external forces. This effect, arguably, would not have been as pronounced without the narrative fusion of Updike's worldview and that of the "potential perpetrator." As Hartnell observes,

> It is hard not to draw the conclusion that what emerges as sinister in Updike's novel are the consequences of a communal faith. Ahmad's attitudes toward Islam are comparable to the workings of a Protestant interiority that Updike can relate to and respect. However, it is the pollution of such interiority by external forces that leads to the assumption of violence. Clearly in this particular case there is every reason to critique and condemn the influence of these external forces; the social system influencing Ahmad here is a form of political Islam that equates acts of violence and the murder of innocents with sacred duty. (Hartnell 2011, 488)

By placing Ahmad at the intersection of these conflicting currents—caught between a secular American identity that never fully accepts him and an "increasingly militant Muslim identity" (Hartnell 2011, 492) that instrumentalises his faith—Updike transforms his protagonist into a figure of liminality and alienation. Ahmad is thus rendered a victim of ideological pollution, a product of forces beyond his control. In this light, he becomes a character with whom readers are not only permitted, but gently encouraged, to sympathise. Updike reportedly told *The New York Times* that readers could not ask "for a more sympathetic and, in a way, more loving portrait of a terrorist" (McGrath 2006). Perhaps that, ultimately, is the legacy Updike sought to leave behind: a deftly constructed narrative that equips readers with the tools, and maybe the moral permission, to empathise with the enemy.

In *Terrorist*, Updike renders the figure of the alleged enemy both inwardly and outwardly legible in ways that defy the dominant modalities of enemy recognition that proliferated in the immediate aftermath of 9/11. Ahmad is "one of us," or more precisely, "among us," a formulation that destabilises the conventional logic of threat not because he hides behind the camouflage of a multicultural society, but because the text encourages us to understand, and even sympathise with, his motivations. His recognisability is psychological, not superficial; the danger he represents is not cloaked in foreignness, but unsettlingly native. In this, Ahmad resists schematic representations of the "enemy." As Slavoj Žižek writes in *Welcome to the Desert of the Real* (2002), "the enemy is by definition [...] invisible, he looks like one of us; he cannot be directly recognised — this is why the big problem and task of the political struggle is providing/constructing a recognisable image of the enemy" (2012, 138). In the wake of 9/11, Žižek argues, the imagination "regained its power by constructing the image of Osama bin Laden, the Islamic fundamentalist par excellence, and al-Qaeda, his 'invisible network'" (2012, 139).

These imaginative constructions function on at least two simultaneous levels. On the one hand, they produce a sharp binary between the visible — the enemy's body, comportment, and surface traits — and the invisible: the presumed malice of his intentions. On the other hand, they associate a limited range of physical markers, beards, turbans, and prayer, with specific acts of violence. In such a context, visual legibility becomes a moral diagnosis. It is no wonder, then, that when Changez, the narrator of Mohsin Hamid's *The Reluctant Fundamentalist*, meets his presumably American interlocutor at the start of the novel, he pre-empts suspicion by insisting he is "a lover of America." The beard, a signifier of faith and cultural tradition in other contexts, is here already encoded with threat, suspicion, and proximity to terror. Ahmad, however, short-circuits this encoding. His recognisability is not predicated on visible difference, but on psychological dissonance, making his potential for violence all the more uncanny.

Aesthetically, the terrorist must be made recognisable to become an object of hatred, and recognition is often coded through ugliness. Much like the villains of fairytales, whose deformity signals their inner depravity, the post-9/11 terrorist figure is rendered grotesque to reflect the horrors of their intentions. "Embodying evil in a person's physical appearance," Colin McGinn observes in *Ethics, Evil and Fiction* (1997), "is simply a vivid way to convey the gruesomeness of their soul" (McGinn 1999, 100). Violence, by this logic, is not only logically reprehensible but also aesthetically repulsive. Those who commit such acts must, in some sense, look the part. "Evil," McGinn notes pointedly, "is *expressed* in evil acts" (1999, 101). In the American political imaginary post-9/11, anyone capable of weaponising passenger planes against civilians—anyone who could harbour such virulent hatred for what George W. Bush called "our freedom of religion, our freedom of speech, our freedom to vote and assemble and disagree with each other" (*The Guardian* 2001)—*must* necessarily be marked by a kind of physical malevolence. The figure of Osama bin Laden, with his beard, turban, and spectral composure, soon became the iconographic crystallisation of this logic: evil made visible.

Updike's *Terrorist*, however, subtly rewires this aesthetic mechanism. Ahmad's physical and ideological construction initially reproduces the logic of suspicion: his dark features, devout religiosity, and social marginality all index him as a potential threat. Yet the novel ultimately backtracks on this encoding. It couples specific physical traits with evil intent only to unravel them through narrative design. Ahmad, though poised to commit an act of terror, is ultimately shown to be morally intact, unable to follow through precisely because of an inner goodness that resists ideological corruption. In this sense, he is restored to moral purity not through rehabilitation, but through a narrative absolution that contradicts the visual and behavioural cues associated with his constructed "otherness." Evil, in Ahmad's case, is not embodied—it is imposed and ultimately rejected.

Nevertheless, Updike explores this issue even more profoundly, especially in the way he constructs his characters. The person who ultimately persuades Ahmad to abandon his plan to blow up the Lincoln Tunnel is his sixty-three-year-old guidance counsellor, Jack Levy—a character whose worldview eerily mirrors Ahmad's own. At times, their inner monologues seem to resonate in perfect, if disturbing, harmony. Consider Levy's own bitter reflections on American life:

> Corner grocery stores have one by one dropped away, leaving the field to franchises whose standardised logos and decors are cheerfully garish, as are the gargantuan full-colour images of their fattening fast food. As Jack Levy sees it, America is paved solid with fat and tar, a coast-to-coast tarbaby where we're all stuck. Ever our vaunted freedom is nothing much to be proud of, with the Commies out of the running; it just makes it easier for terrorists to move about, renting airplanes and vans and setting up websites. (Updike 2007, 27)

Ahmad, too, surveys the world around him through this lens of decay and corruption. He sees the "shabbiness in the streets, the fast-food trash and broken plastic toys, the unpainted steps and porches still dark from the morning's dampness, the windows cracked and not repaired" (2007, 281). Beneath this surface degradation, he perceives a way of life belonging to "infidels," a culture "headed for a terrible doom" (2007, 39). Yet, Updike seems to suggest, the real doom is not where we instinctively look for it.

Despite their shared disillusionment, only Ahmad radicalises and actively plots to blow up the tunnel. At first glance, this might reinforce a narrative that specific individuals, young, from disrupted families, and socially isolated, are more susceptible to radicalisation. This perspective gained traction in the post-9/11 period. Indeed, as Arun Kundnani argues in *The Muslims Are Coming!* (2014), such radicalisation models quickly became "policing tools," employed across the United States to preemptively identify potential terrorists (Kundnani 2014, 133). Yet, in *Terrorist*, the plot Ahmad is drawn into is revealed to be a fabrication orchestrated by the CIA, with his supposed co-conspirators serving as agency patsies. In this way, Ahmad's radicalisation is shown to be less an organic evolution than a dangerous fantasy manufactured and tested by external forces. Updike thus comes perilously close to implying that American society, when sufficiently manipulated, can turn its own latent fears and dissatisfactions against itself.

Only Levy's deep-rooted cynicism prevents him from taking violent action, despite sharing Ahmad's bleak assessment of America. In this final gesture, Updike seems to suggest that the true threat, the enemy "among us," is not embodied in a single, easily recognisable figure, but rather emerges from the very mechanisms of surveillance, coercion, and narrative control that structure

American life after 9/11. This is a society capable of turning inward, engaging in a form of self-inflicted narrative violence in its desperate search for stability and meaning. The act of "coercive integration," then, extends beyond literary technique: it becomes a metaphor for how an entire culture absorbs, manipulates, and ultimately internalises its own anxieties, producing the spectres it most fears.

3.2 Permutations of Everything: The Strange Case of Paul A. Toth's *Airplane Novel*

While writers such as Foer and Updike appear to have exhausted the conventional narrative strategies for addressing 9/11 – and even Nguyen's protagonist can do little more than scoff at their attempts – what if another route existed altogether? Paul A. Toth's *Airplane Novel* (2011) ventures precisely into this unexplored territory. Described as "the Guernica of 9/11 novels," it dares to narrate the events from a truly radical perspective: that of the Twin Towers themselves. The novel's narrator is the South Tower, who, from the outset, pledges to disclose everything, including the inner workings of its own storytelling. "Every author," laments the Tower, who self-identifies as Cary Grant, "tells my story from the outside-in and then pretends to be my friend. A court of skyscrapers convicts them all. Spider monkeys [human beings] see from every vantage point but those of Gary Cooper and Cary Grant. How could they?" (Toth 2011, 13) This narration emerges as a corrective, a definitive version that seeks to reclaim authority over the story from the countless external accounts. After all, who could be more entitled to articulate the truth than the towers themselves?

In this way, Toth's novel functions as a form of narrative retribution – a revenge against conventional perspectives that must now be reconsidered and rescinded. The unlikely narrator gleefully violates literary and narrative conventions, positioning himself as the quintessential anti-writer. "I am not a writer," Grant asserts, "I am a tower. [...] Cary Grant never sought prestige; Cary Grant sought Cary Grant" (2011, 123). His pleasure in defiling narrative standards stems from his conviction that countless other stories have misappropriated his existence, each one an injustice. Hence, when he asks rhetorically whether he should have included footnotes and a bibliography to support his claims, he scoffs: "[all] sources are my sources; they owe me. [...] And here, in this case, no thanks from me will be provided to those who stole my information, every book and film about me an act of plagiarism" (2011, 149). In doing so, he turns his disdain directly toward the readers themselves, implicating them in the cycle of narrative theft and urging them to question their passive acceptance of received accounts.

Cary Grant also acts as a totalising narrator, endowed with a vantage point no human narrator could possess. "My views from every perspective," he declares at the novel's outset, "through windows narrowed to lessen the sense of height, formed a horizon of cubes. I saw permutations of everything, none stable, a floating metropolis of tints and hues in constant shift" (Toth 2011, 11). As readers, we are granted front-row seats to a performance that is, in essence, about us, our blindness, our complacency, and our misapprehensions of what unfolded before and after the catastrophe. The narrator not only recounts but also promises to guide us through these events. "I will explain my life from the inside out," Cary Grant confides, "I must possess a utilitarian reason for existing. I will help you" (2011, 13). This promise of assistance underscores his supposed benevolence: a mission to reveal the more profound truths behind the spectacle we thought we understood.

Yet this "help" arrives in the form of provocations and riddles rather than straightforward clarifications. Within the narrator's fragmented and vividly associative imagination—where sounds and images bleed into each other for rhetorical effect—9/11 is not presented as a singular, exceptional rupture. Instead, Cary Grant places it within a web of different events that punctuated the towers' histories. Among them is the fire of February 13, 1975, which was started by Oswald Adorno, a nineteen-year-old cleaner frustrated by his lack of "proper recognition" (Treaster 1975) at his workplace. "If Oswald seemed to disappear after the fire," Grant recalls, "we towers remembered him as he was not, which is more than he became" (Toth 2011, 20). Space is also given to Owen J. Quinn, who famously parachuted off one of the towers in a defiant stunt. At this point, as onlookers pause to watch Quinn's leap of faith, the narrator abruptly connects this memory to a later, darker scene: the crowds staring upwards as others would "involuntarily jump" (2011, 26) to avoid being burned to death. In merging these moments, Cary Grant collapses temporal and emotional boundaries, forcing readers to confront the continuity of spectacle.

The comparison between the two moments—Quinn pulling the ripcords of his parachute to land softly on the ground and those who chose to jump from the towers on 9/11—is disturbingly provocative. It closely resembles Paul Virilio's suggestion of situating the event within a dialectic of media and art development. In the imagination of Toth's unusual narrator, if Quinn's gesture represented a flight of fancy with an escape hatch ingeniously built into it, those who leapt from the towers on 9/11 performed a parallel kind of flight—an ultimate, terrifying escape hatch. Rather than face the agony of burning alive, they chose the sudden exhilaration and the swift finality of the fall. "Later," the narrator recalls, "many might have dived from me and North and pulled their ripcords— had they been equipped with parachutes—and they would have safely plunged, a sky filled with human sailboats, the world inverted and people falling upward or rising downward" (Toth 2011, 27). In this reinterpretation, Quinn's leap becomes a prototype: by incorporating an escape hatch into his descent, he transformed every subsequent leap into a variation on the same artistic performance. Quinn's allegedly suicidal gesture, the narrator argues, was "no more a suicide than those who would later leap" (2011, 27). Those who chose to burn rather than jump, Grant provocatively suggests, were in fact the ones enacting a kind of suicide.

When considering the final performance—the towers' destruction—these earlier spectacles become preludes to that ultimate act. Viewed together, they lend the final collapse the grandeur and coherence of a culminating spectacle. In this unusual narrator's eyes, that last act was the only one in which the towers were not mere props but genuine protagonists. While other failed spectacles used the towers as symbolic backgrounds, the September 11 attacks implicated them directly and irrevocably.

Yet, within this narrative, the towers are not innocent victims. Their collapse is portrayed as the interruption of a long-developing suicidal trajectory — an act that almost fulfilled an internal drive toward self-annihilation. Over time, the towers had acquired the capacity to absorb and archive the information and experiences coursing through them, forming a collective consciousness. Thus, their end signifies not only architectural destruction but also the termination of a particular way of thinking and an unexpected call for compassion. "I cannot differentiate between one spider monkey and the next," the narrator declares on the novel's final page, "[they] shall raise and bring down new towers that will become beams of light. In the end, your buildings are you. I respect neither claims of outrage nor innocence. But I am compassionate" (Toth 2011, 207). Yet, in this compassion, there is an implicit judgement: not everyone merits the compassion that such an event might seem to demand.

In *Airplane Novel*, those engulfed by the towers' collapse rarely receive the solemnity traditionally afforded to the dead. Instead, Toth's narrator dedicates an entire chapter, tellingly titled "The Blotting Out of Scatteredness," to a fictional character named George Collins, ostensibly an employee at one of the first investment firms to occupy the towers. Both the name and narrative are invented; there is no George Collins listed among the actual victims of 9/11. Yet this fabricated, inverted obituary speaks volumes. Before 9/11, George's life was defined by a failed marriage and a tendency to retreat into the dim anonymity of triple-X theatres for vicarious release. His relationship with his wife, Muriel, "consisted of trips to restaurants. They both turned fat. Eating provided an excuse not to talk. Lust had never been found in the usual dust of perfumes, dying with sweat never beaded, skin untouched by another, and a well-rested breathlessness" (2011, 37). George is, in effect, the quintessential anti-hero: emotionally dulled, physically unremarkable, sexually unsatisfied. He is not someone readers are naturally inclined to mourn, except, perhaps, when his life ends violently and without meaning. "George was an asshole," the narrator insists, "because later everyone would imagine that not one asshole worked and died in North and me. Plenty of assholes worked in us. To deny this is to diminish humanity in all its possibilities" (2011, 38). The point is uncompromising: the narrator rejects the sanctification of the dead. Not all who died were virtuous. Grief, like humanity, is plural, and must allow for the flawed, the petty, the unloved.

This fictional obituary sharply contrasts with the *New York Times'* "Portraits of Grief," which casts the victims of 9/11 as literary heroes, miniaturised hagiographies written in journalistic prose. In those sketches, Thomas Collins (whose surname Toth re-appropriates) is remembered as infectiously vivacious, a man perpetually planning outings for friends and family. "[When] he wasn't trying to get a laugh out of someone," his portrait recalls, "Mr. Collins, 36, an avid skier and outdoorsman, was busy organising weekend adventures for his friends and family" (*The New York Times* 2011). Suria Clarke is depicted as "sunny, vivacious, irreverent," with an unrelenting "appetite for life, for food, for wine" — the kind of traveller who would return from Tuscany with ninety litres of a local vintage (*The New York Times* 2011). Jeffrey Coale is remembered for his dream of opening a restaurant; Leonard Castrianno is remembered as a tireless socialiser who was "relentlessly positive" and always saw "the glass half full." In contrast to Toth's George Collins, these figures are polished into icons, idealised for their passions, personalities, and potential. Toth's narrator disrupts this narrative economy, not out of disdain, but to restore moral complexity to a moment too often filtered through mythic simplification.

Toth's portrayal of George Collins takes a decidedly subversive turn. "Mr. George Collins," the South Tower declares, "'worked' at _____ and was known for knowing nothing. He rocketed to the top of his department via certain erotic and pornographic fixations shared with his manager" (Toth 2011, 197). Another fictional victim, Mr Hollander, is sketched as a man who "saw more violence in his mind than he did in Vietnam, returning to marry his wife Emily and father two children, all of whom he often wished to murder" (2011, 197). Death, the narrator suggests, functions as an automatic redemption: it "improves" the image of the deceased, who are "forgiven when they've been disallowed the courtesy of asking forgiveness" (2011, 196). In this light, even the tower's biting honesty reads as a plea for forgiveness — a confession that its disappearance fundamentally alters how it is remembered, demanding a final absolution from those left behind.

Nevertheless, despite the narrator's self-proclaimed rebelliousness, the novel cannot entirely escape the constraints of its genre or the realities of the publishing industry: the book's cover credits Paul A. Toth, not Cary Grant, as its author. As readers, we are unavoidably aware that the Tower did not, and could not, literally write the story; it is Toth's voice that orchestrates the text. Yet the novel proposes a provocative "exit strategy." "This book," the narrator asserts, "is a natural resource of fading paper and disappearing ink, a constant *disintegration*" (Toth 2011, 13). This motif of the "disintegrating narrator" reemerges toward the novel's close, as the cinematic spectacle of the towers' collapse draws near. As the narrative nears its end, its very structure—mirroring the "disintegrating narrator," who is at once already gone (since 9/11 has irrevocably happened) and actively collapsing while recounting its demise—begins to fracture. The text splinters into competing streams, weaving in quotations from newspaper headlines and editorials. It culminates in a "denouement" that intimates the narrator has always been a kind of disembodied conscience—a lingering spirit that persists long after that physical fall of the Twin Towers.

However, Toth's proposed escape strategy is not without its caveats. Within the broader discourse surrounding 9/11, *Airplane Novel* occupies a somewhat privileged position: it appears well after the initial wave of trial and error that defined early 9/11 fiction, at a point when the cultural narrative had already begun to solidify. This temporal positioning mirrors the evolution of the so-called "war on terror discourse." For example, Mark Doten's *The Infernal* (2015) could not have emerged until after a critical mass of fictional portrayals of the wars in Iraq and Afghanistan had already circulated. Both *Airplane Novel* and *The Infernal*, with their experimental narrative forms and radical narrative voices, function less as direct interventions and more as "discourse regulators." By foregrounding form over content, they do not offer resolutions or moral certainties. Instead, they illuminate the interpretive frameworks that shape how surrounding texts, both contemporaneous and retrospective, should be understood and situated within the cultural imagination.

3.3 The Americanising Gaze: Cultural Intrusions and the 'Third Space' in Ackerman's *Green on Blue*

Thus far, I have argued that a defining characteristic of a culturally selfish event is its capacity to signal a rupture that creates a semiotic void. This void, in turn, demands the absorption of other cultural artefacts until the selfish event secures or imposes a stable discourse for itself. The resulting "cultural stump" engages in a dynamic dialogue with fully developed cultural forms, appropriating their features to such an extent that it contaminates and reshapes them. Consequently, owing to this ethos of appropriation, which is a primary signature of culturally selfish events, subsequent cultural artefacts emerging from these events tend to replicate this very gesture. Such events function as cultural vortices, drawing in and reorganising surrounding symbolic resources to sustain their narrative power in the public imagination.

However, as Homi K. Bhabha argues in *The Location of Culture* (1994), cultural appropriation and hybridity do not operate through simple acts of borrowing or imitation; instead, they unfold within what he calls a hybrid "third space" that "displaces the histories that constitute it, and sets up new structures of authority, new political initiatives, which are inadequately understood through received wisdom" (Rutherford 1990, 211). This "third space" is not merely a site of easy translation or appropriation, but a complex and unstable zone of negotiation where cultural meanings are constantly rearticulated.

Nevertheless, as I have previously discussed, cultural appropriation is rarely a monolithic process. Appropriating a cultural artefact or some of its features involves stepping away from one culture, shedding its familiar markers, and immersing oneself, however incompletely, in another. Yet this process is never purely mimetic or straightforward; it inhabits what Bhabha terms the "third space," a hybrid arena where meaning is negotiated and reconstituted rather than transferred.

The notion of the "third space" highlights that cultural identity is not a fixed essence to be "accessed" through intellectual exertion or documentary research, but rather a shifting, performative act that emerges from moments of translation and transformation. Thus, any claim to authentically "enter" another culture inevitably reveals the instability and porousness of cultural boundaries rather than confirming their accessibility. Indeed, as Gayatri Spivak warns in "Can the Subaltern Speak?," such attempts often risk reinscribing the authority of the Western subject by framing the Other as an object of knowledge rather than an agent of speech (Nelson 2007, 271), thus complicating Bhabha's optimistic vision of hybridity.

This latter assumption, namely that otherness can be penetrated and understood through intellectual means alone, is likely what propelled Elliot Ackerman, "whose five tours of duty in Iraq and Afghanistan left him highly decorated" (Bissell 2015), to write his first novel, *Green on Blue* (2015). Set in Afghanistan and narrated from the perspective of an Afghan soldier fighting to uphold his wounded brother's manly dignity, Ackerman's novel has been repeatedly described by literary critics as an act of cultural appropriation, a move that remains rare, especially within the conventions of war writing. Yet rather than purely appropriating Afghan subjectivity, Ackerman's novel can also be seen as attempting to occupy Bhabha's "third space," albeit problematically. The novel constructs a hybrid narrative standpoint that ostensibly merges an American authorial voice with an Afghan experiential one, thus revealing the tension inherent in this kind of cross-cultural narrative experiment. In doing so, it lays bare both the seductive appeal and the inherent risks of writing from a position that seeks to mediate between radically different cultural imaginaries.

True, novels *about* the enemy are a standard trope in times of war. Yet Ackerman's *Green on Blue* does more than depict an enemy perspective. It invites readers to inhabit, however provisionally, the mind of the enemy—who, by the novel's end, is revealed to be not an enemy in the strict sense, but rather a pawn ensnared in the brutal machinery of a conflict where money itself has become a "weapons system," to borrow Phil Klay's phrase from *Redeployment* (2014). The novel's aim, much like Updike's *Terrorist* and Toth's *Airplane Novel*, is to encourage readers to grasp the larger, often obscured picture by granting access to perspectives that resist the reductive, Manichean distinctions which dominated political and cultural discourse after the September 11 attacks.

Beyond the immediate reactions that a novel written from the viewpoint of the supposed enemy inevitably provokes, and beyond the latent imperial impulse that often informs denunciations of cultural appropriation, I contend that Ackerman's novel offers a significant insight into how discourses surrounding historical events like the 9/11 attacks and the ensuing 'war on terror' enact interpretative intrusions. These intrusions are carried out by establishing a dialogue between cultural artefacts across different traditions. One way to examine the depth of this intrusion is by introducing two contrasting cultural artefacts: one steeped in the culture of the appropriator, Cormac McCarthy's *Blood Meridian* (1985), and the other rooted in the culture of the alleged enemy, Hassan Blasim's collection of short stories *The Corpse Exhibition: And Other Stories of Iraq* (2014).

Although Ackerman has explicitly stated that "while the American West wasn't 'front and centre' in his mind while writing, 'the American counterinsurgency campaign was, and so by default, the Indian Wars became a layer in understanding how Americans behave in these types of war'" (Castner, n.d.), it is crucial to note the novel's covert but persistent references to the American West and the Indian Wars. These references resonate not merely because of the geographical affinities between the Afghan terrain and the American frontier but also because they attest to a tacit cultural recognition of long-standing narrative frameworks. Many veterans, for instance, identify McCarthy's *Blood Meridian* as the novel that most accurately captures the atmosphere of Afghanistan, for reasons that, on closer inspection, are perhaps less surprising than they first appear (Castner, n.d.). Yet, while these intertextual echoes contribute to our understanding of narrative inheritance, it is Ackerman's deliberate narrative choices—his selective use of Western tropes and his invocation of Afghan subjectivity—that ultimately shape the novel's hybrid aesthetic.

The resemblance is particularly striking in the way the landscapes are described in Ackerman's and McCarthy's novels. On one of his first missions with the Special Lashkar, a military group funded by American money to maintain a delicate balance of power and influence in the region, Aziz depicts the Afghan mountains in animalistic terms. He describes them as having a mouth that "swallows" the convoy and a ravine that "rolled out like a sloppy tongue" (Ackerman 2015, 51). These descriptions recall those in McCarthy's *Blood Meridian*, such as "the cotton eye of the moon squatted at broad day in the throat of the mountains" (McCarthy 2015, 81). From this perspective, both *Green on Blue* and *Blood Meridian* portray a geography infused with a sense of fear and foreboding. Nature, in both texts, is not a welcoming or passive backdrop but a stubborn, almost sentient force that resists human intrusion. It obeys its own impenetrable rhythms and cycles, following unwritten laws that disregard human presence.

Along the roads travelled by the protagonists of both novels, one can almost hear the same echoes, the barking of dogs, and see the same "low mud houses" (McCarthy 2015, 90). Sometimes, the reader even encounters similar characters. Consider the old hermit whom "the kid" from *Blood Meridian* encounters at the novel's beginning—an old man remarkably like Mumtaz from *Green on Blue*, both of whom offer comfort to the protagonists. "The family of itinerant musicians" who are "dressed in fools' costumes with stars and halfmoons embroidered on" (McCarthy 2015, 82) reappear in Ackerman's novel as "travelling musicians looking for work" (Ackerman 2015, 96). Even Aziz's demeanour evokes that of "the kid" from McCarthy's work. Both characters are young, inexperienced, and shaped by a lack of formal education that leaves them vulnerable and malleable in a shifting political landscape. The references to the American West culminate when the narrator describes how their military company was divided into two groups with telling names: the Tomahawks and the Comanches. This division, Aziz explains, was implemented not only for tactical reasons but also because their American sponsor, the spectral Mr Jack, "had a great affection for the American West" (Ackerman 2015, 51).

I argue that this lies at the core of the problem with Ackerman's attempt at cultural appropriation. Although the novel is ostensibly narrated from the perspective of an Afghan soldier, Aziz ultimately embodies an American gaze, or more precisely, an *Americanising* gaze. Aziz inherits elements of the myth of the self-made man, which becomes particularly evident toward the novel's conclusion. He emerges as a kind of triumphant figure, reminiscent of a spy in an American thriller, who attains a higher understanding of the war and the forces shaping it despite his limited formal education.

This Americanising gaze is also apparent when Aziz returns to visit his maimed brother under the pretence of having become a respectable merchant in Kabul. His deceit echoes the classic trope of the American hero who conceals hard truths for a perceived greater good. Aziz further exhibits this borrowed behaviour when, while serving with the Special Lashkar, he pounds the roof of a car to signal the driver to depart. This gesture, awkwardly imitative of Hollywood action scenes, rings as hollow as the moment when "the kid" from *Blood Meridian* enters a bar and all the men inside "quit talking when he entered" (McCarthy 2015, 21).

Most importantly, this Americanising spirit becomes unmistakable when Aziz tells his imagined readers that Mr Jack wrongly believed that Afghans "did not understand what it meant to be named after the Indians of his country, but we understood. To us, it seemed a small but misguided sort of insult. For our tribes had never been conquered" (Ackerman 2015, 51). For an ostensibly uneducated Afghan soldier, Aziz displays a remarkably sophisticated understanding of Native American history and cultural symbolism. It is almost as if this is not an Afghan soldier speaking at all, but rather an American voice masquerading in Afghan guise.

Nevertheless, the novel's cultural appropriation reaches its most effective and revealing moments when it turns its attention to members of the US occupation forces. Beyond the occasional American soldiers, whose physicality starkly contrasts with the Afghan soldiers, the most striking American presence is that of Mr Jack. His ghostly, spectral figure resonates with the almost carnivalesque portrayal of the Comanches and Apaches in McCarthy's *Blood Meridian*. Mr Jack emerges only at night in a pitch-dark vehicle, and he is memorable primarily for his blindingly while teeth, his absurdly crisp wardrobe, "his shalwar kameez [that] still held the creases from where it'd been folded in plastic packaging" (2015, 217), and his distinctly American manner of speaking Pashto.

One way to gauge the accuracy and depth of this kind of cultural appropriation is to examine comparable portrayals in narratives produced within the culture being appropriated, thereby observing how they respond and converse with such representations. A striking parallel to Mr Jack can be found in the depiction of "the blonds" (Blasim and Wright 2014, 81) in Hassan Blasim's short story "The Madman of Freedom Square," included in *The Corpse Exhibition*. Although the narrative does not explicitly identify the two blonds as American, the story follows a familiar trajectory: two blonds, likely a reference to their skin and hair colour, arrive in town, and suddenly the local economy flourishes, wages rise, and public infrastructure improves—all standard tropes associated with American financial intervention within the discourse of the "war on terror." Soon enough, much like Mr Jack with his blinding teeth and colourless eyes, the blonds acquire a quasi-mythical aura. As the narrative recounts, the local women

> attributed to the baraka or spiritual power of the blonds the fact that their husbands, who worked sweeping the streets or as school janitors in the city center, had all received pay raises. The husbands, who had been skeptical about the baraka of the two men, soon stopped scoffing, when the government decided to install electricity at the beginning of winter. After all these signs of baraka, the women began a campaign to plant flowers outside their front doors so that the blonds could smell the fragrance as they made their angelic passage through the Darkness district. As for the men, they filled in the puddles so the blonds would not have to walk around them. (Blasim and Wright 2014, 82)

The presence of these two men radiates the same uncanny aura that surrounds Mr Jack in *Green on Blue*. "The children would be even happier," the narrator continues, highlighting the people's fascination with the blond men, "when they would graciously bend down, without stopping their walk, to let the children touch their blond hair" (Blasim and Wright 2014, 84). In "The Nightmares of Carlos Fuentes," the protagonist, an Iraqi man who has escaped to Amsterdam, experiences bizarre dreams, and one night "painted his face like an American Indian, slept wearing diaphanous orange pajamas, and placed three feathers taken from various birds" (2014, 194). In these stories, American figures exert a spiritual rather than physical power over the local populations. When their presence is explicitly described, rather than evoked through indirect metaphor, it is almost always to satirise or expose them, underscoring the absurdity of their mythic status.

However, this mode of depicting American presence has become a cliché and is not confined to fictional accounts. In *The Assassins' Gate* (2005), George Packer employs a similar language when describing a formal meeting between American officials and Iraqi exiles at the London Hilton Metropole in 2002. "Sprinkled among them," Packer writes, "palely lurking, were the Americans. [...] These Americans moved through the throng of Iraqi exiles with the glowing and watchful fervour of missionaries among the converted" (Packer 2007, 88). These few Americans stand in sharp contrast to their Iraqi counterparts. While the Americans' faces display an eager, almost evangelical fervour, the Iraqis resemble "beefy apparatchiks from the old Soviet republics of Central Asia" and evoke "the words 'fatwa' and 'stoning'" (2007, 88). The Americans do not evoke or recall anything; rather, they embody what they have always been: missionaries moving confidently among those they imagine as needing salvation. Taken together, these narrative elements illustrate not only the seductive possibilities of cross-cultural storytelling but also the fragile ethics underpinning such literary experiments.

Ultimately, *Green on Blue* demonstrates how a culturally selfish event like 9/11 continues to shape and demand new narrative forms. By attempting to inhabit Bhabha's "third space," Ackerman's novel reveals both the allure and the limitations of cross-cultural storytelling. While it invites readers into the mind of the supposed enemy, it remains marked by an Americanising gaze that reframes Afghan subjectivity through familiar Western tropes.

Placing Ackerman's work alongside McCarthy's *Blood Meridian* and Blasim's *The Corpse Exhibition* clarifies how different cultural artefacts enter into dialogue, borrowing and reshaping each other in the process. Rather than resolving the tensions inherent in this exchange, *Green on Blue* highlights the ongoing instability and porousness of cultural meanings in the aftermath of conflict. In doing so, it underscores the difficulty, and perhaps the impossibility, of fully escaping the gravitational pull of one's own cultural frameworks when attempting to represent the other.

3.4 Reading Otherwise: Toward a *Reparative Reading* of Selfish Events

A few months before writing this, I was invited by a colleague of my supervisor to meet with a student who was working on an undergraduate thesis about 9/11 and its representation in fiction. The purpose of our meeting was to exchange ideas and recommend further readings that might offer alternative perspectives on the topic. In our email correspondence before meeting in person, I asked the student which texts he had chosen. He replied that he was focusing on "four 9/11 novels": Paul Auster's *Brooklyn Follies* (2005), William Gibson's *Pattern Recognition* (2003), Don DeLillo's *Falling Man* (2007), and Thomas Pynchon's *Bleeding Edge* (2013). His approach was to analyse how these four authors, most, if not all, considered proponents of postmodern poetics, engage with the event and reflect what he described as the decline of postmodernism. In this context, he argued that 9/11 marked the end of postmodernism because it profoundly altered our shared perception of reality. What I neglected to ask him at the time, and now regret not doing, was whether the label "9/11 fiction," which he employed so readily, was derived from an existing critical framework or was instead a category of his own making. Aside from DeLillo's *Falling Man*, which I discussed in an earlier section, I knew the other novels only by reputation and the aura surrounding their authors' names.

Since that conversation over coffee with the student, I have reflected deeply on the label he used and its implications. Labelling a text in one way rather than another inevitably narrows its interpretive possibilities and subtly dictates the kinds of meanings readers may extract. Were these works called "9/11 novels" simply because they were published after the attacks, or did they embody some intrinsic thematic or structural characteristic that warranted such a designation? The real issue does not lie within the novels themselves but rather in the attempt to define and stabilise the category of "9/11 fiction," which is often the first step when grappling with any emerging literary genre.

A cursory search online reveals hundreds of lists purporting to identify "9/11 novels." *The Guardian*, for instance, sidesteps this ambiguity by inviting the Iranian-American writer Porochista Khakpour to compile her own selection of such works. Of the ten novels Khakpour includes, only one—the most obvious choice, DeLillo's *Falling Man*—appears on both her list and the one the student proposed. Yet the fact that *The Guardian* entrusts the creation of such a list to a single individual, rather than to an editorial board or a collective of writers, underscores the subjective and provisional nature of such labels. Ultimately, the formation of such lists depends less on rigid scholarly consensus than on individual sensibilities and interpretive investments.

No authority can decree a definitive canon, whether we might wish for it or not. These lists remain provisional and open to continuous revision, especially as new works that might belong to the so-called 9/11 genre continue to emerge. Consider, for example, the case of the Vietnam War. David Means's debut novel, *Hystopia* (2016)—a counterfactual reimagining of the Vietnam conflict—was published more than forty years after the war's conclusion. Even more revealing is that, despite an extensive body of literature and cinema on Vietnam, critics rarely speak of a "Vietnam War genre" as a distinct category. Instead, they refer more broadly to "war fiction" or "war films." This hesitancy to name a discrete genre suggests that there must be something uniquely specific and formally legible in both content and form to justify the existence of a "9/11 genre."

Several critics, whose work I examine and engage with extensively in this section, have compiled their own influential selections. For instance, in his seminal study *Out of the Blue: September 11 and the Novel* (2009), Kristiaan Versluys, one of the earliest and most authoritative voices in this field, attempted to delineate an initial canon of 9/11 fiction. He identifies four novels and one graphic narrative that, in his view, form the backbone of any critical engagement with this body of work: Don DeLillo's *Falling Man* (2007), Jonathan Safran Foer's *Extremely Loud and Incredibly Close* (2005), Frédéric Beigbeder's *Windows on the World* (2003), John Updike's *Terrorist* (2006), and Art Spiegelman's *In the Shadow of No Towers* (2004). Additionally, Versluys briefly discusses works such as Ian McEwan's *Saturday* (2005), Claire Messud's *The Emperor's Children* (2006), Ken Kalfus's *A Disorder Peculiar to the Country* (2006), and Joseph O'Neill's *Netherland* (2008), suggesting an expanding orbit of texts that might be considered in this emerging canon.

Birgit Däwes's *Ground Zero Fiction: History, Memory, and Representation in the American 9/11 Novel* (2011), regarded as perhaps the most comprehensive and systematic study of post-9/11 fiction to date, proposes an even more expansive corpus. As Däwes notes, "as of late June 2011, at least 231 novels from around the world are available in print which can be classified as '9/11 novels' — that is, the terrorist attacks on New York and Washington provide the entire or a part of the setting, they feature more or less prominently as a historical context (establishing a particular atmosphere or set of themes), or they have a decisive function for the development of the plot, the characters, or the novel's symbolism" (Däwes 2011, 6). Däwes adopts a "story-oriented" approach to classification, prioritising elements such as spatial and temporal setting, "the thematic and/or symbolic relevance of the terrorist attacks," and "the characters' involvement with and/or perception of the event" (2011, 81). Däwes's study thus provides a map of post-9/11 fiction by identifying six categories of novels, a categorisation that could ultimately help readers group the abundance of 9/11 novels.

Däwes's six categories include "metonymic approaches" (those that "substitute the subject [...] by characteristics of that subject or something closely related to it"), "salvational approaches" (those that "explore various narrative methods of preservation from destruction or calamity"), "diagnostic approaches" (those that "contextualize 9/11 within larger historical and/or geographical frameworks"), "appropriative approaches" (those that transcend "the boundary to the Other by constructing the voice of the perpetrator"), "symbolic approaches" (those that use 9/11 "as a symbolic setting and event, which provides a parallel or contrastive background to tales of personal crisis, loss, or decline") and "writerly approaches" (those that transform "the representational challenges into semantic, structural or formal innovations, such as multiple perspectives, extensive allegories, non-linear forms of narration, visual elements, creative layouts, metafictional angles, and various other textual experiments") (2011, 20–22). Each category, however wide-ranging and permissive, comes with many interpretations and, like all categories, a series of prescriptions and provisos. Although Däwes's study, with its almost obsessive attention to minutiae and desire to include every perspective, acquires the aura of a "Bible" of Ground Zero Fiction, we must acknowledge that her system remains contingent on her chosen criteria.

Moreover, certain works of fiction might refer to 9/11 only in passing, without foregrounding it as a central narrative concern. After all, the attacks of September 11, so widely disseminated and absorbed into global consciousness, constitute a shared generational imprint. I recall vividly what I was doing when I first saw the footage on television; many others carry similar memories, often framed as moments of "history in the making" by parents or peers. Should works that merely mention the attacks in passing also be classified as Ground Zero fiction? By invoking the event, even tangentially, do these texts not implicitly participate in a commentary on its cultural resonance? The boundary between what qualifies as Ground Zero fiction and what does not is undeniably porous, requiring a heightened attentiveness from both readers and critics. Though this attentiveness does not demand great mental effort, I believe it is crucial in shaping the integrity of our interpretive practice.

Given the enduring impact that selfish events like the terrorist attacks of September 11 have on the consciousness of those who witnessed them, whether directly or through mediated experience, I argue that such events foster a form of *paranoia* that seeps into interpretative processes, even those that seem ostensibly detached or innocent. Däwes acknowledges this phenomenon when she observes that, in the aftermath of 9/11, "any sight of two aircraft near buildings, and especially of a plane so precariously tilted toward a vertical structure, summons the one association which iconically opened the twenty-first century: the World Trade Centre's spectacular destruction" (2011, 26). We are almost instinctively inclined to map the interpretative framework of the selfish event onto anything that even faintly resembles one of its constitutive elements. In other words, the event functions as a mental shortcut, a pre-established interpretive schema that we activate when confronted with ambiguous or suggestive cultural signs.

One effective way to examine this dynamic is by tracing instances in which such paranoid reading emerges and analysing how it operates, as well as exploring possible strategies to counteract it. Finding these instances is not difficult; they are embedded in a wide range of texts and cultural artefacts. While reading Nell Zink's novel *Nicotine* (2016), I encountered one such moment and realised that I, too, was deploying this interpretative reflex. The novel frequently situates scenes through specific temporal markers—days, times, seasons—without necessarily attaching symbolic weight to them at first glance.

> SUNDAY MORNING, SEPTEMBER 11, 2016.
> In Fort Lee, Matt kicks off his duvet. He picks up his phone, checks his mail and social media, and selects an old Funkadelic MP3 to pipe to the speakers in the kitchen. He picks his way downstairs. There are wineglasses on the open wooden staircase, and dust bunnies, some resting on the remains of the wine. He is thinner, with dark circles under his eyes.
> He dresses carefully, in indigo Levi's, a long-sleeved T-shirt, light fleece jacket, Timberlands, and a solar-powered Timex. It reads nine-thirty-three. (Zink 2016, 262)

That is how Matt marks the fifteenth anniversary of the September 11 attacks. However, the moment I saw the date, I started to expect some reference to that anniversary, some side remark, a snippet of a ceremony on television, and the pompous rhythm of a speech on the radio commemorating those who died in the attacks. I kept reading, but my expectations were never fulfilled. I checked the calendar and confirmed that September 11, 2016, was indeed a

Sunday, affirming that Zink was not referring to a parallel universe. Rather than providing the expected commemorative cues, she denied the reader the anticipated satisfaction, confronting us with our own interpretative habits.

On the other hand, as my frustration persisted, I began to realise that this denial of expectation might be precisely what Zink intended. By withholding overt commemorative references, she opens a space in which the reader becomes acutely aware of their own interpretive habits. The incomplete reference operates as an invitation to reflect on how readily we are drawn into a *paranoid* mode of reading, one that instinctively imports 9/11 into any cultural frame that even remotely gestures toward it. Throughout *Nicotine*, Zink repeatedly plays this game of thwarted anticipation: she builds expectations only to dismantle them, creating characters and narrative arcs that deliberately lead readers into familiar interpretive traps before leaving them unresolved. In this sense, frustration is an integral part of her aesthetic project, a deliberate strategy designed to expose and destabilise our habitual responses and provoke self-awareness.

A more overt example of a text that cultivates and then interrogates paranoid interpretation is Steve Erickson's *Shadowbahn* (2017), which, unlike Zink's *Nicotine*, clearly fits within Däwes's criteria for a 9/11 novel. In Erickson's narrative, the Twin Towers inexplicably reappear in the Badlands of South Dakota twenty years after their destruction, their sudden manifestation prompting a national and existential bewilderment. The novel, composed of brief, often poetic chapters, begins with a seemingly mundane phone conversation about things that "vanish into thin air."

> Things don't just disappear into thin —
> ...but she hangs up on him before he finishes. "What the...?" he says, staring at his cell phone in dismay and trying to remember if she ever hung up on him before. As he finishes filling the tank of his truck and replaces the pump's nozzle, Aaron ponders how this became the kind of argument where his wife hangs up on him. He hauls himself back into the driver's seat thinking maybe this is really the kind of argument that's about something other than what it's about. (Erickson 2017, 3)

Given the context provided by the novel's cover and the critical commentary surrounding it, my immediate assumption was that the "things" vanishing into thin air were a veiled reference to the Towers themselves. Erickson deliberately toys with such assumptions, allowing Aaron to wonder whether the argument is actually about "something other than what it's about." As the narrative unfolds, it becomes increasingly clear that the argument is indeed about something more banal—a lost wallet—rather than an existential meditation on national loss.

> *Is something else wrong?* He wonders. *Is there something else going on with her?* Can this fight actually be about something as trivial as his wallet gone missing, vanished from his jacket? Even if now he's a driver without an identity. [...]
> *If I'm being honest,* Aaron admits to himself ruefully about the conversation with Cilla Ann, *I know it's not true that things don't just disappear into thin air. If I'm honest, and I've learned anything in this life, it's that things disappear into thin air all the time.* (Erickson 2017, 5)

Erickson, once again, shifts between expectation and deferral. In the following chapter, the disappearance of the wallet and the loss of the two towers converge as Aaron ponders "how it is that on this morning of the argument about the wallet vanishing into thin air, he could have overlooked the two skyscrapers, each a quarter mile high, standing on the flat plain before him: the breath of Aaron's homeland, exhaled from the nostrils of Aaron's century" (Erickson 2017, 6). By conflating these two acts of disappearance, Erickson constructs a dialectic of our paranoid readings and provides us with the mental tools to recognise it, while simultaneously enabling a *reparative reading*. In this sense, the novel functions almost like a cognitive-behavioural exercise, allowing the readers to identify their interpretive reflexes and consider alternative modes of engagement. It simultaneously implicates us and offers tools for transcending the mental straitjacket imposed by selfish events.

The idea of a *reparative reading* of cultural artefacts is not new. It was articulated most compellingly by Eve Kosofsky Sedgwick in her writings on affect and critical method, particularly in the essay "Paranoid Reading and Reparative Reading, or, You're so Paranoid, You Probably Think This Essay Is About You," included in

Touching Feeling (2002). In this essay, Sedgwick argues that the "first imperative of paranoia is *There must be no bad surprises*" (Sedgwick and Frank 2003, 130). Paranoia, in her formulation, is "at once anticipatory and retroactive," as it works by constantly rehearsing all the bad things that have happened in order to be prepared for all the bad things yet to come.

In this sense, Sedgwick contends, paranoia "seems to grow like a crystal in a hyper-saturated solution, blotting out any sense of the possibility of alternative ways of understanding or things to understand" (2003, 131). She characterises paranoia as a "strong theory" because it insists on the belief that "everything means one thing," a stance that "permits a sharpened sense of all the ways there are of meaning it" (2003, 136). Paranoia is also a "theory of negative effects," since it is the only mode of knowledge "that has so thorough a practice of disavowing its affective motive and force and masquerading as the very stuff of truth" (2003, 138). Finally, paranoia "places its faith in exposure," in the sense that it places "an extraordinary stress on the efficacy of knowledge per se — knowledge in the form of exposure" (Sedgwick and Frank 2003, 138).

To put it more bluntly, Sedgwick depicts paranoid reading as a means of recanting affect to claim possession of the truth, and it is accordingly described in negative terms as single-minded, self-defeating, hypervigilant, contemptuous, sneering, monopolistic, and ultimately, terrible. Paranoia manufactures expectations and, by doing so, forecloses the possibility of surprise or wonder. Viewed in this light, Sedgwick's critique of paranoid reading becomes an invaluable framework for resisting the interpretative dominance of selfish events, enabling a methodological counterpoint that creates openness rather than interpretive foreclosure.

Considering all these aspects, I cannot help but notice the similarities between what Sedgwick calls "paranoid reading" and my interpretative experience with Zink's *Nicotine* and Erickson's *Shadowbahn*. The moment I see the date in Zink's novel, viewed as a triggering element (much like spotting a plane dangerously close to a building), I instinctively begin to read it in a paranoid mode. Like Sedgwick's crystal in a hyper-saturated solution, the selfish event exerts its gravitational pull, occluding any possibility that Zink might intend to diverge from it. It is September 11, 2016, and therefore, Zink *must* refer to the event. This illustrates how the interpretative vortex of a selfish event exerts a gravitational pull on the reader's imagination, leading us to retrofit any ambiguous sign as evidence of its ongoing cultural dominance. Yet Zink almost defiantly resists this gravitational pull. Had she chosen to remain within its orbit, she would have only reinforced a paranoid reading of her work. Instead, her refusal exposes our own expectations and disarms them, inviting us to acknowledge our interpretative impulses. The exact mechanism operates in Erickson's novel, which actively oscillates between raising and subverting these expectations, prompting us to recognise and reflect on our interpretive habits.

Given Sedgwick's critique of paranoia and my encounters with this mode of reading, it becomes evident that a more generous and open approach to post-9/11 texts is needed, namely, a *reparative reading*. To read reparatively, Sedgwick writes, or "to read from a reparative position is to surrender the knowing, anxious, paranoid determination that no horror, however apparently unthinkable, shall ever come to the reader as new; to a reparatively positioned reader, it can seem realistic and necessary to experience surprise" (Sedgwick and Frank 2003, 146). While this stance may initially seem naïve or overly sentimental, it offers a radical alternative: it foregrounds hope as an interpretive method, a means of refusing the inevitability of trauma's narrative dominion.

> Hope, often a fracturing, even a traumatic thing to experience, is among the energies by which the reparatively positioned reader tries to organise the fragments and part-objects she encounters or creates. Because the reader has room to realise that the future may be different from the present, it is also possible for her to entertain such profoundly painful, profoundly relieving, ethically crucial possibilities as that the past, in turn, could have happened differently from the way it actually did. (Sedgwick and Frank 2003, 146)

Sedgwick also underscores the value of accepting the frustration that arises from unmet narrative expectations. Whereas a *paranoid* reading insists on *inevitability* (Zink *must* be referring to 9/11; Erickson *must* be discussing the Twin Towers when he mentions things that vanish into thin air), a *reparative* reading invites the reader to imagine alternate trajectories. It encourages the belief that Zink and Erickson can indeed refer to something else unrelated to what happened on September 11, 2001. It also promotes the hope that whatever happened that day cannot and will not define what follows.

A reparative reading practice would also temper the culturally expansive tendencies of a selfish event, rescuing us from the compulsion to revisit it obsessively, much like an anxious mind loops through a cascade of negative thoughts that reinforces its own distress. By liberating us from the habit of interpreting every artefact through the lens of the selfish event, reparative reading reopens the field of signification, allowing works to reveal alternative meanings and potentialities. After all, wallets can vanish into thin air without evoking the collapse of towers. "[Things] disappear into thin air all the time" (Erickson 2017, 5). Likewise, planes frequently fly low, and when viewed from below, they may seem to approach skyscrapers without necessarily portending catastrophe. Reparative reading thus invites us to see these moments not as inevitable echoes of past trauma, but as possibilities for new interpretations and forms of meaning-making.

A reparative reading practice, then, would diminish the overwhelming influence of selfish events, freeing us from compulsively revisiting them as if tending to an unhealed wound. It would enable cultural artefacts to signify beyond their immediate gravitational pull, opening them up to new interpretative possibilities. In this way, we might come to see two household objects in a Morandi painting simply as that, or perceive Changez's gaze in *The Reluctant Fundamentalist* as motivated by ambition rather than suspicion. Ultimately, a reparative reading does not merely shift our interpretive focus; it offers a hopeful social ethic, encouraging us to imagine that what has happened does not always determine what comes next.

4. Mapping a Way Out of the Selfish Event: Fiction, Journalism, and the Proximal-Ancillary Continuum

4.1 Theoretical Foundations: From Canons to Continuums

"Canons and cannons," Lynne Hanley provocatively declares in *Writing War: Fiction, Gender, and Memory* (1991), "have more in common than the accident of sounding alike" (Hanley 1991, 18). Embedded within the very notion of the literary canon, Hanley suggests, lies a spirit of belligerence and a latent project of cultural imperialism (1991, 18). Yet, beyond the perennial debates over who possesses the authority to determine which war books deserve canonical status, this hostility does not dissipate; rather, it intensifies and diversifies in the hands of individual war writers. Indeed, many writers deliberately defy convention, crafting alternative narratives that subvert the expectations shaped by established fictional and non-fictional discourses. Ultimately, this belligerence is not eliminated but instead mutates into a subtler, more insidious form of hostility when fictional and non-fictional accounts are intertwined.

Consider, for instance, Kurt Vonnegut's *Slaughterhouse-Five (1969)*, which upends linear narrative conventions by imagining, in a cinematic inversion, American aeroplanes taking off backwards from an airfield in England (Vonnegut 1991, 74). In a similarly playful spirit, Robert Coover's *The Universal Baseball Association* (1968) refrains from directly confronting the Vietnam War, engaging instead in what John Limon describes as "an exercise in mixed, but not mock, nostalgia" (Limon 1994, 165). In stark contrast to Coover's evasiveness, Thomas Pynchon's *Gravity's Rainbow* (1973) compels readers to conceive war as a commercial exchange, where "murdering and violence" are relegated to acts of "self-policing" performed by non-professionals. Pynchon's narrator underscores that "the mass nature of wartime death serves as spectacle, as diversion from the real movements of the War. It provides raw material to be recorded into History so that children may be taught History as sequences of violence, battle after battle, and be more prepared for the adult world" (Pynchon 2014, 107). In Pynchon's reimagining, war, stripped of its didactic and moralising force, becomes a grotesque "celebration of markets" (2014, 107).

In a comparable, though more ironically existential vein, Joseph Heller's *Catch-22* (1961) offers an absurdist critique of war, echoing and expanding on the undertones of Dino Buzzati's *The Tartar Steppe* (1940). Extending this lineage into the contemporary context, Mark Doten's *The Infernal* (2015) depicts modern American warfare as a conflict no longer confined to tangible battlefields but instead unfolding at the informational level, affecting the subjectivities of individuals ensnared in the maelstrom of the "war on terror." Similarly, Elliot Ackerman's *Green on Blue* (2015) resists the fetishisation of the American soldier's experience, narrating the war in Afghanistan through the eyes of Aziz, a young Afghan orphan who joins a U.S.-backed militia to support his wounded brother.

Yet, before we examine how these texts contest and complicate dominant discourses, it is essential to recognise that, despite their diverse narrative strategies and thematic emphases, these works remain fundamentally anchored in the historical event of war itself. One of the most pressing issues in analysing war fiction, and one of the very reasons it occupies a distinctive place within literary fiction, is its foundational reliance on events that are, at least in principle, *verifiable*. This verification is pursued first through parallel reading with non-fictional accounts and then through comparison with other representational modes of the same events. As Hanley astutely observes, while we cannot dispute the authenticity of fictional works like H.G. Wells's novel *The War of the Worlds* (1898) "with the evidence of our own senses" (1991, 4), war narratives invariably invite scrutiny and provoke questions regarding their capacity to capture the truth of wartime experience.

Given these considerations, this chapter seeks to explore what I term *ancillary coverage*: fictional accounts that offer supplementary or alternative perspectives on the American wars in Iraq and Afghanistan. The necessity of introducing this concept arises from the imperative to differentiate between *proximal* (journalistic) coverage of military events and *ancillary* (fictional) coverage. This distinction is not merely an academic exercise; rather, it represents a crucial step toward understanding the complexities of contemporary war narratives. Accordingly, the rest of this chapter develops in three parts: first, a methodological reconsideration of the truth-fiction dichotomy that lays the groundwork for the *proximal-ancillary coverage continuum*; second, an examination of how *proximal coverage* depicted the "war on terror"; and finally, an exploration of *ancillary coverage*, focusing on its operation in works such as Mark Doten's *The Infernal* and Elliot Ackerman's *Green on Blue*. While *proximal* and *ancillary* coverages differ in their narrative methods and claims to truth, it is essential to clarify from the outset that they do not constitute opposing categories, but instead points on a *continuum*. This continuum highlights their mutual capacity to inform and challenge each other, thereby offering a more nuanced understanding of war representation.

4.2 Premises for a Proximal-Ancillary Coverage Continuum

Wars have always engendered significant narrative productions. In this regard, military events may be understood as *selfish events*: they unfold with such velocity and intensity that they preclude the immediate formation of a stable cultural discourse. They are so voracious in their semiotic appetite that they absorb even cultural artefacts ostensibly unrelated to the events themselves. Consider, for example, the immediate aftermath of September 11, the catalyst for the so-called "war on terror." In that moment of collective shock, politicians eagerly invoked the memory of Pearl Harbour to legitimise military reprisals. Lacking an established cultural frame, the "war on terror" initially sought to stabilise itself by borrowing from historical analogies.

As Sandra Ball-Rokeach and Melvin DeFleur argue in their media dependency theory, during periods of acute social and political instability, there is a marked surge in textual and visual production, a phenomenon driven less by the events themselves than by the existential necessity for meaning. In developed media ecosystems, they write, "audience dependency on media information increases as the level of structural conflict and change increases" (Ball-Rokeach and DeFleur 1976, 7). This theoretical framework thus strengthens our continuum model and illustrates how proximal accounts shape public perception immediately, while ancillary narratives emerge later to contest, reinterpret, and deepen the same perception.

Within this landscape of heavy informational exchange, military "mavens" and a broad constellation of specialists—often former state officials—are quickly summoned to interpret events and regulate, if not authenticate, the flood of information. When such authoritative voices are enlisted to fortify credibility, this resembles the rhetorical strategy of medieval writers, who, in their quest for authority, invoked sacred texts to lend legitimacy to their claims.

In this context, the proliferation of insider accounts authored by former officials or those who held pivotal roles in military conflicts is especially noteworthy. These texts wield disproportionate influence on public opinion because they promise an insider's revelation, seemingly transgressing the state's reluctance to disclose sensitive information. Such denials of full allegiance to official structures create the illusion that the account transcends institutional control, thus amplifying its perceived veracity.

However, despite the value such insider accounts have in depicting a military conflict and expanding its discursive outlets, and regardless of the immediacy and presumed accuracy they offer under such difficult circumstances, it is generally believed that this type of coverage does not fully explore the realm of war narration. It often fails to demonstrate how readers can experience the war vicariously. Perhaps the only written accounts that aim to surpass this initial limitation are those focusing on individual war experiences, both from the perspective of the authors themselves (mainly "embedded journalists") and the soldiers or others whose "narratives" are conveyed through those authors.

These hybrid accounts occupy an ambiguous space, as they hover between fiction, given their subjectivity and inevitable selective framing, and journalism, owing to their professed documentary intent. They function as *discourse regulators* that promise to diminish the readers' need for both accurate information *and* emotional engagement. Their "delivery system," to borrow David Palumbo-Liu's phrase, which explains how the notion of *otherness* shifts into *sameness* in the process of reading (Palumbo-Liu 2012, 10), is expected to adhere to the rules dictated by journalism's practices, traditions, and clichés. For clarity, in this chapter, I use 'truth' to refer to factual accuracy and empirical verification typical of proximal coverage. In contrast, 'authenticity' refers to emotional and experiential resonance, typical of ancillary narratives.

A paradigmatic example is Sebastian Junger's *War* (2010). In his *Author's Note*, Junger assures readers that he "was never asked — directly or indirectly — to alter [his] reporting in any way or to show the contents of [his] notebooks or [his] cameras" (Junger 2011, xiii). He even mentions that "many scenes" were "captured on videotape," an implicit invitation for readers to verify his claims, as though journalistic credentials alone could not satisfy the modern reader's hunger for authenticity. Junger's refusal to don a uniform or carry a weapon further underscores his assertion of objectivity: he insists that any compromise would transform him from observer to combatant.

Even more illustrative is Michael V. Hayden's *Playing to the Edge: American Intelligence in the Age of Terror* (2016). In his *Foreword*, Hayden, a former Director of both the NSA and CIA, declares that he "pushed as hard as prudence and the law (and CIA's Publication Review Board) allow" (Hayden 2016, 6). Yet the precise boundaries of this "prudence" remain opaque, quickly swept aside by his claim that intelligence work "deserves understanding, appreciation, and even occasional criticism" (2016, 6). Hayden's self-portrayal aligns him with Prometheus, a heroic figure bringing forbidden fire to humanity, thereby deflecting scrutiny even as he invites it.

Junger's and Hayden's diligence in foregrounding their honesty and disclosing the circumstances under which their accounts were produced is both deliberate and strategically placed. Positioned at the very outset, these declarations serve as explicit invitations to reconsideration and re-examination. They are intended to pre-empt criticism and to frame the accounts within a context of transparency that anticipates the kinds of responses they are likely to provoke. Given their stated purpose of providing accurate information to their readers, these accounts almost inevitably elicit reactions grounded in comparison with alternative versions of events.

Such was the case with the reception of Hayden's book in *The New York Review of Books* shortly after its publication. Charlie Savage, the reviewer, observes that although Hayden "is good at projecting the impression that he is laying out everything you need to know about a topic," (2016, 8) he ultimately suggests that the General's judgment may be clouded by his deep-seated idealism and allegiance to the state apparatus he continues to serve, even in a text purporting to be personal and candid. Moreover, though Hayden acknowledges that intelligence agencies are subject to "political winds" and "political elites," Savage cautions that readers might "question whether he sometimes lets his defence of espionage agencies against such criticism [...] interfere with his candour" (Savage 2016, 8). Savage's remarks on the trustworthiness of Hayden's account thus not only undermine the structural stability of the narrative but also symbolically attach a "mental red tag" to its content, prompting readers to approach it with a heightened degree of scepticism.

Bearing in mind this initial limitation, namely the inability of these accounts to exhaust the narrative possibilities of war, another widespread postulation emerges: an exploration of the cultural significance of war requires not merely accepting the immediacy and claims to authenticity offered by *proximal coverage* but venturing beyond them, into the realm of narratives crafted in the aftermath of military conflict. While such accounts provide facts, it is narratives that are tasked with recreating experience. As Catharine Savage Brosman argues in "The Functions of War Literature," what fundamentally distinguishes fictional renditions of war from non-fictional portrayals is their "emphasis upon the experiential dimension" (Brosman 1992, 85). These narratives, Brosman explains, record "not simply the causes and conduct of armed conflict or individual battles but the manner in which they are lived, felt, used, and transformed by participants" (1992, 86). The power of these narratives resides primarily in their capacity to generate a sense of authenticity that does not arise from a desire to ascertain factual accuracy but rather from readers' identification with the feelings and interior worlds of the characters through the exercise of imagination:

> [The] impressions left by literature derive from shaping, which narrative histories, as opposed to mere records, also entail, but which is usually more radical in poetry and fiction. In the case of poetry, rhythm, rhyme, stanza form, images, condensation, irony, and other means of formalising experience can create, from destruction, violence, and fear, psychological and aesthetic fulfilment. In fiction, the linear movement of plot — even if loose — and of prose itself, and the unavoidable interpretation of material that comes from selection and shaping, create a fictional rationality that tends to overcome formlessness and thus seems to ratify experience. (Brosman 1992, 86)

One need not engage in exhaustive archival research to unearth an abundance of "objective" data regarding the Vietnam War, nor to find ample documentary material that is undoubtedly far less evocative than, for example, Tim O'Brien's *The Things They Carried* or Coppola's film *Apocalypse Now*. Yet, despite the wealth of purportedly objective data, it is far more likely, from a cultural perspective, that our collective memory of a war's significance will be cemented through the lens of structured narratives rather than through newspaper accounts or, in contemporary times, through the deluge of information circulating across digital media. This is chiefly because, as Hanley observes, since we as readers are unable to verify their "authenticity with the evidence of our own senses," narratives "shape our memories of the past, and they create memories of pasts we have never had, of experiences not even remotely like anything that has ever happened to us" (Hanley 1991, 3-4).

From this perspective, literary fiction not only offers readers a sense of cultural closure and vicarious participation but also proves invaluable in providing a wider range of cultural reflections on war, supporting this claim on multiple occasions. However, this does not necessarily mean that an *ancillary coverage* of war diminishes in any way the importance and centrality of *proximal coverage*. While both stem from the same source, namely the military conflict itself, and thus lie on a continuum where *ancillary coverage* aims to complement *proximal coverage*, their paths towards becoming part of a larger discourse are inherently different, highlighting essential features of that discourse.

4.3 *Proximal Coverage*: From Functional Truth to Spheres of Consensus

In *The Elements of Journalism* (2001), Bill Kovach and Tom Rosenstiel outline what they believe are the ten fundamental principles of journalism, thereby providing a guideline for both news professionals and the public. At the top of their list stands the principle by which "journalism's first obligation is to the truth" (Kovach and Rosenstiel 2014, 49) and the idea that its ultimate purpose is to offer a practical and functional form of truth that would fundamentally create "a map for citizens to navigate society" (2014, 242) irrespective of the fact that such truth might prove to be uncomfortable to the higher echelons of the political establishment. The two authors further argue that journalism must also be loyal to the citizens it seeks to inform. As such, it must simultaneously maintain a "discipline of verification" (Kovach and Rosenstiel 2014, 98) and an "independence from those they cover" (2014, 142). Journalism must also "serve as an independent monitor of power" (2014, 171). Additionally, besides providing "a forum for public criticism and compromise" (2014, 197), the aspects that it covers must be significant and relevant, "comprehensive and in proportion" (2014, 242), as well as deriving from the journalist's "personal conscience" (2014, 272).

In theory, Kovach and Rosenstiel's principles appear to be as sturdy and sound as principles can be, but in practice, different situations require applying these principles in varying ways. Albeit the attacks of 9/11 and the "war on terror" could have constituted an excellent opportunity for a relaunch of American journalism after it had fallen into the throes of *infotainment*, they also marked a shift toward what Michael Schudson calls a "sphere of consensus" (Zelizer and Allan 2011, 48) within the American press, in the sense that American journalists "moved into what might even be called a priestly or pastoral mode" (2011, 48). What Kovach and Rosenstiel advocate as one of the most substantial principles of good journalism was quickly abandoned for what Schudson perceives as a "quiet, solemn tone as if speaking at a funeral" (2011, 48).

Thus, when it came to reporting on the "war on terror," the American media apparatus, as Robert W. McChesney argues, "proved to be a superior propaganda organ for militarism and war" (Zelizer and Allan 2011, 105). Journalists were no longer asking the tough questions nobody else was willing to address, just as they were no longer looking for scapegoats different from those offered on a plate from "above." American journalists limited themselves to simply echoing the conceptions and views of the elite opinion by engaging in what Adam Hodges calls "a chain of authentication" (Hodges 2011, 98), a process through which critical phrases uttered by those who have "symbolic capital" within a specific network (i.e. politicians) "enter into media circulation and provide inertia for the accrual of a shared cultural narrative" (2011, 98). Tethered to their alleged professionalism implicit in the notion of "reporting" and afraid of being accused of nurturing anti-American sentiments at a time when such sentiments were policed in an almost McCarthyite manner (Silberstein 2004, xiv), journalism in the United States fell short when it came to exercising their "watchdog principle" (Kovach and Rosenstiel 2014, 171).

Further evidence of this restriction comes from a study that examines the "war on terror" framing process through interviews with journalists at USA Today. This newspaper has the widest circulation in the United States and "seeks to speak with a national voice." Conducted by Seth C. Lewis and Stephen D. Reese, the survey asked journalists "to define the War on Terror, reflect on the phrase's use in the news media, and offer thoughts on how such issues should be presented in the press" (Lewis and Reese 2009, 89). The study's results, published in the *Journalism and Mass Communication Quarterly* (Spring 2009), reveal that most of the journalists interviewed "expressed frustration with the difficulty of defining the War on Terror" mainly because "the phrase had become a convenient (yet unfortunate) shorthand for Bush administration policies since 9/11" (2009, 90). However, despite this frustration, "the U.S. media not only transmitted President Bush's preferred phraseology but also reified and naturalised the policy, making it an uncontested and unproblematic 'thing'" (2009, 90). Due to "sourcing patterns" that give primacy to "'official' accounts," Lewis and Reese conclude, "reporters tend to cast their work within a 'web of facticity' that lends particular gravity and validity to the words of authority figures; hence, the news is that the President said X, not whether X is empirically accurate" (2009, 88). Thus, whatever official figures stated, they were echoed in and authenticated by the press.

At the root of this identification of the notion of reporting with the "words of authority figures" stand at least two factors worth mentioning in this context. The first factor refers to how information, ideally akin to wealth in a capitalist system, trickles down within a system of knowledge. To explain the process, Robert M. Entman proposes the model of "cascading activation" (Entman 2003, 415), a model "designed to explain how thoroughly the thoughts and feelings that support a frame extend down from the White House through the rest of the system" (2003, 419). Entman argues that ideas produced at the administration level "possess the greatest strength" (2003, 420). The administration, on the other hand, is distinguished within this model from the *other elite*. This network is comprised of "insiders who do not work in the executive branch" (2003, 420) but still retain some framing abilities. Among these stand members of Congress and their staffs, former government officials, think tank denizens, university sages, interest groups, and public relations firms. "Elites," Entman argues, "heavily influence the media, which in turn significantly shape public opinion—that is why the public occupies the bottom level of the cascade after all" (Entman 2003, 421).

A curious aspect of Entman's model of the modes in which ideas and frames circulate is that the media lacks the means to directly influence other elites and, by extension, the administration. It can only do so by creating and reinforcing news frames, which, in turn, can indirectly impact the upper levels, including the administration. Thus, Entman implies that the media *transmits* frames from the upper levels of the knowledge system. At the same time, they cannot directly influence how those frames reverberate once they have reached the lower levels of that same system, as Entman imagined.

The second factor that underlies this identification with the needs of those who fall within the system's upper levels is socioeconomic, as Glenn Greenwald explains. Leading American journalists, Greenwald says, "live in the same neighbourhoods as the political figures and financial elites over which they ostensibly serve as watchdogs" (Greenwald 2014, 234). In Greenwald's view, American journalism has ceased to be an "outside force." Like all "courtiers," journalists are always "eager to defend the system that vests them with their privileges and contemptuous of anyone who challenges that system" (2014, 235). This protective stance is so deeply ingrained within US establishment journalism that, in an interview with *The Guardian*, Pulitzer Prize-winning reporter Seymour Hersh harshly condemned "the timidity of journalists in America" as well as their "failure to challenge the White House" in matters of political and social significance. The solution, Hersh says, would be to endorse those editors who cannot be financially and politically manipulated and to dismiss those "chickenshit editors" who do the Administration's bidding (O'Carroll 2013). However, the covert manipulation Greenwald refers to extends beyond the individual level and into the institutional level. As Noam Chomsky and Edward S. Herman point out in their well-known study on media bias, *Manufacturing Consent: The Political Economy of the Mass Media*, complete identification also implies a "technical legal dependency" since "radio-TV companies and networks all require government licenses and franchises and are thus potentially subject to government control and harassment" (Herman and Chomsky 1994, 13).

Once caught within Hodges's "chain of authentication," which reuses soundbites taken from official sources and repeats them *endlessly* until they become naturalised and taken for granted, the American press proved incapable of escaping, at least up to a certain point. However, this was mainly due to the structural rigidity that journalism suffers from. Sometimes, reporting on a specific aspect requires repeating the information multiple times. Essentially, since the press is at least theoretically an intermediary between political elites and the public, particular frames were quickly accepted and further transmitted. Essentially, one of the weaknesses of the American press was its failure to create an institutional space for debate. This discussion would have ultimately mapped out in moral terms a contested area in the discourse surrounding the "war on terror."

4.4 *Ancillary Coverage*: Personal Truth and the Demands of Narrative

In contrast to proximal coverage, fiction is generally perceived as a form of textual production that operates with greater freedom from institutional constraints. While journalism and other forms of proximal coverage are often subject to political, economic, and temporal pressures, fiction has long enjoyed a reputation for its ability to elude such limitations. This is due, in part, to the temporal lag that typically separates an event from its fictional reimagining: unlike the immediacy demanded of journalists, novelists are afforded time to reflect, interpret, and transform. More crucially, fiction is governed by literary conventions rather than by standards of empirical verification or factual accuracy. As Jerome Bruner argues in *The Narrative Construction of Reality* (1991), "narratives are a version of reality whose acceptability is governed by convention and 'narrative necessity' rather than by empirical verification and logical requiredness, although ironically, we have no compunction about calling stories true or false" (Bruner 1991, 18). The novelist, unlike the journalist or historian, follows a different ethos—one focused on narrative coherence and emotional resonance. Jane Smiley, in *Thirteen Ways of Looking at the Novel* (2005), draws this distinction:

> The historian is required to give up dramatic interest in the pursuit of accuracy, but a novelist must give up accuracy in the pursuit of narrative drive and emotional impact. Even if the novel is based entirely on what the novelist himself has experienced, he will rework the experiences to make them more vivid and evocative, and, indeed, more logical and comprehensible. In reworking them, he will betray, or transcend, the original experience. (Smiley 2006, 21)

Whereas reviews of journalistic texts often centre on factual credibility and political accountability, reviews of fiction are more likely to assess narrative craftsmanship, stylistic choices, or thematic depth. Fiction writers are often regarded, perhaps romantically, as autonomous editors of experience, free from the immediate financial, political, and social constraints that journalists must negotiate. While the publishing industry does exert forms of gatekeeping, particularly in its sifting through the "slush pile" of unsolicited manuscripts (Doten 2015, 275), its allegiances differ from those that guide proximal coverage. The novel is seldom burdened with the same degree of ethical or epistemological scrutiny when it comes to the social consequences of its representations, and this relative detachment affords fiction a unique discursive space, one that is imaginative, reflexive, and often subversively illuminating.

Fiction has always offered something different. While at times its ideas proved consequential, its role in discussions about universal human values, or morality, to be precise, could sometimes be overlooked, with its results disregarded. One of the unique values of fiction is, as Wayne C. Booth explains, "its relatively cost-free offer of trial runs" (Booth 1988), and although these "trial runs" may sometimes be risky because they "deliver us out of our 'comfort zone'" (Palumbo-Liu 2012, 10), they also provide "both a relative freedom from consequence and, in their sheer multiplicity, a rich supply of antidotes" (Booth 1988, 485). This illustrates how, for example, literature produced under totalitarian regimes often exploited the chance to remain unseen by categorising their work as fiction. Since literature served as a means of escape from the mental and cultural uniformity fostered by such regimes, it is not surprising that many books were banned under these circumstances. In a way, the witch hunts against writers and free thinkers under totalitarian regimes have demonstrated that literature plays a vital role in shaping our perception of reality.

In his *Author's Note* to *The Infernal* (2015), Mark Doten warns his readers that even though "real-world people and events" are rendered in the novel "to use a legal phrase, which also happens to be true—this is a work of fiction, and all incidents and characters are either fictional or used fictitiously." To put it differently, the only "truth" that the reader can entirely give credence to is that what they physically hold in their hands is nothing more than a work of fiction and that they should act accordingly. Nevertheless, the mere fact that a fictional representation such as this one does contain an "author's note" with legal undertones further signals that Doten's novel, as Linda Hutcheon notes in *A Poetics of Postmodernism* (1988), falls into the category of fictional representations that "install and then blur the line between fiction and history" (Hutcheon 1988, 113). Though they are both narratives, fiction and history are generally separated by their "frames [...], which historiographic metafiction first establishes and then crosses, positing both the generic contracts of fiction and history" (Hutcheon 1988, 109–10).

Unlike Junger and Hayden, who went to great lengths to ensure they receive proper recognition for their work, Doten subtly suggests that what we, as readers, access are mere "omnosyne outputs," pages produced by a machine whose flaws are evident not only because of our own encounters with technology but also due to the chaotic sequences of code scattered throughout the book. This adds an extra layer to the author's *effacement,* implying both that since a machine randomly prints these pages, the ideas of selection and framing seem peculiar, and that the author somewhat disclaims responsibility for what readers may interpret from his work, as he is simply a messenger offering no moral judgment or accusations.

A similar form of *effacement* is present in Elliot Ackerman's Afghanistan war novel *Green on Blue* (2015) at the very beginning of the narrative when the protagonist overtly states that many of his peers and acquaintances would call him a "dishonest man" (2015, 3), even though he has always kept faith with himself. This tendency towards dishonesty is further reinforced when the protagonist, who is initially nameless and only identifies himself as "Ali's brother" (2015, 3), tells his readers how his mother entrusted him with the secret of her smoking habits. "The truth is," the narrator admits later, "she recognised in me her own ability to deceive" (2015, 4). Our initial response as readers would be to dismiss the narrator quickly by labelling him "unreliable," a term coined by Booth.

Nevertheless, this serves as a warning on at least two levels. Considering that Ackerman, an American writer, is engaging in cultural appropriation by choosing to write from the perspective of an Afghan soldier in *Green on Blue*, this may reveal a fundamental issue with such appropriation. Cultural appropriations are often seen as derogatory because they suggest, on the one hand, that different cultures can be accessed through intellectual effort, and on the other hand, that anyone can objectify and turn that other culture into their own asset. Additionally, since the novel is written in the first person, it offers a one-sided account. As a result, we are given insight into the part of the self that the protagonist has always remained loyal to. We are also reminded that the narrative does not aim to present any ultimate truths about the war.

Additionally, and returning to the set of commonly held beliefs regarding war writing, the writer's lack of expertise in specific topics also plays a vital role in the likelihood of this possibility of *effacement*. Although concerning particular issues careful research is needed on the part of the writer, the findings of such research usually place that writer among outcasts, who are never quite *there*, wherever that may be. The writer who has not taken part in a military event technically could not write "truthfully" about that event, which would position him or her as "unreliable," just as a soldier is readily cast as "unreliable" due to his or her lack of writerly skills.

In the case of war literature, particularly when written by war veterans about their own experiences, it is, to a certain extent, part of an effort to preserve that status and to bring war literature as a genre closer to direct coverage on the proximal–ancillary continuum. Such accounts of war experience, similar to the journalistic renderings and written accounts mentioned earlier, function as discourse regulators. Following this reasoning, a somewhat traditional approach has been established in the context of most military events. On an imaginary scale of literary worthiness and truthfulness, accounts of war written by veterans or by those who have had direct contact with the war generally rank higher, and this idea has gained traction, especially in the case of war literature. However, as Phil Klay, another war veteran turned writer, argues in the Sunday Review section of *The New York Times*, the very idea that "the veteran is an unassailable authority on the experience of war shuts down conversation" and "believing war is beyond words is an abrogation of responsibility — it lets civilians off the hook from trying to understand, and veterans off the hook from needing to explain" (Klay 2014).

Klay is not the only one who points out this tendency, which he sees as detrimental and limiting. "The difference with war literature," David A. Buchanan argues in *Going Scapegoat: Post-9/11 War Literature, Language and Culture* (2016), "may be that, unlike other subjects, strong voices (usually veterans) protect the field of war literature from being penetrated by the noncombatant voice when they argue about the distracting details and issues of authenticity and accuracy" (Buchanan 2016, 17). Following James Campbell's notion of "combat gnosticism" (Campbell 1999, 203), Buchanan further explains that when it comes to war literature both critics and readers tend to overlook or even to silence civilian voices because they do not constitute authorities in the field. For instance, Peter Molin's blog *Time Now: The Iraq and Afghanistan Wars in Art, Film, and Literature*, which makes a very comprehensive list of war writers and books at the end of each year, never mentions Mark Doten's novel *The Infernal*, although it has been repeatedly publicised as a war novel. Writing for the *Los Angeles Times*, Nathan Deuel called Doten's novel "a darkly twisted take on [the] Iraq War" (Deuel, n.d.). Doten is not a war veteran turned writer, and *The Infernal* seems to have been excluded from the canon.

Although nearly seventeen years have passed since Campbell first discussed "combat gnosticism" and its influence on literary creation and perception, the concept remains relevant and alive. Perhaps Molin's omission of Doten's novel from his collection of contemporary war literature reflects this. Nonetheless, there is a strong movement towards entirely abolishing it, based on the fact that wars have evolved. "[It] is becoming increasingly obvious," Buchanan contends, "that the very nature of the fighting in Iraq and Afghanistan (and now Syria) denies anything we may try to call an experience of war" (2016, 29). The term "combat gnosticism" has become increasingly problematic for both critics and readers. This is not only because of the realisation that war literature as a genre has become more permissive, but also because employing combat gnosticism as a kind of Occam's razor for determining who belongs in the war literature canon is rather undemocratic. Combat gnosticism, as Campbell originally defined it, refers to the belief that only those who have participated directly in combat possess the legitimate epistemological authority to speak about war.

Buchanan further explains that, on the one hand, the ideology behind it does not suggest, as one might expect, a definitive answer to questions of veracity and verisimilitude, and it refuses "to admit that the factual nature of the answer doesn't matter" (2016, 29). On the other hand, "combat gnosticism ignores the fact that many voices can speak fictionally about the facts of war and that they can come from any quarter of war's experience" (2016, 30). Its ideology manipulates the notion of authority, "one conferred by the dubious term 'combat' while the epistemology it puts forward as superlative is no less suspicious than the loudest and unadorned pro-war propaganda" (2016, 30).

However, considering these points, it does not necessarily mean that *ancillary coverage* is entirely free of constraints or failures, unless we imagine, as Noam Chomsky did with his journalist from Mars, a writer from some other planet (Chomsky 2002, 69), preferably a planet where writers reside. This does not imply that, in the case of war literature, non-veteran writers are less trustworthy if we use the notion of trust. On the contrary, the latter has been shown to extend beyond war experience and to raise further issues related to war literature as a genre and *its coverage*. Moreover, even if accounts of war written by veterans are considered to offer the highest degree of verisimilitude, those written by non-veterans challenge how that verisimilitude is perceived.

Written mainly because the Iraq War "pissed the writer off," Mark Doten's novel *The Infernal* is an unconventional take on the "war on terror" that goes against both existing fictional representations of the American "war against terrorism" as well as those representations of the war that circulated in the media. One illustrative example in this sense is the novel's representation of war veterans and how its portrayal of them essentially avoids the fetishisation of war trauma. With the portrayal of Tom Pally, "soldier of the Gallant arms" (2015, 3), Doten is not imagining, as Brian Turner did in *My Life as a Foreign Country* (2014), a war veteran haunted by the hordes of "the wounded, and the maimed, and the traumatised, and the frightened and the shattered, and the shivering and the bruised, and the broken and the disfigured" (Turner 2014), but rather one whose most pressing issue is the fact that he is unable to secure dinner reservations on Valentine's Day at a restaurant that had been repeatedly mentioned by one of his comrades during their service in Iraq.

Matters turn even more uncanny when Pally realises he cannot keep the conversation going while still on the phone with the restaurant manager because "a mass of pale maggots was churning behind [his] lips and teeth" (Doten 2015, 112). The cause or the source of the maggots is never fully explained. However, the narration seems to suggest that even though Pally indirectly blames it on his service in Iraq, the maggots might indicate either that he is dead and what the readers see on the page are but the words of a ghost veteran or that he is metaphorically rotting on the inside.

The former suggestion, however, is somehow invalidated by the introductory "Dramatis Personæ" where Pally is described as "[a] soldier of the Gallant Arms; wife and son dead" (2015, 3), and where the fact that the author chooses to signal the death of Pally's wife and son seems to refute Pally's death. On the contrary, the latter suggestion is somewhat shyly supported by Pally's lifestyle and his way of relating to his family and friends. An alcoholic and a keen consumer of internet pornography who sometimes forgets to wipe his Internet browser's history, as well as somebody who cannot take the blame for not making those dinner reservations in time, Pally discovers that his mother lives on with the belief that he had died in combat. This final confession comes from his father, who imagines a gradual comeback for the prodigal son into the bosom of the family, first as "a *door-to-door salesman of world classics*" (2015, 214) and then as a lost-and-found son to be rewarded with "[a] full meal" (2015, 216). On this line of reasoning, with Tom Pally, Doten seems to be singling out the tendency of war veterans toward self-aggrandising by denying them the status of heroes and demonising them.

Essentially a remake of Dante's *Inferno* with characters taken from the Bush Administration, *The Infernal* is narratively disruptive and graphically visceral. At the core of its many storylines lies a sinister device called the "omnosyne," a technological apparatus designed for advanced torture and intelligence extraction. The omnosyne is less a machine than a metaphor—a chilling embodiment of the data-driven apparatus of modern warfare. Built to "reverse the entropy that humans throw off with every word and every thought," the device aims to generate a new, angelic language: "a superfluid new type of information... to speak as angels speak, in beams of light without friction or distortion" (Doten 2015, 184). Once connected to a living body, the machine extracts a "kernel of belief" (2015, 23), supposedly embedded deep within nerves and bone, by administering "terrible pain" (2015, 282). If the subject converts pain into pleasure, the machine readjusts, "they cut off the pleasure so that again it is pain" (2015, 282). However, just like a mad scientist who sees beauty even in the most gruesome experiments, Jimmy Wales, the inventor of the omnosyne, explains that the end of the process justifies the means: the subject ultimately reaches a point where "he is OK with himself at last" and "[a] look comes into the face, of such grace, such light—even with the mouth split open by the Jennings gag. That open mouth is no longer expressive of a demented rictus but of something else—total understanding" (Doten 2015, 283).

Nevertheless, Doten's Jimmy Wales is not merely a mad scientist worthy of a solitary castle hidden within a dark forest but also the puppeteer in a "spectacle of power" (Scarry 27). As Elaine Scarry explains in her seminal work *The Body in Pain: The Making and Unmaking of the World* (1985), through its very practice, torture "bestows visibility on the structure and enormity of what is usually private and incommunicable, contained within the boundaries of the sufferer's body" (Scarry 1987, 27). The omnosyne, in its monstrous impersonality, pushes this idea to its logical extreme by removing the concept of consent. Once a body is connected, there is no way to prevent information from being leaked; there is no intermediary consciousness between the source of the information, which is the prisoner's body, and the torturer. The body is not even allowed to die, as the machine will keep it alive until all information has been collected.

What Wales describes in his notebooks as the transformations that the body undergoes under torture, "the eyes on the twisted-back head darting and squeezing shut, the mouth wide, tongue swelling, the body jittering madly as though touched by high-voltage wires" (Doten 2015, 283), is essentially the rendition of an objectified "vision of suffering" that is further converted "into the wholly illusory but, to the torturers and the regime they represent, wholly convincing spectacle of power" (Scarry 1987, 27). Written in the first person, Wales's account of the omnosyne torture, along with the entire range of narratives the novel includes, has a further uncanny effect in that, at least for the duration of the read, readers find themselves inside the minds of both the torturer and the tortured, and then become representatives of that regime of power.

As extreme and as disturbing as these aspects portrayed in the novel might seem at first glance, it is worth pointing out that Doten's novel was published at a time when discussions on the ethics of torture had been rekindled by the release of the *Committee Study of the Central Intelligence Agency's Detention and Interrogation Program* in late 2014. *The CIA Torture Report*, as it came to be called in the international press, contained information about the agency's use of "enhanced interrogation techniques" that included "rectal feeding and rehydration," "confinement in a box," "the use of cold water," "sleep deprivation," "beatings and threats," and "waterboarding" (Laughland 2015), to mention just a few. In this context, Doten's novel and the "theory of the omnosyne" (Doten 2015, 23) bring to the whole discussion of torture an extended annotation, challenging the reader to imagine the ultimate consequences of the use of torture.

Although a vast amount of information is gathered through torture, Doten's narrative suggests that this information is of little value to those involved in the process: the tortured individual dies, and the torturer or reader is left with a chorus of voices speaking of different things and offering no meaningful closure. The kind of dialogue the novel engages in with *The CIA Torture Report* prompts a re-evaluation of both texts, making it impossible to determine which one influences the other. Although we know which is fictional and which is not, both seem to occupy the same space within our memory.

Nevertheless, despite the disruptive tendencies with which *The Infernal* engages the discourse surrounding the "war on terror," Doten's novel occupies a somewhat privileged position. Freed from the institutional responsibilities typically associated with proximal coverage, ancillary coverage enjoys a cumulative power of a different kind—more diffuse, more recursive, and perhaps more insidious. Its logic resembles a *snowballing effect*: whereas proximal coverage tends to accumulate facts and interpretations from individuals endowed with considerable symbolic, social, and cultural capital (Hodges 2011, 97), ancillary coverage goes further. It extends the process by absorbing and refracting elements of proximal coverage itself, or at least some reaction to it. *The Infernal* is no exception to this logic. Among the documents compiled by the Omnosyne is an entry attributed to Andrew Breitbart, labelled a journalist in the "Dramatis Personæ." His 'testimony,' however, amounts to little more than a repeated onomatopoeic "oink" embedded within random sequences of code, stretching over three pages. Ironically, the account concludes with the prompt to "EXPAND to see all 817 pages" (Doten 2015, 321), suggesting that the same nonsensical utterance continues across hundreds of blank digital screens. This is not journalism—not even a parody of it—but a metatextual reaction to something the fictional Breitbart might have said, a gesture that strips his words of consequence and reduces them to animalistic noise, as irrelevant to the discourse on war as the grunt of a pig.

Another striking example of this snowballing effect lies in Doten's portrayal of Osama bin Laden, rendered in imagery reminiscent of horror cinema. Despite this apparent deviation from what Charles D'Ambrosio, via Leslie Jamison, has called "the truth of the thing" (Jamison 2014), the representation remains remarkably faithful to—and critical of—the media constructions of Islamic fundamentalism that proliferated in the aftermath of September 11. Doten is not interested in depicting Osama bin Laden per se, but in interrogating how that figure was perceived, consumed, and weaponised. His portrayal becomes a critique of the cultural fantasy that reduced bin Laden to a symbol of essentialised evil, severed from any serious political or theological context. In doing so, the novel reflects, and distorts, the contours of a media spectacle designed not to inform, but to inflame.

This cumulative layering of discourse in The Infernal, along with the broader argument that fictional and non-fictional representations of the "war on terror" exist along a non-exclusionary continuum — at least from the reader's perspective — resonates with Linda Hutcheon's definition of historiographic metafiction. Like the texts Hutcheon identifies, Doten's novel deploys extensive parodic intertextuality and foregrounds its own metafictional architecture. With its cavalcade of "real people and events" and its mimicry of media soundbites and political rhetoric, The Infernal exemplifies what Hutcheon describes as the relocation of textual meaning "within the history of discourse itself" (Hutcheon 1988, 126). Meaning, in other words, is not forged solely between author and text, but between text and reader. Furthermore, Doten's novel, like Hutcheon's examples, underscores "art's critical relation to the 'world' of discourse — and through that to society and politics" (Hutcheon 1988, 140). The result is a novel that not only deconstructs its sources but also aspires to a didactic function, forcing readers to examine the ideologies embedded in the texts and images through which war is mediated and remembered.

An image is malleable, Doten seems to suggest, so malleable that we can do whatever we want with it. Apart from his occasional moments of prophetic madness, in Doten's infernal imagination, bin Laden appears as a sadist — like a vampire who needs to be fed daily with the fresh blood of his disciples, who, in turn, seem to be pulled from a circus act. Doten's bin Laden envisions a world shaped by the labyrinthine structure of his hiding place — a cave system where many followers get lost and are never found again. However, this does not come as a surprise to those familiar with how Islamic fundamentalists were portrayed in the media. "Prejudice against a group," Martha C. Nussbaum argues, "always involves fantasy" (Nussbaum 2012, 166). In his portrayal of the founder of al-Qaeda, Doten pushes the demonisation of the enemy that followed September 11 to its extremes and ridicules it as nonsensical.

Though it might seem excessively hyperbolic, Doten's portrayal of Osama bin Laden closely follows, and simultaneously interrogates, the conventions surrounding the depiction of Muslims in the post-9/11 media landscape. Over the past two decades, Farish A. Noor has argued, there has been a pronounced "inflation of the notion of the Muslim as a potential threat to society," to the point where Muslims are often endowed with superhuman traits. These exaggerated attributes serve to legitimise what Noor calls the "creation, expansion and perpetuation of the military-industrial complex" (Noor 2010).

> It would seem as if in the context of the 'war on terror' discourse Muslims have been endowed with a superhuman subjectivity that presents them with an extraordinary degree of agency, intelligence, endurance, the capacity to mobilize themselves and of course the super-human capability to withstand attack by conventional weaponry (which necessitates the purchase and use of greater weapons of destruction). Muslims have, in short, been re-invented as a super-human threat that can no longer be contained and defeated by conventional means alone. (Noor 2010)

This logic of containment and defeat is particularly salient when one considers the intensified surveillance Muslim communities have faced across the United States, especially in New York City, in the aftermath of 9/11. In *This Muslim American Life: Dispatches from the War on Terror* (2015), Moustafa Bayoumi documents how, following a series of leaks, it was revealed that the NYPD had embedded confidential informants in seven Muslim Student Associations (MSAs) at local colleges—including Brooklyn College, where Bayoumi himself teaches, and Baruch College. The same leaks listed forty-two "persons of interest," deemed dangerous not because of any overt actions but rather due to personality traits or social influence. One such individual, Mohammad Elshinawy, was singled out because, as the leaked memo reads, the "TIU [Terrorism Interdiction Unit] believes that [Mohammad] is a threat due to the fact that he is so highly regarded by so many young and impressionable individuals," as though personal charm itself constituted a potential weapon (Bayoumi 2015). In the logic of Noor's argument, it would.

In this context, Doten's fictionalisation of bin Laden does more than parody—it exposes the grotesque elasticity of post-9/11 representations. To borrow Judith Butler's vocabulary from *Precarious Life* (2004) and *Frames of War* (2009), Doten's depiction enacts a "differential distribution of precariousness and grievability" (Butler 2010, 31). By reducing bin Laden to a fictional caricature, the novel renders transparent the symbolic work that representation performs. The label "fictional character" allows Doten to exert ironic control over the exact mechanisms of dehumanisation that the media wielded in earnest. In doing so, he reframes the discussion: outside the fictional realm, certain lives, especially those cast as enemy or Other, are excluded from the sphere of grievability. They become lives that, in Butler's words, are "not 'regarded' as potentially grievable, and hence valuable," and are instead made to endure "starvation, underemployment, legal disenfranchisement, and differential exposure to violence and death" (Butler 2010, 25).

The reader, then, is not prompted to sympathise with a fully fleshed-out character, but with a phantasm—a composite image forged by years of media demonisation. Doten's "delivery system," to adopt David Palumbo-Liu's term, is overloaded with otherness (Palumbo-Liu 2012, 10–15). The text delivers too much, too quickly, and with too many competing referents, creating a sense of ethical dislocation. In that dislocation, however, lies the possibility of critical reflection. This saturation of representation forces the reader to reconsider the interpretive positions they may have previously adopted. Rather than facilitating identification, Doten's narrative produces what might be called a reparative *dis*identification. As Daniel O'Gorman argues, literature can challenge readers to "think about the framing of contemporary reality in ways that may help more radical 'new constellations' to begin to emerge" (2015, 22), placing them "in a better position to make informed decisions about the ideas and interpretations of reality to which [they wish] to subscribe" (2015, 50). Ultimately, Doten's novel asks an uncomfortable yet urgent question: have we, as readers and citizens, come to derive a kind of cathartic pleasure from the cruelty enacted in the "war on terror" simply because the so-called terrorist has been rendered so recognisably inhuman?

This shift of the reader to the centre of interpretation is revealing in war fiction, mainly because, as I have argued earlier, when it comes to the textual representation of specific events such as military conflicts, fiction does not hold a dominant position but is inherently part of a broader network of information sources. However, this dislocation does not necessarily cause an ideal reader to rely solely on the claimed truthfulness of *proximal coverage*, especially if that reader is aware of the limitations of such coverage.

Exiled, as it were, from the dominion of either wholly factual or wholly fictional registers, the reader encounters what might be termed a *parallax effect*. *This* refractive dynamic emerges from the interplay between proximal and ancillary coverage. This effect is most vividly observed in the way ancillary narratives echo, distort, or refract fragments of proximal discourse, re-situating them within altered imaginative landscapes. For instance, the image of a "thirsty dog that was lapping up a puddle of human blood" (Finkel 2011, 3) in the opening of David Finkel's non-fiction work *The Good Soldiers* reappears, eerily transformed, in Phil Klay's short story "Redeployment," where the protagonist is forced to shoot his dying dog after returning from Iraq. The image recurs, yet is made to resonate differently. A similar logic underpins Ben Fountain's *Billy Lynn's Long Halftime Walk* (2012), where grandiose political rhetoric about "freedom" and the so-called "clash of civilizations" is punctured by gallows humour and soldierly irreverence: "Dude," says one character, "maybe they don't hate our freedoms, maybe they hate our fat!" (Fountain 2012, 165). Likewise, the phrase "I'm the best friend you're ever going to have" (Fountain 2012, 178) echoes across both fictional and non-fictional terrains—from Fountain's novel to Sebastian Junger's *War*—its valence shifting with each contextual recalibration.

In light of these intertextual dynamics, it becomes increasingly plausible to extend Robert Entman's model of "cascading network activation" to encompass fictional narratives from ancillary coverage. If, as Entman suggests, news frames shape public understanding through a cascading hierarchy of institutional discourse, then ancillary narratives might be seen as participating in this cascade—albeit from a displaced or refracted vantage point. In the case of proximal coverage, works such as those by Junger or Hayden tend to provoke *post-factum* critical feedback by offering interpretations that can be directly compared with competing accounts. Ancillary coverage, by contrast, resists such comparison. Because these narratives are not accountable to factual veracity in the same way, their relationship to events and persons is often deliberately obscured or effaced through aesthetic strategies. As a result, the feedback they generate operates differently: rather than interrogating their fidelity to actual occurrences, readers engage with their internal "narrative necessities" — their linguistic architecture, their formal cohesion, and the coherence of the imaginative world they construct.

Considering all these factors and revisiting the initial question about the importance of structured narratives in achieving a cultural understanding of a military conflict, it is reasonable to assume that a balanced approach to *proximal* and *ancillary coverage* should not seek to prioritise *ancillary coverage* over *proximal coverage*. Instead, these two aspects should be viewed as *points on a continuum* rather than as separate levels. The shift towards *ancillary coverage* does not diminish the significance of *proximal coverage*; instead, it is within this *continuum* that a comprehensive understanding of the event can be achieved. War fiction challenges Hodges's "chain of authentication" (2011, 98) by presenting varied, non-fictional accounts against different backdrops. However, it does so to underscore the malleability of discourse and the inherent inaccessibility of war to both war writers, whether direct participants or not, and their readers.

This process ultimately offers a tentative answer to two key questions about war writing and reading. For those contemplating how to write about war, it emphasises the importance of establishing certain discourses before beginning to write. It underscores the necessity of constructing and interrogating discursive frameworks before committing experiences to the page. For readers of war texts, it uncovers the deep trauma experienced by war participants. Most importantly, accessing this through literature does not equate to comprehending the full horror of war, its absurdity, its irrevocable loss of life, or the vast and fragmentary constellation of individual experiences. Instead, it entails confronting the combatant's struggle to impose coherence or achieve closure. "Traumatic memory is not narrative," Jonathan Shay argues in *Achilles in Vietnam*, "it is experience that reoccurs, either as full sensory replay of traumatic events in dreams or flashbacks, with all things seen, heard, smelled, and felt intact, or as disconnected fragments" (Shay 2010).

Ultimately, the relationship between journalism and fiction in war writing is more about dialogue than opposition. *Proximal coverage* may provide immediacy and factual basis, but it is through ancillary *coverage* that we glimpse the deeper fractures, hesitations, and emotional truths of conflict. Fiction does not aim to "correct" journalism; instead, it questions the frames through which wars are perceived and remembered. By exploring voices at the margins and reimagining the unspoken, *ancillary coverage* complicates our understanding and keeps open the possibility of rethinking what war truly means. Perhaps it is this very openness, this refusal to close off interpretation, that makes fiction essential within the broader continuum of war discourse. In this sense, rather than offering final answers, war fiction invites us to remain uneasy, to read and reread, and to confront the persistent difficulty of truly understanding the war experience.

5. The Peacekeeping Novel Is a War Novel: Ancillary Coverage of the "War on Terror" as a Form of Cultural Selection

5.1 Men Against "Roaches" and Other Enemies

Stripe is portrayed as an exemplary soldier, entirely committed to his duty. Despite experiencing a recurring dream in which a girl confesses her love for him, Stripe remains stoic and unemotional. When asked about his feelings when pulling the trigger, he asserts he feels nothing. The racial and gender dynamics within his team seem inconsequential, as they unite in their fight against the "roaches," a common enemy threatening humanity. The soldiers' interactions are notably harmonious, free from power struggles or romantic entanglements. Their sole focus is the battle. The only difference between the protagonist and the other team members is that Stripe is a novice and still has much to learn. Viewers of *Black Mirror*'s fifth episode (season 3), "Men Against Fire," will not give him the benefit of the doubt because everything around him is constructed to reinforce a specific view of his fellow combatants and the war they are fighting. These soldiers appear entirely devoted to their cause, a devotion that becomes increasingly uncanny as the episode unfolds. The situation depicted in the episode also feels eerily familiar.

In that episode, as the soldiers wake up, they are informed that Her Falls, one of the villages under their supervision, has been attacked again and that they need to investigate. It is Stripe's first time out, and apart from the recurring dream, we know nothing about his past or his reasons for joining the army. However, as they discuss their mission, he seems to be firmly opinionated regarding the "roaches," who had raided the village and contaminated food storage, and who were assisted by a local man with "some interesting views on roaches" (Verbruggen 2016). On their way to Mr Heidekker's place, whose benevolence towards the "roaches" is blamed on some unidentified mental health issue, one of the soldiers argues that these benevolent locals only make their job more difficult. "Out here," the soldier explains, "you got rustic fucks throwing them scraps. No wonder it's taken so long to mop shit up" (Verbruggen 2016). Stripe agrees: "But how can anyone be dumb enough to help a fucking roach?" As we get a first glimpse of the "roaches," we can almost concur.

The "roaches," human-like but sharp-toothed and unable to use language except for guttural screams that resemble those of animals, are terrifying and grotesque. The first reaction they trigger is *revulsion*. Their faces are a mix of alien-like features, with skin so tight that it seems to hide any sign of emotion, human or otherwise. As one of them runs away, it could be mistaken for a woman. "There's shit in their blood," the platoon commander tells Heidekker while she tries to squeeze information out of him, "that made them that way. The sickness they're carrying. That doesn't care about the sanctity of life or the pain, or about who else is gonna suffer. We don't stop the roaches in five, ten, twenty years from now, you're still gonna get kids born that way, and then they're gonna breed" (Verbruggen 2016). They are ideal scapegoats: easily recognisable and driven by malicious intent that surpasses their appearance. Their looks reflect their character, so killing them causes no remorse.

Mr Heidekker, whose name bears a resemblance to Heidegger, is also intimidating and somewhat familiar. His bearded face is seen against a white wall on which a cross is on display, and his almost religious stubbornness in cooperating with the soldiers recalls those of Islamic fundamentalists seen on television in the aftermath of 9/11. Furthermore, because we are not given access to his motives, except for the ones we infer from his portrayal, Heidekker becomes as evil as those he is trying to protect. The feeling is reinforced even further when the soldiers find a "roach nest" on the top floor of the house. The man is *obviously* lying about the whereabouts of the alleged "roaches."

The soldiers are equally terrifying in their machine-like perfection. An implant into their brains not only makes communication simple and more effective but also turns them into perfect killing machines. They can shoot accurately even from vast distances and do not seem to have emotions other than the desire to serve their purpose, purging the country of "roaches." "Hunting's in my blood," one of the female soldiers says when another soldier calls her "farm girl," "some of us are naturals." Later, the same farm girl says that if she manages to kill two "roaches" in one go, she would want "to come for, like, an *hour*" (Verbruggen 2016). After detaining Heidekker and killing two of the roaches, the soldiers boast about their mission. Stripe is the one with the beginner's luck: his first time out, he gets to kill two roaches. The other members of his platoon almost envy him. "You lucky motherfucker, man," one of the soldiers exclaims as they head out of Heidekker's house, "sweet dreams for this asshole" (Verbruggen 2016). When Stripe visits Arquette, the shrink, the latter tells him he has done a big thing and should be proud of himself.

However, everything begins to unravel for Stripe. One of the "roaches" he manages to kill in action exposes him to a green light that seems to tamper with the system on which the soldiers operate. Following the exposure, his body begins to show signs of fatigue and loss of focus. One night, as he wakes up from his idyllic dream, he suddenly realises that all his team members are doing the same thing: dreaming in unison. Then, he begins to be affected by the sounds and smells around him, elements he had not even been aware of before. It is almost as if the machine is letting him be affected by emotions. Fear begins to creep into his bones as his commander is killed in action. Then, as Stripe's implant goes berserk, the "roaches" killed so ruthlessly by the "farm girl" are suddenly human, and the "farm girl" begins to resemble a killing machine indeed. The grunts and guttural sounds that seemed so threatening become comprehensible language, and the language they speak is the same as that spoken by the villagers in Her Falls. Stripe attacks the "farm girl," who keeps telling him they are "roaches" and must be exterminated.

"The whole thing is a lie," Stripe tells Arquette towards the end of the episode. It was the "Mass Implant" that made the soldiers perceive the "roaches" as mindless and diseased animals. The green light to which Stripe is exposed at the beginning of the episode is, in fact, a virus that shuts down the implant from within.

"Roaches," a battered Stripe tells Arquette, "they look just like us." Arquette's reply is as terrifying as Stripe's discovery: "Of course they do. That's why they're so dangerous" (Verbruggen 2016). In this final confrontation between the regular soldier and the mastermind of military tactics, Arquette also briefly mentions the "Mass implant" and places it within a dialectics of war. In the two World Wars, Arquette explains, only fifteen per cent of people fired to kill, while most of them missed on purpose. That percentage went up in the Vietnam War, but the soldiers who came back suffered from crippling mental health issues. The "Mass Implant" makes it easier to kill because it controls what soldiers see and what they feel. "It's a lot easier," Arquette smugly explains, "to pull the trigger when you're aiming at the bogeyman" (Verbruggen 2016). Moreover, the "roaches" are the perfect embodiment of the bogeyman. They are repulsive, and setting up a dialogue with them is impossible.

Besides these minor revelations about modern warfare, "Men Against Fire" also examines how the enemy is defined through discourse. The term used to label them, "roaches," influences the soldiers' perception of these alleged enemies. Typically, roaches are considered pests that must be eradicated, and this belief is reinforced by the "Mass Implant," which conditions soldiers to think and act accordingly. When Stripe flees from the "farm girl," who seems to have gone on a killing spree, he is rescued by one of the "roaches" in an underground shelter. Catarina, the now humanised "roach," tells Stripe that even civilians without the "Mass implant" despise them "because it's what they've been told":

> Ten years ago, it began. Post-war. First the screening program, the DNA checks, then the register, the emergency measures. And soon everyone calls us creatures. Filthy creatures. Every voice. The TV. The computer. Say we have we have sickness in us. We have weakness. It's in our blood. They say that our blood cannot go on. That we cannot go on. My name was Catarina. He was Alec. Now we're just roach. (Verbruggen 2016)

The name brings a host of consequences that make the lives of those who bear it impossible. They are hunted down like the deer the "farm girl" refers to during their missions. Their very existence has been criminalised. They have been turned into scapegoats, and although the war in "Men Against Fire" cannot be historically placed, the situation portrayed in it bears a familiar resemblance. The term used to describe the enemy, "roach," recalls the "hajji" of the wars in Iraq and Afghanistan. Akin to "roach," the term "hajji," which was used extensively to denote both civilians and combatants, particularly in Iraq, is "another iteration of the American habit to devise a slur and use it to describe an enemy, particularly an enemy that is seldom seen or that is rarely identifiable as a martial unit of a recognised nation-state" (Buchanan 2016, 155). The terms "hajji" and "roach" have several precedents in this sense. "Similar to 'charlie' and 'gook' and 'kraut' and 'Jap'," Buchanan argues in this sense, "the word *hajji* has become the latest epithet for the United States' enemy Other" (2016, 155). It is not necessarily a code name intended to facilitate communication; however, it is a term that implies a certain amount of contempt.

Thus, "Man Against Fire" is not just a war film but also a visual analysis of the discursive practices surrounding war, which influence how war is understood. It functions as a discursive practice through its dialectics of before and after, also relocating the enemy. The "roaches" are not the enemy but the war machine that initially turned them into "roaches." Once this discursive machine's operation is exposed, it portrays the enemy as clever enough and equipped with the means to prevent the ordinary soldier from believing they are fighting against an imagined enemy or for the wrong side of the conflict. The film criticises the war not for the carnage it causes but because it is fought for all the wrong reasons. "Men Against Fire" does not wage war on war because the war depicted in the film does not yet exist; instead, it warns about how much modern warfare relies on technological advances and discursive practices. Modern warfare involves more sophisticated weapons *and* establishing a consensus about who the enemy truly is.

5.2 The Peace Within War and the War Within Peace: A Literary Genealogy of the "War on Terror"

War narratives, much akin to war films, often appear to wage war on the wars they seek to portray, so much so that critics and readers alike define them as anti-war. This feature is most salient, particularly when these narratives do not seem to shy away from the gruesomeness of amputated limbs and the frailty of human lives and morals. Ultimately, there is not much choice when it comes to writing about war since, as Elaine Scarry puts it, the sole purpose of every war strategy is to "out-injure by injuring and disarming" the other (Scarry 1987, 69). However, despite their gruesomeness and because of the literary contract that obliges readers to conceive of these texts as literary texts on account of their claims, war narratives also foster the sense that the reader can always opt out when matters become excessively gory. "The act itself of writing about war," Lynne Hanley argues in *Writing War: Fiction, Gender, and Memory* (1991), "no doubt misrepresents war by promoting a false sense of security" (Hanley 1991, 5). If a war veteran wrote the work, the reader is somewhat reassured that the author has survived to tell the tale and that, once the book concludes, both the reader and author will be alive and well. "However vivid and gripping the account," Hanley rightly suggests, "a reader's experience of war will never include one of war's most definitive emotions: the immediate and entirely legitimate fear of losing one's life, limbs, or sense, or of seeing the person next to one lose his" (1991, 5). Given this false sense of security, as well as the unexpurgated portrayal of death, defining war narratives as anti-war has almost become the default mode in literary criticism.

However, defining these narratives as anti-war, aside from being an easy way out of a theoretical quagmire, also presents a moral stance that seems questionable when taken for granted, as it often is. According to this moral view, since war narratives highlight the physical and psychological damage wars can inflict on readers, it is almost a moral duty for both the reader and the critic to believe that these narratives are anti-war. Furthermore, because they depict such damage as absurd and unnecessary, they must be seen as condemning the wars they portray. The more graphic and vivid the descriptions in a war novel, the stronger its pacifist message appears to be. These narratives cannot be pro-war because that would imply endorsing the destruction that wars embody.

Therefore, reading war literature becomes a moral act that opposes forgetting, aims to memorialise the damage, and ensures its persistence by passing it on to future generations. The brutal iconography of war, with its bloodshed and victims, thus challenges the role of art and aesthetics by refusing to frame itself aesthetically. Although some imagery in these novels might seem awe-inspiring, it cannot "for reasons of piety and respect for the victims—be framed in aesthetic terms" (Däwes 2011, 3). Reading war literature takes on didactic overtones. Reading it differently would be regarded as a sign of moral laxity.

The moral stance behind pacifist readings of war literature is fundamentally problematic: it is both limiting and, at times, dangerously close to ideological propaganda. Such interpretations often impose a prescriptive path on the war writer, demanding that they persuade the reader that a pacifist stance is not only different from, but also morally better than, the violent nature of war itself. This supposed distinction, presented as clear and straightforward, promotes a reductive approach where war texts are categorised by their perceived moral position or the emotional responses they aim to provoke. However, this framework risks oversimplifying the complexity of war narratives, reducing their aesthetic and epistemological subtleties to an unchallenged moral directive. Instead of shedding light on the human experiences of conflict, such an approach reduces literature to a tool for moral teaching.

In practice, however, the distinction between pro-war and anti-war stances is far less clear-cut than one might hope. In *Waging War on War* (2015), Giorgio Mariani argues that the anti-war concept in literary studies remains inadequately theorised because it is "largely a reactive, negative concept, whose lack of substance is implicit in its parasitical nature" (2015, 10). Unlike war, which can be identified as a tangible and historically verifiable phenomenon, anti-war is not anchored in an equally objective or ontologically stable foundation. Instead, it functions primarily as an effect produced in the reader through specific narrative and rhetorical strategies (2015, 11). From this perspective, if an anti-war effect is indeed the goal, then writers might logically be compelled to depict war as vividly and grotesquely as possible: the more violent and blood-soaked the narrative, the more forcefully it might repulse the reader and induce a moral rejection of warfare.

However, this approach is fraught with complications. Excessive violence can easily be dismissed as gratuitous or manipulative, undermining the very message it seeks to convey. As Mariani observes, the anti-war concept is fundamentally "disruptive and dubious," perpetually at risk of collapsing the aesthetic and ethical complexities of a literary text into the blunt instrumentality of propaganda (2015, 7). Paradoxically, overtly didactic anti-war sentiments often provoke greater discomfort among critics and readers, who recoil from what they perceive as moral coercion rather than genuine artistic engagement.

The concept is difficult to pin down because, as Mariani asserts, "war literature, including literature commonly considered to be 'anti-war,' always entertains an ambivalent, contradictory, troubled relation with the violence it is asked to represent" (Mariani 2015, xi). Indeed, Mariani continues, "[all] war texts are at risk of feeding on the very violence they purportedly wish to denounce" (2015, xi). This paradox has led many to argue that war texts are not inherently anti-war; instead, they acquire a pacifist essence only through subsequent interpretation and analysis. The cultural and political context in which such decoding occurs is crucial. As Mariani notes:

> Whether a poem, a novel, or a film may be said to be anti-war or not ultimately depends on the way they are decoded—and the way they are decoded, to a considerable extent, hangs in turn on the protocols of reading sponsored by a given culture, whether hegemonic or resistant. Within pacifist circles, *The Iliad* may be read as an anti-war text; within an imperialist culture, it is a poem extolling the manly virtues of the warrior. (2015, 6)

This inherent simultaneity leads Mariani to suggest that war novels should be read as "war-and-peace novels" (2015, 20), an ostensibly inclusive but ultimately evasive formulation. Rather than resolving the issue, this designation sidesteps it, replacing conceptual clarity with an unproductive ambiguity. If war narratives can be understood as simultaneously pacifist and belligerent, it follows that they are, in effect, neither one nor the other—a position that risks nullifying any critical or ethical stance altogether.

While this duplicity might hold for recent war narratives—or at least for contemporary interpretations—it becomes more tenuous when applied to "older" narratives such as *The Iliad*. As Catharine Savage Brosnan contends, there is little doubt that early war texts and chants served specific functions: alongside commemorating military exploits as collective history, they also set standards of martial conduct and inspired a spirit of warlike valour (Brosman 1992, 86). While some men enlisted primarily out of familial duty, "for many of the most sensitive and reflective among young men, literary texts seem to have been a crucial factor in their love of the military and their enthusiasm for war" (1992, 87). These narratives, in their idealisation of war and their portrayal of "vital themes of self and manhood," functioned effectively as *invitations* to military life (1992, 88). From this perspective, they can be understood as indirect yet potent instruments of war propaganda.

Compared to these older texts, contemporary war narratives, particularly those emerging since the Vietnam War, have evolved in markedly distinct ways. "The purpose," Brosman argues, "of telling the war 'as it is' and not as it is supposed to be, may come from the desire to demystify a phenomenon that centuries of history had glorified," and in doing so, to support pacifism. Describing war as "a phenomenon of half-organised, half-random destruction and death" is not necessarily anti-patriotic; rather, by adopting this approach, a writer can challenge the vestiges of heroic and patriotic traditions inherited from the past (Brosman 1992, 89).

One manifestation of this demystifying tendency, which Brosman does not explicitly address, is the way contemporary war narratives increasingly foreground the soldier's life after returning home. While battlefield scenes may still echo the grandeur found in older texts, it is the soldier's re-entry into civilian life that provides the crucial counterpoint, tempering, or even neutralising any lingering sense of martial heroism. What emerges as most striking in these narratives is not only the shallow gratitude of well-meaning civilians but also the profound existential void and alienation that the returning soldier experiences. Indeed, in many of these works, it is not the horror of combat but rather the impossibility of resuming an ordinary life that most compellingly draws the soldier back toward the battlefield. Paradoxically, it is the ideal of civilian "bliss" that transforms into the most persuasive invitation to military life.

A crucial point worth emphasising in both Brosman's and Mariani's arguments is how they conceptualise peacefighting and pacifism, which, in my view, are distinct, if not outright opposed, notions. While Brosman maintains that war narratives can be considered pacifist when they reveal and critique the discursive construction of war, Mariani argues that such narratives become pacifist only through our interpretive frameworks—that is, when we read them in ways conditioned by our cultural and historical contexts. Furthermore, Brosman's model permits at least a conceptual separation between pacifism and belligerence, suggesting that the two can coexist but remain fundamentally distinct. Mariani, by contrast, sees these categories as mutually constitutive or, at the very least, existing on a fluid continuum.

Brosman, in contrast to Mariani, addresses the problem at a more conceptual level. When she argues that contemporary war narratives demystify war and therefore display pacifist tendencies, she implies that what is being demystified are "the heroic and patriotic *traditions* of the past" (1992, 89), not war itself in its entirety. Peacefighting, according to Brosman, is thus not about preventing future wars or negating war as such; rather, it is about transforming our perception of how wars are represented and mythologised. In this view, war narratives are pacifist only insofar as they expose the internal contradictions and inconsistencies inherent in patriotic and heroic portrayals of war. Mariani, too, gestures towards this idea when he observes that certain war novels—such as Hemingway's *A Farewell to Arms*—may critique "the emptiness of an older martial rhetoric," but can do so only by adopting "a new rhetoric that will inevitably be in a relation of both opposition and proximity to war" (Mariani 2015, 19). However, I would argue that Brosman's focus is not on martial rhetoric *per se*, but instead on how this rhetoric is harnessed to sustain and propagate the myth of war itself.

At first glance, Brosman's position suggests that pacifist tendencies in war literature are inherently retroactive, a consequence of the evolving functions of such texts. Modern war writing, she argues, has transformed into "a way of resolving, or attempting to resolve, war experiences whose recurring drama must be relived, reexamined, and, through an apparent catharsis, accepted" (1992, 90). Thus, in Brosman's framework, pacifism does not necessarily entail persuading readers that wars are intrinsically harmful or unjust. Instead, it implies an emphasis on revisiting and dissecting past conflicts, precisely because these wars are already concluded and therefore safer to examine. From this perspective, peace-fighting in fiction is not so much a preventative measure against future conflicts as it is an educational project: a means of re-educating readers about the mechanisms through which war discourse is constructed and perpetuated. Alternatively, in a more pragmatic sense, it functions as an exercise in cultivating compassion towards veterans who must navigate the aftermath of these historical traumas.

However, even as modern writers strive to expose the vacuity of martial rhetoric, Brosman suggests such efforts are ultimately insufficient. "[War] remains," she explains, "an enduring cultural myth as well as a continuing human experience, and thus is still preeminently a topic for literature" (Brosman 1992, 95). Disrupting this mythic continuity and dismantling the cultural mythology of war does not necessarily redirect literary interests toward explicitly pacifist themes. On the contrary, "whether in the form of initiation," Brosman further observes, "metamorphosis, purification, sacrifice, or death and rebirth, the war experience is made up of other mythic patterns, sometimes in a powerful form; and it is hard to imagine that readers can be dissuaded from the pull of such experiences" (1992, 95). Irony, too, offers no resolution: war language and myth persist, even when ironised. Ultimately, Brosman seems to suggest that the only viable solution lies not merely in acknowledging the myth's enduring power but in constructing a counter-myth potent enough to rival, and perhaps subvert, the myth of war itself.

5.3 The War Narrative Before the War: *The Things They Carried*, *Hystopia*, *The Sympathiser*, and *Anatomy of a Soldier*

Though it might be tempting to argue that the "true" pacifist novel, in Brosmanian terms, originated with Tim O'Brien's *The Things They Carried* (1990), I fear the issue is far from settled. Nevertheless, it is reasonable to suggest that the Vietnam War's literary representation marked a pivotal development in this direction. Perhaps the singular nature of that conflict demanded a new narrative approach, or perhaps broader evolutions in fiction created the necessary conditions for O'Brien's work to emerge. *The Things They Carried* not only demystified the war experience itself but also became a cultural artefact, a kind of unruly dog that could be positioned wherever debates about war experience and representation might arise. Part of its cultural resonance stems from its formal innovations. "Whether only a few pages long or spanning an entire book," Stefania Ciocia notes in *Vietnam and Beyond: Tim O'Brien and the Power of Storytelling*, "his stories frequently unfold through multiple, interweaving narrative strands, each covering a different temporal dimension or exploring the relationship between facts, memory and imagination, or even providing various perspectives on the same theme and separate accounts of the same events" (Ciocia 2012, 185). Yet, perhaps its most remarkable achievement lies in O'Brien's capacity to conceive storytelling itself as a "viable epistemological tool" (2012, 185).

Returning to Elaine Scarry's conception of war — as an activity designed to "out-injure by injuring and disarming" the adversary (Scarry 1987, 69) — we can see why war, as a discursive practice, is an inherently non-viable epistemological tool: it does not seek the establishment of shared knowledge but instead enforces silence through domination. While one might describe war metaphorically as a "dialogue," given its underlying logic of exchange, its ultimate purpose resembles a trial by combat, where the hegemony of one interlocutor is established by obliterating the other. As Scarry puts it, "war is in the massive fact of itself a huge structure for the derealisation of cultural constructs and, simultaneously, for their eventual reconstitution. The purpose of the war is to designate as an outcome which of the two compelling cultural constructs will by both sides be allowed to become real, which of the two will (after the war) hold sway in the shared space where the two (prior to war) collided" (Scarry 1987, 137).

For Brosman, undermining this violent structure requires not merely contesting it but building a parallel framework capable of surpassing it—a project that O'Brien arguably undertakes in *The Things They Carried*. Mark A. Heberle, in *A Trauma Artist: Tim O'Brien and the Fiction of Vietnam*, argues that O'Brien's collection does not simply rewrite his earlier works; it also continually revises itself in a self-reflexive interrogation "upon its own status and purpose as imaginative writing" (Heberle 2001, 181). If war, as a discursive practice, aims to annihilate its interlocutor, O'Brien's stories conjure a paradoxical figure: an interlocutor who has been both obliterated and yet reified, allowing for a fragile, ambiguous dialogue to persist.

Another narrative that rigorously interrogates this dynamic is David Means' novel *Hystopia* (2016). Set in the late 1960s, the novel—presented in Nabokovian fashion as a manuscript discovered in a drawer—depicts a treatment called "enfolding," designed to suppress painful memories and thus assist war veterans in coping with depression and post-traumatic stress disorder. In one of the interviews included in the "Editor's Note," Markus Decourt mentions a drug called Tripizoid, a chemical catalyst integral to the enfolding process. "Pop one of those suckers," Decourt explains, "go through the reenactment of your original trauma—we're talking controlled, man, scripted, staged right down to the gestures, the whole show run by these Shakespearean motherfuckers—and you'd come out cured" (Means 2016, 11). Strikingly, however, the reenactment does not involve each veteran's unique "original trauma" but rather a standardised one: "We were doing scenes from the *Iliad*," Decourt adds, "Hector and all that" (2016, 11).

Eugene Allen, the purported author of the manuscript, elaborates further:

> The process of reenacting particulars of the causal/trauma events turns (enfolds) the drama/trauma inward. Confusion is undoubtedly an element of the curative process: a mysterious blurring of the line between what happened and what is reenacted. One folds into the other, and during the period of adjustment the patient typically experiences disjunction and bewilderment. He or she may vehemently reject the curative process, making statements to the effect of "This is pure bullshit. I remember everything. Nothing has been tucked away. I'm the same old screwup. You can't just yank me in here, make me reenact a bunch of the shit I went through, in a lame-assed way, not even close to what it was really like, and expect me to forget about it." But in most cases, the patient does forget about it, becoming fully immersed in the reenacted trauma's nullification of the real trauma. (Means 2016, 18)

Embedded within the convoluted folds of Means's narrative is a trenchant critique of those stories that, as Brosman suggests, exploit the heroic mode. In Means's view, such narratives attempt to rewrite or reshape veterans' experiences to the point where the line between fact and fiction becomes dangerously blurred. In Eugene Allen's words, the reenactment of trauma within these narratives ultimately nullifies the original trauma itself. Consequently, Allen's narrative emerges as a desperate attempt to reclaim what has been effaced, to recover authentic war memories that these distortions threaten to obliterate.

If we apply Brosman's terminology, *Hystopia* would indeed serve as a compelling example of a narrative with pacifist inclinations. Published roughly forty years after the end of the Vietnam War, Means's novel can afford to diverge significantly from earlier fictional portrayals of the conflict and its historical contours. By depicting a parallel America where President Kennedy serves a third term, the novel rehearses—almost in a frustrated, pastiche-like manner—the gestures of older war narratives while simultaneously critiquing them. Stewart Dunbar, one of the interviewees quoted in the "Editor's Note," articulates this tension:

> History has always had a hard time allying itself to the novel. [Eugene Allen's] creative effort, disturbed though it might be, is realistic to the extent that it captures the tension of history meeting the present moment. Is it not possible that someone looking back at the past, even the very recent past, and bending it this way and that [...] might actually rearrange the—No, I can't express the thought without getting Einsteinian and saying that

retelling the past, as the young man does in this novel, might actually change the past. But perhaps that is exactly what I mean. (Means 2016, 15–16)

A similar, and perhaps even more sophisticated, "creative effort" to change our perception of the past appears in Viet Thanh Nguyen's novel *The Sympathizer* (2015). Like *Hystopia*, Nguyen's novel engages with questions of war representation and memory and might also be read as a pacifist novel in a Brosmanian sense. Its narrative strategy is particularly striking. Told from the perspective of a nameless narrator who is half-Vietnamese, half-French, and educated in the United States—a country for which he harbours both love and contempt—the novel deliberately foregrounds divided identity. As the title suggests, the narrator is a "sympathiser," yet, as the story unfolds, it becomes clear that his sympathies shift as capriciously as the wind. "I am simply able to see any issue," he remarks of himself with almost sideshow curiosity, "from both sides" (Nguyen 2016, 1). This very fluidity renders him ultimately incapable of taking a definitive stance.

When offered a job as a consultant on a Hollywood film about the Vietnam War, the narrator seizes the opportunity to challenge American-centric representations and to amplify Vietnamese perspectives. As Philip Caputo observes in his review for *The New York Times*, "the more powerful a country is, the more disposed its people will be to see it as the lead actor in the sometimes farcical, often tragic pageant of history" (Caputo 2015). The United States, he argues, is emblematic of this tendency, having long viewed the Vietnam War as an exclusively American drama, reducing Vietnam to an exotic backdrop and its people to mere extras. Nguyen's narrator attempts to subvert this narrative but nearly dies when an on-set explosion erupts prematurely.

In this battle over cultural hegemony waged on the film set, it is the Americans who hold the means of production—and thus control the dominant version of the war. They even romanticise the act of representation itself. Much like the reenactments in *Hystopia*, the film in *The Sympathizer* serves as a surrogate for a war experience. As the film's pompous director proclaims to the crew, "It is the moment when we show that making this movie was going to war itself.

When your grandchildren ask you what you did during the war, you can say, I made this movie" (Nguyen 2016). In this formulation, every war movie becomes a new war—an aesthetic conquest masquerading as commemoration.

The irony implicit in the director's statement is multilayered and operates on at least two distinct levels. On the one hand, it ridicules the ease with which a "powerful country," to borrow Caputo's phrase, so readily produces aestheticised images of war—images that not only stand in for but claim to surpass the reality of combat itself. It also exposes a pervasive belief that beautifully crafted war narratives are somehow equivalent to, or even more authentic than, what James Campbell famously termed "combat gnosticism," the notion that only those "who have actively engaged in combat have access to certain experiences that are productive of, perhaps even constitutive of, an arcane knowledge" (1999, 204). On the other hand, the irony simultaneously lays bare Hollywood's profoundly formative role in shaping American cultural consciousness. Its echo of the 1915 British recruitment poster—which sought to induce guilt in those who refrained from military service—implies that creating a cultural artefact about an actual event can assuage, or even nullify, any lingering sense of moral culpability. In the director's egomaniacal imagination, making a film about war becomes synonymous with waging war itself:

> The Movie was just a sequel to our war and a prequel to the next one that America was destined to wage. Killing the extras was either a reenactment of what had happened to us natives or a dress rehearsal for the next such episode, with the Movie the local anaesthetic applied to the American mind, preparing it for any minor irritation before or after such a deed. Ultimately, the technology used to actually obliterate natives came from the military-industrial complex of which Hollywood was a part, doing its dutiful role in the artificial obliteration of natives. (Nguyen 2016)

From this vantage point, *The Sympathizer* emerges as a biting critique of the American way of perceiving war and of the institutions that so eagerly manufacture and disseminate its imagery. Hollywood, as one of these prime meaning-machines, becomes an easy yet essential target for the narrator's scathing commentary. "Yes, art eventually survives war," the unnamed narrator ruminates after the director's self-aggrandising speech, "its artefacts still towering long after the diurnal rhythms of nature have ground the bodies of millions of warriors to powder, but I had no doubt that in the Auteur's egomaniacal imagination he meant that his work of art, now, was more important than the three or four or six million dead who composed the real meaning of the war. They cannot represent themselves; they must be represented" (Nguyen 2016). With its shrewd deconstruction of the cultural machinery behind war narratives, *The Sympathiser* is a novel with strong pacifist tendencies. Although these tendencies are *retroactive*—in that they revisit past conflicts and seek to resolve lingering issues—they also function prophylactically, aiming to immunise readers against future iterations of triumphalist or aestheticised war discourse.

Harry Parker's *Anatomy of a Soldier* (2016) also belongs to this category of texts that aim to liberate the reader by constructing an alternative discursive framework. Set primarily in Afghanistan, the novel is narrated from the perspective of various objects that come into contact with the protagonist, Tom Barnes, a British army captain. In contrast to Tim O'Brien's short story "The Things They Carried," Parker narrates the story through the "eyes" of these inanimate objects, a narrative technique reminiscent of Richard Dawkins's concept of the "selfish gene," wherein agency is diffused among seemingly passive elements. For instance, the first three chapters are told by a tourniquet, a bag of fertiliser, and a boot.

In Parker's narrative universe, each object is granted a distinct voice, distinguished not only by the poetic inflexion of its language but also by its relational proximity to Captain Barnes. The body armour, for instance, expresses itself in a markedly more lyrical register than a running shoe, and even an explosion becomes an occasion for alliterative flourish. However, all this is executed with deliberate intention: Barnes himself is rendered primarily as an object—an assemblage of flesh, metal, and medical intervention—whose humanity is repeatedly mediated and fragmented by the implements of war. Whereas in O'Brien's text soldiers are defined by the objects they carry, Parker extends this notion by transforming them into objects altogether, thus collapsing traditional hierarchies within war narratives.

This radical levelling between soldiers and objects produces further effects. On the one hand, it underscores the idea that in war, human lives often assume the status of objects, an idea echoed in the technological and affective flattening depicted in "Men Against Fire." The objectification—or at least the systematic suppression—of human qualities facilitates what Elaine Scarry might call more "efficient" or "productive" wars, wherein the moral and corporeal weight of violence is obscured. On the other hand, this narrative strategy illuminates the fragile boundary between pacifism and belligerence. By articulating the relationship between objects and people, and consequently between intention and outcome, Parker invites the reader to interrogate what truly constitutes an anti-war stance, as opposed to a covert perpetuation of militaristic logic.

One striking example of this relationship is evident in the fourth chapter, where an improvised explosive device recounts its own story. This brief, at times poetic narration—punctuated by fragmented dialogue among its makers—traces the "life" of the IED from its construction to the moment it fulfils its fatal purpose: the explosion that sends Captain Barnes to the hospital. Unlike other objects that encounter Barnes, the IED maintains a chilling detachment from the human beings upon whom it inflicts violence. The relationship between the explosive device and the soldiers who tread upon it is depicted as a purely mechanistic encounter, akin to the interaction of two substances in nature that, upon contact, produce an inevitable reaction:

> Eventually, I felt vibrations—the rhythm of walking—that were faint at first but then converged towards me. A weight pressed down. The dry mud above me flexed, cracked down and pushed my metal strips together. A circuit was created that filled my wires instantly.
> I was alive.
> The metal rod at the heart of me detonated, a controlled high-explosive force that triggered the mix in me to react.
> I functioned. (Parker 2017, 19)

The device resembles a force of nature, set into motion by a chain of reactions, and the soldiers who step on it are reduced to mere catalysts—anonymous weights pressing down, indistinguishable and interchangeable. They are not portrayed as soldiers with agency, but rather as interchangeable triggers; it might just as easily have been an animal or a civilian.

Other objects, however, relate to Captain Barnes in markedly different ways. For instance, the fifth chapter is narrated by a breathing tube, recounting the moments immediately following the IED explosion. Here, the relationship is rendered almost as one of gentle respect:

> A man fed a laryngoscope into your mouth, and another lifted your head back. Your tongue was held open, and I was pushed into you. Your mouth had dirt in it and a blade of grass. I slid past the laryngoscope that directed me into you. I scraped down through you, grazing your voice box, past your glottis, down through your trachea, until I reached the top of your lungs. One of them was smaller and collapsed. A nurse inflated my balloon cuff that puffed out and held me inside you. (Parker 2017, 22)

In this instance, the reaction between the object and the soldier is no longer overtly violent, save for minor scrapes and grazes. The narrative voice of the breathing tube assumes an almost paternal, protective tone, inhabiting what might otherwise have been a blind spot in the soldier's own perception. Since Barnes is unconscious during this scene, the tube assumes the role of narrative custodian, preserving not only the soldier's life but also the continuity of his story. The breathing tube exists simultaneously to save the soldier and to sustain the narrative thread itself.

Parker elevates these objects beyond simplistic moral binaries of good and evil by defining them solely in relation to the human intentions that animate them. Their ethical value is not intrinsic but contingent upon the purposes of those who wield them; they exist merely as extensions of human will, much like the "unmanned aerial vehicle" that narrates chapter thirty-three. These tools are never inherently instruments of war, just as language itself is not *inherently* martial or pacific. Instead, both objects and language are fluid media, capable of embodying conflicting impulses depending on context and intention. From this vantage point, war literature cannot be said to be genuinely "about war" in any essential sense unless the social and political environment that produces and receives it is itself marked by conflict.

Mariani's perspective on peacefighting in fiction diverges subtly yet significantly from Brosman's. Drawing on James Dawes's distinction between the "disciplinary model" of war texts—where violence and language are understood as "mutually constitutive"—and the "emancipatory model," which views rhetoric and force as "mutually exclusive" (Dawes 2002, 1), Mariani contends that we should interpret "war writings as ways to 'handle' the intractable reality of war and that we distinguish them, like proverbs, on the basis of their prevalent rhetorical strategies" (Mariani 2015, 16). In his view, some war novels function therapeutically or cathartically, akin to proverbs intended to console; others adopt a more explicitly admonitory tone, examining war from a critical distance. Peacefighting, in his view, demands not a mere rhetorical flourish but a more sophisticated deployment of language capable of reshaping our comprehension of war's brutal reality and its discursive underpinnings.

However, Mariani's proposal is weakened by the implication that one might establish a kind of evaluative system to weigh and measure rhetorical strategies and thereby determine a text's moral or political valence. According to this logic, if a war text's dominant rhetorical strategy promotes a pacifist agenda, it must be categorically anti-war, and vice versa. Yet Mariani's framework, like Dawes's, places undue responsibility on readers or critics to define what precisely constitutes the "dominant" strategy. The so-called "peace novel," unlike the overtly propagandistic "pacifist novel," is "a war novel one reads with the intention of assessing not only its representation of war but also what image of 'war's other' (as Nick Mansfield aptly describes peace) the text either implicitly or explicitly constructs" (Mariani 2015, 20). Mariani seems to imply that the text itself is ultimately devoid of intrinsic intention and becomes meaningful only through the interpretive lens applied to it. In this formulation, the peace novel risks becoming an unread war novel—an abstraction that fails to resolve the underlying problem. Indeed, this raises further questions: Do we all share the same understanding of "prevalence" in rhetorical strategy? Are all war narratives latent peace narratives awaiting our decoding? Should we develop an algorithm to quantify and adjudicate these strategies? If we were to discard the moral stance implicitly assumed in reading war literature, would the balance tip decisively, or would it collapse altogether?

The brief answer to this crucial question is that it would not simply tip the balance in one direction or another; rather, it would completely upend the balance. While Mariani views pacifist and belligerent tendencies as coexisting—or existing "along a continuum" (Mariani 2015, 63)—thus enabling readers to oscillate between them depending on a text's dominant rhetorical strategies, I contend that, in the context of literature addressing the American "war on terror," these two categories are not only inseparable but essentially *coterminous*. They must therefore be replaced by a third category, or at the very least redefined, to account for these texts more adequately. This necessity arises primarily from a profound displacement in how we conceive of war and its representations today, as well as from what Buchanan describes as the "genre's incoherence [that] has never resolved the running battle that has long existed regarding experience, authenticity, and aesthetics" (Buchanan 2016, 21). Indeed, displacement and incoherence emerge as central motifs in the texts examined in the remaining part of this chapter, signalling a need to move beyond the inherited dichotomy of pacifism and belligerence toward a more nuanced interpretive framework.

5.4 The War at Hand and the War Literature That Is Not

In *Authoring War: The Literary Representation of War from the Iliad to Iraq* (2011), Kate McLoughlin proposes a similar line of reasoning when she asserts that "the language of war can be simultaneously emancipatory and disciplinary, that it obfuscates even as it aims to illuminate, and vice versa" (McLoughlin 2011, 20). However, like many critics of war literature, she ultimately succumbs to the default perspective. "While war literature may dazzle," she immediately adds, "with its technique and resourcefulness, its subject matter can—should—sadden and horrify" (2011, 20). Although she observes that these two elements are undoubtedly intertwined in an "ethical-aesthetical nexus," she also indirectly implies that the subject matter is what renders it primarily an ethical issue. "The dazzlement's raison d'être," McLoughlin concludes her introduction, "is to keep the horror in view" (2011, 20). Even humour and irony are acceptable, provided that a particular war text keeps the horror of war in focus. "References to laughter in the war zone," McLoughlin argues later in her book, "strike a jarring note," and they might seem "not only callous but inhuman, puerile, and even in bad taste" (2011, 165). According to McLoughlin, the only thing that redeems such references is when they underscore the absurdity of war. Beneath the laughter, the horror of war must persist.

What makes this issue particularly challenging is the relationship this type of narrative maintains with the reality it aims to depict. Because it retains strong ties to the reality it constantly references, the genre must attend to both ethics and aesthetics. It must be ethical because it engages with human affairs and can influence the very reality it seeks to portray or critique. At the same time, it must adhere to specific aesthetic standards, given its literary nature. If one attempted to resolve this dilemma through pure logic pushed to its extreme, the only way these narratives could be unequivocally pacifist or belligerent would be by altering their relationship with the reality they depict. The absence of wars in "real life," or even the lack of any knowledge of war, would render these narratives seemingly pro-war, while the absence of peace, in any form, would conversely make them appear anti-war. Alternatively, if responsibility were once again placed on readers—such that reading these narratives during peacetime would make them seem pacifist, while reading them during wartime would render them belligerent—the entire approach would become deeply problematic.

Nevertheless, even this solution, however improbable, is problematic. To some critics of war literature, removing the "real war" from the equation would strip these narratives of what makes them compelling as war stories in the first place. If a novel does not exist without the war it depicts, Wallis R. Sanborn argues in *The American Novel of War: A Critical Analysis and Classification System* (2012), then it cannot truly be classified as a war novel. "A novel of war," Sanborn explains, "must have war and the physical, psychological, spiritual, social, and cultural effects of war; otherwise, it is not a novel of war. A novel of war must be born of war; otherwise, it is not a novel of war" (Sanborn 2012, 12).

To some extent, Sanborn suggests that it is precisely the war depicted in these stories that grants them aesthetic and literary value. The novels he examines, including but not limited to Stephen Crane's *The Red Badge of Courage* (1895), Thomas Alexander Boyd's *Through the Wheat* (1923), and Karl Marlantes' *Matterhorn* (2009), were chosen for their "literary presentation of war." While a number of these texts, he admits, might not be historically celebrated for their literariness—however one may define that term critically or popularly—they nonetheless present war in a distinctly literary fashion (Sanborn 2012, 12). It is almost as if the violence they depict is what renders them worthy of serious attention. "*The Red Badge of Courage* and *Through the Wheat*," Sanborn contends, "are seminal texts in that each work, early in the American canon, showed the violence—and bloody cost—of war realistically for a readership that, up to that particular point in history, had not been exposed to war violence in such a realistic mode" (2012, 12). By extension, given that these narratives cannot exist independently of the wars that provide their aesthetic value and cultural status, it follows that they inevitably perpetuate—if only discursively—the very conflicts they portray. As a result, they cannot be truly considered pacifist narratives.

However, the root of this dilemma, a factor that Mariani and Sanborn overlook, at least when addressing contemporary war literature, precedes any debate on the pacifist or belligerent nature of war texts. The fundamental issue lies in the labels assigned to these works, which ultimately shape how they are analysed and understood. Even when we speak of pacifist or belligerent tendencies in fiction, the very theoretical framework of war literature compels us to think in belligerent terms. Any discussion of peacefighting necessarily references the war it concerns, just as any debate about pacifist tendencies in literature must implicitly acknowledge the prior failure of pacifism.

If there are traces of peacefighting in Tim O'Brien's *The Things They Carried* (1990), they did not prevent the Vietnam War from unfolding, nor did they forestall subsequent conflicts. These texts are fundamentally war narratives, only later categorised into opposing moral camps. It is as if we claim they are inherently belligerent because we first label them as war novels, yet still insist they *can* be pacifist. Ultimately, I argue that without proper attention to how we label these texts, we must reconsider the entire theoretical framework on which future analyses rest—a move that would render many prior distinctions obsolete.

At its most basic level, the label of "war literature," a term used carefully regarding these texts, invites scrutiny. Attentive readers may have noticed that "war on terror" is often enclosed in quotation marks. This is not accidental; it signals a deliberate critical stance by those who employ it. The quotation marks serve to indicate distance from both the context in which the phrase was coined and from those who adopted it unquestioningly. "Captivated by a powerful master narrative after 9/11 and in the run-up to the Iraq war," Seth C. Lewis and Stephen D. Reese observe in "Framing the War on Terror: The Internalization of Policy in the US Press," "American journalists found it difficult to resist being drawn into the national anxiety and general pro-Bush patriotic fervour" (Reese and Lewis 2009, 778). Those who chose to distance themselves from this collective fervour often placed the phrase in quotation marks, signalling it as a ready-made, ideologically loaded construct rather than an objective descriptor.

The phrase "war on terror," contrary to what many might assume, was not coined by George W. Bush in his address to the nation ten days after the 9/11 attacks. Its origins reach back to the Reagan administration. In 1984, President Reagan first invoked the phrase to justify legislation aimed at countering terrorist groups in the wake of the 1983 Beirut barracks bombings, an attack that claimed the lives of 242 Americans. What ultimately compelled Reagan to sign the National Security Decision Directive 138, however, was the abduction and subsequent torture of the CIA's Beirut station chief, William Buckley, in March 1984. "The signal success of this war on terror," John Arquilla notes in *Foreign Policy*, "came in a campaign against the Abu Nidal Organisation [...] which was conducting terrorist hits for hire on behalf of Iraq, Libya, and Syria"

(Arquilla, n.d.). When portions of Reagan's directive were later declassified, it became clear that it authorised the use of paramilitary squads to wage *de facto* wars against guerrillas, an aggressive element somewhat obscured by the seemingly broad and ambiguous umbrella term "war on terror."

Then, as now, the phrase concealed a multitude of unnecessary military actions, partly because of the nature of the events that provoked it. Like Reagan's use, Bush's adoption of the phrase "emerged as a powerful ideological frame" (Lewis and Reese 2009, 85). Its deliberate vagueness regarding who the enemy was or where the conflict might unfold, coupled with its "flexibility and good-versus-evil judgment," provided crucial moral cover for pre-emptive military action (2009, 86). "More broadly," Seth C. Lewis and Stephen D. Reese argue in "What is the War on Terror," the phrase "took on ideological dimensions, not only providing linguistic cover for widespread political change in the name of national security but also offering an institutionalized way of seeing the world—a frame as influential as it was subtle" (2009, 85). Or perhaps, one might say, as influential as it was catchy.

The phrase was self-explanatory. Like the Death Star in the *Star Wars* franchise, it functioned as a blunt narrative device that simplified reality, much like an effective advertisement. It divided the world into two sharply opposed camps. In the language of the Bush administration, Farish A. Noor argues in his analysis of the "war on terror" discourse, "the world was carved into two neat, oppositional blocs that could not possibly be engaged in any meaningful debate or dialogue with each other, simply because the constitutive Other of 'terror' or the 'forces of terror' was something that one could not engage with rationally in the first place" (Noor 2010). Viewed through the lenses of this rhetoric, Noor explains, the world became monochromatic; the line separating the Muslim world and the West turned into a perpetually shifting frontier. The phrase also cast the Other, against whom this war was waged, as inherently irrational and primitive in both thought and action. "The irrationality of the Other," Noor further notes, "meant that the Other also could not speak to and of itself, which allowed the 'West' to comment on the ontological state of the Other as the negative Other" (Noor

2010). As a discursive instrument, the "war on terror" did not merely describe a conflict but entrenched "the cultural and historical biases that have long served as obstacles to genuine intra-cultural and inter-cultural dialogue between the West and the Muslim world" (Noor 2010). Once coined, the phrase magnetically attracted reality to itself, as cultural artefacts gather around a selfish event.

As the phrase gained wider circulation in the media, it acquired legitimacy and authority. It became, as Lewis and Reese put it, "a socially shared organising principle" (2009, 86). Supported by the press, "the Bush administration effectively framed the march toward war in Iraq as an extension of the War on Terror, allowing the Iraq war to achieve levels of public support that were nearly as high as those for the war in Afghanistan" (2009, 87). By characterising 9/11 as a declaration of war, Adam Hodges argues in *The "War on Terror" Narrative: Discourse and Intertextuality in the Construction of Sociopolitical Reality* (2011), and framing the response as a "war on terror" (rather than an investigation into terrorist crimes), the administration accomplished a "discursive achievement [that] has naturalised one characterisation of 9/11 and America's response to terrorism as the dominant way to talk about the issue" (Hodges 2011, 23). With each repetition and reuse, the phrase gathered momentum, eventually shaping reality in its own image.

Although the intellectual elite eventually disavowed the phrase, the damage had already been done, and it continued to circulate widely. Moreover, the criticisms raised against it often targeted the phrase itself rather than the concrete actions it justified — actions that were, in many cases, deeply contested. Despite the multitude of objections, John Brenkman identified four principal arguments that emerged over time. The first, repeatedly advanced by Noam Chomsky, concerned the assertion that "[armed] force was an unnecessary and excessive reaction to the September 11 attack" (Brenkman 2007, 80). As Chomsky argued, the most appropriate response would have been a trial akin to the Nuremberg proceedings, which would have brought the perpetrators to justice through legal, rather than military, means.

The second argument, closely related to the first, advocated for intervention by the United Nations, which "would have been a more appropriate and/or more effective mechanism for responding to September 11 than a U.S.-led military and diplomatic offensive" (Brenkman 2007, 80). Similarly, in the January/February 2002 issue of *Foreign Affairs*, Michael Howard, the eminent Anglo-American military historian, maintained that rather than launching a "crusade against evil," as President George W. Bush framed it, "many people would have preferred a police operation conducted under the auspices of the United Nations on behalf of the international community as a whole, against a criminal conspiracy whose members should be hunted down and brought before an international court, where they would receive a fair trial and, if found guilty, be awarded an appropriate sentence" (Howard 2002). Yet such an approach was one the American administration would never have accepted.

Brenkman, however, contends that both arguments are flawed, primarily because there is a profound difference between the events of 9/11 and the conflicts addressed by trials such as Nuremberg. Those trials took place only after a "cessation of hostilities" on both sides; they were retrospective closures, not ongoing battles. In contrast, following 9/11, "the Islamic terrorists were still active, their planning of violent acts ongoing, and their leaders 'at large'" (Brenkman 2007). Hostilities persisted, rendering the "war on terror" a continuing rather than concluded affair. Conducting a trial similar to Nuremberg would have first required apprehending the alleged perpetrators and bringing them into custody — a closure that was not only impractical but impossible in the immediate aftermath. As Brenkman underscores, "If they can be found — that, of course, was the question of the hour: not only whether they could be found, but how" (Brenkman 2007, 91). Even the eventual killing of Osama bin Laden, the alleged mastermind behind 9/11, failed to deliver the sense of closure that such a trial might have offered.

Howard, like Brenkman, considers such alternative approaches fundamentally unsuitable to the situation at hand. Not only does he recognise that the United States has "little respect" for an international body such as the United Nations, but he also argues that the attacks had grievously wounded American pride. "Such an insult to American honour," Howard contends, "was not to be dealt with by a long and meticulous police investigation conducted by international authorities, culminating in an even longer court case in some foreign capital, with sentences that would then no doubt be suspended to allow for further appeals" (Howard 2002). The elusive perpetrators had to be brought to justice swiftly and decisively. While the involvement of international agents was occasionally invoked, it was articulated only in vague, ideological terms. When George W. Bush addressed the nation ten days after the attacks, he declared that the United States would seek support from police forces, intelligence services, and banking systems worldwide, but strictly as deemed appropriate and under American direction, framing this cooperation as part of a larger civilizational struggle. "The civilised world," Bush announced midway through his State of the Union address, "is rallying to America's side" (*The Guardian* 2001).

The very nature of the event, with its profound immediacy, is again underscored by both Howard and Brenkman. As Howard explains, when the media demanded "immediate stories of derring-do, filling their pages with weapons, ingenious graphics, and contributions from service officers," even suggesting an alternative course of action was "dismissed as 'appeasement' by politicians whose knowledge of history is about on a par with their skill at political management" (Howard 2002). There was simply no time, or willingness, to invoke historical precedent or caution; the event's urgency dictated a response perceived as both bold and immediate. As Brenkman asserts, the imperative in the aftermath was to weaken terrorist networks without delay because "[the] dangers of the terrorist offensive were immediate, while the task of removing its causes or sources is the work of decades" (Brenkman 2007, 84).

The third argument advanced against the idea of a "war on terror," an argument shared not only by Chomsky but also by prominent intellectuals such as Susan Sontag—articulated most famously in her brief response to 9/11 published in *The New Yorker* and later reflected upon in her essays collected in *Styles of Radical Will* (1969)—posits that "U.S. actions past and present are the true cause of the terrorist attack, and, therefore, addressing the grievances in the Arab and Islamic world is the most appropriate (or only justifiable) course of action to take" (Brenkman 2007, 80). Closely related to this is the fourth argument, which attributes the rise of Islamic fundamentalism to the unresolved Palestinian-Israeli conflict. According to this line of reasoning, the proper solution — one that the United States ought to have pursued — would have been to resolve that conflict, including the establishment of a Palestinian state, rather than embarking on a military offensive against al Qaeda (Brenkman 2007, 80). However ideal such solutions might have appeared, they would have transformed what many saw as an urgent act of self-defence into a series of protracted diplomatic negotiations. In the charged climate of the time, such negotiations were swiftly dismissed as a form of "appeasement," insufficient to satisfy a public impatient for retribution and immediate results.

Thus, the phrase "war on terror," though amorphous in substance, functioned like a cognitive puzzle, akin to the mind-training games in which one must name the colour of a word rather than read the word itself. While it did not describe an actual "war" in any traditional sense, its rhetorical force was undeniable and persistent. So pervasive was its grip on the public imagination that when U.S. military interventions escalated in Iraq and Afghanistan, the literature emerging from these theatres was readily classified as literature of the "war on terror," and by extension, as war literature. The transition seemed almost natural. These texts were often written by American soldiers returning from foreign deployments, grappling with the psychic scars of violence and the burdens of post-traumatic stress disorder. Since President George W. Bush had already declared it a "war," the texts were seamlessly categorised as war narratives, reinforcing the semantic power of the phrase itself.

Labelling these texts as war narratives is not entirely mistaken. If we follow Sanborn's definition of war literature, most of them fit comfortably into this category. Their central focus is "the war at hand," and the violence they depict is concrete and immediate, not symbolic, metaphorical, verbal, or merely imagined (Sanborn 2012, 12). These narratives also rely heavily on war rhetoric: their narrators and characters "continually use such rhetoric — war lingo, war slang, war clichés, war abbreviations and acronyms, and [...] war propaganda and obfuscation" (2012, 13). Death, whether of fellow soldiers or noncombatants, is an omnipresent spectre, and destruction is a dominant theme woven into their fabric. The "dyad between occupying/invading forces and the indigenous/local people" is clearly articulated, as is the hierarchy between officers and enlisted men (2012, 16). Finally, these narratives often reference prostitution, since, as Sanborn provocatively asserts, there cannot be "war and warriors — and texts of war — without prostitution" (2012, 18). Yet, the ease and almost automatic certainty with which we assign these labels should give us pause. Or, to borrow Dr. House's sardonic phrasing, calling a bear a dog does not make it a dog.

What prompts my hesitation is precisely the first criterion Sanborn identifies in his definition, which resonates with my earlier reflections on the relationship these narratives have with the reality they depict. When Sanborn contends that the central subject of a war narrative must be "the war at hand," he implicitly suggests that these texts cannot exist independently of the wars they represent. If we were to sever this connection between the conflict and its textual representation, it is the text that would suffer most, bereft of its very *raison d'être*. This foundational dependence becomes the *sine qua non* condition for categorising a work as a war text, or at least as the war text of a particular conflict. A novel like *Hystopia*, although thematically centred on the Vietnam War, transcends this restrictive framework and gestures towards a broader meditation on the nature and legacy of war itself.

This does not necessarily mean that all wars share the same core, or that each war is merely a variation on some eternal, immutable conflict. Instead, it may suggest that all war narratives — or indeed narratives more broadly — can absorb and incorporate events, whether military or social. Conversely, these events can shape the narratives in return. *Hystopia* can resonate with the "war at hand," such as the "war on terror," just as *The Sympathizer* can. It is almost as if, to follow Brosman's historical perspective on the evolving purposes of war literature, modern writers have recognised that the tighter the connection between a specific war and its textual representation, the more rapidly that text risks becoming obsolete.

One creative response to this problem has been to adapt the war genre in a way that makes it highly receptive to hybridisation with other genres. A particularly compelling choice has been investigative fiction. John Renehan's novel *The Valley* (2015), for example, recounts the story of Lieutenant Black, who is sent to a remote combat outpost in Afghanistan to conduct an after-action report. Peter Molin, in his review of Renehan's novel, observes that it "maps the highly structured form of a crime novel onto the equally structured form of a war novel," a combination that in Renehan's hands "feels harmonious and productive" (Molin 2015). The investigation unravels a series of unexpected and disruptive issues: rogue sergeants have divided the platoon, and a poppy-growing and heroin-distribution network implicates some of the soldiers.

As Molin further explains, the novel "reads as if Renehan had grafted J.K. Rowling's *The Cuckoo's Calling* onto Joydeep Roy-Bhattacharya's *The Watch*, and then mixed in elements of Aaron Gwyn's *Wynne's War*" (Molin 2015). All three of these novels, although distinct in style and approach, share Afghanistan as their setting and are all shaped by the conventions of the crime genre. As we shall see, Afghanistan has proven especially fertile ground for this narrative strategy. Moreover, if one assumes that these fictional investigations focus exclusively on the so-called "enemy" — in this case, the Taliban — one is likely to be surprised. A closer examination of literature emerging from the "war on terror" reveals curious, even unsettling, features not only in narratives about Afghanistan but also in those set during the war in Iraq.

The first of these peculiar aspects, which makes me see these novels as decisively departing from the traditional war story, is that the supposed enemy is displaced, out of place in a manner that feels both strangely ancient and starkly modern. In war fiction, the enemy often appears as a source of profound unease, much like Mr Hyde in Robert Louis Stevenson's *The Strange Case of Dr Jekyll and Mr Hyde* (1886), who invariably provokes "a visible misgiving of the flesh" in those who encounter him (Stevenson and Mighall 2002, 58). When American journalist Mary Douglas, the protagonist of Martha Gellhorn's *A Stricken Field* (1940), arrives in the newly occupied Czech capital from Paris, one of the first sights that strikes her upon disembarking is the brash confidence of a group of German tourists:

> The regular transport plane from Berlin had landed a few moments before their plane from Paris, and the customs was crowded with German tourists, wearing belted suits and swastika lapel buttons. They carried cameras, by straps slung over their shoulders, and seemed very much at home. The people from the Paris plane stood apart and watched the Germans without friendliness. The Czech customs officials appeared to be embarrassed by the Germans who talked loudly with each other and argued about having to open their suitcases. Then, the Germans drove from the airport in a special bus, and the place became quieter. (Gellhorn 2011, 4)

In Gellhorn's narrative, the enemy's belligerence is, at first, overlooked, as if such arrogance could not be reconciled with any more profound understanding of shared humanity. Yet as the story unfolds and Douglas begins to realise the Germans' intentions are deadly serious, it becomes clear that the initial "visible misgiving of the flesh" felt by the Parisians is far from unfounded. Horrified by what she witnesses, Douglas comes to align herself fully with the Czech citizens, recounting a narrative of Nazi atrocities that confirms and justifies their sense of dread and resistance.

In Ben Fountain's *Billy Lynn's Long Halftime Walk* (2012), by contrast, the enemy against whom the "war on terror" is ostensibly waged is conspicuously absent, existing only as a spectral presence in the memories of the Bravo Squad soldiers. In the novel, the soldiers are not ducking bullets on a distant battlefield but find themselves in Dallas, Texas, "deep within the sheltering womb of all things American—football, Thanksgiving, television, about eight different kinds of police and security personnel, plus three hundred million well-wishing fellow citizens" (Fountain 2012, 21). They are there because, back in Iraq, they participated in a firefight that was serendipitously captured on film by a journalist. The footage went viral, transforming them into national heroes and sending them on a propaganda tour. They are even promised a Hollywood movie adaptation of their exploits, a promise that quickly evaporates because films about Iraq had "underperformed" at the box office (2012, 6). The values of the American public they encounter on this tour seem bewilderingly misaligned with those of the soldiers themselves, highlighting a profound disconnect between lived experience and its mediated spectacle.

This misplacement of the enemy has led writers and critics such as Karl Marlantes to conclude that Fountain's novel is, at its core, a critique of "the American way of watching war" (Tait 2012). This critique is especially evident not only in the soldiers' propaganda tour—staged to bolster the morale of a nation already wavering in its belief in the wars in Iraq and Afghanistan—but also in the grotesque spectacle of their marching alongside cheerleaders and dancers during the halftime show of a football game. Like the cheerleaders, the soldiers are transformed into mere entertainers, absorbed into the machinery of mass entertainment.

When these two discourses, that of the soldiers and that of the performers, are narrated simultaneously, it is the latter that ultimately drowns out the former. In Fountain's novel, the enemy does not manifest as a group of menacing insurgents but rather as the insatiable, complicit mass of well-wishing Americans at home, who crave spectacle above all else. "They hate our freedoms?" the protagonist wonders bitterly. "Yo, they hate our actual guts! Billy suspects his fellow Americans secretly know better, but something in the land is stuck on teenage drama, on extravagant theatrics of ravaged innocence and soothing mud wallows of self-justifying pity" (Fountain 2012, 11). Ultimately, Bravo Squad is redeployed to Iraq without securing the movie deal they had hoped for, their momentary fame dissipating as swiftly as it was manufactured.

6. Families and Their Soldiers, Soldiers and Their Families

6.1 Now Survive the Homecoming: Phil Klay's *Redeployment*

This *misplacement of the enemy* blurs the boundary between homeland security and battlefield threat. It redefines peace as another kind of hostility, as returning home becomes a new form of conflict. This idea is evident in Phil Klay's short story "Redeployment," which opens his National Book Award-winning collection of the same title. When Sergeant Price hands in his rifle upon returning home, he does not know what to do with his hands: "First I put them in my pockets," he explains, "then I took them out and crossed my arms, and then I just let them hang, useless, at my sides" (Klay 2014, 6). The gesture evokes the unsettling sensation of a phantom limb, an absent part that can still be felt as if it were present.

Even simple, well-meaning questions, meant to comfort, become sharp and accusatory. "How are you?" morphs into "How was it? Are you crazy now?" (Klay 2014, 8). Each interaction carries a latent suspicion, echoing the wary tension soldiers learn to associate with enemy encounters. The war experience estranges even the most intimate gestures, turning warmth into mechanical ritual. "I moved in and kissed her," Price recounts of his wife, Cheryl. "I figured that was what I was supposed to do. But it'd been too long, and we were both too nervous, and it felt like just lip on lip pushed together" (2014, 8). To Cheryl, Price becomes a figure to be feared rather than embraced.

This silent estrangement between two people who once knew each other as intimately as their own skin unsettles the belief that war exists only on foreign fronts. Instead, the narrative demands a redefinition of both "fronts," suggesting that the true enemy may not be foreign at all but found in the returning soldier's inability to rebuild a world untouched by the knowledge of war. Or rather, it is the soldier's trained incapacity to reconcile the imagined homeland longed for on the battlefield with the alienating reality of the homeland to which they return. "And glad as I was to be in the States," Price confesses, "and even though I hated the past seven months and the only thing that kept me going was the Marines I served with and the thought of coming home, I started feeling like I wanted to go back. Because fuck all this" (Klay 2014, 11). The real enemy becomes the realisation that one cannot erase the violence of war, not only from the soldier's body but also from the idealised image of home itself. "We took my combat pay," Price says with biting irony, "and did a lot of shopping. Which is how America fights back against the terrorists" (2014, 11). Any lingering illusion of a pure or ideal war is dismantled in two short, devastating sentences.

The misplacement of the enemy goes hand in hand with the individuation of the soldier-turned-civilian, who must now confront this new adversary alone. On the battlefield, as Sebastian Junger explains, each soldier bears a duty to the group they belong to, and "every soldier had a kind of de facto authority to reprimand others—in some cases even officers" because "there was no such thing as personal safety out there; what happened to you happened to everyone" (Junger 2011, 160). In Wilmington, while shopping with his wife, Price relives the battlefield experience—but now without his squadmates, which renders the experience all the more disorienting and threatening. Like the father in McCarthy's *The Road*, Price cannot imagine a world in which knowledge of what happened is absent. Those who lack that knowledge embody an ignorance that is both disheartening and almost offensive to those who survived and to the memory of those who did not:

> In Wilmington, you don't have a squad, you don't have a battle buddy, you don't even have a weapon. You startle ten times checking for it and it's not there. You're safe, so your alertness should be at white, but it's not.
> Instead, you're stuck in an American Eagle Outfitters. Your wife gives you some clothes to try on and you walk into the tiny dressing room. You close the door, and you don't want to open it again.
> Outside, there're people walking around by the windows like it's no big deal. People who have no idea where Fallujah is, where three members of

your platoon died. People who've spent their whole lives at white. (Klay 2014, 12)

Reality, in this context, is perceived at different speeds and intensities, shaped by profound changes in a soldier's brain chemistry. "I could spot a dime in the street," Price explains, "twenty yards away. I had antennae out that stretched down the block" (Klay 2014, 12). Unlike McCarthy's father and son, who wander through a world physically altered to the point of near-erasure, Price's homeland remains unchanged in its material form. Yet its details become more salient, even estranged. As Dexter Filkins notes in his review of Klay's collection, "armed conflict so fundamentally alters the environment it takes hold of that no aspect of life escapes undistorted: not love, not friendship, not sleep, not trust, not conversation" (Filkins 2014). What changes is the homeland's failure to evoke the same powerful ideals that first inspired these soldiers to enlist and sustained them throughout their time in combat.

However, Klay's relocation of the enemy, which parallels his critique of American society at large, goes deeper still, reaching a point where the narrator's rancour ultimately turns against the reader in the closing paragraphs of the collection's first story. On the surface, Price takes his dog, Vicar, to a place where he plans to euthanise it due to an illness that has left the dog in constant pain. As he looks at Vicar, he recalls an episode from his deployment, when all the other Marines opened fire on an insurgent hiding in "a big round container filled a quarter way with liquid shit" (2014, 15), while he stood frozen. Yet, as he prepares to aim his AR-15 at the ailing dog, his training takes over, and his mind shifts away from the animal to consider a very specific "you," a second-person figure at both ends of the gun. The narrator almost instructs the reader on how a human body would react to being shot:

> The first two [shots] have to be fired quick, that's important. Your body is mostly water, so a bullet striking through is like a stone thrown in a pond. It creates ripples. Throw in a second stone soon after the first, and in between where they hit, the water gets choppy. That happens in your body, especially when it's two 5.56 rounds traveling at supersonic speeds. Those ripples can tear organs apart.

> If I were to shoot you on either side of your heart, one shot…and then another, you'd have two punctured lungs, two sucking chest wounds. Now you're good and fucked. But you'll still be alive long enough to feel your lungs fill up with blood.
> If I shoot you there with the shots coming fast, it's no problem. The ripples tear up your heart and lungs and you don't do the death rattle, you just die. There's shock, but no pain. (Klay 2014, 15–16)

Although seemingly harmless on the page, this display of force offers the story a disappointing, even anticlimactic, ending, departing from the kind of resolution readers might expect. The reader is cornered, led into a conclusion as inevitable and pitiful as Price's dying dog. The narrative converges on this moment, compelling the reader to imagine themselves as the target, thus providing the closest approximation to the sensation of going to war. At the same time, this is the narrator's bitter recognition that, however harrowing or menacing the narrative may seem, it cannot inflict real violence on the reader beyond the realm of imagination. Once the story ends, the "attack" in the reader's mind also ceases. Alongside this realisation lies the belief that with each reading, the looming threat will not fade into familiarity but instead grow more acute. This risk-free display of force aims to instil a lingering, unsettling sensation in the reader—an unease that persists long after the story has concluded.

War narratives serve as a means of sharing combat experiences with those who have not witnessed them firsthand. By extension, these stories are generally intended for non-combatants, since those who have lived through war seldom feel the need to revisit those memories or the emotions tied to them. This exchange of stories has also remained, for the most part, a male domain. Apart from a few notable exceptions, most contemporary war stories are written by men. Out of fifty-four titles listed by Peter Molin at the end of 2017, forty were authored by male writers. Although the emergence of "war on terror" literature, beginning with Nadeem Aslam's *The Wasted Vigil* in 2008, was initially marked by a significant presence of female writers (with 2013 standing out as a particularly prolific year for women), the genre gradually became dominated once again by men. The year 2014 was especially emblematic in this regard, with the publication and immediate success of Atticus Lish's novel *Preparation for the Next Life* and Phil Klay's short story collection *Redeployment*. Klay's work, in particular, seemed to open the floodgates for a new generation of male war writers. His debut collection, which won both the National Book Award for Fiction and the National Book Critics Circle's John Leonard Award in 2014, quickly established itself as a cornerstone of the emerging literary canon.

However, it was not the accolades that set Klay's work apart. The significance of *Redeployment* lay in something prior to any formal recognition: it was the narrative voice that distinguished it. Several factors contributed to this impact: Klay served in Iraq as a Marine, and he possessed the rare ability to write in a voice that was both compelling and intimate—one that felt personal yet representative, masculine yet reflective. His tone resembled that of an old war veteran who cannot recall everything but remembers just enough vivid details to convey an entire world within a few lines. "It was Klay's story's immediately established voice," Donald Anderson writes in his review for *WLA: War, Literature and the Arts*, "that caught me" (Anderson 2014). It was a voice that commanded attention—not with force, but with the quiet authority of a comrade confiding in another.

Although it may seem trivial or self-evident, the narrator's voice in war narratives plays a decisive role in shaping how the story is received and interpreted. This is not to suggest that narrative voice is unimportant in other genres; however, in war literature, it operates under a unique tension. There is a fine line between a narrator whose voice sounds boastful or self-aggrandising—thus shutting off any meaningful connection with the reader—and one who remains aware of both the weight of their story and the reader's capacity for empathy and attention. In many cases, the inherent gravity of war as a subject imposes a kind of narrative etiquette on this relationship, demanding sincerity and moral accountability. While other genres might allow for, or even thrive on, unreliable narrators, war narratives often insist on a certain degree of earnestness to maintain their ethical force.

Although some might contend that ironic approaches to war do exist—as exemplified by Joseph Heller's *Catch-22* (1961) or David Abrams's *Fobbit* (2012)—it is crucial to recognise that even in these instances, the absurdity on display is not a dismissal of war's seriousness but rather a mirror reflecting its intrinsic contradictions and irrationality. These ironic narratives do not trivialise war; on the contrary, they amplify and expose the grotesque bureaucracy, perverse logic, and existential absurdity that often define armed conflict. Thus, even when irony is employed, it reinforces the demand for a narrative voice that is at once serious, perceptive, and profoundly aware of the stakes involved.

Phil Klay's collection of short stories is often compared to Tim O'Brien's *The Things They Carried*. In his review of Klay's *Redeployment*, Dexter Filkins argues that although Klay writes about a different war, he "aims for a similar effect: showing us the myriad human manifestations that result from the collision of young, heavily armed, Americans with a fractured and deeply foreign culture that very few of them even remotely understand" (Filkins 2014). Yet, it is not only the effect that binds O'Brien and Klay so closely; it is also the voice of their narrators. Consider, for instance, the opening of O'Brien's *The Things They Carried*:

> First Lieutenant Jimmy Cross carried letters from a girl named Martha, a junior at Mount Sebastian College in New Jersey. They were not love letters, but Lieutenant Cross was hoping, so he kept them folded in plastic at the bottom of his rucksack. In the late afternoon, after a day's march, he would dig his foxhole, wash his hands under a canteen, unwrap the letters, hold them with the tips of his fingers, and spend the last hour of light pretending. (O'Brien 1991, 3)

In a few lines, O'Brien's narrator creates a world that is both structurally and psychologically credible, defining both the home front and the battle front. These first few lines sketch a whole generation of American soldiers and their experience in Vietnam. In *Fighting and Writing the Vietnam War* (1994), Don Ringnalda contends that American soldiers in Vietnam discovered, akin to the contented prisoners in Plato's cave, "two sets of shadows." One shadow was "the myth of the righteous warrior making the world safe for democracy," which ultimately revealed itself as a "tautological reflection of a national lie." The other shadow was the belief that America could "make sense of and impose its will on Vietnam with a Western Positivist strategy," which proved to be a manifestation of "cultural arrogance" (Ringnalda 1994, 94). All these elements subtly surface in O'Brien's opening lines. One can discern them in the way Lieutenant Cross holds the letters as if they are sacred remnants of a homeland that deserves his reverence—a ritual object rather than a tangible promise. Despite the physical and emotional exhaustion of combat, he meticulously washes his hands before touching these tokens, transforming this act into a private liturgy. In that "last hour of light" (O'Brien 1991, 3), he engages in a fragile, almost devotional imagining of a future that is not a true promise but a shimmering illusion. Within this ritual, Cross convinces himself that by continuing to pretend, his imagined relationship with Martha might one day become real.

An echo of this voice, as well as of its encapsulating capacities, can be seen in the opening lines of Phil Klay's *Redeployment*:

> We shot dogs. Not by accident. We did it on purpose, and we called it Operation Scooby. I'm a dog person, so I thought about that a lot.
> First time was instinct. I hear O'Leary go, "Jesus," and there's a skinny brown dog lapping up blood the same way he'd lap up water from a bowl. It wasn't American blood, but still, there's that dog, lapping it up. And that's the last straw, I guess, and then it's open season on dogs. (Klay 2014, 1)

In just a few lines, the entire American effort in Iraq is distilled. Though seemingly ironic, juxtaposing military terminology ("operation") with a beloved cartoon dog ("Scooby-Doo"), this brief passage encapsulates the disorientation and moral disarray of the conflict. The enemy is absent, and in that void, soldiers seek new, often grotesque, outlets for their aggression. These lines also gesture toward the home front, where such actions would be unequivocally condemned. The narrator's inner conflict underscores the jarring dissonance between civilian moral codes and the battlefield's brutal logic, revealing how easily those codes collapse under the strain of war.

Yet these narrative voices, as inviting and confessional as they seem, also compel the reader into a morally fraught conversation.

They do not simply indict the violence of the battlefield or the corrupted ethics of war itself; instead, they expose the unsettling complicity and moral blindness of those at home. Here, the comparison with O'Brien's short story is particularly illuminating:

> They carried the common secret of cowardice barely restrained, the instinct to run or freeze or hide, and in many respects, this was the heaviest burden of all, for it could never be put down, it required perfect balance and perfect posture. They carried their reputations. They carried the soldier's greatest fear, which was the fear of blushing. Men killed, and died, because they were embarrassed not to. It was what had brought them to the war in the first place, nothing positive, no dreams of glory or honor, just to avoid the blush of dishonor. They died so as not to die of embarrassment. (O'Brien 1991, 18–19)

O'Brien deftly dismantles the myth that men go to war to become heroes, drawing instead a painful parallel between soldiers and civilians. Although this comparison might seem to bring them closer, O'Brien subtly introduces an emotional snare. Elsewhere, O'Brien has confessed that what ultimately kept him from fleeing to Canada to evade the draft was the dread of being perceived as a coward by his hometown community. This disclosure implicates the reader in a deeply uncomfortable moral terrain: safe in their civilian lives, they can never truly grasp the soldier's burden. In this framework, the burden of proof is always placed on the reader. The soldier's shame, however degrading, is validated by their status and experience. For those who merely watch—readers included—there is no such justification.

Klay likewise prefigures the reader, placing them in an equally uncomfortable and destabilising position, particularly when he highlights the gulf between soldiers and those "who have no idea where Fallujah is" (Klay 2014, 12). Although the reader might be invited to sympathise with the soldier who goes shopping with his wife, they are cast into a different and more unsettling role. The reader is prompted to perceive civilians as a kind of enemy. The narrator describes these civilians, "walking around by the windows like it's no big deal," as utterly unable to grasp the constant dread every soldier carries (2014, 12). In the narrator's feverish discourse, civilians have "spent their whole lives at white" (2014, 12).

This reference to the colour code, used to indicate levels of alertness, places civilians and soldiers along a continuum or even on opposing poles. Existing perpetually at white, civilians embody a state of blissful ignorance, immune to vigilance and danger, and therefore appear to have relinquished any claim to genuine anxiety or existential threat.

By contrast, soldiers live perpetually at orange or even red, navigating a heightened state of awareness that renders civilian life a lumbering, oblivious mammoth, an existence seemingly destined for extinction. Against this backdrop of nuanced emotional tension between the reader and the civilian, it is almost unsurprising that Klay concludes his short story with a symbolic act of mock killing. In the final paragraphs, the narrator contemplates whether to inflict the excruciating pain of two sucking chest wounds or to deliver two quick shots that would tear organs apart and ensure a swift death to the elusive "you" continually invoked throughout the story. "That's how it should be done," the narrator insists after dispatching Vicar, the dog, with two rapid shots, "each shot coming quick after the last so you can't even try to recover, which is when it hurts" (Klay 2014, 16). The parallelism here is deliberately ambiguous, a tension Klay sustains through the shifting pronoun "you." Who, ultimately, is meant to recover? Is it the victimised "you," forced into sudden, brutal awareness of mortality? Or is it the shooter, compelled to shepherd the victim through the transformation from living being to lifeless body?

Considering the title of the short story and Klay's implied idea—that soldiers never truly return from the battlefield—the answers to all these questions might appear bleak. Yet, they hold the key to understanding the profound transformations that war imposes on the human psyche. The parallels woven throughout Klay's collection do not merely redefine war as an event that disrupts civilian life; they depict it as an invasive force that almost irreversibly alters it. Moreover, they compel us to reconsider the concept of the enemy. In this reframing, the enemy is not only the insurgent who, from an American perspective, fails to grasp the supposed nobility underpinning the American invasion, but also the American who fails to look beyond those professed noble intentions. In this context, both enemies stand on equal footing.

The "you" addressed in the title story remains deliberately ambiguous, encompassing both civilians and combatants. In its ambiguity, the pronoun gathers all entities under its umbrella, whether friend or foe. "It was another three weeks before I got home," explains the narrator of "Bodies," another story in the collection, "and everybody thanked me for my service. Nobody seemed to know exactly what they were thanking me for" (Klay 2014, 63). This "service," defined by noble intentions as a matter of course, ultimately suppresses the very conversation that writers and soldiers like Klay wish to have with civilians, the kingdom to which they can never fully return.

6.2 The War Seen Through Somebody Else's Eyes: Elliot Ackerman's *Green on Blue*

This relocation of the enemy may partly explain why contemporary literature on the wars in Iraq and Afghanistan exhibits such a strong affinity with the investigative genre. Since the enemy is elusive — constantly shifting, adapting, and assuming new forms — these narratives become investigations into the very nature of enmity itself. Within the context of war, these stories suggest that the line dividing friend from foe is never as clear-cut as one might assume; indeed, the enemy may be much closer to home than we care to admit. A particularly compelling example is Elliot Ackerman's novel *Green on Blue* (2015), which not only adopts the perspective of the "enemy" but also argues that the war in Afghanistan is, as the title implies, an inside job. Although Ackerman does not focus on what happens after the war, he radicalises Klay's idea of returning home as a form of redeployment. In Ackerman's narrative, war becomes a means of survival, yet not survival in Klay's sense of returning to Wilmington to shop at the mall, but rather survival as the preservation of one's basic humanity.

The first and most striking aspect Ackerman underscores throughout the novel is the almost stubborn refusal, evident from the very first pages, to link any belligerence on the part of the "enemy" to the supposed hatred of American freedoms. Ackerman subtly but insistently suggests that the reality is far more complex, and any simplification, such as George W. Bush's claim in his post-9/11 address, fails to account for the actual dynamics in Afghanistan. Aziz, the novel's first-person narrator, does not join the special Lashkar, a group fighting against the Taliban, because he despises American freedom. When he is recruited, he has no real understanding of what American freedom even entails. Instead, he joins for deeply personal rather than political reasons, and because he is too young to comprehend the broader stakes. Aziz and his brother, Ali, are orphaned after a military raid kills their parents, forcing them to beg on the streets of Orgun to survive. Later, Ali is crippled in an attack and requires intensive hospital care. Faced with unaffordable medical bills and driven by loyalty to his brother, Aziz joins the special Lashkar with the promise that, as long as he continues fighting, Ali will receive treatment. Taqbir, a member of the Lashkar who wears an American uniform, assures Aziz that all expenses will be covered.

The American uniform worn by a non-American soldier emerges as a potent symbol at this point in the narrative. Only twelve pages into the novel, the narrator offers readers a stark glimpse of the Afghan battlefield's grim realities. "Militants," the narrator explains in a rare moment of lucid synthesis, "accused men of being informants and beheaded them in front of their families," while "Americans accused men of being militants and disappeared them in the night on helicopters. The militants fought to protect us from the Americans, and the Americans fought to protect us from the militants, and being so protected, life was very dangerous" (Ackerman 2015, 12). Almost immediately after Aziz joins the special Lashkar, the vicious cycle of American intervention in Afghanistan rises unmistakably to the surface, transforming the entire situation into a kind of mise-en-abyme of the American "war on terror."

The special Lashkar is tasked with pursuing a singular enemy named Gazan—an elusive figure whom the Americans intend to capture or kill. Yet Gazan's presence remains spectral, perpetually receding behind shifting acolytes, conflicting interests, and misleading intelligence. Mr Jack, the only conspicuously drawn American character in the novel, supplies Sabir, the commander of the special Lashkar, with new rifles and uniforms and, it is whispered, increases the Lashkar's budget for the coming fighting season (2015, 40). From the outset, it is subtly suggested that the Lashkar's true interest lies in prolonging the hunt for Gazan rather than ending it decisively, thereby ensuring that American funds continue to flow into their coffers.

The novel suggests that Americans have established a miniature military-industrial complex within Afghanistan. Once Gazan is portrayed as an existential threat, every action—no matter how costly—is deemed necessary to eliminate him. Those who joined the special Lashkar did so because they were persuaded by an official figure clad in an American uniform that their suffering would end once they had exacted revenge on Gazan. Yet they also fought for money. Aziz articulates this reality in one of his sombre reflections:

> As long as I stayed a soldier and my pay went to the hospital, my brother would be cared for. My war was as simple and honest as that. There was no cause in it except the cause of survival. Had I killed for money? Perhaps. Perhaps it was a round from my machine gun that had killed the man on the ridge a few days ago. I had no feud with him. If I killed him, I did it for money. Atal sold information to Mr. Jack for money, too, the money to care for Fareeda. What could be corrupt in that? Yet that money also paid for his large house, generator and Hilux. Still, the truly corrupt have unreliable motivations, and money is one of the most reliable. (Ackerman 2015, 85)

Chasing the enemy across Afghanistan's unforgiving terrain becomes an end in itself. At the same time, the outpost that Commander Sabir is so determined to build serves as a means to secure a continued source of income once the Americans depart. Although the villagers strongly oppose its construction, Sabir believes that by establishing it, he could "extend his control over a large swath of the border, regulating anything and anyone who wished to cross" (Ackerman 2015, 99). The annihilation of Gazan would also mean relinquishing this control, as the enemy's very existence empowers the Lashkar to dominate the villagers. Even those soldiers who have, in some sense, already avenged themselves choose to remain, as the war has become essential to their survival. In a rare moment of candour, Sabir confides to Aziz that "war can be a life," suggesting that the revenge Aziz seeks so fervently, even at the risk of his own life, is ultimately meaningless unless he has "made a life in this war" (Ackerman 2015, 123–24), as Atal has done.

In this context, peace is always a theoretical possibility. However, it is ultimately unproductive. To justify his outpost and maintain control over the area, "Sabir secretly supplies Gazan and keeps him on the attack, mortaring our village and mining our roads" (Ackerman 2015, 223). The vicious circle thus reveals itself fully: Sabir receives money from the Americans, who pay him and the soldiers of the special Lashkar to fight Gazan, who, in turn, is secretly supplied by Sabir to perpetuate the conflict and keep the financial pipeline open. By the novel's end, when Aziz decides to kill Gazan, Mr Jack, and Atal as they attempt to negotiate peace terms, the significance of the title becomes entirely clear:

> No one would know this killing had been a green on blue.
> But as I thought about it, I felt uncertain it was. I no longer wore a uniform. Still, I'd been a member of the Special Lashkar, something the Americans made. I then recalled how Commander Sabir kept Gazan in business, and how the Americans kept Commander Sabir in business. And as I thought of all the ways one could be killed in this war, and of all those who could do it, I couldn't think of a single way to die which wasn't a green on blue. The Americans had a hand in creating all of it. (Ackerman 2015, 226)

Yet Aziz does not break this vicious cycle by killing the three men; instead, he does so precisely because he does not wish to see it broken. Like Sabir, Aziz has come to perceive war as a form of employment, one that provides tangible benefits, including the costly medicine he will need to procure for Fareeda after Atal's death. When Aziz assures Fareeda that he will find the medicine necessary to keep her illness at bay — a disease that has already disfigured parts of her body — she looks at him with undisguised hatred. "The hate," Aziz reflects, "was in the need. She was a prisoner of her needs, and I'd become the master of them" (Ackerman 2015, 229). Ultimately, Aziz transforms into a new incarnation of Gazan, but one who is even more ruthless, for he comprehends the logic and machinery of war fully.

From this perspective, Ackerman's novel can be interpreted as a bildungsroman, tracing the development of Aziz and his brother from childhood into adulthood. The bildungsroman is a common narrative framework not only because of the protagonists' age but also due to the profound, often violent, transformation that war imposes upon them. Even if one were to disregard the characters' youth, war narratives invariably evoke the essence of the bildungsroman. Regardless of age, characters gain new and often harrowing insights by the end of the story. In Ackerman's novel, Aziz emerges stronger and more perceptive than his peers, not merely due to physical maturation but because war has fundamentally reshaped him. Like the protagonists themselves, the reader, too, emerges transformed, confronted with a deeper, more unsettling understanding of the human condition and the psychological landscapes shaped by violence.

Furthermore, akin to the experience of war itself, war narratives aim to recreate the rupture between a "before" and an "after" — a decisive break that irrevocably transforms both characters and readers. In this context, one way to evaluate a war narrative's belligerent or pacifist tendencies is by examining how it frames the information it conveys. Do these narratives represent such information as inherently valuable? If the information is portrayed as unique, irreplaceable, and unattainable by other means, then the narrative may lean towards a belligerent stance, implicitly valorising the experience of war as a necessary crucible for acquiring such knowledge. However, paradoxically, if that information is presented as valuable yet already acquired and shared with a broader public, it could also function as a powerful deterrent, dissuading future engagement in war by exposing its brutal realities. As I have already discussed in reference to Mariani's argument, whenever the burden of proof shifts onto the reader, the interpretive outcomes invariably oscillate, depending on the sociocultural and historical context in which the narrative is consumed. As I shall further argue in this chapter, one possible resolution lies in examining how these narratives explore the "physical" knowledge produced through war, particularly in their representation of human bodies.

The bodies of Fareeda and Commander Sabir exemplify the kind of conflict Ackerman depicts in *Green on Blue*. An obscure disease ravages Fareeda's body, its deformities rendering her a living metaphor for Afghanistan itself. When Aziz first encounters her, he is struck by her right hand, which "was grotesque, the thumb and index finger engorged as though they were about to burst, the fingernails yellow and brittle" (Ackerman 2015, 64). Fareeda's disfigurement transforms her into a corporeal symbol of her nation's protracted suffering. In an interview with Sean Purio for *WLA: War, Literature and the Arts*, Ackerman elaborates on this symbolism:

> Fareeda is a symbol of Afghanistan, at least that's how she developed in the book. One remarkable thing about the country is that it has been at war for thirty-seven years. The average life expectancy for an Afghan male is around sixty. That means the generation of Afghans who are currently dying were in their early twenties when the Soviets invaded in 1979. They are the last Afghans who can remember their country at peace, none of the young people can. For this reason, peace in Afghanistan is not an act of returning to a previous state, which everyone can remember. Instead, conjuring peace has become an act of sheer imagination. (Purio 2016)

When Aziz tells Fareeda that she should not speak of death and killing because she is "young and a woman," she counters fiercely, asserting that survival is not merely the province of soldiers; she, too, is engaged in a daily battle. "I fight every day to keep this from killing me," she declares, referring to the illness consuming her from within. "[It] spreads across me, and without medicine, it will consume me" (Ackerman 2015, 113). Fareeda's disease, much like the Special Lashkar operating in Afghanistan, demands constant intervention and a continuous influx of financial resources to be held at bay, though never truly eradicated.

Ackerman's *Green on Blue* is not the only novel to depict the body as a locus of struggle—a struggle often interpreted as a metaphor for infirmity, weakness, or deeper societal maladies. Brian Van Reet's *Spoils* (2017) frequently engages with this idea, suggesting that physical infirmity embodies a weakness rooted in national and historical failings. When Cassandra, one of the novel's multiple protagonists, observes a group of children at play, she immediately notices their congenital disabilities. "For the first time," the third-person narrator remarks, "Cassandra notices the defect in his other arm [...] shrivelled and misshapen. Without a hand or fingers, it tapers to a diminutive paddle like a fleshy spoon" (Van Reet 2018, 76). Haider, the boy with the malformed arm, reveals that he has a sister who is gravely ill and in need of urgent medical care, and he offers to become an informant for the American forces in exchange for assistance. Shortly thereafter, Cassandra notices yet another child: "a girl with a stooped back who throws out one leg in an exaggerated circular motion with each step" (2018, 80).

These deformed bodies stand in stark contrast to those of the American soldiers, seemingly underscoring an inherent flaw within the Iraqi system—one that the Americans, despite their military might and technological superiority, cannot rectify overnight. They can intervene and offer aid, but such efforts do not liberate these children from their deformities, nor do they erase the underlying historical and societal traumas that have contributed to them. Unlike the Americans, whose bodies symbolise power and resilience, these local bodies appear irreparably marked by forces beyond any individual's control, embodying a collective, tormented past. The novel thus intimates that military intervention, however well-intentioned, cannot "cure" congenital afflictions or heal deep-seated historical wounds.

Commander Sabir's disfigured body, much like Fareeda's, emerges as another potent symbol of Afghanistan's condition. However, unlike Fareeda, who is depicted as an innocent victim, Sabir's disfigurement signifies recognition and a certain perverse respect. His "mangled bottom lip," which exposed a row of teeth behind it, together with "the scars, paunches, and calluses of the other men, gave the group an honest authority, one greater than shining medals and rank" (Ackerman 2015, 41). Sabir's physical description evokes the image of a drug addict who can no longer distinguish between reality and hallucination—an apt metaphor for his dependency on war. For Sabir, war confers dignity and purpose; any other occupation would not only seem worthless but might also threaten to undermine his sense of masculinity and self-worth.

The notion of war as a legitimate occupation—an inherited profession rather than a temporary deviation—is reinforced through what initially appears as a somewhat dismissive comparison. For Sabir, war is a family trade, passed down almost as an heirloom. His brother Jazeem, whom the Americans called James, founded the Special Lashkar. Following Jazeem's death, Sabir assumed his role to support his financially struggling family. In a parallel fashion, Aziz steps into the vacuum left by Gazan's death, effectively 'inheriting' both his men and his mission in the larger scheme orchestrated by Sabir and driven by his relentless pursuit of prosperity.

Conversely, those who do not perceive war as a form of employment are portrayed as incapable of transcending their misfortunes. "These people have nothing," Tawas tells Aziz as they watch two boys begging for food, "[they] are ignorant even of their suffering. This is the worst poverty" (Ackerman 2015, 60). Members of the Special Lashkar—such as Aziz, Tawas, and Mortaza—are considered superior precisely because their participation in the Lashkar signifies an awareness of their suffering and an active response to it. "You've done something to lift yourself up," Tawas tells Mortaza when confronting his arrogance, "[these] people do nothing. [...] Their indifference stares back at you. It is in their mud houses, overfilled sewers, and dirt-faced children who are stupid and unknowing" (2015, 60–61). Mortaza fails to recognise that, much like the unknowing children who merely "need an example of strength" and have been paralysed by American charity, he too has ultimately become a victim of that same charity, trapped within a system that sustains rather than liberates.

Compared to the men in the Special Lashkar, those who pursue occupations unrelated to war are depicted as having forfeited their sense of manhood. Atal, who oscillates between serving American interests and those of the local community, is portrayed as effeminate and lacking authority. "His dress was neat," the narrator observes upon first meeting Atal, "and his body perfumed so heavily that his scent caused in me a spinning moment of drunkenness. He extended his hand as though we should kiss it" (Ackerman 2015, 62). On another occasion, the soldiers of the Special Lashkar derive particular pleasure from belittling the local population. When a group of itinerant musicians is captured—not for any legitimate reason but simply for being in the wrong place at the wrong time—the musicians appear diminished and fragile when confronted face-to-face with the soldiers. When two of them stand before Yar, "their clothes filthy and hair now matted with fine dust," Yar laughs at them—not at their pitiable state but at his absolute power over them (Ackerman 2015, 96). In the eyes of the Special Lashkar, their profession commands no respect; their presence merely reaffirms the soldiers' superiority.

The war Ackerman portrays in *Green on Blue* is not a traditional conflict between two clearly defined sides. The supposed enemy is not driven by a hatred of freedom but is instead someone arbitrarily cast into the role of adversary. In this narrative, war transcends simplistic categories of friend and foe. "War is a mother to men such as us," Sabir tells Aziz near the novel's end, "[it] is a mother whose generosity brought you Badal [revenge] and will bring me my outpost. Men who forget about her generosity wind up like the three you just left" (Ackerman 2015, 232). Like a capricious goddess, war demands loyalty and service; those who serve it are rewarded, while those who forsake it—such as Atal, Gazan, and Mr Jack—are ultimately destroyed. Those caught in its vortex, particularly the villagers, become akin to Fareeda: prisoners of their own needs, willing to follow whoever offers sustenance and protection. "They'll follow whoever clothes them," Sabir reminds Aziz, "feeds them, and arms them. I do all of this, and you will do all this through me" (2015, 232). Thus, Ackerman suggests that the identity of the enemy is fluid and constructed, shaped by the desires and financial interests of those who wield power.

The emptiness of any higher ideals that might justify war is further underscored by Aziz's final realisation that *Badal*—the concept of revenge he had so fervently pursued—can shift its meaning depending on the circumstances. When Aziz accidentally kills the brother of one of his fellow combatants during a skirmish, he recognises that the surviving brother might now swear *Badal* against him. "I fought to avenge my brother," Aziz reflects painfully, "but I'd just killed the brother of another man, a friend. I'd taken from him just what Gazan had taken from me" (Ackerman 2015, 143). However, Sabir dismisses this moral crisis almost perfunctorily, assigning Aziz a mission that takes him away from the base. Given Sabir's long-standing record of moral corruption and manipulation, it even appears plausible that this entire episode was orchestrated as a strategy to compel Aziz to accept the morally fraught mission of eliminating Atal. Thus, once more, someone is conveniently cast into the role of the enemy, revealing the ultimate arbitrariness and moral bankruptcy at the heart of the war machine.

6.3 Parallel Views: Michael Pitre's *Fives and Twenty-Fives*, Matt Gallagher's *Youngblood*, and Roy Scranton's *War Porn*

In other narratives, the enemy is not always a foreign combatant on the battlefield but sometimes occupies the highest echelons of command. In Michael Pitre's novel *Fives and Twenty-Fives* (2015), Lieutenant Donovan and his team are assigned the hazardous task of disposing of a series of barrels containing chemical substances of unknown origin and purpose, simply because no other unit is willing to undertake it. Forced to wait for more than six hours under the scorching Iraqi sun, they are eventually met by a confident Mr Moss, described as a "twentysomething kid with a pleasant smile" and an "upper-class Texas accent" (Pitre 2015, 279), who provides them with a cursory and incomplete briefing that contradicts their original orders. When pressed for clarification about the true nature of the mission, Mr Moss dismisses their concerns, curtly reminding them that they are "losing daylight. And air-conditioning, too" (2015, 279). Bound by their orders, the soldiers have no choice but to proceed.

The site of the mission eerily resembles an American suburb. "The dirt road curved around a low bluff," Lieutenant Donovan recalls as they approach, "and a walled subdivision, like something out of the American Southwest, complete with stucco tract housing and cul-de-sacs, appeared in the windshield" (2015, 280). The illusion is so powerful that Donovan must blink twice to convince himself he is not hallucinating. "I couldn't help feeling," he admits, "as if I were on my way to see a friend in Alabama. The sensation deepened when the Suburbans ahead of us wagon-wheeled into a loose perimeter at the end of a cul-de-sac, and the Iraqi trucks parked in adjacent driveways" (2015, 281). However, the comforting mirage of suburban normalcy soon shatters when the soldiers realise they are neither adequately equipped nor physically prepared to execute the mission, and that the chemicals they are meant to handle have already begun to affect their bodies:

> Through my clouded vision, I could see the Marines on security standing against a backdrop of houses not dissimilar from the ones in which they might have grown up, and they appeared to me as the children they had been just a few years earlier. I pictured them passing footballs in the street. Walking up to front doors wearing tuxedos, carrying flowers for their homecoming dates. I even let myself picture the impossibility of Gomez coming to the door in a dress, accepting her corsage.
> I blinked the tears free, and they were Marines again, with eyes wide and jaws slack at the sight of the solid and impervious Zahn, broken by the mere smell of the chemicals in that backyard pool. (2015, 282–83)

Pitre's critique operates on at least two levels. On a micro level, the narrative functions as a war story that exposes the stark disconnect between the abstract orders issued from high command and the actual capabilities and vulnerabilities of soldiers in the field. Here, Pitre makes it clear who the real enemy is: it is not a band of bloodthirsty jihadists, but instead figures like Mr Moss, who reprimands Donovan and his team for failing to complete an impossible mission. Mr Moss's reproach, delivered from the comfort of his air-conditioned vehicle, underscores his sanitised and naive understanding of the war's brutal realities. In his view, recovering the barrels represents "an opportunity to win the war, just a little. To show the Iraqis that we are here to help. To show them what Americans are all about. Hard work" (2015, 284). The dramatic irony and hypocrisy embedded in this declaration are unmistakable. While Mr Moss extols the virtues of American hard work, he remains utterly inactive, embodying the detachment and performative idealism of those far removed from the battlefield.

At a macro level, as a critique of American society, Pitre's narrative hinges on the revealing parallel between the fabricated American suburb in Iraq and the idyllic memories it evokes in the soldiers' minds. In Pitre's subtle yet incisive vision, the American suburb nostalgically recalled by the soldiers is as toxic as the one they encounter abroad. Furthermore, if the suburban mirage in Iraq perplexes the soldiers with its unsettling familiarity, the sounds and sights of the battlefield continue to haunt them even after they return home. For instance, when hospitalman Lester Pleasant goes out to watch the fireworks with his girlfriend, the explosive sounds immediately evoke memories of gunfire. In this sense, the enemy is not confined to the distant battlefield of the so-called "war on terror" but is also present on American soil, rendering the distinction between "here" and "there" increasingly porous. Ultimately, the two spaces collapse into one another, becoming coterminous and, in effect, cancelling each other out.

However, Pitre's narration also underscores that, in this war, the true battlefield is not the simulated American suburb, nor is it some far-flung city overseas. Instead, it resides within the soldiers' own bodies and their ongoing internal struggle between comfort and discomfort, safety and vulnerability. When the narrator of Phil Klay's short story "Redeployment" mentions the colour codes that signify a soldier's level of alertness on duty, he implicitly refers to the corresponding intensity of fear each level entails. That fear, ultimately, is a fear for one's own body, an instinct amplified to overwhelming proportions by the constant threat of violence. Pitre thus shifts the focus of the battlefield inward, emphasising the primacy of the soldier's corporeal experience and its deep interconnectedness with the bodies of his comrades. Lieutenant Donovan's decision to defy orders from above, motivated by the danger posed to his marines' physical well-being, embodies not the cold calculation of a strategist but the protective impulse of a father or a friend, deeply invested in the lives entrusted to him.

The focus on the inner lives of soldiers — and on how they individually grapple with the trauma of war upon returning home — also distances Pitre's narrative from the seductive allure of "combat gnosticism." Pitre himself, as a former U.S. Marine captain and veteran of two tours in Iraq, is acutely aware of this danger. His decision to structure the novel through multiple points of view, including that of an Iraqi man, serves as a narrative system of checks and balances against the tendency to romanticise combat as a source of esoteric, exclusive knowledge. This concern is further evident in the way he handles military jargon, a recurring feature in war fiction that is often approached in two distinct ways: either deployed sparingly, creating a jarring effect when it appears, or used excessively for dramatic emphasis, as Phil Klay does in "OIF," a short story included in *Redeployment*, to underscore its dryness and inherent absurdity.

In *Fives and Twenty-Fives*, Pitre adopts an innovative approach that combines both strategies. He fragments the narrative into different points of view, with each new section introduced by a short note, letter, official report, or even commentary from Dodge/Kateb's thesis on *Huckleberry Finn*. These narratives move fluidly back and forth, revisiting the war in Iraq and then following the Marines as they attempt to reconstruct their lives after their service has ended. The text is replete with flashbacks, typically triggered by mundane events in the present, some of which become almost predictable in their recurrence: Doc Lester Pleasant recalls "the machine-gun range" when he hears fireworks on New Year's Eve; Donovan is haunted by memories of a perilous chemical disposal mission while working on his "solid reports" at his civilian job; the smell of grass in Lizzy's room prompts Lester to remember "the grass down at Nasr Wal Salam. That's right. Thickest damn grass I ever saw" (Pitre 2015, 154). It is as if each detail of the present serves as an inadvertent conduit back to the battlefield, as though the present moment cannot be fully experienced without the omnipresent shadow of combat knowledge. Each aspect of civilian life is thus imbued with a resonance alien to its ordinary context but profoundly authentic to the former Marine.

Some of these flashbacks are so absurd and ironic that they border on the unbelievable. Others verge on the comedic, such as the episode when Dodge (Kateb) first encounters Lieutenant Pederson in "All Smiles, All Friendship," and the lieutenant's interpreter takes considerable liberties with his role. "This guy? Pederson?" the interpreter says in Arabic during their meeting, "he is going to fuck your whole world. Fuck you hard up the ass. Tell him where you have the weapons hidden. He's Fifty Cent's cousin. I'm not lying" (Pitre 2015, 211). Of course, Pederson utters none of these crude threats, nor does he invoke 50 Cent. This encounter becomes a crucial moment for Dodge, who gains the Americans' trust by revealing his fluency in English and exposing the interpreter's playful, subversive mistranslations.

Most of these episodes function as detailed commentaries on the terse notes or reports that precede them, as if they exist to provide context and illuminate the more profound emotional truths behind the official record. Many of these notes are couched in dry, impersonal military jargon—for example, the frequent "findings of fact," which are nothing more than sterile lists of observations. The stories that follow transcend these impersonal documents, exposing the emotional undercurrents and moral complexities that inform the decisions and experiences behind the factual façade.

These stories exhibit a remarkable openness towards the reader, an openness that could never be conveyed through the rigid, impassive language of military bureaucracy. They reveal a narrative preoccupation with the reader's engagement, as if urging this attentiveness to become a sustained ethical practice. At least during the act of reading, the reader is invited to inhabit the fractured present of those who carry the indelible marks of past battles. In doing so, a space for authentic dialogue emerges, reinforcing the idea that seemingly benign aspects of civilian life, such as the sound of fireworks, can trigger profound trauma for veterans. This type of narrative dialogue underscores the notion that war veterans often find themselves fundamentally unable to return to their previous mental and physical states. For most, returning home is not a simple closing of a narrative arc but rather a continuous process of spiralling outward and inward, marked by both dislocation and introspection.

In these narratives, it is often the case that, for the grunts in the lower ranks, the orders issued from high up in the chain of command are as cruel as they are absurd. At times, these orders stand in direct conflict with the soldiers' moral principles. In Matt Gallagher's *Youngblood* (2016), for instance, a group of soldiers is dispatched to disperse a large gathering of angry locals in Ashuriyah "by any means necessary" (Gallagher 2016, 316). Upon arrival, however, the soldiers quickly realise that they are not only vastly outnumbered by the locals—who have gathered around a bonfire, armed with torches and assault rifles—but also that they have been tasked with a mission as vague and impenetrable as the darkness of the surrounding desert:

> A small group had gathered in front of the crowd, under the eyes of the arch. They kept pointing to us and gesturing. After a minute or so, five of the men walked our way, carrying small torches and flashlights and assault rifles. The many locals behind them gathered around the bonfire and faced out, chanting with raised fists. I guessed them to be about four hundred meters or so away—definitely within distance of a decent shooter with a scope. (Gallagher 2016, 318)

Later in the novel, Lieutenant Porter, the squad leader, learns that the mob had actually been after him and that he and his men had narrowly escaped by sheer luck. Yet it was not luck alone that saved them, but rather Porter's and his men's ingenuity and restraint. When the angry mob corners them, the soldiers do not resort to violence; instead, they choose to reveal their vulnerability. "I took off my helmet," Porter recounts, "and looked up at the bodies through the black of night, trying desperately to show neither fear nor aggression" (2016, 320). The other soldiers follow suit, and, remarkably, the crowd disperses. Towards the novel's conclusion, when Porter questions a local woman, Alia, about the whereabouts of one of his intelligence sources, she responds that they do not need the Americans' help; instead, they want them to leave.

Gallagher's novel is permeated by instances of discursive simultaneity, where disparate images and thoughts converge and overlap. While reflecting on why he and his brother, Will, had joined the army—and thinking tenderly of his grandmother—Porter looks out at the Iraqi landscape. Raising a cigarette, he uses it to blot out a distant minaret. "A curl of smoke drifted from it," he narrates, "and I narrowed my eyes until the minaret fell out of focus and looked like a burning Twin Tower on a television screen" (2016, 149). In this moment, two images collapse into one: the minaret in Iraq and the iconic image of the burning Twin Towers. Yet, if 9/11 had once compelled Porter to enlist and fight for his country, that original motivation now seems remote and hollow. The Twin

Towers appear not in the sky before him but on a television screen, symbolically distancing Porter from the very event that catalysed the war in which he finds himself entangled.

Gallagher's novel also functions as an extended commentary on the entanglement of combat and masculinity. From its very title, *Youngblood*, the narrative signals a raw, visceral engagement with war, framing it as a proving ground for young soldiers seeking to construct and assert their manhood. Central to this exploration is the fraught relationship between Lieutenant Jack Porter, the narrator, and his staff sergeant, Chambers. Beyond serving as a bildungsroman, the novel also unfolds as a detective story—chronicling the protagonist's efforts to investigate "dark rumours about the past conduct of [...] Chambers, whom Jack worries will get his own platoon into trouble" (Kakutani 2016)—and as a love story, further complicating its thematic texture.

The tension between Porter and Chambers is evident from the novel's outset, where Chambers effortlessly commands the attention and admiration of the platoon. This tension escalates dramatically when Chambers shoots the goat belonging to the "Barbie Kid," an underage informant who sells goods to American soldiers and locals while wearing a sweatshirt adorned with a Barbie doll. At first glance, the goat's death appears accidental. "If that thing had been a suicide bomber," Chambers shouts amidst the commotion, "you'd be explaining to Saint Peter why the fuck you're so stupid" (Gallagher 2016, 13). The goat, of course, posed no threat; it was merely the boy's pet. What truly disturbs Chambers is the Barbie Kid's perceived femininity, "all ninety pounds of him" (Gallagher 2016, 320), and the unsettling absence of a tangible enemy to keep the platoon alert and unified in aggression. Moreover, Chambers' exaggerated, almost ritualistic gestures, pounding his chest and hooting, suggest a performative display intended to reinforce his dominance and masculine bravado. This performance is further contextualised by the earlier curiosity of the soldiers about Chambers' tattoos and the circulating rumours that he bore a mark for every enemy he had killed.

Chambers's obsessive need to assert his masculinity also serves to reinforce his claim to superior experience, rooted in a previous deployment he insists was far more brutal than the current one. Chambers laments what he perceives as a decline in the standards of manhood within the army. This belief is particularly evident in a conversation he has with Lieutenant Porter concerning their captain's alleged homosexuality:

> "So," he said. "It true our commander's a fag?"
> "I guess." I'd met Captain Vrettos' purported boyfriend many times before we left. A CrossFit coach, he'd come in and led physical training once, and could bench more than anyone, even Sipe. That'd stopped most of the gay jokes.
> Chambers shook his head. "What the fuck has happened to my army." (Gallagher 2016, 22)

However, Gallagher's critique extends well beyond the soldiers' internal dynamics. His critical eye turns toward broader aspects of American ideology and cultural assumptions, often articulated through the perspectives of Iraqi characters. When Porter visits Saif for a briefing, Saif notes that Iraqi officers intentionally keep themselves separate from lower-ranking soldiers to maintain discipline—an approach at odds with American military egalitarianism. "[We're] big on equality," Porter responds, "[all] for one, one for all sort of thing. Goes back to George Washington, I think." Saif's retort is sharp and incisive: "'George Washington?' Saif raised an eyebrow. 'One of your slave-owner presidents, yes?'" (Gallagher 2016, 140). The subtlety and biting irony of Saif's remark are entirely lost on the young American lieutenant, revealing a profound disconnect between American self-mythology and the critical perceptions of those they claim to help.

An even more biting critique of American society and military leadership appears in Phil Klay's short story "Money as a Weapons System," included in *Redeployment*. When the protagonist asks his translator why everyone refers to him as "the Professor," the translator's response is devastatingly revealing: "Because I was a professor," he replies, "before [Americans] came and destroyed the country" (Klay 2014, 85). The absurdity deepens when the protagonist learns that Gene Goodwin, "the mattress king of northern Kansas" (2014, 94), has donated baseball uniforms intended to transform baseball into Iraq's "soon-to-be national pastime" (2014, 99). The protagonist is then tasked with photographing a group of malnourished Iraqi children wearing these uniforms:

> The kid swung as though he were using the bat to beat someone to death, lifting it overhead and bringing it brutally down. I wanted to send that shot to [Gene Goodwin], but instead I showed the kid how to swing correctly and went back to taking photos. The timing was difficult, but after about twenty swings I got it perfect, the bat blurry, the batter's face pure concentration, and a look of worry from the catcher, as if the batter has just connected with a pitch. I turned the camera's display around and showed the picture to the Professor and the kids.
> 'Look at that,' I said.
> The Professor nodded. 'There you are,' he said. 'Success.' (Klay 2014, 117)

For Gene Goodwin—who becomes a symbol of American naivety and self-congratulatory ignorance—it is irrelevant that the locals lack running water or that local women desperately need medical facilities. On a broader scale, America's so-called success in the "war on terror" is encapsulated in that carefully staged photograph of Iraqi children playing baseball: an image meticulously crafted to project triumph while ignoring fundamental, life-sustaining needs. Here, the true enemy is not a faceless insurgent but the sprawling military-industrial and cultural apparatus at home, sustained by delusion and performative gestures.

Roy Scranton's novel *War Porn* (2016) underscores this issue even more starkly, placing the notion of the "enemy" in a radically different and unsettling light. When Aaron, recently returned from Iraq, shows Matt—a civilian entirely unconnected to the military—photographs of tortured Iraqi men and women (who are later revealed to have been detained without cause), he repeatedly insists that he was merely the one holding the camera, emphasising that everyone involved in these atrocities was simply "doing their jobs":

> We didn't *decide* to do this shit. We didn't *ask* for the torture detail. Staff Sergeant Cortázar told us to do this shit because Lieutenant Viers told *him* to do this shit, and Captain Weems, the company commander, told *him* to do this shit and so on up the fucking chain of command. [...] They say jump, we don't ask how high, we don't ask shit. We jump. [...] Think about this fact: if we decide to talk to somebody, show somebody pictures, we better damn well think about who exactly is going to be getting it in the ass. Bush? Rumsfeld? The general? The CO? Or your battle buddy? (Scranton 2016, 314)

Here, a hierarchy of blame is presented, yet the ultimate figure responsible remains frustratingly elusive. Blame is thus dispersed among all participants, creating a moral opacity that prevents clear accountability and transparency. Scranton appears to suggest that the true culprit is not merely an individual but the psychological and systemic damage inflicted on those compelled to participate in these acts.

However, Scranton navigates a perilous line in addressing this topic. His depiction of blame as shifting perpetually upwards through the chain of command risks being perceived as a convenient rationalisation for acts that are, in themselves, unjustifiable and gratuitous. Aaron, in this context, is a clear victim of what psychologists term "groupthink," a condition in which individuals surrender their moral judgment to the collective mentality of the group, leading them to commit actions they would otherwise unequivocally condemn. As Susan David asserts in *Emotional Agility* (2016), "conformity and loyalty are key concepts in military culture [but] under stressful conditions, members of tightly knit military units can fall prey to dangerous groupthink, exhibiting violent and dehumanising behaviour that in other contexts they would condemn as wrong" (David 2016, 124). Nonetheless, acknowledging Aaron's susceptibility to cognitive bias does not absolve the moral violation perpetrated against human dignity. Crucially, Aaron is not a whistleblower exposing atrocities in the hope of seeking justice or sparking moral reflection. Instead, he shares the photographs with Matt as a form of grotesque boasting, a demonstration of power rather than a gesture of accountability.

The context in which Aaron shows the photographs further undermines, rather than supports, his implicit self-justification. Eager to play the perfect host, Matt invites Aaron into his home and proudly presents the project he has been developing, a sophisticated computer program designed to predict weather patterns by synthesising data from various sources into visually accessible models. The idealism and constructive ambition behind Matt's work stand in stark contrast to Aaron's contribution. In response, Aaron offers to share "some real war shit," as he describes it, while waving a thumb drive: "[you] show me the future. I'll show you the past" (Scranton 2016, 303). The "future" is represented by Matt's utopian project, a hopeful tool for human benefit. The "past," as Aaron wishes to present it, is far more sinister, evoking the abuses of Abu Ghraib and other notorious detention centres:

> "We did a bunch of stuff in Iraq," Aaron said, "including working at several different internment camps. This is Camp Crawford. We called it the Pit. It was north of Baghdad, not far from Taji, and it was specifically for insurgents and intel targets. It's not like Cropper, or BIAP, which was high-value, or Abu G, which had a bunch of different shit. We were supposed to get hard cases from other assets in the north and northwest, a lot of hadjis from Fallujah and Tikrit and Baqubah, a lot of Sunni triangle shit."
> "Hadjis?"
> "Iraqis. You get real racist over there." (Scranton 2016, 307)

Aaron's language betrays him completely. While he obliquely suggests that the circumstances forced his hand, his vocabulary reveals that his attitudes have remained unchanged. Aaron is no longer "over there," yet he continues to use the same dehumanising, racist language without hesitation. The context has shifted, but his moral framework has not evolved; the violence lives on within him, unexamined and unrepentant.

Incidentally, when Susan David discusses the phenomenon of groupthink in *Emotional Agility*, she explicitly references Abu Ghraib, but in a manner that offers no support to Aaron's defence. On the contrary, David highlights the example of Sergeant Joseph Darby, who, at only twenty-four years old, was able to break free from the collective mentality and act in accordance with his internal moral compass. By "staying aligned with his values," Darby not only rejected the group's abusive behaviour but also found the courage to expose it by handing over a CD containing incriminating photographs to his superiors, thereby revealing the atrocities to the public (David 2016, 124). In stark contrast, Aaron exemplifies the soldier who forfeits his values entirely, succumbing to groupthink to secure a place within the group's hierarchy. Unlike Darby, who acted as a true whistleblower in defence of human dignity, Aaron engages in a grotesque exchange, handing over his thumb drive of photographs in a moment of dark, almost playful exhibitionism.

Aaron also confesses that many of the atrocities were committed simply out of boredom—a revelation that further undermines his attempt to deflect blame onto higher command. "[One] of our OGA dudes came from Abu G," Aaron continues, even as Matt begins to show signs of disgust, "and he gave us guidance on a bunch of shit he said worked really well over there. Naked Dog-Pile, Electric Wire Box, Fake Menstrual Wipe, shit like that. But a lot of shit we did 'cause we were bored" (Scranton 2016, 318). Aaron's familiarity with such acts of evil, coupled with his casual, dismissive attitude, is so grotesque that it becomes almost surreal. It is as if Scranton deliberately crafts Aaron's character to repel any possible sympathy from the reader. In this way, Aaron resembles Tom Pally, the veteran in Mark Doten's *The Infernal*, who is unable to imagine a world without suffering and whose perception of reality is profoundly warped. Scranton's novel culminates in an equally harrowing scene that mirrors the images Matt viewed on Aaron's thumb drive: Dahlia, Matt's wife, is tied to the bed with a phone cord and sexually assaulted by Aaron.

When Aaron leaves the house—having cut the phone cord that bound Dahlia—he shows no trace of remorse. In this final gesture, Scranton ensures that no space remains for forgiveness or redemption. With *War Porn*, as Sarah Hoenicke observes in her review for the *Los Angeles Review of Books*, Scranton "defies the American cultural tenet that our military is lawful, moral, and organised, depicting it instead as it more probably is: needlessly brutal, a blunt instrument rather than a refined machine" (Hoenicke, n.d.). Hoenicke further argues that Scranton aims to force readers to confront history and "the choices they've made" (Hoenicke, n.d.). However, I would contend that Scranton's provocation operates on a more intricate level than Hoenicke and others are perhaps willing to acknowledge. *War Porn*, as the title suggests, is not merely an exposé but a calculated provocation designed to unsettle. It compels readers to feel discomfort not only with the realities of war and its inherent violence but also with their own complicity in consuming war as entertainment. By explicitly linking war with the aesthetics of pornography, Scranton offers what readers might subconsciously crave: a novel that dwells on brutality while simultaneously keeping their attention balanced on a perilous edge, forcing them to interrogate their own gaze and appetite for violence.

The novel might also be read as the culmination—or perhaps the coronation—of Scranton's frustration with the publishing industry. Although *War Porn* was completed by 2011, it remained unpublished for five years because Scranton struggled to secure a publisher. The hardback cover is as provocative as the title itself: it depicts the tip of what appears to be a bullet or missile, whose lower half has been replaced by a charred corn on the cob resting on a barbecue grill. Coupled with the title, this image evokes a phallic shape, further accentuating the book's deliberately confrontational allure, a visual provocation seemingly designed to elicit discomfort in the viewer.

Yet perhaps this is precisely the point Scranton aims to make regarding the pressures exerted by the publishing industry and, more broadly, the demands of war narrative readership. Much like in Ben Fountain's *Billy Lynn's Long Halftime Walk* (2012), war must often share the stage with entertainment to be rendered palatable to the general public. The fact that we sometimes expect literary finesse from war writers—many of whom are themselves veterans—underscores the extent to which we privilege the medium over the message. This dynamic reveals an unsettling truth: the consumption of war narratives is frequently shaped more by aesthetic expectations and market demands than by a genuine confrontation with the subject matter's ethical and human dimensions.

Beyond his critique of the publishing industry, Scranton also directs his attention to an even more influential cultural construct: the myth of the trauma hero. In a comprehensive article for the *Los Angeles Review of Books*, Scranton argues that this myth has profoundly shaped not only the interpretation of war literature, films, and visual culture but also the very act of war writing itself, becoming, in his words, a kind of "perpetual motion machine." According to Scranton, this myth functions as a cultural scapegoat, "discharging national bloodguilt by substituting the victim of trauma, the soldier, for the victim of violence, the enemy," to such an extent that it has become the central axis around which war literature revolves.

The myth has grown so pervasive that it has "turned from being a frame for understanding reality into a mirroring surface that reflects back only our own expectations" (Scranton 2015). It persuades us that war experiences occupy a privileged place within the hierarchy of human experiences, conferring upon veterans a presumed monopoly on certain "truths" accessible only through firsthand exposure to violence — truths that then legitimise their authority as narrators and interpreters of war.

The myth of the trauma hero, according to Scranton, has its origins in British Lieutenant Wilfred Owen's seminal poem "Dulce et Decorum Est" (1920), which implicitly asserts that the most profound truth of war resides in the visceral, personal experience of the soldier. In Scranton's genealogy of the myth, Ernest Hemingway's *A Farewell to Arms* builds on Owen's foundational gesture, introducing the notion that "the soldier's truth becomes a formal truth: it determines not only who can speak, but what words can be spoken" (Scranton 2015). Scranton further contends that Tim O'Brien's *The Things They Carried* partially resists this supremacy by presenting the soldier's truth as a "mystic truth" that cannot be fully articulated or understood, only felt. In contrast, Kevin Powers's *The Yellow Birds* (2012) reinforces the myth's core tenets by suggesting that "the conventional tropes of war lit are not a means of conveying truth, but the truth of war itself" (Scranton 2015). In Scranton's analysis, each of these works, in varying degrees, contributes to the consolidation and perpetuation of this self-reinforcing myth.

Yet, if one assumes that Scranton reserves his sharpest critique for Powers — whose lyricism he dismisses as banal — he saves his most incisive argument for last. "The most troubling consequence," Scranton warns, "of our faith in the revelatory truth of combat experience and our sanctification of the trauma hero [is] that by focusing so insistently on the psychological trauma American soldiers have had to endure, we allow ourselves to forget the death and destruction those very soldiers are responsible for" (Scranton 2015). Phil Klay's short story "Redeployment" exemplifies this danger, offering readers a narrative that inadvertently allows them to sidestep the grim reality that, beyond shooting dogs, American soldiers also killed human beings. The story's opening line, "We shot dogs," functions similarly to lines such as "We built schools" or "We brought democracy," foregrounding a peripheral detail while subtly deflecting attention away from the larger, more unsettling truths of American intervention in Iraq. In doing so, it invites a selective empathy that absolves rather than interrogates.

It is no wonder, then, as Scranton points out, that Sergeant Price's dog in "Redeployment" is named "Vicar," because "[a] vicar is a representative or substitute, as the Pope is the Vicar of Christ, and in 'Redeployment,' the tumorous Vicar is a substitute for the narrator's trauma and guilt" (Scranton 2015). It is as if Klay intentionally invites readers to care more deeply about the dog and the emotional suffering of Sergeant Price than about the countless Iraqi victims of the war. These texts, in effect, make the grotesque realities of the Iraq and Afghanistan wars more palatable by using the soldiers' emotional trauma as a convenient stand-in for the collective complicity shared by the public in a war of aggression waged in their name.

According to Scranton, the problem does not lie solely with the writers themselves but rather with a readership that expects war writers to conform to a specific narrative and emotional framework. The failure of war literature, he argues, "belongs to all the readers and citizens who expect veterans to play out for them the ritual *fort-da* of trauma and recovery, and to carry for them the collective guilt of war" (Scranton 2015). In this sense, Scranton's *War Porn* deliberately withholds this form of emotional surrogacy: it refuses to replace the readers' shared complicity with Aaron's personal trauma. As I have previously argued, Aaron cannot be absolved of responsibility for the horrific acts documented in the photographs he carries, not on the grounds of diffused responsibility up the chain of command, nor through any appeal to psychological trauma.

Unlike a whistleblower, Aaron does not reveal these images to seek justice or provoke moral reckoning; instead, he deflects blame onto higher authorities without the slightest introspection. The novel's ending offers no redemption for Aaron, and his final act of sexual violence against Dahlia eliminates any possibility of moral substitution or escape. In this way, *War Porn* denies readers the comforting illusion of transference, compelling them instead to confront their own implication in the structures of violence it depicts.

The soldiers depicted in these texts embody a third morality, which I propose to call *operative realism* — a framework that is neither wholly pacifist nor strictly belligerent, but rather practical, functional, and disturbingly relatable for the reader. Whereas survivors of the Holocaust often described their experiences in Nazi concentration camps as unspeakable, lamenting that those at home were either unable or unwilling to listen, these contemporary war narratives reveal a different kind of refusal: a refusal rooted not in ignorance, but in a preconceived and commodified vision of war. Civilian audiences already "know" what they wish to hear because they have been saturated with simplified, sanitised representations that leave no room for complexity or moral ambiguity. The soldiers, in turn, are denied the luxury of genuine introspection; their choices are predetermined or driven by impulses so deeply personal and immediate that they defy articulation.

These narratives further suggest that the most debilitating affliction confronting these soldiers does not arise merely from their exposure to violence and bloodshed, but from the necessity of returning to a civilian value system incapable of truly reintegrating them. This system offers no clear option for embracing either complete pacifism or total belligerence. Their return home — aptly captured by the title of Phil Klay's short story collection *Redeployment* — becomes, in effect, a redeployment to a new and insidious battlefield, governed by shifting and contradictory moral standards. In this inverted landscape, home ceases to be a place of peace, and the battlefield no longer functions as a clearly defined site of conflict. Within this framework, the literature of the "war on terror" transcends its literal meaning, emerging instead as a series of discursive practices that seek to reshape our collective understanding of war through the lens of *operative realism*.

Considering all these aspects, it might be more precise to argue that debating whether these texts should be classified as pacifist or belligerent is, if not entirely fallacious, then at least deeply problematic. As evidence, these narratives, by presenting what I have called discursive simultaneity, ultimately carve out a third position—one that is neither pacifist nor belligerent, but rather grounded in *operative realism*: a practical and functional moral stance that resists traditional ideological binaries. The only way to continue categorising them within pacifist or belligerent frameworks would be to redefine those terms to accommodate such narrative complexities radically. In this sense, a truly pacifist narrative would not simply reject violence abstractly but would forcefully foreground the harm that war inflicts on the bodies of all participants, acknowledging both the dead and the living. It would compel the reader to confront the potential damage to their own body and sense of self, thereby eliciting a visceral empathy that transcends rhetorical condemnation.

Alternatively, drawing on Judith Butler's theoretical framework, a pacifist narrative would attempt to apprehend "as living" those lives that are either injured or lost. "If certain lives," Butler explains, "do not qualify as lives, or are, from the start, not conceivable as lives within certain epistemological frames, then these lives are never lived nor lost in the full sense" (Butler 2010, 1). In contrast, a genuinely belligerent narrative might acknowledge such damage but interpret it as a necessary means to an end that transcends the validity and reality of those individual bodies. Crucially, a belligerent narrative does not necessarily exhort the reader to participate in war, just as a pacifist narrative does not merely plead for abstention. Instead, a belligerent narrative accounts for bodily loss but refuses to recognise these bodies as discrete, individual "ends." Instead, it aggregates them into undifferentiated masses, treating them as symbolic or instrumental. Such narratives resemble the Angel in Tony Kushner's *Angels in America* (1991), who remains "too far off the earth to pick out the details" (Kushner 2013, 230). Belligerent narratives thus stubbornly eschew individual stories, favouring sweeping visions of grandeur or functioning as extended meditations on humanity's enduring martial spirit.

Additionally, by displacing and reconfiguring the notion of the enemy, these narratives challenge traditional ways of representing war in literature and thus occupy a position distinctly different from that of conventional war narratives. Their function within the broader discourse of the American "war on terror" resembles, in many ways, the role that Harper Lee's *To Kill a Mockingbird* (1960) played within the Civil Rights Movement, rather than that of classic war novels such as Stephen Crane's *The Red Badge of Courage* (1895). Much like Lee's novel, these contemporary "war" narratives appear committed to demonstrating that peacefighting is not fundamentally a political endeavour in the narrow sense but rather an endeavour in which the political is inextricably bound to the personal.

These narratives suggest that peacefighting does not consist merely in persuading people that war is wrong; instead, it operates by instilling fear and a profound sense of disquiet in those who have not experienced war firsthand. The parallels they draw underscore the impossibility of returning to a prior, unblemished state. Just as the return home is not a simple closing of a circle but rather a spiralling both outward and inward, these texts expose the ultimate failure of any true "homecoming." Their ambition is to create a point of no return within the reader's consciousness, a rupture that mirrors the psychic dislocation experienced by returning soldiers. A genuinely pacifist narrative, then, enables readers to comprehend the complexities and moral ambiguities of war, opening a space where the reader may return "home" with the same sense of estrangement and unfamiliarity that haunts the veteran.

While on the surface novels such as Ben Fountain's *Billy Lynn's Long Halftime Walk*, Michael Pitre's *Fives and Twenty-Fives*, and Roy Scranton's *War Porn* engage directly with the wars in Iraq and Afghanistan, they appear to do so primarily because these conflicts provide them with visibility and cultural capital that would otherwise be absent. Beneath this surface engagement lie deeper, more urgent concerns—psychological, moral, and existential—that might have otherwise remained unnoticed. Perhaps most importantly, these narratives seem to perform a preparatory function for the civilian audience: they preemptively define the shape and terms of the dialogue that might take place between returning combatants and the society they re-enter, shaping how civilians understand, receive, and respond to the psychic and moral burdens veterans carry home.

When Lieutenant Donovan, one of the protagonists in Michael Pitre's *Fives and Twenty-Fives*, refuses to discuss the war with friends and acquaintances, it is not because he is a brooder or someone repressing his emotions. Instead, it is because they fundamentally do not wish to hear what he has to say. "That's why," Donovan explains, "I always keep two or three stories on deck, harmless and cute, to distract and move the conversation elsewhere. The million dollars burning on the side of the road is a real winner. Fred the Scorpion works well, too" (Pitre 2015, 174–75). These prepared anecdotes function as social armour, allowing him to deflect genuine inquiry and protect his interlocutors from truths they are unwilling or unable to confront.

Although these "harmless and cute" stories *are* part of the bigger picture, they remain consistently marginal, never reaching the core of the issue. By the end of the novel, the reader might realise that they have not been presented with the story involving the million dollars burning on the side of the road, but rather that they have been armed or inoculated against that kind of story, or against the expectation of encountering such narratives at all.

In sum, these contemporary narratives of the "war on terror" resist easy categorisations and instead demand a more attentive, nuanced reading—one that recognises the hybrid moral terrain they traverse. By displacing the enemy, emphasising bodily vulnerability, and unsettling expectations of confession or redemption, these texts articulate a form of *operative realism* that challenges both our ethical frameworks and the cultural narratives through which war is so often filtered. Rather than affirming a simple dichotomy between pacifism and belligerence, they reveal the insufficiency of such terms, offering instead a moral logic grounded in pragmatic necessity and deep psychological ambivalence. In doing so, they do not provide closure or consolation; instead, they implicate the reader in the very structures of complicity they might prefer to overlook. These works do not offer a window onto a distant battlefield; instead, they function as mirrors, reflecting back to us the stories we demand, the silences we preserve, and the moral shortcuts we too willingly accept.

6.4 The Enemy at Home: Families at War

In the previous sections, I have argued that many of the narratives emerging from the wars in Iraq and Afghanistan hinge upon a fundamental misplacement of the enemy. This displacement becomes particularly pronounced in one of the pivotal texts of the "war on terror," Phil Klay's short story "Redeployment," where the return home is reimagined as another kind of "redeployment," and where, perhaps counterintuitively, family members themselves are momentarily perceived as "enemies." In this reversal between battlefield and homeland, the family, traditionally viewed as the locus of recovery and sanctuary, emerges as the most problematic space, in urgent need of re-examination and reform. The very values that define the notion of "home" are subjected to scrutiny, as seen not only in Klay's story but also in Ben Fountain's *Billy Lynn's Long Halftime Walk* (2012) and other texts discussed earlier. Across these narratives, returning home is depicted not as a smooth process of reintegration but rather as a profoundly destabilising experience, fraught with emotional and moral tension for both soldiers and their families.

Another significant text in this regard is George Saunders' short story "Home," included in his collection *Tenth of December* (2013), which underscores the alienation soldiers often face upon returning to the supposed "haven" of their families. In this story, Mike returns from an unnamed war to find that everything he once knew has become unrecognisable. His devout, church-going mother has cycled through boyfriends and is now being evicted after failing to pay rent for four months. His former wife has reorganised her financial life and is raising their child with another man, whom Mike pointedly refers to as "Asshole." Even the domestic objects he encounters, such as a mysterious product called "MiiVOXmax," whose purpose is never explained, deepen his sense of estrangement. These elements of confusion and disorientation do nothing to alleviate the post-traumatic stress disorder that pervades his inner life. Instead, they compound it, turning the supposed sanctuary of home into a new, bewildering battleground.

Mike is not the only one frustrated by the changes he encounters upon his return home. Readers of Saunders's short stories often find themselves grappling with a similar sense of frustration and disorientation. Many aspects of Mike's past remain unexplained: we are never told why he enlisted in the army or chose to go to war, nor do we learn the reasons behind his girlfriend's departure. We are informed only vaguely that Mike did something in Al-Raz (Saunders 2014, 192), but the specifics of this event remain entirely obscured. Likewise, the purpose of the mysterious product, MiiVOXmax, sold by the two clerks, remains unclear. Yet, despite, or precisely because of, this deliberate ambiguity, Saunders succeeds in recreating the disorienting confusion that returning soldiers so often experience. The sharp contrast between the external world and the intimate space of the family, Saunders explains in an interview for *The New Yorker*, is intentionally constructed to produce this effect:

> So here's our affluent, materialistic culture buzzing along, everything branded and corporate and glossy, bankers running roughshod over the rest of us, wealth continuing to drift upward, the middle-class vanishing ... and meanwhile this group of overworked and underpaid (mostly young) people are doing absolutely heroic labours in our name, while, in some small number of cases, doing horrific things in our name, to people who didn't ask for us to be there in the first place and to whom we must occasionally look completely otherworldly and Darth Vaderesque. (*The New Yorker*, 2011)

By narrating the story from Mike's perspective, Saunders seeks to portray the sense of alienation and disappointment felt by returning soldiers—a frustration born from confronting a homeland that utterly fails to embody or uphold the values exalted by militaristic rhetoric.

One trope Saunders employs, common across narratives about soldiers' return home, is the civilian compulsion to perform gratitude by incessantly thanking veterans for their service. In *Home*, everyone who learns of Mike's military service repeats the phrase "thank you for your service" with almost mechanical zeal. When the landlord and the sheriff arrive to evict Mike's mother, she indignantly invokes her son's military status as a shield: "This is my son," she insists, pointing to Mike, "[who] served. Who just came home. And this is how you do us?" (Saunders 2014, 180). In response, both the landlord and the sheriff dutifully echo the refrain, thanking Mike for his service even as they proceed with the eviction. The mother's new boyfriend underscores the perceived injustice, accusing the landlord of lacking sufficient gratitude for Mike's supposed heroism. Even the two young clerks selling the cryptic MiiVOXmax thank Mike for his service, despite having no knowledge of where, how, or why he fought.

The issues that returning soldiers face extend far beyond the battlefield. While deployed, they often experience an acute sense of purpose: their presence is justified by a clear, immediate objective, often as stark and urgent as the simple imperative to stay alive. Once home, however, that sense of purpose begins to erode, eventually disappearing altogether. One of the most painful realisations for these returning soldiers is that the world they imagined as their anchor—the world that gave meaning to their survival—has changed in fundamental ways during their absence. Girlfriends have moved on with new partners; wives have left or betrayed them; families have reconfigured their orbits around new centres. For someone who has spent months or years in a context where their very life hung in the balance, this sudden irrelevance can be profoundly harrowing.

This experience of dislocation is so pervasive that Sebastian Junger dedicates an entire book to it, albeit a concise one. In *Tribe: On Homecoming and Belonging* (2016), Junger argues that a soldier's return home is distressing above all because "[modern] society has perfected the art of making people not feel necessary" (Junger 2016, xvii). This pervasive sense of superfluousness exacerbates mental health struggles, such as post-traumatic stress disorder (PTSD), compounding their psychological burden and impeding reintegration. For Junger, the root of this problem lies not in individual pathology but in the deeper structure of modern society itself, which has severed individuals from the communal bonds that once sustained them and affirmed their value.

To substantiate his argument, Junger returns to the early history of the United States, specifically drawing on the observations of Benjamin Franklin. Writing in 1753, Franklin noted with fascination that Native American children, once exposed to tribal life, refused to return to white communities, despite having been raised and educated there. "The frontier," Junger elaborates, "was full of men who joined Indian tribes, married Indian women, and lived their lives completely outside civilisation" (2016, 9). These individuals seemed to believe that the material advantages of Western civilisation paled in comparison to the profound communal intimacy and shared sense of purpose found within Native American societies. In this light, Junger suggests that the returning soldier's profound alienation is not merely a personal struggle but a symptom of a broader societal failure to provide the sense of belonging and necessity that is essential to human flourishing.

What drew these people most powerfully to the lifestyle of Native American tribes was their "fundamental egalitarianism," which defined social status as something accessible to every member of the community. Personal property was also limited, making it difficult for gross inequalities of wealth to accumulate (Junger 2016, 14). Most importantly, Junger argues that advantages of any kind could not be inherited from parents, siblings, or other relatives, allowing individuals within the community to enjoy a far greater sense of freedom than in so-called "civilised" societies, where private property and inheritance are central. Moreover, whereas in many tribal cultures young people must "prove themselves by undergoing initiation rites that demonstrate their readiness for adulthood," for the average American young man, particularly one from a family able to afford an education, going to war is less an obligation than "a chance to be part of something bigger" (2016, 37). "To the extent that boys are drawn to war," Junger explains, "it may be less out of an interest in violence than a longing for the kind of maturity and respect that often come with it" (2016, 38). This pull may also arise from a desire to escape troubled family situations or, conversely, from a sense of continuity, especially when fathers or older brothers have also served in the military.

From this vantage point, wars can have a paradoxically positive effect on mental health. In contrast to modern, peaceful societies, which often leave individuals feeling worthless and unable to contribute meaningfully, war offers soldiers a clear sense of purpose. This perspective may also help explain why so many white men historically preferred the tribal societies of Native Americans. To further develop this point, Junger introduces Charles Fritz, an American scientist who dedicated his career to disaster research during and after World War II. Fritz's theory posited that large-scale disasters produce mentally healthier people because "modern society has gravely disrupted the social bonds that have always characterised the human experience, and disasters thrust people back into a more ancient, organic way of relating" (2016, 53). Disasters—whether wars or natural catastrophes—create what Fritz called a "community of sufferers," thereby strengthening individual connections to others within the group.

On the battlefield, under harsh conditions, a platoon or military unit effectively mimics what Junger calls a "community of sufferers." It strengthens the bonds between individual soldiers because what befalls one can potentially befall them all. "Self-interest," Junger explains, "gets subsumed into group interest because there is no survival outside group survival, and that creates a social bond that many people sorely miss" (2016, 66). Often, soldiers returning to civilian life find themselves longing for the war and the adrenaline it provides—a longing that sometimes compels them to return to combat. By contrast, modern society, with its extensive safety nets and protections, has largely eliminated "many of the situations that require people to demonstrate a commitment to the collective good," to the extent that "an urban man might go through his entire life without having to come to the aid of someone in danger—or even give up his dinner" (Junger 2016, 59). The abrupt transition from one world to the other, from collective interdependence to isolated individualism, is, unsurprisingly, a profoundly disorienting and painful experience for many soldiers.

Recovery from the trauma of war must therefore take these social dynamics into account, as the roots of recovery lie as much in community as in individual psychological treatment. As various studies show, the primary difficulty is not necessarily the trauma experienced on the battlefield—indeed, even those who never see combat often suffer from PTSD, depression, and other mental health struggles—but rather the challenge of "reentry into society"

(2016, 90). "In the United States," Sharon Abramowitz of the Peace Corps tells Junger, "we valorise our vets with words and posters and signs, but we don't give them what's really important to Americans, what really sets you apart as someone who is valuable to society—we don't give them jobs. All the praise in the world doesn't mean anything if you're not recognised by society as someone who can contribute valuable labour" (Junger 2016, 100). When these soldiers return home, they are often perceived as incapable of functioning "normally" in civilian life, and in many cases they genuinely struggle to do so. Yet this perception fails to address the deeper need: they "need to feel that they're just as necessary and productive back in society as they were on the battlefield" (Junger 2016, 102).

This does not mean, however, that we must engage in warlike activities to maintain our mental health. Rather, it reveals something crucial about how we approach mental health treatment and the kind of society we must envision for ourselves and for our veterans. "Today's veterans," Junger concludes,

> often come home to find that, although they're willing to die for their country, they're not sure how to live for it. It's hard to know how to live for a country that regularly tears itself apart along every ethnic and demographic boundary. The income gap between rich and poor continues to widen, many people live in racially segregated communities, the elderly are mostly sequestered from public life, and rampage shootings happen so regularly that they only remain in the news cycle for a day or two. […] In combat, soldiers all but ignore differences of race, religion, and politics within their platoon. It's no wonder many of them get so depressed when they come home. (Junger 2016, 124–25)

What this suggests is that, rather than parading our veterans as symbolic tokens, as Mike's mother does before the sheriff and her landlord, or merely thanking them for their service in a hollow ritual, we might begin by restoring the sense of purpose they once experienced on the battlefield. The prominence of family narratives in literature emerging from the American "war on terror," narratives that frequently refuse to portray the family as a sanctuary, suggests that the family could function as an intermediary space between the battlefield and the broader society into which veterans seek to reintegrate. As these narratives demonstrate, the narrower the gap between war and civilian life, the smoother the transition between them. Acknowledging and addressing the psychological impact of war on returning soldiers not only facilitates more effective treatment for mental health issues such as PTSD and depression but also fosters a society better equipped to respond to veterans' physical and emotional needs.

War narratives themselves point toward this direction; if they do not overtly criticise the phrase "thank you for your service," they at least create situations in which the phrase feels painfully inadequate or out of place. Moreover, they illuminate the challenges families face in coping with a soldier's return home. In their function as "trial runs," to borrow Booth's term, these narratives can sometimes serve as practical guides, as in works often written by army spouses, such as Siobhan Fallon's *You Know When the Men Are Gone* (2011), which I will discuss in the following pages. Before analysing these texts, however, some theoretical considerations are necessary.

Most often, when we consider the connection between *war* and *family*, we unconsciously assume that it is always *war* that affects the *family*: military events involving overseas deployment disrupt the fabric of the family, with far-reaching implications for its cohesiveness as an emotional and social unit. Wars are almost always seen as intrusive events, violently invasive, to the extent that they tend to tarnish or distort the concept of family. Families change in the process: they lose members, marriages collapse, and children become estranged.

The idea that war affects the concept of family is grounded in a series of beliefs that are not necessarily sustainable upon closer examination. The first of these beliefs is inherently *ethical*. It relies, through a shortcut of availability heuristics, on a stark division between the two concepts: within the war–family dichotomy, one is assumed to be fundamentally opposed to the other. If we were to imagine these notions on a spectrum ranging from comfort to discomfort, they would naturally be positioned at opposite ends of the spectrum. Politically and socially, they must remain opposed, for wars would lose much of their perceived purpose without this opposition. Wars are ostensibly fought to preserve the comfort, safety, and reassurance that families provide; indeed, it is often precisely this image of familial comfort that motivates individuals to enlist in the military in the first place.

Most of us are inclined to accept this ethical argument because it aligns with our civilian mindset, which fosters a strong impulse to thank veterans for their service and an equally powerful curiosity to understand "what it was like" for them to participate in an event whose primary purpose, as Elaine Scarry so incisively notes, is to "alter (to burn, to blast, to shell, to cut) human tissue" (Scarry 1985, 10). The means available to understand "what it was like" are necessarily limited yet readily accessible through fictional and nonfictional war accounts. This leads to my second argument, which in some respects undergirds the first: what I will refer to as the argument from *ancillary coverage*. To clarify this idea further, I will break down this argument into two key elements.

The first element pertains to war literature as an institution that sets specific limits on how texts are both produced and received. Military events reach us through images and words — a mode of delivery that, echoing our spectrum of comfort and discomfort, is at once invasive and urgent. Wars are invariably brought to our attention, and we consume these representations in part because we believe it is our moral obligation to do so, and in part because of the cultural and ethical principles underpinning the depiction of war. "The reasons that make war's representation imperative," Kate McLoughlin argues in *Authoring War: The Literary Representation of War from the Iliad to Iraq* (2011), "are as multitudinous as those which make it impossible" (McLoughlin 2011, 7). Besides imposing a discursive order "on the chaos of conflict and so to render it more comprehensible," war representation also aims "to inform civilians of the nature of battle to facilitate the reintegration of veterans into peacetime society" (2011, 7). In order to understand war and support this reintegration, we feel compelled to read about it, which in turn generates a widespread demand for acceptable representations. Within the genre of war literature, David A. Buchanan notes in *Going Scapegoat: Post-9/11 War Literature, Language and Culture* (2016), "all such literature faces an aesthetic tension, one based on popular demands and expectations" (Buchanan

2016, 8). We are constantly bombarded with war news and narratives, and a refusal to engage is often interpreted as a lapse in moral responsibility.

The second element relates to *what* is being delivered to us as readers of war literature. The narratives we consume about military events actively shape the kind of intrusiveness that war exerts on the concept of family. These accounts frequently construct stories of families disrupted and destabilised by war, to the point where we are confronted with the militarisation of the family space itself.

One of the most poignant texts in this regard is Phil Klay's short story "Redeployment," included in the collection of the same title, which I have discussed earlier. This story is particularly symptomatic because the "redeployment" in its title does not signify a return to active duty; on the contrary, it narrates a soldier's return home after serving in Iraq. Here, the traditional roles of war and family are strikingly reversed, as the narrator focuses on the rites of passage that soldiers from Bravo Company must undergo upon returning home. In the military limbo between boarding a plane in Kuwait and waking up in America, soldiers are expected to shed their military identity and relinquish their rifles—a moment that symbolises their transition but also reveals their disorientation. "I didn't know where to rest my hands," the narrator explains after handing in his combat rifle, "first I put them in my pocket, then I took them out and crossed my arms, and then I just let them hang, useless, at my sides" (Klay 2014, 6). This transitional moment marks the first signs of profound inadequacy: soldiers become awkward within their own bodies, and this awkwardness inevitably extends into their reunions with family members.

Family members, on the other hand, often appear utterly terrified. Cheryl, the narrator's wife, manages to handle the homecoming relatively well, unlike Lance Corporal Curtis's wife, who had spent "all his combat pay before he got back, and she was five months pregnant, which, for a Marine coming back from a seven-month deployment, is not pregnant enough" (2014, 10). In an attempt to ease the shock and awkwardness of the reunion, the narrator and Cheryl go shopping—an act he wryly describes as "how America fights back against the terrorists" (2014, 11). Yet the shopping centre, the site of his ironic "redeployment," fails to deliver its supposed calming effect. "You're safe," the narrator tells himself, "so your alertness should be at white, but it's not" (2014, 12). Military conditioning proves stubbornly persistent. As he admits, it takes "a fucking long time before you get down to white" (2014, 13). This heightened vigilance continues to infiltrate civilian and family life long after a soldier's physical return. Soldiers who survive the battlefield must then undertake the equally fraught task of surviving homecoming.

This motif recurs throughout Siobhan Fallon's collection of short stories, *You Know When the Men Are Gone* (2011), written from the perspective of an army wife. In "Leave," one of the most striking stories in the collection, Fallon narrates the experiences of Chief Warrant Officer Nick Cash, who breaks into his own home and secretly lives in the basement for several days to determine whether his wife is being unfaithful. After a friend informs him that Mark Rodell, the new gym teacher, has been seen at his house, Nick's military training takes over. He tells his wife he is giving up a leave so that a mate can take it instead, only to return home unannounced, hoping to catch her in the act.

While hiding in the basement of his own home, Nick sleeps in unsanitary conditions, using his daughter's discarded toys as pillows. He listens intently to his wife's daily routine and eats small, almost imperceptible amounts of food from the refrigerator. Although he is fully aware that he is "investigating" his wife and daughter, his mind repeatedly drifts to scenes of intelligence gathering from the war. In Nick's eyes, Trish, his wife, becomes a suspect. "He knew from experience that the only way to prove anything beyond a reasonable doubt was to get inside the suspect's house, to find the sniper rifle under the bed, the Iranian bomb-making electronics in a back shed, the sketches of the nearest U.S. military base in a hollow panel of the wall" (Fallon 2012, 169). This parallel between his intelligence missions in Iraq and the "mission" he is now conducting at home persists throughout the story, even after he discovers his wife peacefully asleep beside another man in their bedroom. "Here it was," the protagonist reflects as he observes the scene, "after all this searching, after all the lies and lies and lies, the shifty informants with their misinformation and subtleties lost in translation. Here, in his own home, was a single and undeniable truth" (Fallon 2012, 186–87). Yet, Fallon leaves the ending deliberately open-ended; we never learn what Nick ultimately decides. What lingers is the haunting image of his knife moving from hand to hand, reminiscent of a raised "judge's gavel" (2012, 187).

Nevertheless, in Fallon's collection, the militarisation of the family and domestic space extends beyond the mere transfer of military training into the home. The family space is thoroughly militarised in nearly every story in *You Know When the Men Are Gone*. Set on the American army base at Fort Hood, Texas—a kind of military limbo where soldiers prepare for deployments to Iraq and Afghanistan—these stories portray the lives of army wives as they struggle to manage their husbands' absences. Amid the silence of their new homes, food casseroles, and Family Readiness Group meetings, these families live under rules dictated by the army. When another army wife asks Meg, the protagonist of the opening story, for a loan, Meg's ingrained "army wife" training instinctively kicks in:

> This was taboo. If a wife was in need, there were rules; you were supposed to call the rear detachment commander, and he could approve an official Army Emergency Relief loan. Or, if you didn't want your husband or his command to find out, there were the shifty money shops on Rancier Avenue that let you borrow, at interest, until the next paycheck came through. (Fallon 2012, 7)

Like their husbands or boyfriends on the battlefield, these women must rely on each other, knowing instinctively what the others are enduring. "Mingling too often with the civilian world," the omniscient narrator observes, "so full of couples, of men nonchalantly paying bills, planning vacations, and picking kids up after ball games—those constant reminders of what life could be, would drive an army spouse crazy" (Fallon 2012, 9). Observing other army spouses enduring the same struggles creates the "community of sufferers" that Charles Fritz describes, ultimately making their burdens more bearable.

In "Remission," Fallon portrays another army wife, Ellen Roddy, who is fighting her own battle against breast cancer, which has already claimed one of her breasts. While waiting for a routine check-up at the hospital—and doing her best to ignore a hysterical baby nearby—she struggles to resist the impulse to assess "the rank of the woman's husband by her clothes or level of parenting skills" (Fallon 2012, 73). The army permeates every level of family life, enforcing a system of checks and balances and the "ever-present chain of command" (Fallon 2012, 74). Observing those waiting with their wives, Ellen notes that they "were usually better-looking than their spouses, which was the curse of an army base where women were scarce and the enticement to get laid all too often led to the altar" (2012, 75). Like a ghost inhabiting every shell of domestic life, the army seems to make choices for these families, shaping even the most intimate corners of their existence.

The army trickles into their sexual lives as well. For these army wives, the threat of death that their husbands face daily is not the only looming fear. In "Inside the Break," as these women watch their husbands depart, they suddenly register another kind of threat, casually boarding one of the supply buses: "That supply bus held a threat that had never occurred to any of them when they thought of faraway insurgents and bombs and helicopters crashing. That supply bus with its fifteen women" (2012, 105). Some army wives, like Kailani Rodriguez, ultimately decide that this additional threat is not worth confronting, even after discovering a stray message from a female soldier in her husband's army email account.

In another story, included in *Fire and Forget: Short Stories from the Long War* (2013) and suggestively titled "Tips for a Smooth Transition," Fallon depicts yet another army wife preparing for her husband's return from Afghanistan. She turns to *Battle Spouses' Tips for a Smooth Transition*, a guide reminiscent of "The Good Wife's Guide" published in the May 1955 issue of *Housekeeping Monthly*. "Typically," Fallon's fictional manual explains, "a 'honeymoon' period follows in which couples reunite, but not necessarily emotionally. Sexual intimacy may take time. Be patient and communicate— you and your spouse may have expectations that are not met right away" (Scranton and Gallagher 2013, 25). The guide also offers advice on managing jealousy and infidelity, among other potential challenges, portraying the homecoming not as a joyful resolution, but as a fraught and negotiated return to an uncertain domestic equilibrium.

Now, after examining these examples of how the idea of family becomes militarised, a compelling question emerges: could we also speak of a "familiarisation" of the army and of war itself? Does the concept of family exert an influence on the military institution and the practice of war? The quick answer is *yes*; we can. However, the reassurance offered by this affirmative answer does not come from the ancillary coverage of the "war on terror." Most narratives that engage with this issue reveal that "familiarisation" typically does not extend beyond the Forward Operating Base (FOB) — a kind of military limbo where soldiers acclimate to the battlefield while maintaining tenuous ties with their families back home. Beyond the FOB, familial connections are often replaced by the immediate and intense bonds formed among soldiers as a means of collective survival. A more comprehensive answer to this question emerges from the *proximal coverage* of the war, specifically in how the idea of family has prompted institutional changes within the American military system.

Some of the most significant institutional changes within the American military, as paradoxical as it may seem, were prompted by none other than toddlers. "In the decade that followed the Gulf War," Rachel Maddow observes in *Drift: The Unmooring of American Military Power* (2012), "preschool kids ended up being the most effective shock troops in the assault on the last remaining constraints keeping us from going to war all the time" (Maddow 2013, 157). The toddlers themselves had no agency in these transformations, yet because they are integral members of army families, the Army had to account for their needs, often at enormous financial cost. Soldiers, for their part, were more willing to accept deployment anywhere in the world if they felt assured that their families would be adequately cared for in their absence.

Maddow explains that to address this problem, the Army faced two possible solutions: downsize or cut costs. They chose the latter: "Outsourcing. Privatisation. Civilian Augmentation. In other words, can't we get someone in here who doesn't come with day-care costs?" (2013, 159). In Maddow's view, the privatisation of the

Army, which began soon after the Gulf War, has had severe long-term consequences for the way the United States has conducted its wars ever since. It has led to a complete separation between war and civilian life, to the extent that by 2001, "the spirit of the Abrams Doctrine—that the disruption of civilian life is the price of admission for war—was pretty much kaput" (2013, 187). In an article for the *Los Angeles Times*, David Zucchino and David S. Cloud argue that most Americans have "experienced little, if any, personal impact from the longest era of war in U.S. history. However, those in uniform have seen their lives upended by repeated deployments to war zones, felt the pain of seeing family members and comrades killed and maimed, and endured psychological trauma that many will carry forever, often invisible to their civilian neighbours" (Zucchino and Cloud 2015). This widening separation has profoundly altered how civilians perceive the military and the service it provides.

This brings us full circle to the central thread of my argument. If the militarisation of family space is, as Maddow describes, part and parcel of the "disruption of family life," then that militarisation becomes essential in maintaining a system of checks and balances concerning a nation's capacity and willingness to wage war, an issue of paramount importance in today's increasingly unstable global context. As these narratives suggest, the narrower the gap between war and civilian life, the more meaningful and effective the dialogue between the two spheres can become. Coming to terms with the psychological and emotional impact of war on those who serve not only facilitates the development of more effective treatments for mental health issues such as post-traumatic stress disorder and depression but also helps to foster a society genuinely equipped to address the physical and emotional needs of its veterans.

Conclusion

The field of literature this book aims to explore continues to evolve. The terrorist attacks of September 11, 2001, and the subsequent military interventions in Iraq and Afghanistan have left a lasting impact on those who experienced them, whether directly or indirectly. These events, with their profound significance, will continue to challenge our imagination and inspire new perspectives. The mental imprint of these happenings will inevitably lead to more books being published and more films and documentaries being produced, reflecting not only the events themselves but also how we come to understand and reframe them. These literary and visual media will also inevitably reshape the events by situating them within a context that, while acknowledging what occurred, also seeks to redefine the social practices surrounding them. Even after all these years, the Vietnam War still appears in works of fiction, and much like the Vietnam War, 9/11 will remain a source of fascination for years to come, with even the slightest detail triggering a host of memories and related ideas.

The sheer abundance of material also renders it increasingly difficult to navigate the cultural, ethical, and aesthetic complexities these events entail. Unless one chooses to narrow the scope and address only a single facet, as many scholars have done, it becomes nearly impossible to offer a comprehensive and unified perspective. For this reason, among others, this book has adopted a different methodological approach: rather than fixating on the volume of texts or the minutiae of how they represent these events, it proposes an "event-centric" view of cultural production, much like Richard Dawkins' gene-centric view of evolution. Rather than categorising these texts through rigid typologies, as Birgit Däwes suggests, this study argues that these works are profoundly shaped by the very nature of the events they depict. They function as protective membranes—cultural skins—that both shield and transmute the event, ensuring its ongoing survival and continual metamorphosis within collective memory.

While Däwes emphasises the role these fictional texts play in "the shaping and installation of the cultural memory of 9/11" (Däwes 2011, 6), my analysis has instead sought to examine how 9/11 itself exerts pressure on these texts, shaping their form, reception, and cultural function. In so doing, this book aims not merely to chart a genealogy of representations but to reveal the intimate, reciprocal entanglement between catastrophic events and their narrative afterlives. By foregrounding this dynamic, I hope to invite readers to consider not only how we narrate trauma, violence, and rupture but also how these narratives, in turn, shape the very contours of our collective moral and cultural imagination.

The idea that *selfish events* have agency might be hard to accept. Like Dawkins' concept of selfish genes, it suggests that these events possess a form of consciousness and agency, even though we know this is not the case and could never be the case. Events occur as a result of a series of actions carried out over different periods. They do not decide to happen consciously, as imagining so would be absurd. Nonetheless, even purely for intellectual curiosity, considering the possibility that an event like 9/11 has its agency could help us understand some of its paradoxes and why it is regarded as a *transformative* event.

Additionally, that agency might stem from actions taken by different actors, such as intellectuals, politicians, and other figures with social capital. Being able to identify it as an "agent," however unlikely that might be, helps in understanding its inner workings and mechanisms of reinforcement, which in turn makes it easier to find ways to *dismantle* it. The effects of this could be liberating for some, while appearing suspicious and dismissive to others. However, it might also free those cultural artefacts that are unrelated to it from the influence of the event's agency. Most importantly, the idea of *selfish events* aims to be, much like Sedgwick's theory of affect, *empowering*.

The *proximal-ancillary coverage continuum* further emphasises the fluid relationship between an event and its cultural impact, potentially providing a framework for analysing the textual representation of other events. Although the continuum is often seen as an extension of Marxist critique or a reimagining of the traditional divide between fictional and non-fictional portrayals of an event, it offers more than that. Usually, literature related to an event remains limited to academic circles or is dismissed as mere entertainment. While entertainment does play a role, especially in what gets published and what does not, it is only one aspect of these works. *Event literature* should be regarded as an integral part of understanding a particular event, rather than merely an aside or commentary. The "non" in non-fictional draws a boundary, beyond which lies a no man's land ruled by rules as fictional as the entities they depict. Conversely, the *proximal–ancillary coverage continuum* views these two types of texts as interconnected, informing and giving meaning to each other.

The *proximal-ancillary continuum* also highlights the social role of texts. By refusing to accept a clear division between fiction and non-fiction, it argues that since discursive practices shape social practices and vice versa, texts can be used to correct social behaviours and even create new ones. This process is especially evident in literature related to the wars in Iraq and Afghanistan, where specific texts serve not only as descriptions of the reality of war or its outcomes but also as means of engaging with social issues both locally and internationally. These texts can also offer valuable insights into how we perceive war and how this influences our approach to fighting wars. This is not to imply that these texts directly lead to political action; instead, they can equip us with the mental tools to recognise the extent to which discursive practices influence our experience of war's reality. The potential significance of this research is considerable, as it can offer a new perspective on the cultural influence of significant events and their depiction in literature.

The theoretical framework discussed in this book is by no means complete, nor does it claim to be exhaustive. Further work is needed to refine it and expand it beyond a simple series of observations based on a sequence of texts. An interesting avenue would be to explore whether these notions could be applied to events like the Second World War or the Vietnam War, or to literature concerning events not directly connected to the United States. Additional work should also examine what I refer to in my book as "foreign discourse regulators," namely, texts by Iraqi and Afghan authors about the wars in Iraq and Afghanistan, which I allocated limited space to. Incorporating these texts could strengthen the framework because they often challenge how events are portrayed by the U.S. press and publishing industry. Including these texts would also demonstrate that, while firmly rooted in reality, an event's significance always arises at the intersection of different streams of thought, constantly shifting, evolving, and remaking itself, as if it possesses a life of its own.

Bibliography

Abrams, M. H. 1999. *A Glossary of Literary Terms*. 7th ed. Fort Worth: Harcourt Brace College Publishers.

Ackerman, Elliot. 2015. *Green on Blue: A Novel*. First Scribner hardcover edition. New York: Scribner.

Alexander, Jeffrey C., ed. 2004. *Cultural Trauma and Collective Identity*. Berkeley, California: University of California Press.

Althusser, Louis. 1984. *Essays on Ideology*. London: Verso.

Amis, Martin. 2009. *The Second Plane: September 11: Terror and Boredom*. New York: Vintage International.

Anderson, Donald. 2014. 'You Can't Come Home Again: Phil Klay's Redeployment'. *WLA; War, Literature and the Arts*, 1 January 2014.

Anderson, Jack. 1982. 'Lawsuit Forces CIA Confession on MK-ULTRA'. *Washington Post*, 28 August 1982. CIA Electronic Reading Room.

Arquilla, John. n.d. 'Three Wars on Terror'. *Foreign Policy* (blog). Accessed 9 January 2018. https://foreignpolicy.com/2012/09/10/three-wars-on-terror/.

'Astoria Park Highlights—General Slocum Disaster: NYC Parks'. n.d. Accessed 17 October 2017. https://www.nycgovparks.org/parks/astoria-park/highlights/19029.

Badiou, Alain, and Cécile Winter. 2011. *Polemics*. Translated by Steve Corcoran. London; New York: Verso.

Ball-Rokeach, S.J., and M.L. DeFleur. 1976. 'A Dependency Model of Mass-Media Effects'. *Communication Research* 3 (1): 3–21.

Banita, Georgiana. 2012. *Plotting Justice: Narrative Ethics and Literary Culture after 9/11*. Lincoln: University of Nebraska Press.

Baudrillard, Jean. 2012. *The Spirit of Terrorism: And Other Essays*. Translated by Chris Turner. Radical Thinkers. London; New York: Verso.

Bayoumi, Moustafa. 2008. *How Does It Feel to Be a Problem? Being Young and Arab in America*. New York: Penguin Press.

———. 2015. *This Muslim American Life: Dispatches from the War on Terror*. New York: New York University Press.

Berger, James. 2003. 'There's No Backhand to This'. In *Trauma at Home: After 9/11*, edited by Judith Greenberg, 52–59. Lincoln, NE: University of Nebraska Press.

Bissell, Tom. 2015. "Elliot Ackerman's 'Green on Blue.'" *The New York Times*, 27 February 2015, sec. Sunday Book Review. https://www.nytimes.com/2015/03/01/books/review/elliot-ackermans-green-on-blue.html.

Blasim, Hasan, and Jonathan Wright. 2014. *The Corpse Exhibition and Other Stories of Iraq*. New York: Penguin Books.

Bleiker, Roland. 2006. 'Art after 9/11'. *Alternatives: Global, Local, Political* 31 (1): 77.

Booth, Wayne C. 1988. *The Company We Keep: An Ethics of Fiction*. Berkeley: University of California Press.

Bottum, J. 23:01. 'Sontagged'. *Weekly Standard*. 23:01. http://www.weeklystandard.com/sontagged/article/1615.

Brenkman, John. 2007. *The Cultural Contradictions of Democracy: Political Thought since September 11*. Princeton: Princeton University Press.

Brosman, Catharine Savage. 1992. 'The Functions of War Literature'. *South Central Review* 9 (1): 85–98. https://doi.org/10.2307/3189388.

Bruner, Jerome. 1991. 'The Narrative Construction of Reality'. *Critical Inquiry* 18 (1): 1–21. https://doi.org/10.1086/448619.

Buchanan, David A. 2016. *Going Scapegoat: Post-9/11 War Literature, Language and Culture*. Jefferson, North Carolina: McFarland & Company, Inc., Publishers.

Butler, Judith. 2010. *Frames of War: When Is Life Grievable?* Paperback Edition. London; New York: Verso.

Campbell, James. 1999. 'Combat Gnosticism: The Ideology of First World War Poetry Criticism'. *New Literary History* 30 (1): 203–15.

Caputo, Philip. 2015. '"The Sympathizer," by Viet Thanh Nguyen'. *The New York Times*, 2 April 2015, sec. Book Review. https://www.nytimes.com/2015/04/05/books/review/the-sympathizer-by-viet-thanh-nguyen.html.

Carter, Shan, AM, and A. Cox. 2011. 'One 9/11 Tally: $3.3 Trillion'. *The New York Times*, 8 September 2011. http://www.nytimes.com/interactive/2011/09/08/us/sept-11-reckoning/cost-graphic.html.

Castner, Brian. n.d. 'Afghanistan: A Stage Without a Play'. Los Angeles Review of Books. Accessed 28 February 2018. https://lareviewofbooks.org/article/afghanistan-stage-without-play/.

Chabon, Michael. 2007. 'After the Apocalypse'. *The New York Review of Books*, 15 February 2007. http://www.nybooks.com/articles/2007/02/15/after-the-apocalypse/.

Chapman, Loren J., and Jean P. Chapman. 1969. 'Illusory Correlation as an Obstacle to the Use of Valid Psychodiagnostic Signs.' *Journal of Abnormal Psychology* 74 (3): 271–80. https://doi.org/10.1037/h0027592.

Chomsky, Noam. 2002. *Media Control: The Spectacular Achievements of Propaganda*. 2nd ed. An Open Media Book. New York: Seven Stories Press.

– – – . 2011. *9-11: Was There an Alternative?* An Open Media Book. New York: Seven Stories Press.

Chossudovsky, Michel. 2008. "Al-Qaeda and the 'War on Terrorism.'" Global Policy Forum. 20 January 2008. https://www.globalpolicy.org/component/content/article/154/26821.html.

Cilano, Cara, ed. 2009. *From Solidarity to Schisms: 9/11 and after in Fiction and Film from Outside the US*. Internationale Forschungen Zur Allgemeinen Und Vergleichenden Literaturwissenschaft 126. Amsterdam: Rodopi.

Ciocia, Stefania. 2012. *Vietnam and beyond: Tim O'Brien and the Power of Storytelling*. Liverpool: Liverpool University Press.

Cole, David, "The Priority of Morality: The Emergency Constitution's Blind Spot" (2004). *Georgetown Law Faculty Publications and Other Works*. 925. https://scholarship.law.georgetown.edu/facpub/925.

Colman, Andrew M. 2009. *A Dictionary of Psychology*. 3rd ed. Oxford Paperback Reference. Oxford; New York: Oxford University Press.

'Commemoration | National September 11 Memorial & Museum'. n.d. Accessed 13 October 2024. https://www.911memorial.org/connect/commemoration.

Cordesman, Anthony H. 2017. 'Islam and the Patterns in Terrorism and Violent Extremism', October. https://www.csis.org/analysis/islam-and-patterns-terrorism-and-violent-extremism.

Croft, Stuart. 2006. *Culture, Crisis and America's War on Terror*. Cambridge; New York: Cambridge University Press.

Crouch, Ian. 2016. 'George Carlin's Shocking Prescience on the Nights Before 9/11'. *The New Yorker*, 10 September 2016. https://www.newyorker.com/culture/culture-desk/george-carlins-shocking-prescience-on-the-nights-before-911.

Cusk, Rachel. 2014. 'The Blazing World by Siri Hustvedt – Review'. *The Guardian*, 15 March 2014, sec. Books. http://www.theguardian.com/books/2014/mar/15/blazing-world-siri-hustvedt-review.

D'Angelo, Paul, and Jim A. Kuypers, eds. 2010. *Doing News Framing Analysis: Empirical and Theoretical Perspectives*. Communication Series. New York; London: Routledge.

Daniels, Roger. 2002. 'Incarceration of the Japanese Americans: A Sixty-Year Perspective'. *The History Teacher* 35 (3): 297. https://doi.org/10.2307/3054440.

David, Susan A. 2016. *Emotional Agility: Get Unstuck, Embrace Change, and Thrive in Work and Life*. http://www.myilibrary.com?id=949648.

Däwes, Birgit. 2011. *Ground Zero Fiction: History, Memory, and Representation in the American 9/11 Novel*. American Studies 208. Heidelberg: Winter.

Dawes, James. 2002. *The Language of War: Literature and Culture in the U.S. from the Civil War through World War II*. Cambridge, Mass: Harvard University Press.

Dawkins, Richard. 2006. *The Selfish Gene*. 30th anniversary ed. Oxford; New York: Oxford University Press.

DeLillo, Don. 2001. 'In the Ruins of the Future'. *Harper's Magazine*, December 2001. https://harpers.org/archive/2001/12/in-the-ruins-of-the-future/.

— — —. 2011. *Falling Man: A Novel*. London: Picador.

Deuel, Nathan. n.d. "Mark Doten's 'The Infernal' a Darkly Twisted Take on Iraq War." Latimes.Com. Accessed 26 January 2018. http://www.latimes.com/books/jacketcopy/la-ca-jc-mark-doten-20150308-story.html.

Didion, Joan. 2003. *Fixed Ideas: America since 9.11*. New York: New York Review Books.

— — —. 2007. *The Year of Magical Thinking*. 1st Vintage International ed. New York: Vintage International.

Doten, Mark. 2015. *The Infernal: A Novel*. Minneapolis, Minnesota: Graywolf Press.

Douglas, Mary. 2002. *Purity and Danger: An Analysis of Concepts of Pollution and Taboo*. New York, NY: Routledge.

Drell, Cady. n.d. "'Stranger Things': The Secret CIA Programs That Inspired Hit Series." *Rolling Stone*. Accessed 17 October 2017. http://www.rollingstone.com/culture/features/stranger-things-inside-shows-real-life-cia-inspirations-w432945.

Eberstadt, Fernanda. 2014. '"The Blazing World," by Siri Hustvedt'. *The New York Times*, 28 March 2014, sec. Sunday Book Review. https://www.nytimes.com/2014/03/30/books/review/the-blazing-world-by-siri-hustvedt.html.

Edgers, Geoff. n.d. 'Fifteen Years after 9/11, We Can Hear the Only Bit George Carlin Ever Cut for Taste'. *Washington Post*. Accessed 10 October 2017. https://www.washingtonpost.com/entertainment/fifteen-years-after-911-we-can-hear-the-only-bit-george-carlin-ever-cut-for-taste/2016/09/07/40e0312c-745c-11e6-8149-b8d05321db62_story.html.

Einstein, Albert, Robert W Lawson, and Nigel Calder. 2006. *Relativity: The Special and the General Theory*. New York: Penguin Books.

Eleey, Peter. 2011. *September 11*. New York, NY: MoMA PS1.

Entman, Robert M. 2003. 'Cascading Activation: Contesting the White House's Frame After 9/11'. *Political Communication* 20 (4): 415–32. https://doi.org/10.1080/10584600390244176.

Erickson, Steve. 2017. *Shadowbahn*. New York: Blue Rider Press.

Faber, Michel. 2005. 'Extremely Loud & Incredibly Close by Jonathan Safran Foer'. *The Guardian*, 3 June 2005. http://www.theguardian.com/books/2005/jun/04/featuresreviews.guardianreview22.

Fairclough, Norman. 2009. *Discourse and Social Change*. Reprinted. Cambridge: Polity Press.

Fallon, Siobhan. 2012. *You Know When the Men Are Gone*. New York: New American Library.

Faludi, Susan. 2007. *The Terror Dream: Fear and Fantasy in Post-9/11 America*. 1st ed. New York: Metropolitan Books.

Faulkner, William. 1995. *Absalom, Absalom!* Fiction. London: Vintage.

Filkins, Dexter. 2014. '"Redeployment," by Phil Klay'. *The New York Times*, 6 March 2014, sec. Sunday Book Review. https://www.nytimes.com/2014/03/09/books/review/redeployment-by-phil-klay.html.

Finkel, David. 2010. *The Good Soldiers*. Atlantic Books Ltd.

Foer, Jonathan Safran. 2006. *Extremely Loud & Incredibly Close*. London: Penguin Books.

Fountain, Ben. 2012. *Billy Lynn's Long Halftime Walk*. 1st ed. New York: Ecco.

Gallagher, Matt. 2016. *Youngblood: A Novel*. First Atria Books hardcover edition. New York: Atria Books.

Gellhorn, Martha. 2011. *A Stricken Field*. Chicago Press ed. Chicago: The University of Chicago Press.

Gessen, Keith. 2005. 'Horror Tour'. *The New York Review of Books*, 22 September 2005. http://www.nybooks.com/articles/2005/09/22/horror-tour/.

Gray, Richard J. 2011. *After the Fall: American Literature since 9/11*. 1st ed. Blackwell Manifestos. Chichester, West Sussex; Malden, MA: Wiley-Blackwell.

Greenberg, Paul. 2008. 'Recipes for Disaster - Essay - World Made by Hand - James Howard Kunstler - Books - Review'. *The New York Times*, 20 April 2008, sec. Sunday Book Review. https://www.nytimes.com/2008/04/20/books/review/Greenberg-t.html.

Greenwald, Glenn. 2014. *No Place to Hide: Edward Snowden, the NSA, and the U.S. Surveillance State*. New York: Metropolitan Books.

Gross, David. 2000. *Lost Time: On Remembering and Forgetting in Late Modern Culture*. University of Massachusetts Press.

Habermas, Jürgen, and Jacques Derrida. 2003. *Philosophy in a Time of Terror: Dialogues with Jürgen Habermas and Jacques Derrida*. Edited by Giovanna Borradori. Chicago: University of Chicago Press.

Halbwachs, Maurice, and Mary Douglas. 1980. *The Collective Memory*. Translated by Francis J. Ditter and Vida Yazdi Ditter. First edition. Harper Colophon Books, CN 800. New York, Cambridge, Hagerstown, Philadelphia, San Francisco, London, Mexico City, Sydney: Harper & Row, Publishers.

Hamid, Mohsin. 2008. *The Reluctant Fundamentalist*. Boston; New York: Mariner Books/Houghton Mifflin Harcourt.

Hanley, Lynne. 1991. *Writing War: Fiction, Gender, and Memory*. Amherst: University of Massachusetts Press.

Hartnell, Anna. 2011. 'Violence and the Faithful in Post-9/11 America: Updike's Terrorist, Islam, and the Spectre of Exceptionalism'. *MFS Modern Fiction Studies* 57 (3): 477–502. https://doi.org/10.1353/mfs.2011.0066.

Hayden, Michael V. 2016. *Playing to the Edge: American Intelligence in the Age of Terror*. New York: Penguin Press.

Heberle, Mark A. 2001. *A Trauma Artist: Tim O'Brien and the Fiction of Vietnam*. University of Iowa Press.

Herman, Edward S., and Noam Chomsky. 1994. *Manufacturing Consent: The Political Economy of the Mass Media*. A Vintage Original. London: Vintage.

Hodges, Adam. 2011. *The 'War on Terror' Narrative: Discourse and Intertextuality in the Construction and Contestation of Sociopolitical Reality*. Oxford Studies in Sociolinguistics. New York: Oxford University Press.

Hoenicke, Sarah. n.d. "When the Hurlyburly's Done: Roy Scranton's 'War Porn.'" *Los Angeles Review of Books*. Accessed 23 February 2018. https://lareviewofbooks.org/article/when-the-hurlyburlys-done-roy-scrantons-war-porn/.

Holloway, David. 2008. *9/11 and the War on Terror*. Representing American Events. Edinburgh: Edinburgh University Press.

Howard, Michael. 2002. "What's In A Name? How to Fight Terrorism." *Foreign Affairs*, 1 January 2002. https://www.foreignaffairs.com/articles/2002-01-01/whats-name-how-fight-terrorism.

Huntington. 1993. 'The Clash of Civilizations? | Foreign Affairs'. *Foreign Affairs*, 1993. https://www.foreignaffairs.com/articles/united-states/1993-06-01/clash-civilizations.

Hustvedt, Siri. 2014. *The Blazing World: A Novel*. New York, NY: Simon & Schuster.

Hutcheon, Linda. 1988. *A Poetics of Postmodernism: History, Theory, Fiction*. New York: Routledge.

Huyssen, Andreas. 2009. *Present Pasts: Urban Palimpsests and the Politics of Memory*. Repr. Cultural Memory in the Present. Stanford, Calif: Stanford Univ. Press.

Jamison, Leslie. 2014. "Instead of Sobbing, You Write Sentences: An Interview with Charles D'Ambrosio." *The New Yorker*, 26 November 2014. https://www.newyorker.com/books/page-turner/instead-sobbing-write-sentences-interview-charles-dambrosio.

Junger, Sebastian. 2011. *War*. Fourth Estate paperback edition. London: Fourth Estate.

— — —. 2016. *Tribe: On Homecoming and Belonging*.

Kahneman, Daniel. 2011. *Thinking, Fast and Slow*. 1st ed. New York: Farrar, Straus and Giroux.

Kakutani, Michiko. 2005. 'A Boy's Epic Quest, Borough by Borough'. *The New York Times*, 22 March 2005, sec. Books. https://www.nytimes.com/2005/03/22/books/a-boys-epic-quest-borough-by-borough.html.

— — —. 2016. '"Youngblood," an Urgent Novel About the Iraq War'. *The New York Times*, 21 January 2016, sec. Books. https://www.nytimes.com/2016/01/22/books/review-youngblood-an-urgent-novel-about-the-iraq-war.html.

Keeble, Arin. n.d. 'Why the 9/11 Novel Has Been Such a Contested and Troubled Genre'. Accessed 3 February 2018. http://www.independent.co.uk/arts-entertainment/books/features/911-novel-thomas-pynchon-twin-towers-september-11-don-delillo-a7236091.html.

Kelman, Mark. 2011. *The Heuristics Debate*. New York, NY: Oxford University Press.

Klay, Phil. 2014a. 'After War, a Failure of the Imagination'. *The New York Times*, 8 February 2014, sec. Opinion. https://www.nytimes.com/2014/02/09/opinion/sunday/after-war-a-failure-of-the-imagination.html.

— — —. 2014b. *Redeployment*. New York: The Penguin Press.

Kovach, Bill, and Tom Rosenstiel. 2014. *The Elements of Journalism: What Newspeople Should Know, and the Public Should Expect*. Revised and updated third edition. New York: Three Rivers Press.

Kumar, Amitava. 2006. 'The Last Days of Muhammad Atta'. *Amitava Kumar Blog* (blog). 21 April 2006. http://amitavakumar.blogsome.com/2006/04/21/the-last-days-of-muhammad-atta/.

Kundnani, Arun. 2014a. *The Muslims Are Coming! Islamophobia, Extremism, and the Domestic War on Terror*. London: Verso.

— — —. 2014b. *The Muslims Are Coming! Islamophobia, Extremism, and the Domestic War on Terror*. London; New York: Verso.

Kunstler, James Howard. 2009. *World Made by Hand*.

Kushner, Tony. 2013. *Angels in America: A Gay Fantasia on National Themes*. First Revised Combined edition. New York: Theatre Communications Group.

Laughland, Oliver. 2015. 'How the CIA Tortured Its Detainees'. *The Guardian*. 20 May 2015. http://www.theguardian.com/us-news/2014/dec/09/cia-torture-methods-waterboarding-sleep-deprivation.

Levithan, David. 2010. *Love Is the Higher Law*. New York, NY: Knopf.

Lewis, Seth C., and Stephen D. Reese. 2009. "What Is the War on Terror? Framing through the Eyes of Journalists." *Journalism & Mass Communication Quarterly* 86 (1): 85–102. https://doi.org/10.1177/107769900908600106.

Limon, John. 1994. *Writing after War: American War Fiction from Realism to Postmodernism*. New York: Oxford University Press.

LUAG. n.d. 'George Segal: Woman on Park Bench, 1998'. *Lehigh University Art Galleries* (blog). Accessed 17 October 2017. http://www.luag.org/event/george-segal-woman-on-park-bench-1998/.

Maddow, Rachel. 2013. *Drift: The Unmooring of American Military Power*.

Mariani, Giorgio. 2015. *Waging War on War: Peacefighting in American Literature*. Global Studies of the United States. Urbana: University of Illinois Press.

McCarthy, Cormac. 2010. *The Road*. London: Picador.

– – –. 2015. *Blood Meridian*.

McDougall, Christopher. 2010. *Born to Run: The Hidden Tribe, the Ultra-Runners, and the Greatest Race the World Has Never Seen*. London: Profile Books.

McGinn, Colin. 1999. *Ethics, Evil, and Fiction*. Oxford: Clarendon Press.

McGrath, Charles. 2006. 'Updike Explores Mind of a Terrorist'. *The New York Times*, 31 May 2006, sec. Arts. https://www.nytimes.com/2006/05/31/arts/31iht-updike.html.

McKelvey, Tara. 2013. 'Spies Like Us'. *The New York Times*, 11 October 2013, sec. Books. https://www.nytimes.com/2013/10/13/books/review/enemies-within-by-matt-apuzzo-and-adam-goldman.html.

McLoughlin, Catherine Mary. 2011. *Authoring War: The Literary Representation of War from the Iliad to Iraq*. Cambridge, UK; New York: Cambridge University Press.

McMahon, April. 2010. *An Introduction to English Phonology*. Reprinted. Edinburgh Textbooks on the English Language. Edinburgh: Edinburgh Univ. Press.

Means, David. 2016. *Hystopia*. First edition. New York: Farrar, Straus and Giroux.

Miller, Michael H. 2011. 'An Associative Trip At MoMA PS1's "September 11" Exhibition | Observer'. Observer. 9 September 2011. http://observer.com/2011/09/an-associative-trip-at-moma-ps1s-september-11-exhibit/.

Mishra, Pankaj. 2007. 'Pankaj Mishra on 9/11 Fiction'. *The Guardian*. 18 May 2007. http://www.theguardian.com/books/2007/may/19/fiction.martinamis.

Molin, Peter. 2015. 'War Crime: John Renehan's The Valley'. *Time Now* (blog). 22 September 2015. https://acolytesofwar.com/2015/09/22/war-crime-john-renehans-the-valley/.

Naqvi, H. M. 2011. *Home Boy*.

Nelson, Cary, ed. 2007. *Marxism and the Interpretation of Culture*. Nachdr. Urbana, Ill.: Univ. of Illinois Press.

New York Magazine. n.d. 'Days of Terror: A September 11 Photo Gallery'. Accessed 20 October 2017. http://nymag.com/news/articles/wtc/.

Nguyen, Viet Thanh. 2016a. *Nothing Ever Dies: Vietnam and the Memory of War*. Cambridge, Massachusetts; London, England: Harvard University Press.

― ― ―. 2016b. *The Sympathizer*.

― ― ―. 2017. *The Refugees*. First Grove Atlantic hardcover edition. New York: Grove Press.

Noor, Farish A. 2010. 'Analysing the Discourse of the "War on Terror" and Its Workings of Power'. *Human Architecture* 8 (2): 47.

Nora, Pierre. 1989. 'Between Memory and History: Les Lieux de Mémoire'. *Representations*, no. 26, 7–24. https://doi.org/10.2307/2928520.

Nunn, K. 2002. "Race, Crime and the Pool of Surplus Criminality: Or Why the 'War on Drugs' Was a 'War on Blacks.'" In. https://www.semanticscholar.org/paper/Race%2C-Crime-and-the-Pool-of-Surplus-Criminality%3A-Or-Nunn/be54448a4b6edb8ba34eb81b76c8626e08f28ee4.

Nussbaum, Martha Craven. 2012. *The New Religious Intolerance: Overcoming the Politics of Fear in an Anxious Age*. Cambridge, Mass.: Belknap Press of Harvard Univ. Press.

O'Brien, Tim. 1991. *The Things They Carried*. London: Flamingo.

O'Carroll, Lisa. 2013. 'Seymour Hersh on Obama, NSA and the "pathetic" American Media'. *The Guardian*. 27 September 2013. http://www.theguardian.com/media/media-blog/2013/sep/27/seymour-hersh-obama-nsa-american-media.

O'Gorman, D. 2015. *Fictions of the War on Terror: Difference and the Transnational 9/11 Novel*. Springer.

Packer, George. 2007. *The Assassins' Gate: America in Iraq*. London: Faber & Faber.

— — —. 2009. *Interesting Times: Writings from a Turbulent Decade*. http://rbdigital.oneclickdigital.com.

— — —. 2014. 'Home Fires: How Soldiers Write Their Wars'. *The New Yorker*, 4 July 2014. https://www.newyorker.com/magazine/2014/04/07/home-fires-2.

Palumbo-Liu, David. 2012. *The Deliverance of Others: Reading Literature in a Global Age*. Durham; London: Duke University Press.

Parker, Harry. 2017. *Anatomy of a Soldier*. London: Faber & Faber.

Pinker, Steven. 2008. *The Stuff of Thought: Language as a Window into Human Nature*. Penguin UK.

Pitre, Michael. 2015. *Fives and Twenty-Fives: A Novel*.

Poster, Jem. 2006. 'Terrorist by John Updike'. *The Guardian*, 5 August 2006. http://www.theguardian.com/books/2006/aug/05/shopping.fiction.

'Publications | Intelligence Committee'. n.d. Accessed 18 October 2017. https://www.intelligence.senate.gov/publications/committee-study-central-intelligence-agencys-detention-and-interrogation-program.

Purio, Sean. 2016. 'Crossings and Connections: A Conversation with Elliot Ackerman'. *WLA; War, Literature and the Arts*, 2016. https://www.questia.com/read/1P3-4296363761/crossings-and-connections-a-conversation-with-elliot.

Pynchon, Thomas. 2014. *Gravity's Rainbow*. New York: The Penguin Press. http://search.ebscohost.com/login.aspx?direct=true&scope=site&db=nlebk&db=nlabk&AN=1123618.

Randall, Martin. 2011. *9/11 and the Literature of Terror*. Edinburgh: Edinburgh University Press.

Rashid, Ahmed. 1999. 'The Taliban: Exporting Extremism'. *Foreign Affairs* 78 (6): 22–35.

Redfield, Marc. 2007. 'Virtual Trauma: The Idiom of 9/11'. *Diacritics* 37 (1): 55–80. https://doi.org/10.1353/dia.0.0020S.

— — —. 2009. *The Rhetoric of Terror: Reflections on 9/11 and the War on Terror*. 1st ed. New York: Fordham University Press.

Reese, Stephen D., and Seth C. Lewis. 2009. 'Framing the War on Terror: The Internalization of Policy in the US Press'. *Journalism* 10 (6): 777–97. https://doi.org/10.1177/1464884909344480.

Reet, Brian Van. 2018. *Spoils*. London: Vintage.

Ringnalda, Don. 1994. *Fighting and Writing the Vietnam War*. Jackson: University Press of Mississippi.

Roman, David. n.d. 'The Ethical Game: Morality in Postapocalyptic Fictions from Cormac McCarthy to Video Games'. Los Angeles Review of Books. Accessed 3 February 2018. https://lareviewofbooks.org/article/the-ethical-game-morality-in-postapocalyptic-fictions-from-cormac-mccarthy-to-video-games/.

Rutherford, Jonathan, ed. 1990. *Identity: Community, Culture, Difference*. London: Lawrence & Wishart.

Said, Edward. 2001. 'Islam and the West Are Inadequate Banners'. *The Guardian*, 16 September 2001. http://www.theguardian.com/world/2001/sep/16/september11.terrorism3.

Sanborn, Wallis R. 2012. *The American Novel of War: A Critical Analysis and Classification System*. Jefferson, NC: McFarland & Company.

Saunders, George. 2014. *Tenth of December*. Paperback ed. London: Bloomsbury.

Savage, Charlie. 2016. 'General Hayden's Offensive'. *The New York Review of Books*, 26 May 2016. http://www.nybooks.com/articles/2016/05/26/general-haydens-offensive/.

Scarry, Elaine. 1985. 'Injury and the Structure of War'. *Representations*, no. 10, 1–51. https://doi.org/10.2307/3043799.

— — —. 1987. *The Body in Pain: The Making and Unmaking of the World*. First issued as a paperback. Oxford Paperback. New York, NY: Oxford University Press.

Scranton, Roy. 2015. "The Trauma Hero: From Wilfred Owen to 'Redeployment' and 'American Sniper.'" *Los Angeles Review of Books*, 25 January 2015. https://lareviewofbooks.org/article/trauma-hero-wilfred-owen-redeployment-american-sniper/.

— — —. 2016. *War Porn*. New York, NY: Soho.

Scranton, Roy, and Matt Gallagher, eds. 2013. *Fire and Forget: Short Stories*. Boston: Da Capo Press.

Sedgwick, Eve Kosofsky, and Adam Frank. 2003. *Touching Feeling: Affect, Pedagogy, Performativity*. Series Q. Durham: Duke University Press.

Shay, Jonathan. 2010. *Achilles in Vietnam: Combat Trauma and the Undoing of Character*. Simon & Schuster.

Silberstein, Sandra. 2004. *War of Words: Language, Politics and 9/11*. This paperback ed. 1. publ. London: Routledge.

Smiley, Jane. 2006. *Thirteen Ways of Looking at the Novel*. New York: Anchor Books.

Staff, Guardian. 2017. 'Truck Attack in New York City: What We Know so Far'. *The Guardian*, 1 November 2017, sec. US news. http://www.theguardian.com/us-news/2017/nov/01/truck-attack-in-new-york-city-what-we-know-so-far.

Stepanova, Ekaterina Andreevna. 2008. *Terrorism in Asymmetrical Conflict: Ideological and Structural Aspects*. SIPRI Research Report 23. Oxford: Oxford University Press.

Stevenson, Robert Louis, and Robert Mighall. 2002. *The Strange Case of Dr Jekyll and Mr Hyde and Other Tales of Terror*. London: Penguin. http://site.ebrary.com/id/10006941.

Sturken, Marita. 2007. *Tourists of History: Memory, Kitsch, and Consumerism from Oklahoma City to Ground Zero*. Duke University Press. https://doi.org/10.1515/9780822390510.

Tait, Theo. 2012. 'Billy Lynn's Long Halftime Walk by Ben Fountain—Review'. *The Guardian*, 6 July 2012, sec. Books. http://www.theguardian.com/books/2012/jul/06/billy-lynn-ben-fountain-review.

The Guardian. 2001. 'Text of George Bush's Speech', 21 September 2001, sec. US news. http://www.theguardian.com/world/2001/sep/21/september11.usa13.

The New York Times. 2011. 'Portraits of Grief', 10 August 2011. https://www.nytimes.com/interactive/us/sept-11-reckoning/portraits-of-grief.html.

The New Yorker. 2001. 'Tuesday, and After', 17 September 2001. https://www.newyorker.com/magazine/2001/09/24/tuesday-and-after-talk-of-the-town.

———. 2011. 'Summer Fiction: George Saunders'. *The New Yorker*, 9 June 2011. https://www.newyorker.com/books/page-turner/summer-fiction-george-saunders.

Toth, Paul A. 2011. *Airplane Novel*. First edition. Bowie, MD: Raw Dog Screaming Press.

Treaster, Joseph B. 1975. 'Suspect, 19, Is Charged With Trade Center Fires'. *The New York Times*, 21 May 1975, sec. Archives. https://www.nytimes.com/1975/05/21/archives/suspect-19-is-charged-with-trade-center-fires.html.

Turner, Brian. 2014. *My Life as a Foreign Country*. London: Jonathan Cape.

Updike, John. 2005. 'Mixed Messages'. *The New Yorker*, 7 March 2005. https://www.newyorker.com/magazine/2005/03/14/mixed-messages.

———. 2007. *Terrorist*. Paperback ed. London: Penguin Books.

Verbruggen, Jakob, dir. 2016. *Men Against Fire*. Drama, Sci-Fi, Thriller. http://www.imdb.com/title/tt5709234/.

Versluys, Kristiaan. 2009. *Out of the Blue: September 11 and the Novel*. New York: Columbia University Press.

Virilio, Paul. 2002. *Ground Zero*. London; New York: Verso.

Vonnegut, Kurt. 1991. *Slaughterhouse-Five or the Children's Crusade: A Duty-Dance with Death*. New York, NY: Dell Publ.

White, Hayden V. 1973. *Metahistory: The Historical Imagination in Nineteenth-Century Europe*. Baltimore: Johns Hopkins University Press.

Willis, Susan. 2005. *Portents of the Real: A Primer for Post-9/11 America*. London; New York: Verso.

Wright, Robert. 2015. 'The Clash of Civilizations That Isn't'. *The New Yorker*, 25 February 2015. https://www.newyorker.com/news/news-desk/clash-civilizations-isnt.

Zelizer, Barbie, and Stuart Allan, eds. 2011. *Journalism after September 11*. 2nd ed. London; New York: Routledge.

Zink, Nell. 2016. *Nicotine*. First edition. New York: Ecco, an imprint of HarperCollins Publishers.

Žižek, Slavoj. 2012. *Welcome to the Desert of the Real: Five Essays on September 11 and Related Dates*. Radical Thinkers. London: Verso.

Zucchino, David, and David S. Cloud. 2015. 'U.S. Military and Civilians Are Increasingly Divided'. *Los Angeles Times*, 24 May 2015. http://www.latimes.com/nation/la-na-warrior-main-20150524-story.html.

Acknowledgements

This book would not have been possible without the kindness, support, and patience of many people who have stood by me throughout this lengthy process.

First of all, I am deeply grateful to my parents. Their moral and financial support made this research possible, but more importantly, they taught me the value of hard work and integrity.

To my husband: thank you for being my steadfast supporter and my safe place. Your patience and love carried me through every moment of doubt.

I am also grateful to the Università di Torino for the institutional support that enabled me to undertake this work, and especially to my supervisor, Andrea Carosso. Thank you for trusting my choices, for giving me the freedom to explore, and for always believing in the direction I wanted to take.

A special thank you goes to Giorgio Mariani at the Università "La Sapienza" di Roma. His advice, our rich discussions, and his generosity in writing the foreword have been invaluable. More than that, he has been an intellectual model and an example of the kind of scholar and person I aspire to become.

I am also indebted to the Graduate Centre at the City University of New York (CUNY), and particularly to Ashley Dawson and Moustafa Bayoumi, whose work and guidance demonstrated to me what an engaged and courageous academic life can look like.

My heartfelt thanks go to the John F. Kennedy Institute for North American Studies at the Freie Universität Berlin and Bergische Universität Wuppertal for welcoming me and allowing me to utilise their excellent library resources at a crucial moment in this project.

To all of you: thank you. This book is, in many ways, as much yours as it is mine.

ibidem.eu